Women and Politics

This textbook presents a much-needed exploration of the many ways that women in the United States have used their voices in the political process.

Written in a concise and accessible style, *Women and Politics* equips students with the necessary skills and knowledge to understand the political involvement of women as individuals and their efforts to achieve political and economic equity as a group. This textbook is both historical, examining trends, and contemporary, focusing on participation and the public policy concerns of women in the early decades of the 21st century.

Key content and features:

- Exploration of diverse actions women have taken to achieve empowerment and gender equity
- Surveys women as voters, as candidates for elected office, and as interest group organizers lobbying for equity in public policy and for global women's rights
- Chronicles protest actions against unequal practices of economic and governmental elites
- Highlights the actions of women with few economic resources that join together to challenge local power structures.

Readers will appreciate Burrell's valuable insights on the multiple political voices of American women and the challenges of economic inequality in their quest for political equality.

Barbara Burrell is Professor Emerita of Political Science at Northern Illinois University. She has taught women and politics classes at both the undergraduate and the graduate level. Burrell has researched and written extensively on women engaging in politics in the United States, including studies on women as candidates for public office and public opinion and the first ladyship. The Midwest Political Science Association's Women's Caucus awarded Professor Burrell a lifetime career achievement award in 2012.

Routledge Series on Identity Politics
Series Editor: Alvin B. Tillery Jr., *Rutgers University*

Group identities have been an important part of political life in America since the founding of the republic. For most of this long history, the central challenge for activists, politicians, and scholars concerned with the quality of U.S. democracy was the struggle to bring the treatment of ethnic and racial minorities and women in line with the creedal values spelled out in the nation's charters of freedom. In the midst of many positive changes, however, glaring inequalities between groups persist. Indeed, ethnic and racial minorities remain far more likely to be undereducated, unemployed, and incarcerated than their counterparts who identify as White. Similarly, both violence and workplace discrimination against women remain rampant in U.S. society. The Routledge series on identity politics features works that seek to understand the tension between the great strides our society has made in promoting equality between groups and the residual effects of the ascriptive hierarchies in which the old order was rooted.

Women and Politics

A Quest for Political Equality in
an Age of Economic Inequality

Barbara Burrell

NEW YORK AND LONDON

First published 2018
by Routledge
711 Third Avenue, New York, NY 10017

and by Routledge
2 Park Square, Milton Park, Abingdon, Oxon, OX14 4RN

Routledge is an imprint of the Taylor & Francis Group, an informa business

Library of Congress Cataloging-in-Publication Data
Names: Burrell, Barbara C., 1947– author.
Title: Women and politics : a quest for political equality in an age of
   economic inequality / Barbara Burrell.
Description: New York, NY : Routledge, 2018. | Series: Routledge series on
   identity politics | Includes bibliographical references and index.
Identifiers: LCCN 2017021114 | ISBN 9781138856547 (hardback : alk.
   paper) | ISBN 9781138856554 (pbk. : alk. paper)
Subjects: LCSH: Women—Political activity—United States. | Women
   political candidates—United States. | Feminism—United States. | Women's
   rights—United States.
Classification: LCC HQ1236.5.U6 B8753 2018 | DDC 320.082/0973—dc23
LC record available at https://lccn.loc.gov/2017021114

ISBN: 978-1-138-85654-7 (hbk)
ISBN: 978-1-138-85655-4 (pbk)
ISBN: 978-1-315-71953-5 (ebk)

Typeset in Sabon
by Apex CoVantage, LLC

Contents

Boxes and Sidebars

Text Boxes

Sidebars

Figures

Tables

Pictures

1 Introduction

A half-century has passed since the emergence of what is commonly referred to as the second women's rights movement in the United States. Over the decades that followed, the movement has profoundly affected women's political lives. Women are now not only the majority of voters but also vote in higher percentages than men. Winning the "women's vote" has become a key focus of political campaigns across the country and at all levels of public office. Hillary Clinton won a majority of the popular vote in 2016 as the Democratic Party nominee, although her opponent, Republican Donald Trump, won the Electoral College vote, giving him the presidency. Thus, the last political glass ceiling remains to be broken. Women have become governor, secretary of state (but not defense), and Speaker of the U.S. House of Representatives. In 2015, three of the nine U.S. Supreme Court justices were women. A woman also chaired the Federal Reserve Board. Beginning in January 2016, all combat jobs in the military were opened to women. Women's groups have organized to raise huge amounts of money for female candidates and to recruit and train them to be successful office seekers. A host of laws have been enacted, dismantling discriminatory public policies and mandating political equity for women.

At the same time, after all these decades, women as political leaders and issues of particular concern to women are still subjects of political debate. In the second decade of the 21st century, the major political parties became engaged in what has been popularly called a war on women battle in a public policy dispute encompassing social and economic issues. Illustrative of this "war" is a debate that occurred on April 8, 2011, in the midst of a budget showdown between Democrats and Republicans in the U.S. Congress with a government shutdown imminent. Nine female Democratic U.S. senators held a press conference in which they accused Republican members of Congress of promoting a federal budget that would "throw women and children under the bus," a phrase repeatedly used in their briefing. In response, fourteen Republican female representatives held an opposing conference later that same day with the dominant theme that sound fiscal policy and cutting spending would help their children and their grandchildren. The Democratic budget proposal was not fiscally sound, they argued.

In these competing press briefings, the senators stressed how their party's position would help women and how the other party's approach would hurt women. A key sticking point that day to solving the immediate budget impasse from the perspective of the female Democratic senators was the Republican insistence that no federal money go to Planned Parenthood. As the federal government was about to be shut down, Republicans demanded that any legislation keeping the government operating bar federal dollars for Planned Parenthood, the country's largest abortion provider but also a major provider of reproductive and other health care for low-income women. The overarching issue Democratic Senator Barbara Mikulski iterated was that the Republicans "want to cut funding for prenatal care by fifty million dollars . . . they want to take our mammograms away from us; they want to take prenatal care away from us, take counseling and family planning away from us and we just say 'no.'" Senator Dianne Feinstein added that the Republican cuts "hurt women and we women in the Senate will not let it happen. What is at stake is about the ability of poor American women to get health services."

In response, as Republican Representative Shelley Moore Capito of West Virginia put it, "The argument is about spending and there is nothing more important to the health of my granddaughter who is going to be one next week, my daughter and every woman in America is good sound fiscal policy and that the women of America are not swallowed up by a huge debt and deficit . . . that is about healthy women." Each of the speakers reiterated this theme, relating spending cuts to creating a healthy future for children and grandchildren.

This event illustrates several significant features of the contemporary engagement of women in American politics. This event, which was part of a larger policy debate between Democrats and Republicans, highlighted women's prominence as policy makers. Their sex also had symbolic meaning in advocating for public policy. In addition, it highlights public policy continuing to have a gendered nature to it, with economic and social politics both being important in the debate. Further, the public presentations of Democratic female U.S. senators and Republican female U.S. representatives were meant to send a message to the American public that each group saw itself as representing women in the political process. It was female leaders speaking for women, but the substance of their arguments was starkly different between the parties, with social and economic policy implications. Related to that point, it showed the importance of women as a voting bloc to which the parties needed to appeal. It highlights the continued significance and unsettling of "women's issues" in national debates a half-century after the emergence of the second women's rights movement and the engagement of women in the political process.

Although a proposed Equal Rights Amendment (ERA) banning discrimination based on sex had never become part of the Constitution, major legislative enactments and judicial rulings in the latter quarter of the 20th century contributed greatly to making women more equal citizens with men. Thus, "women" being an issue at the beginning of the second decade of the 21st century seemed strange and out of place. As one commentator put it during the 2012 election, "Women ponder how they became a campaign issue" (Arrillaga 2012). In 2016, the country came very close to electing the first woman to the presidency of the United States.

> ## Sidebar 1.1 The Equal Rights Amendment
>
> The Equal Rights Amendment as approved by Congress and sent to the states for ratification in 1972 read as follows:
>
> *Section 1. Equality of rights under the law shall not be denied or abridged by the United States or by any State on account of sex.*
> *Section 2. The Congress shall have the power to enforce, by appropriate legislation, the provisions of this article.*
> *Section 3. This amendment shall take effect two years after the date of ratification.*

Political Voice and Practice

This book is about how women practice politics and use their voices in contemporary American politics. Political voice refers to engagement in political practices "to communicate information about preferences and needs and generate pressure on public officials to respond" (Schlozman et al. 2005, 2). It is the heart of the democratic process. The women's rights movement of the last decades of the 20th century following the civil rights movement profoundly influenced public policy and political leadership in the United States through women organizing to raise their voices for greater political equality. *Women and Politics: A Quest for Political Equality in an Age of Economic Inequality* describes the many ways in which women have used their voices in the political process in the United States. *Women and Politics* is about both the involvement of women as individuals in the political process and group efforts to achieve equity and become empowered. It also places political involvement in an age of increasing economic inequality that has impacted the contours of that quest. It is both historical, examining trends, and contemporary, focusing on participation and public policy of specific concern to women in the early decades of the 21st century. The text is divided into three sections. This chapter and the two that follow take a historical and conceptual perspective. Then Chapters 4 through 7 examine various ways of participating in the political process. Chapters 8, 9, and 10 focus on representation and public policy. The book concludes with Chapter 11, which assesses the comparative political status of U.S. women and looks to the future as the United States approaches the 100th anniversary of the passage of the 19th Amendment giving women the right to vote.

The political involvement of women as individual citizens and as groups promoting equal rights and empowerment are important and intriguing facets of American political history and contemporary politics. This text takes a broad view of what constitutes political practice, an essential task if one is to take women's citizenship seriously; assesses trends in their involvement and their current status in the public realm; and considers their efforts to achieve equality a half-century after the beginning of the second women's rights movement in the 1960s. Several diverse political practices are given attention in the chapters of this text to provide readers with a broad sense of what it means to engage in politics and how access to different resources across class and race have affected the practice of politics for women.

A second parallel phenomenon of this era—an economic one—also has significantly affected Americans' lives. We now live in a time of increasing economic inequality. In the past half-century, Americans have "become vastly richer and vastly more unequal" (Bartels 2008, 1). From 1980 to 2005, more than 80 percent of the total increase in Americans' income went to the top 1 percent (Noah 2010). The United States is unique among advanced countries in its growth in economic inequality. This growth in inequality is at the center of much political and economic debate.

These two societal phenomena, the second women's rights movement and the age of increasing economic inequality, have continued into the second decade of the 21st century as prominent and challenging features of American public life. The contours of economic inequality and women's quests for greater political influence and equality are certainly intertwined, yet these two trends have rarely been considered together in the political history of contemporary women's lives. What have been the implications of this growing economic divergence across income classes on women's quests for a greater political voice and involvement in the public life of the nation? Connecting questions center on how the increased divergence in American income across classes has impacted, conditioned, and constrained the movement toward political equality between men and women. What distinctive impact has it had on women's economic status and across groups of women? In what ways have women's greater participation in the political and economic life of the nation mitigated or exacerbated income inequality? The chapters in this book consider these questions as they explore women's political voices and practices and quests for political equality. Cohen et al. (1997, 2–3) have posed the question in the following terms:

> How do we explain the fact that many women's lives have significantly improved in the United States during the last two decades, and that all women have seen their legal status enhanced, while for many women daily life has become more tenuous and threatening?

In a very narrow legal sense, women have always been considered citizens along with men. Their numbers were included when representation in the U.S. Congress was allocated according to population among the states in the initial adoption of the U.S. Constitution. But that citizenship did not give them a political voice in what public policy should be or who should be the governors. They were not considered political beings. Well into the 20th century, women's political voice was only a whisper, even after winning the right to vote in 1920. Their seemingly different natures and abilities from that of men's, plus their distinctive social roles, limited their sense of a political self and political activism. In this regard, they were second-class political citizens. Throughout these years, women's participation in political activities such as voting, contacting elected officials, and contributing to political causes lagged far behind men's. Women running for and being elected to public office was a rare event. Few championed equal rights for their sex.

The 1960s marked a turning point for the gender dynamics of mass politics in the United States. Women's voices became stronger in the public realm. Advances in women's educational attainment and substantial increases in their employment outside the home stimulated greater parity with men in political engagement. Women also became more conscious of their second-class citizenship and organized to demand equal status with men in the public realm. Thus began a movement toward first-class, full, and effective political citizenship.

What constitutes participation in the political process? This text explores a variety of ways in which women have expanded their involvement in the public life of the nation since the second women's rights movement began in the 1960s. Participation in the political process consists of many different actions and a variety of ways of having one's voice heard. Political scientists have grouped several political practices under the rubric of conventional acts, focusing primarily on electoral politics and between elections on groups lobbying and advocating for particular policies. The American National Election Study (ANES) has surveyed participation in several electoral activities over the entire time frame of the contemporary women's rights movement. These activities center on attending a political meeting, trying to influence others' voting decisions, wearing a campaign button, putting up a yard sign for a candidate, contributing financially to a party or campaign, and of course, voting. Chapter 4 presents trends in the activism of men and women in this domain of political engagement.

In contrast to these conventional electoral political practices are a group of unconventional or contentious actions involving protest demonstrations and social movements challenging dominant political structures. Women have been participants in these latter activities throughout American history, from involvement in the Revolutionary War and the abolitionist movement against slavery, to the very recent Tea Party and Occupy Wall Street protests and Black Lives Matter movements centered on economic and social justice issues within the United States, to participation in transnational peace and antiglobalization movements. Women have also formed their own movements promoting women's rights, notably the suffrage movement of the 19th and early 20th centuries to win the right to vote and the second women's rights movement seeking more general political, social, and economic equality that emerged in the 1960s and that has continued since then, including efforts to affect women's rights globally.

Importantly, feminist scholars have also called attention to the "invisible politics" of working-class, minority, and poor women by challenging power systems in their communities. "Doing politics" is a distinctive way in which feminists have characterized this engagement in the public realm by challenging traditional ideas of what engaging in politics means. They challenge the private/public boundary. Women challenging community and economic power structures alter the traditional divide between private and public. Thus, surveying the political practices of women must include attention to invisible politics and "doing politics" actions, not just the conventional actions centered on elections. Our lens on political participation requires setting its sights on the many examples of women engaging in activities to gain control over their lives and those of their families by challenging the power structures in their communities. These practices have often involved actions women with few resources have taken to make their voices heard. I group this loose collection of activities together under the concept of *empowerment*.

Empowerment activities as described in this work center on efforts to upend power relations within one's community. Bookman and Morgen (1988) defined empowerment as consisting of "a spectrum of political activity ranging from acts of individual resistance to mass political mobilizations that challenge the basic power relations in our society" (4). Challenges to local power structures that individual and diverse groups of women have undertaken encompass fascinating, innovative, and sometimes dangerous actions that attack many aspects of their disempowerment. It is an area of participation that has received minimal attention in other texts focusing on American women and politics. This domain is distinctive in that it centers on women who most often have few of the traditional resources used to gain political influence. Their activities involve efforts regarding economic challenges within their communities, fighting for their families, and protesting against violence. Researchers have shown that women engaged in empowerment activities have often not even viewed them as political actions but more as civic involvement and survival mechanisms (see, for example, Naples 1998). They are not included in major surveys of political participation. But they are many, varied, and often actions minority groups and low-income groups have undertaken throughout the country to gain voice and achieve policy changes. Shining a spotlight on women's engagement in these "invisible" activities provides for a broader understanding of citizenship and its inequalities and challenges for women across classes and among minority groups. They greatly expand what it means to "do politics." The work of feminist scholars and reporters has brought public attention to these actions. Text Box 1.1 provides an example of reporting on women's issues.

Text Box 1.1 Women's eNews

Womensenews.org has made visible for attentive publics much of the invisible acts of women daring to challenge local power structures. It also casts a global lens on women's power struggles. The National Organization for Women's Legal Defense and Education Fund (LDEF) launched *Women's eNews* as a nonprofit online news service in 1999. "Looking out at the media's coverage of women, we saw a tremendous void in women's voices, in women as opinion shapers, and in the coverage of all the things that women do in society. So we decided to show the media what they were missing. Not to go on a blame campaign, but to do the ground work, actually do the reporting, and go back to these media outlets and say, 'Here's what we're talking about when we say you're not covering women's issues.'"

Women's eNews describes itself as an "award-winning nonprofit news service covering issues of particular concern to women and providing women's perspectives on public policy. With writers and readers around the globe *Women's eNews'* audience stretches from New York City to New Delhi and all points between, reaching an estimated 1.5 million readers each year." In 2003, it launched Arabic *Women's eNews*. It publishes every day with reports and commentary. In addition to daily reports and perspectives, *Women's eNews* includes special series with more in-depth coverage.

Not only have women sought empowerment at the local level and influence in national politics but also groups have formed to advocate for global women's rights and to participate in transnational feminist actions. Globalization is a central feature of contemporary political, social, and economic life and advocacy for women's rights globally and has become a major political movement of the past several decades. An assessment of the political participation of American women is enhanced through an exploration of their efforts to affect women's rights at the international level and the nature of those efforts. These efforts are the subject of Chapter 7.

Gender and Political Voice

Women's participation and voice in the political process and the public realm is a powerful aspect of citizenship on its own. How their muted voices have grown stronger and more assertive in the political process is a subject of great import in the study of democratic politics. Thus, exploring trends in women's activism across domains of political engagement and their participation across economic classes and racial and ethnic groups is the major focus of this text. It is their sex and the implications of that sex on their ability to engage in and affect the political process that is key to the whole idea of "women and politics" and "female political activity." It is about how women came to question the limitations that being a woman had in exercising a public voice and how, as a group based on their sex, women have raised their voices and organized to achieve equality and influence in governance.

A second lens compares the involvement of women with that of men, which introduces the concept of gender into the political realm. Considering their participation separate from that of men's participation only tells half the story of women's political practice. Placing their participatory acts in a comparative context with that of men's political activism, power, and influence provides a more complete picture of democratic politics. Gender analysis involves comparisons between men and women as they engage in the political, social, and economic realms and how observers perceive those differences.

The concepts of sex and gender are distinct. Sex is biological, whereas gender is socially constructed. Exploring the gendered aspects of politics centers on an interpretation of a political action when a man performs it compared to when a woman engages in it. Gender is something that men and women do. For example, Hillary Clinton's 2016 campaign for the Democratic presidential nomination and Sarah Palin's vice presidential nomination in the 2008 election had gendered aspects when they were questioned about their electability, their appearance, their voices, and their ability to be "commander in chief," all because they were women seeking a power position that only men had ever held. Sometimes they were treated crudely on the campaign trail in gendered terms such as the male shout-out at a Clinton campaign event that she should "iron his shirts." This shout-out was actually

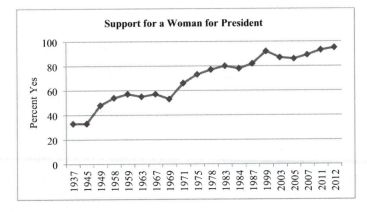

Figure 1.1 Trends in General Public Support for a Woman President
If your party nominated a generally well-qualified person for president who happened to be—, would you vote for that person? Gallup.com

one of the less crude attacks aimed at her. (For other examples, see Carlin and Winfrey 2009; Lawrence and Rose 2010.) Further, Clinton was accused negatively of "shouting" by her male opponents during the 2016 campaign. As Clinton cleverly responded to one such instance, "I have been told to stop, and I quote, 'shouting about gun violence.' Well, first of all, I'm not shouting. It's just when women talk, some people think we're shouting" (Dittmar 2016, 808).

All kinds of gendered questions have been posed when women have run for public office. Do they receive distinctive and less media coverage, should they talk about their children, how aggressive should they be on the campaign trail, and what differences do voters see in their ability to affect policy in diverse political areas? Are they viewed as outsiders and more honest than male politicians? Are they less politically ambitious than men? A media focus on "hair, hemlines, and husbands" has been a catch phrase scholars of campaign stereotypes have used to capture this challenge for women seeking political authority.

In 1937, the Gallup organization surveyed a national sample of the American public asking if they would "vote for a woman for president if she were qualified in every other respect." Thirty-three percent responded affirmatively. Since the latter part of the 1930s, Gallup has periodically asked the public a variation of that question. Figure 1.1 shows the trend in support as an illustration of changing attitudes toward women in political leadership and as an example of a stereotypical question.

The "gender gap"—that is, differences in the opinions, party affiliations, and voting behaviors between men and women—has become a major feature in studies of American elections in the past few decades. Regarding political participation and voice from a gendered perspective, trends in the rates of involvement of men and women and their distinctiveness of their opinions on public policy issues are examined in this text. Chapter 4 describes how the gender gap became a political phenomenon and explores its implications on electioneering.

Looking Ahead

The chapters that follow investigate the many ways in which women "do politics." Their quests to have their voices heard and to gain political influence are presented and embedded in the constraints of the age of economic inequality that characterizes contemporary

America. Trends in their public involvement across a variety of domains of political action are presented, and those trends are embedded in a gender perspective comparing the degree of involvement of women with that of men who have long dominated the public realm.

This text surveys the "how" and the "what" of women's political practice. The broad sweep of political action central to this work focuses on the *how* of women's activism, stressing diversity in political engagement. The voices of women in terms of political demands and public policy centers readers' attention on *what* it is that women have organized to achieve, protested against, and lobbied for and for which they have sought political leadership. From the early days of the 1960s with the enactment of the 1963 Equal Pay Act through the 1994 passage of the Violence Against Women Act (VAWA), the women's rights movement worked to pass national legislation to give women greater equality in the economic, educational, and public life of the nation and to expand their rights. Whereas the latter half of the 20th century should be known as a *women's policy era*, this book also asks readers to consider what public policies are still on the women's rights agenda in the 21st century and how they are being debated. Advocates continue to introduce legislation regarding economic equity and fairness. Reproductive rights, too, continue to be at the center of much recent legislative and electoral debates and have become even more aggressively contested throughout the political system. The 112th Congress (2011–2012) and the 2012 presidential election will long be remembered for what has been called the war on women, as noted in this chapter's introduction. The "war" continues. What constitutes this war on women, how it emerged, and the leadership roles female politicians have played on various sides of the "war" are fundamental questions.

Winning the women's vote has also become a major feature of campaigns for public office. Contemporary political life is filled with empowerment issues and diversity among women as to what constitutes equality. Spotlighting the most recent debates and controversies within the subject matter of each chapter is a major feature of this work, integrating economic inequality, political action, and the public voices of women.

Chapter 2 provides a historical presentation of the two remarkable movements women have undertaken to gain greater citizenship and voice in the United States—the suffrage movement and the women's rights movement. The women's rights movement continues into the 21st century. The essence of this chapter is on the political practices of women who organized these movements and the myriad ways in which they sought to gain power and influence. The campaign to gain women the right to vote lasted seventy-two years. Carrie Chapman Catt, president of the National American Woman Suffrage Association at the time of its ultimate victory, counted that it took 56 state referendum campaigns, 480 efforts to get state legislatures to allow state referenda, 47 campaigns for suffrage at state constitutional conventions, 277 attempts to include votes for women in state party platforms, and 19 campaigns to get a federal amendment through Congress and then to obtain the requisite three quarters of the state legislatures to ratify it (Kraditor 1965). Chapter 2 provides a survey of these historical efforts to impress readers with the strategies these women engaged in and the challenges they faced. When they began the campaign for greater equality in the life of the nation, women did not have public voices. But some had the courage to speak before groups in isolated communities where they were jeered, driven off platforms, and had their lives placed in jeopardy during campaigns to win the right for women to vote in state campaigns. In the latter years of the campaign, suffragists also chained themselves to the White House fence and were beaten and sent to jail, where they were force-fed as they attempted to win a national constitutional amendment to have the right to vote, which we all take for granted today. Their campaign to win the vote was stunning in the range and creativity of its strategies and the audacity of their campaign actions. It was also mainly, although not completely, a middle-class women's movement. It was predominantly a White women's movement, with racist overtones and actions. Some used racist arguments in promoting the vote for women, and African American women often were discouraged from participating in suffrage events and adding their voice to the cause. The major White suffragist organizations rebuffed African American women seeking the vote as a means to protect their rights. At the same time, African American female activists argued that they needed the vote for protection much more than White women.

Forty-some years after women gained the right to vote, a second women's rights movement arose, this one much broader in scope and more complex in its aims. It grew out of women's engagement in other political movements of the time and out of changing educational and economic aspects of their lives. The second section of Chapter 2 presents its origins and introduces readers to the range of activities proponents of women's rights have undertaken as the movement grew and diversified and was challenged throughout the rest of the century. It highlights its diversity, strategies, and goals. Looking ahead to the continued political contestation centering on equity issues in the early years of the 21st century, the chapter concludes with a section on the debates about the current status and character of the movement.

Chapter 3 integrates the quest for equal rights and a greater political voice on the part of women that has characterized the last half-century with the age of rising inequality that has defined the economic life of the nation since the 1970s. The women's rights movement should not be considered in isolation and separate from this large economic change. The challenges and constraints of economic inequality on quests for greater political equality and public influence are significant. Chapter 3 describes the economic trends representing the age of inequality and presents a gendered focus on them to highlight their distinctive effect on women's economic position and efforts to pursue political equality. Women have made remarkable gains within the workforce over this time frame, but they have also been disproportionately hurt by economic changes that, among other things, resulted in the "feminization of poverty." The chapter lays out what constitutes the age of inequality generally and explains how women more specifically have been affected by it. It also explores how trends in women's participation in the workforce have affected economic inequality.

The chapter also examines the Great Recession of 2007 from a gendered lens and the collective responses of women to its impact on their economic lives within the public realm. The involvement of women in two of the major economic protests of the recent past—the Tea Party movement and the Occupy Wall Street movement—are explored. These two movements represent the most recent challenges to the economic and governmental system from opposite perspectives during the economic downturn of the latter part of the first decade of the 21st century. Women have been active and taken on leadership roles in both movements. These movements have offered contrasting spectacles of citizen groups in recent years dominating national politics stemming from contrasting economic perspectives. The Occupy Wall Street movement most specifically challenged economic inequality and marched under the banner "We are the 99%." The slogan refers to the increased concentration of income and wealth since the 1970s among the top 1 percent of income earners in the United States and anger about this disparity. Thus, the chapter's contemporary section explores the involvement of women in the Occupy Wall Street and Tea Party movements, examining their leadership, the gendered aspects of their political demands, and their racial and class diversity.

The character of the age of increasing economic inequality is integrated into presentations of women's activism in various political practices throughout the chapters that follow. The focus varies depending on the nature of the practice being highlighted. In some cases, analysis by class is the important feature, and in other instances, it is more the story of women with unequal political and economic resources seeking a political voice that frames the political practice being investigated.

Chapter 4 begins the second section of this text and focuses on distinctive participation arenas. It explores women's voice in what has traditionally been called conventional political activities centering on electoral politics. First, readers' attention is turned to women as voters, the central political act that the suffragists worked so long and hard to obtain. It traces women's engagement in this most central of political acts in a democratic system. Women are the majority of the population and have long been the majority of voters. Since 1980, they have come to participate at a higher rate than men. Voting is now a civic act that women engage in more than men. (The suffragists would be cheering.) This chapter first explores the turnout rates of men and women and then compares trends in the turnout rates of women based on demographic characteristics such as age, education, race, and ethnicity. Class distinctions are of special importance. Has increasing income inequality affected women's participation rates based on their economic position? Census Bureau surveys that date back to 1964 chronicle women's and men's voting participation and serve as the basis for this analysis. The chapter also presents a comparative trend analysis of the participation of men and women in the various campaign activities beyond voting chronicled across the decades of the contemporary women's rights movement in the American National Election Studies.

Second, the chapter surveys the public policy preferences of women and men. The gender gap in public opinion and voting behavior has become part of the political landscape in the past three decades since the 1980 presidential election, receiving much media and campaign attention and scholarly assessment (see, for example, Lois Whitaker's edited volume, *Voting the Gender Gap* 2008). This chapter chronicles the story of how the gender gap became a political phenomenon in American politics and describes the nature of the gap in public opinion across issue domains and in the making of voting decisions since 1980. It focuses on perspectives on economic policy and perceptions of class and inequality between the sexes.

"Winning the women's vote" has also become a central focus of contemporary presidential campaigns. Thus, the third section of this chapter describes such efforts, as they certainly speak to responses to women's voice and political participation. A good example of such activities was the "W Stands for Women" effort from George W. Bush's 2000 presidential campaign. A second example is the Council on Women and Girls that the Obama administration created as he sought to win reelection. Added to this historical overview, the nature of the gender gap in the 2012 election and the attempts of the presidential candidates to win the "woman's vote" are spotlighted, as are the continued efforts in the 2014 midterm campaign and the 2016 presidential election. The extent to which women have become the center of so much electoral strategy is extraordinary.

Party politics dominate the political life of Americans, and the two major party organizations—Democrats and Republicans—have structured electoral politics and our governing institutions. Chapter 5 centers on the rise of women as important players and leaders in the national parties' organizations, a significant but often neglected means of political influence for women. Scholar Jo Freeman (2000, 7) explains the historical process by which women entered party politics as a "room at a time," describing the process this way:

> With suffrage, women could enter the polls, but voting was just the foyer to the political house, not the living room where candidates were chosen, nor the dining room where the spoils were divvied up, not the kitchen where the deals were made. To enter these rooms women had to pass through several doors; the doorkeepers were the major political parties.

The history of the political parties as organizations has included a long period of dominance in electioneering and governance, and a period of decline occurring roughly at the same time that the second women's movement emerged. Candidate-centered campaigns became the principal approaches for those seeking elective office, especially national positions. In recent decades, however, national party organizations have been reinvigorated, emerging once again as major players in elections and governing. Indeed, by the 1980s, the Republican Party was credited with developing the "strongest party organization in American history" (Jacobson 1985, 603). The contemporary era is also one of major policy polarization between the parties, including social and economic issues of particular concern to women, culminating in the "war on women" debates of recent years. This chapter chronicles women's movement into leadership positions within the various party organizational entities and provides an overview of party efforts to elect women to national office and public relations' efforts to appear as champions of women. It also surveys women's organizational activism outside the parties to pressure them to advance women and to adopt policies reflective of women's interests variously conceptualized.

Chapter 6 trains a different lens on women's voice and practice of politics. It centers on grassroots organizing and community-level action as well as on national initiatives of groups with little political power and few of the traditional resources to be major players in the policy-making process. Women have long been active in efforts to improve, better, and reform their communities. This chapter focuses attention on the empowerment of women at the grassroots level rather than spotlighting more traditional participation emphasized in preceding chapters. Challenges to local power structures that individual women and diverse groups of women have undertaken encompass fascinating, innovative, and sometimes dangerous actions attacking many aspects of their disempowerment. It is an area of participation that has received minimal attention in other texts focusing on women and politics in the United States. It is especially important in a work that seeks to highlight the linking of political participation and economic inequality. Exploring grassroots women's activism in their communities expands readers' ideas of power and political engagement. It should stimulate a desire to observe, perhaps become involved in, and appreciate grassroots initiatives. Empowerment as defined earlier is the principal organizing concept of this chapter.

The political life of American women has come to not only involve quests for individual political leadership and movements for gaining political equality for women in the United States but also engagement in activities and the joining of networks for global women's rights and the improvement of women's and girls' status. Globalization is a central feature of contemporary political, social, and economic life, and women's rights globally have become a major political movement of the past several decades. Thus, including attention on their efforts to affect women's rights at the international level and the nature of those efforts enhances an understanding of the political participation of American women.

Chapter 7 explores the activity of U.S. nongovernmental organizations (NGOs) working to achieve equal rights for women on a global scale. It surveys the nature of these groups, their stimulus for organizing, and their goals. They are incredibly diverse, engaging in a vast array of activities to achieve their aims. Their interests range from eliminating violence against women and energizing women's economic positions to changing legal systems and boosting women's political leadership presence. Their practices include awareness campaigns, governmental lobbying, training women to be leaders in other countries, and working within transnational advocacy networks. Examples of such organizations and their missions include the Coalition Against Trafficking in Women with the mission of "promot[ing] women's human rights. It works internationally to combat sexual exploitation in all its forms, especially prostitution and trafficking in women and children, in particular girls."[1]

Vital Voices, whose mission is to "identify, invest in and bring visibility to extraordinary women around the world by unleashing their leadership potential to transform lives and accelerate peace and prosperity in their communities,"[2] and Women for Women International, which "provides women survivors of war, civil strife, and other conflicts with the tools and resources to move from crisis and poverty to stability and self-sufficiency, thereby promoting viable civil societies,"[3] are other examples. This text's coverage of the diversity of work in this area should raise readers' awareness of women's rights as human rights beyond equality issues within the United States and encourage them to ponder the nature and extent of the work of U.S. women's rights organizations outside our borders.

In section 3, Political Representation and Policy, the political practices and voices of women turn to women's quests to be public leaders and to the making of public policy. Chapter 8 explores women's quests for elective office. It presents trends in women's election to public office, compares their quests for political leadership with that of men, and centers much of its attention on efforts to elect more women to legislative and executive positions. Women have achieved political leadership at all levels of U.S. government except the presidency. It is now commonplace for women to serve as chief executives in the states, be congressional leaders, run federal cabinet departments, and be judges. Women candidates in contemporary elections are as sophisticated and strategic as male candidates. They organize professional campaigns and raise money to finance those campaigns to the same extent as men do. Yet men still vastly outnumber women as political candidates and elective office holders. Women do not seem to be as politically ambitious as men are and do not appear to be recruited to run for public office as often as men. Thus, exploration of the role of gender in contemporary political campaigns is an important part of Chapter 8.

Chapter 8 also surveys women's organizational efforts to elect women to public office. A distinction of recent elections has been the formation of groups to recruit, train, and support female candidates and to stimulate the interest of younger women in political leadership. Local, state, and national campaign trainings have proliferated. Partisan groups and academic organizations have become involved as well as nonpartisan women's organizations. One group, the Women Under Forty Political Action Committee, supports the candidacies of younger women, whereas Political Parity works to get older women to run for office. The Women's Campaign Forum (WCF) offers an online program, She Should Run, in which individuals can complete a questionnaire suggesting a woman who should be considered as a potential candidate. WCF then follows up. Whereas liberal groups have been most active in this domain, conservative women's groups now promote women as candidates for public office as well. Sarah Palin's "mama grizzly" effort, initiated in the 2010 election, is the most colorful of these conservative endeavors.

Chapter 9 chronicles the distinctive 2016 campaign of former U.S. Senator and Secretary of State Hillary Clinton to become the first woman president. She was routinely considered the most likely Democrat to seek this office after the 2012 election. She won the Democratic Party nomination after a hard-fought campaign against independent Senator Bernie Sanders and was the frontrunner during most of the general election campaign. Although winning nearly three million more votes than Republican nominee Donald Trump, she lost the all-important Electoral College vote, which gave the election to Trump. Gender was a factor in this campaign in ways not imagined at the beginning of the campaign season. Chapter 9 highlights the gendered aspects of the 2016 presidential election.

What has all the political activity chronicled in these chapters produced in the way of substantive representation of issues of particular concern to women in the policy-making process and the enactment of laws centering on women's rights and equity? Chapter 10 focuses on public policies. It asks what women in elective office have achieved for women. What are the ways in which female lawmakers have affected the policy-making process?

This question is addressed through several lenses. The first section of this chapter centers on their styles as lawmakers and trends in their formal legislative leadership. The second section explores the substantive impact on policy making. In keeping with the central theme of this work, it pays particular attention to the economic aspects of public policy. This section begins with a historical perspective on public policies regarding equality for women. It takes readers back to the era before women began to organize for political equality and describes the limitations and public constraints on women acting as independent actors in the economic and political life of the nation, even after obtaining the vote. The "great" laws enacted in the second half of the 20th century, such as Title VII of the 1964 Civil Rights Act, which bans sex discrimination in employment, Title IX of the 1972 Education Amendment Act, and the 1994 Violence Against Women Act, are chronicled. The third section of this chapter explores equality issues on the legislative agenda in the contemporary era of the early decades of the new millennium. Examples of recent legislation include the Lilly Ledbetter Fair Pay Act of 2009 and the renewal of the Violence Against Women Act of 1994. Legislation introduced in recent congresses includes the Pregnant Workers Fairness Act, the Paycheck Fairness Act, and the Campus Sexual Violence Elimination (SaVE) Act. Thus, legislative remedies regarding inequality continue to be part of the policy-making landscape, and in many cases continue to be controversial.

Chapter 11, the book's concluding chapter, places American women's quest for political equality and influence in a comparative context. According to data assembled by the Inter-Parliamentary Union (www.ipu.org), the United States lags far behind other democracies in the percentage of its national legislators who are women. Scholars have explored many theories to explain the variation in women's office holding cross-nationally. The chapter explores what we have learned about why the United States lags behind so many other nations. It then considers that although women are vastly underrepresented in Congress, the U.S. Congress is one of the most powerful and independent policy-making institutions globally. Therefore, whereas their numerical representation may be trailing from a comparative perspective, female representatives in the United States perhaps have more opportunities to influence policy making than their fellow female legislators in many parliamentary systems. How they have used these opportunities is consequential for political and economic equality. *Women and Politics* concludes with an overview and assessment of the active citizenship of women in the United States.

On many fronts, the contour of women's lives in the United States has changed dramatically over the course of the second half of the 20th century and the early decades of the 21st century. In 1960, only 6 percent of women aged twenty-five and older had completed four or more years of college. In 2013, that number had risen to 31 percent. The educational attainment of women now outpaces that of men.

Women's labor force participation has increased significantly. In 1950, one third of adult women were in the workforce; in 2015, that number rose to 56 percent. The labor force participation of men remains higher than women's, but men's participation has fallen over time, whereas women's participation has increased, contributing to the closing of the employment gap.

In 1960, female full-time workers earned fifty-nine cents for every dollar men earned. By 2015, they were earning seventy-nine cents, a large narrowing of the pay gap but still a substantial gap. At the same time, women were two thirds of minimum wage workers. Occupational segregation continues to have a negative impact on the gaining of wage equality. Further, at all age levels, women are more likely to live in poverty than men are.

In 1950, one member out of the one hundred U.S. senators was a woman. Nine women were U.S. representatives, 2 percent of its membership. In 2017, 21 percent of the U.S. Senate were women, and 83 of the 435 members of the U.S. House of Representatives were women, 19 percent of its membership. Women now vote at higher rates than men. All these trends—political and economic—are of great substantive importance in American political, social, and economic life. The goal of this book is to make them visible and to center readers' attention on their implications in the quest for equality.

Notes

1. http://catwinternational.org/.
2. www.womenforwomen.org/.
3. www.womenforwomen.org/.

References

Arrillaga, Pauline. 2012. "Women Ponder How They Became a Campaign Issue." *The Associated Press*, May 12.

Bartels, Larry. 2008. *Unequal Democracy: The Political Economy of the New Gilded Age*. New York, NY: Russell Sage Foundation.

Bookman, Ann and Sandra Morgen. 1988. *Women and the Politics of Empowerment*. Philadelphia, PA: Temple University Press.

Carlin, Diana B. and Kelly L. Winfrey. 2009. "Have You Come a Long Way, Baby? Hillary Clinton, Sarah Palin, and Sexism in 2008 Campaign Coverage." *Communications Studies*, 60, 4: 326–343.

Cohen, Cathy J., Kathleen B. Jones, and Joan C. Tronto. 1997. "Introduction: Women Transforming U.S. Politics: Sites of Power/Resistance." In *Women Transforming Politics*, eds. Cathy J. Cohen, Kathleen B. Jones, and Joan Tronto. New York, NY: New York University Press, 1–12.

Dittmar, Kelly. 2016. "Watching Election 2016 with a Gender Lens." *P.S. Political Science & Politics*, October.

Freeman, Jo. 2000. *A Room at a Time: How Women Entered Party Politics*. Lanham, MD: Rowman & Littlefield.

Jacobson, Gary. 1985. "Party Organization and Distribution of Campaign Resources: Republicans and Democrats in 1982." *Political Science Quarterly*, 100, 4 (Winter): 603–625.

Kraditor, Aileen. 1965. *Ideas of the Woman Suffrage Movement, 1890–1920*. New York, NY: Columbia University Press.

Lawrence, Regina G. and Melody Rose. 2010. *Hillary Clinton's Race for the White House: Gender Politics and the Media on the Campaign Trail*. Boulder, CO: Lynne Rienner.

Naples, Nancy. 1998. *Community Activism and Feminism Politics: Organizing Across Race, Class and Gender*. New York, NY: Routledge.

Noah, Timothy. 2010. "The Great Divergence: What's Causing America's Growing Income Inequality?" *Slate*, September 3.

Schlozman, Kay, Benjamin Page, Sidney Verba, and Morris Fiorina. 2005. "Inequalities of Political Voice." www.apsanet.org/portals/54/Files/Memos/voicememo.pdf.

Whitaker, Lois. 2008. *Voting the Gender Gap*. Urbana, IL: University of Illinois Press.

2 The First and Second Women's Rights Movements

On Friday, November 1, 1872, Susan B. Anthony, one of the preeminent leaders of the campaign to win the right to vote for women in the 19th century, led fourteen women in Rochester, New York, to the local barbershop that was set up as the local registry and polling station to register to vote in the presidential election that would occur five days later. They convinced the election officials that they had the right to vote. They then "dared to vote" the following Tuesday (Hull 2012). In a letter to fellow women's suffragists, she wrote, "Well I have been & gone & done it! Positively voted the Republican ticket—strait this a.m. at 7 O'clock."

Their action was legally challenged a few days later. They were charged with having "knowingly, wrongfully, and unlawfully voted for a representative to the Congress of the United States." Anthony then traveled around the region lecturing on the principles on which she claimed the right to vote, hoping to affect public opinion before her jury trial. At the trial, however, the presiding judge summarily decided she was guilty. He did not allow the jury to deliberate. On appeal, he fined Anthony $100, which she refused to pay, but she never went to jail for nonpayment. Anthony was the only woman to be tried in a federal court for the crime of voting. She contended that voting was a fundamental right or privilege of citizenship.

The Constitution the founding fathers wrote left it up to the states to decide who could vote. It was state laws that limited voting to men. The U.S. Constitution had not been amended to explicitly give women the franchise nor had any state passed legislation to give women the right to vote, including the state of New York by 1872 when Anthony and her companions sought to exercise that right. Today, male and female citizens eighteen years of age and older take the right to vote for granted. Indeed, in contemporary elections, women are more likely to turn out to vote than men.

The 14th Amendment to the Constitution enacted in 1868 as part of the civil rights amendments states,

> All persons born or naturalized in the United States, and subject to the jurisdiction thereof, are citizens of the United States and of the State wherein they reside. No State shall make or enforce any law which shall abridge the privileges or immunities of citizens of the United States.

A major constitutional question that emerged centered on what were the *privileges* of citizenship. Was the right to vote one of those privileges, as Susan B. Anthony and others argued?

In the nearly quarter century of women's rights activity that had preceded the enactment of the 14th Amendment, suffragists, as those who advocated for women's right to vote were called, had petitioned Congress for a constitutional suffrage amendment and engaged in lobbying campaigns in state legislatures for voting rights. But this amendment provided the suffragists with a "new departure" or strategy regarding the voting rights of women. Rather than having to petition for the right to vote, perhaps the 14th Amendment already gave women that right if voting was determined to be a fundamental privilege of citizenship. They set out to test this idea.

Intricacies of the law did not allow Anthony to appeal her conviction to a higher court to make constitutional arguments, but in Missouri, Virginia Minor had been denied the right to register to vote that same year, and she and her husband, a lawyer, undertook a civil lawsuit that did go to the U.S. Supreme Court, arguing that the elective franchise was a privilege of citizenship under the 14th Amendment and that denial of that right violated the Constitution. The Supreme Court affirmed that women were citizens, but it went on to unanimously rule that the right to vote was not a privilege of that citizenship. The Constitution did not enumerate privileges nor had it created voters, the judges stated, but left that matter up to the states. "The United States has no voters of its own creation," Chief Justice Morrison Waite wrote. Missouri law had barred women from voting and could continue to do so, the court decided. In addition, unfortunately for women seeking to find in the Constitution and its amendments the right to vote, the 15th Amendment had guaranteed citizens the right to vote regardless of race, color, or previous condition of servitude—but not sex. The 15th Amendment's failure to list sex as one of the characteristics that could not be used to deprive a citizen the vote worked against the suffragists in their claim to a constitutional right to vote.

How were women to win the right to vote if it was not already guaranteed in the U.S. Constitution? How could a group without political power—that is, without the vote and without the right to run for and hold elective office and to lead party organizations—obtain such power from those who already had it (Kraditor 1981)? How did women win the vote? How would they convince men who held political power to give them that right and to stimulate interest among women socialized to not see themselves as independent actors in the public sphere? As noted in Chapter 1, female activists undertook myriad campaigns over seventy years to gain the vote. This chapter describes the political practices—tactics and strategies—the suffragists adopted in these various campaigns. As women began to engage in the public realm, they were met with ridicule, hostility, and even bodily harm. Suffragists endured many defeats in their long quest for the vote. They often had to rethink their strategies (Marilley 1996).

In the early decades of the republic, separate spheres characterized men's and women's lives. Women's place was limited to the private sphere of raising children and domestic work, whereas men's place was in the public sphere of politics and business. Women were not allowed to go to school, speak in public, own property, sue in court, sign a will, or have legal custody of their own children. They could not keep the salaries they earned but had to turn them over to the husbands or fathers who "owned" them. A woman could not leave her husband's home without danger of being forcibly or legally returned. Husbands had a right to physical discipline. Women were considered minors in terms of their intellectual ability.

But women had participated in the American Revolution. Their involvement was central to the success of boycotts of imported products and in the production of household manufactures. They ran the farms and businesses in their husbands' absence. Examples of groups of women angered at what they viewed as wartime price-gouging forcing storekeepers to charge just prices have been recounted. Women also took part in urban crowd actions, organized petition campaigns, and formed groups to help soldiers and widows (Baker 1984).

When women became active in the reform movements of the early decades of the 19th century, they began to question the limitations of a public role for women. Over the course of that century, the demographics of women's lives began to change. Women began to work outside the home with the arrival of the Industrial Revolution. Particularly notable was rural New England, where women began to work in the textile mills. They experienced unequal wages and restricted job openings. They went on strike and formed "associations to fight for better working conditions and hours" (Parker 2002, 25). They also began to seek greater educational opportunities beyond a primary education. By the beginning of the 20th century, women increasingly received extensive education, worked outside the home, entered professional careers, had fewer children, and divorced. The term *the new woman* described the movement of women from the home to the public sphere.

Reform causes that brought women into the public realm included temperance, equal education, workplace inequality, and most significantly, abolition of slavery. Their involvement in these movements gave women rhetorical and practical skills for public leadership. Well before they began to organize for equal rights for themselves, "women circulated thousands of petitions and gathered millions of signatures on petitions for various political causes" (Carpenter and Moore 2014, 479). At the same time, for the most part, they were not allowed leadership in organizations such as the Anti-Slavery Society. Disgruntlement with the limited role they were allowed to play in the abolition movement led to a call for broader women's rights.

Organizing the first women's rights meeting was a remarkable undertaking. It was held in Seneca Falls, New York, in 1848. The announcement of the meeting read a "Woman's Rights Convention—a convention to discuss the social, civil and religious rights of woman." The five organizers, Elizabeth Cady Stanton, Lucretia Mott, Mary Ann McClintock, Jane Hunt, and Martha Wright, wrote a Declaration of Principles based on the Declaration of Independence. At that time, along with being barred for the most part from speaking in public, women were deprived of property rights and control of any earnings they made in employment outside the home, were denied guardianship of their children, were not allowed to vote, could not sign contracts, and were not permitted to testify in court. The participants in this meeting were principally concerned with acquiring greater economic and social rights. The idea of suffrage was considered most radical, but in the end, it was included in their list of demands after the Black abolitionist Frederick Douglass spoke in its favor. Seneca Falls produced a women's rights agenda for its time. The Seneca Falls Declaration adopted by the participants in this meeting included a lengthy list of demands, as Text Box 2.1 enumerates. More than three hundred individuals, men and women, participated in the Seneca Falls meeting.

Text Box 2.1 Seneca Falls Declaration of Sentiments

When, in the course of human events, it becomes necessary for one portion of the family of man to assume among the people of the earth a position different from that which they have hitherto occupied, but one to which the laws of nature and of nature's God entitle them, a decent respect to the opinions of mankind requires that they should declare the causes that impel them to such a course.

We hold these truths to be self-evident: that all men and women are created equal; that they are endowed by their Creator with certain inalienable rights; that among these are life, liberty, and the pursuit of happiness; that to secure these rights governments are instituted, deriving their just powers from the consent of the governed. Whenever any form of Government becomes destructive of these ends, it is the right of those who suffer from it to refuse allegiance to it, and to insist upon the institution of a new government, laying its foundation on such principles, and organizing its powers in such form as to them shall seem most likely to affect their safety and happiness. Prudence, indeed, will dictate that governments long established should not be changed for light and transient causes; and accordingly, all experience hath shown that mankind are more disposed to suffer, while evils are sufferable, than to right themselves by abolishing the forms to which they are accustomed. But when a long train of abuses and usurpations, pursuing invariably the same object, evinces a design to reduce them under absolute despotism, it is their duty to throw off such government, and to provide new guards for their future security. Such has been the patient sufferance of the women under this government, and such is now the necessity which constrains them to demand the equal station to which they are entitled.

The history of mankind is a history of repeated injuries and usurpations on the part of man toward woman, having in direct object the establishment of an absolute tyranny over her. To prove this, let facts be submitted to a candid world.

He has never permitted her to exercise her inalienable right to the elective franchise.

He has compelled her to submit to laws, in the formation of which she had no voice.

He has withheld from her rights which are given to the most ignorant and degraded men—both natives and foreigners.

Having deprived her of this first right of a citizen, the elective franchise, thereby leaving her without representation in the halls of legislation, he has oppressed her on all sides.

He has made her, if married, in the eye of the law, civilly dead.

He has taken from her all right in property, even to the wages she earns.

He has made her, morally, an irresponsible being, as she can commit many crimes with impunity, provided they be done in the presence of her husband. In the covenant of marriage, she is compelled to promise obedience to her husband, he becoming, to all intents and purposes, her master—the law giving him power to deprive her of her liberty, and to administer chastisement.

He has so framed the laws of divorce, as to what shall be the proper causes of divorce; in case of separation, to whom the guardianship of the children shall be given; as to be wholly regardless of the happiness of women—the law, in all cases, going upon the false supposition of the supremacy of man, and giving all power into his hands.

After depriving her of all rights as a married woman, if single and the owner of property, he has taxed her to support a government which recognizes her only when her property can be made profitable to it.

He has monopolized nearly all the profitable employments, and from those she is permitted to follow, she receives but a scanty remuneration.

He closes against her all the avenues to wealth and distinction, which he considers most honorable to himself. As a teacher of theology, medicine, or law, she is not known.

He has denied her the facilities for obtaining a thorough education—all colleges being closed against her.

He allows her in Church as well as State, but a subordinate position, claiming Apostolic authority for her exclusion from the ministry, and, with some exceptions, from any public participation in the affairs of the Church.

He has created a false public sentiment, by giving to the world a different code of morals for men and women, by which moral delinquencies which exclude women from society, are not only tolerated but deemed of little account in man.

He has usurped the prerogative of Jehovah himself, claiming it as his right to assign for her a sphere of action, when that belongs to her conscience and her God.

He has endeavored, in every way that he could to destroy her confidence in her own powers, to lessen her self-respect, and to make her willing to lead a dependent and abject life.

Now, in view of this entire disfranchisement of one-half the people of this country, their social and religious degradation,—in view of the unjust laws above mentioned, and because women do feel themselves aggrieved, oppressed, and fraudulently deprived of their most sacred rights, we insist that they have immediate admission to all the rights and privileges which belong to them as citizens of these United States.

In entering upon the great work before us, we anticipate no small amount of misconception, misrepresentation, and ridicule; but we shall use every instrumentality within our power to effect our object. We shall employ agents, circulate tracts, petition the State and national Legislatures, and endeavor to enlist the pulpit and the press in our behalf. We hope this Convention will be followed by a series of Conventions, embracing every part of the country.

Firmly relying upon the final triumph of the Right and the True, we do this day affix our signatures to this declaration.

Women's rights proponents primarily engaged in yearly conventions from 1848 to 1860 to advance their goals of greater equality. The conventions promoted reform campaigns, generated publicity for women's rights issues, and inspired public debate. The major goal of the women's rights movement was to change public opinion regarding women's capacities and rights and to act in the public sphere. Activists lectured and wrote many articles, pamphlets, and books. Major newspaper coverage of their activities, often from a negative frame, generated most of the publicity about their cause. They also began a campaign to acquire signatures to petitions to state legislatures to change the laws aimed at women, particularly those regarding property rights (Parker 2002). Obtaining signatures was an extraordinarily laborious task in those times, involving primitive travel conditions, much hostility, and apathy. As described by Susan B. Anthony's biographer, Rheta Dorr (1928, 92),

> Like itinerant tin pedlars or book agents they trampled the streets and country roads, knocking at every door, presenting their petitions, arguing with women who half the time slammed the door in their faces with the smug remark that they had husbands, thank God, to look after their interests, and they needed no new laws to protect their rights. After each rebuff the women simply trudged on to the next street, the next row of houses, the next grudgingly opened front door.

After the Civil War, activists turned their attention more single-mindedly to gaining the right to vote until ratification of the federal suffrage amendment in 1920. As noted in Chapter 1, the suffrage organizations participated in campaigns that included a wide range of tactics and actions at the local, state, and national levels. They engaged in demonstrations, legal quests, and political actions. They tried to convince state legislators, members of Congress, local officials, and political party organizations of the rightness of their cause. They employed "insider" and "outsider" strategies to convince lawmakers and the general public that women ought to have the vote. Insider strategies involved activities suffrage proponents used to persuade political insiders—lawmakers or politicians—that movement demands ought to be met. These tactics included personally lobbying state legislators, writing letters to them, giving speeches in state legislatures, and gathering signatures on petitions to present to state legislatures. They also employed strategies targeted at political "outsiders"—that is, nonpoliticians. The suffragists engaged in a variety of such activities. To build membership,

> [they] held regular state suffrage conventions, organized various social events, and put trained organizers in the field. To persuade the general public that women should be given the right to vote, suffragists gave public speeches, distributed handbills, advertised in newspapers, held suffrage parades, and set up booths at local fairs.
>
> (McCammon and Campbell 2001, 61)

By the time the 19th Amendment was ratified in 1920, fifteen states had already granted women full suffrage, two southern states had given women the right to vote in primary elections, and thirteen states had awarded women the right to vote for president.

The suffrage movement had to overcome several hurdles in its attempt to gain the right to vote for women. First, even among early women's rights advocates, petitioning for suffrage was considered too extreme of a measure. Second, in the aftermath of the Civil War, as Congress considered the 15th Amendment to the Constitution granting voting rights to Black men, debate ensued over whether the right of women to vote should be included or whether it was the Black man's time. An inclusion of women in the amendment was too controversial, and many believed it would lead to the defeat of the amendment. Third, advocates split over strategy in the years after the war and losing the fight to include sex in the 15th Amendment. Should all energies be put into a 16th Constitutional Amendment granting women the right to vote, or should campaigns be waged in individual states to gain the franchise?

This last question split the movement into two associations in 1869. Susan B. Anthony and Elizabeth Cady Stanton organized and led the National Woman Suffrage Association (NWSA), comprised exclusively of women, which had the sole objective of securing a 16th Amendment to the Constitution that would enfranchise women. They targeted both middle- and working-class women and focused their efforts on lobbying Congress rather than on organizing state campaigns. The leaders of the NWSA regarded women's rights as a broad cause in which the vote was of primary importance, but other matters such as divorce and prostitution were also significant (Flexner 1974, 153). The second organization, the American Woman Suffrage Association (AWSA), included men and women and centered its efforts on a state-by-state approach to women's suffrage. It concentrated solely on winning the vote and dismissed broader social issues. It built a national communications network through its newsletter, the *Woman's Journal*. Neither group made much progress over the next two decades. Thus, in 1890, they merged into the National American Woman Suffrage Association (NAWSA), with work continuing at both the state and national levels. Suffragists organized associations in every state except Wyoming (which had granted women the vote as a territory in 1869), typically one of the first steps in launching a suffrage movement in a state.

By the turn of the century, suffragists began to hold informal, open-air meetings. They engaged in speeches "standing on soap boxes on street corners or on the backs of open

---

Sidebar 2.1 The 19th Amendment

The right of citizens of the United States to vote shall not be denied or abridged by the United States or by any State on account of sex.

Congress shall have power to enforce this article by appropriate legislation.

automobiles allowing the activists to appeal to those who might not otherwise ever consider voting rights for women or who even might be hostile to the issue" (McCammon 2003, 791). Suffrage parades also became a new, prominent tactic at this time. "Marching in public was a bold step for the suffragists" (McCammon 2003, 788). Between 1908 and 1916, suffragists held parades in twenty-four states. The parades allowed the suffragists to

> present themselves to onlookers as serious and dignified and in possession of the courage to appear publicly to make their demand. The suffrage parades were not festive nor frivolous, but rather the women marched typically in formation, wearing white dresses and carrying banners and signs with their rationales for the vote printed on them.
>
> (McCammon 2003, 791)

The most infamous of all the suffragist parades, organized by what at that time was the Congressional Union, a subgroup of NAWSA, took place in Washington, DC, in 1913, when five thousand women marched the day before Woodrow Wilson's inauguration as president, a day when visitors from around the country were converging on the city. A large crowd attacked the marchers, overwhelming the police staffing the route. The suffragists received tremendous publicity and much supportive public opinion as a result of their ill treatment. Pilgrimages were then organized to Washington from all over the country, with petitions collected at the grassroots level. The pilgrimages culminated in an automobile procession to the Capitol on July 31, 1913, which presented a group of senators with suffrage petitions carrying two hundred thousand signatures.

Public demonstrations or protests challenging established policies were not part of the suffragists' early repertoire of actions with one major exception. In 1876, the United States celebrated its centennial with a large exposition in Philadelphia, including a Fourth of July celebration in Independence Hall. As Flexner (1974), recounts, "The National Women Suffrage Association hope to use the occasion to draw attention to the still inequitable position of women, and also to bring women from all over the country together to exchange their experiences and knowledge" (170). No women were scheduled to speak at the gathering. At a key moment in the program, uninvited Susan B. Anthony led five women to the platform, where they proceeded to hand the program chair a parchment setting out a Declaration of Rights for Women. They left, scattering large handfuls of printed broadsides of their declaration throughout the hall, causing chaos.

As Anthony and Stanton describe the event,

> The declaration of 1776 was read by Richard Henry Lee, of Virginia, about whose family clusters so much of historic fame. The close of his reading was deemed the appropriate moment for the presentation of the women's declaration. Not quite sure how their approach might be met—not certain if at this final moment they would be permitted to reach the presiding officer—those ladies arose and made their way down the aisle. The bustle of preparation for the Brazilian hymn covered their advance. The foreign guests, the military and civil officers who filled the space directly in front of the speaker's stand, courteously made way while Miss Anthony in fitting words presented the declaration. Mr. Ferry's face paled, as bowing low, with no word, he received the declaration which became part of the day's proceedings. The ladies turned, scattering printed copies, as they deliberately walked down the platform. On every side eager hands were stretched, men stood on seats and asked for them.
>
> (Stanton et al. 1885, 30)

Outside the hall, they took advantage of an empty bandstand and a large crowd milling around. Anthony proceeded to read the declaration "in a clear voice that carried far out across the listening throng" (Flexner 1974, 171).

The suffrage movement entered into "the doldrums" for several decades at the end of the 19th century and into the first decade of the 20th century. It took on new life in the second decade. World War I greatly impacted the movement and its push for voting rights. Carrie Chapman Catt became the president of the NAWSA and adopted what became known as the "winning plan," while Alice Paul led a faction that broke away into the Congressional Union and then the Women's Party, which engaged in more militant but nonviolent protest actions.

Catt's winning plan, adopted in 1916, centered on an aggressive nonpartisan lobbying effort in Congress for a constitutional amendment while still working on passing suffrage laws in the states. An important feature of the plan was the creation of "suffrage schools" to train women to be effective leaders in NAWSA at all levels.

> Schools addressed how to work with ordinary citizens and professional politicians, how to deal with (and, if possible, use) the press, and the fundamental techniques of skillful public speaking . . . how to organize down to the last practical detail of circulating petitions.

The aim was to develop a sophisticated lobbying effort at every level of government. NAWSA recruited a membership of two million individuals.

Alice Paul first formed a congressional committee, the Congressional Union, under the auspices of the NAWSA, focusing on a constitutional amendment and advocating a more militant but nonviolent strategy. The Congressional Union worked solely for a constitutional amendment. It insisted on holding "the party in power" responsible for failure to pass the women's suffrage bill or to act to further its passage through Congress (Flexner 1974, 267). Because the Democratic Party held the presidency and the majority in Congress, the Congressional Union centered it actions against it as bearing responsibility for the lack of voting rights for women. They organized the National Woman's Party in the twelve states that had granted women the presidential vote to urge women to vote in a bloc against the Democratic Party in the 1914 and 1916 elections, regardless of whether a Democratic congressional candidate supported women's suffrage. The number of women participating in the franchise had grown to four million by the 1916 presidential election. The National Woman's Party also opposed President Wilson's reelection (Ford 2002).

In 1917, the National Woman's Party began to picket the White House, heckling and embarrassing President Wilson in order to shame him into pressuring Democratic members of Congress to pass a constitutional amendment granting women the right to vote. As the United States entered World War I, this group of suffragists began to stand outside the White House carrying banners "calling attention to the lack of congruence between American democratic war aims and American undemocratic practice in denying self-government to half its citizens" (Kraditor 1981, 239). They also ceremoniously burned Wilson's speeches. They chained themselves to the White House fence and blocked traffic on Pennsylvania Avenue by lying in the street. Their tactics were militant but nonviolent actions, but they were met with violent police and bystander reaction. They were arrested, tried for "obstructing traffic" in front of the White House, and sentenced to jail terms. Between mid-1917 and early 1919, 168 women suffrage protesters were arrested in various demonstrations, mostly in Washington, DC. At first, the jailed suffragists received sentences of a few days. But then, in the fall of 1917, they began to receive sixty-day sentences and sent to the wretched Occoquam Workhouse in Virginia, where they went on hunger strikes.

In suffragist history, November 10, 1917, became known as the "night of terror" when more than 150 women picketing the White House were assaulted, brutally beaten, and

Picture 2.1 1917 Suffragist White House Picket

"The first picket line—College day in the picket line," 1917.

Courtesy of the Prints and Photographs Division, Library of Congress. Reproduction Number LC-USZ62–31799.

jailed for protesting Paul's confinement in a mental ward. Determined to escalate their struggle, the militants refused to give their names until they could present their demand to be considered political prisoners to the superintendent. Enraged guards clubbed and beat the women prisoners, from sixty-year-old Lavina Dock, who was pushed down some stairs, to the youthful writer and activist Dorothy Day, who was beaten and choked. Once released from jail, they generated publicity by touring the country in prison garb on "the Prison Special."

Finally, in 1919, both the U.S. Senate and the U.S. House of Representatives approved the Susan B. Anthony amendment by a two-thirds vote and sent the proposed amendment to the states for ratification. On August 18, 1920, the state legislature of Tennessee became the thirty-sixth state to vote for ratification, giving the proposed amendment the necessary three quarters of states needed to become part of the constituent. More than eight million women voted for the first time in the 1920 presidential election. But it is estimated that only 26 percent of eligible women actually voted that year, a far lower percentage than men (Simon and Danziger 1991). This lower turnout is perhaps not surprisingly given that so many women had been socialized not to consider themselves political beings. As we will see, it took many decades for the underrepresentation of women in the suffrage to disappear. On the other hand, women in Wyoming had been voting for half a century and those in Colorado for twenty-five years when the 19th Amendment was enacted in 1920. Twelve states had already granted full political rights to women, and seventeen additional states had some form of women's suffrage for presidential elections (Cox 1996).

Class and Race in the Suffragist Movement

The suffrage movement was primarily a middle-class and elite women's movement. Over the course of the long campaign to win the vote, some efforts were made to bring working-class women into the campaign and to improve labor conditions for employed women. But lower-class women struggled for the most part on a separate plain for economic rights and improved working conditions as they entered the labor force. The female labor force grew throughout the 19th century. By the 1890s, more than four million women were gainfully employed (Flexner 1974, 193). Long hours, overwork, and poor working conditions characterized women's industrial work throughout the 19th and early 20th centuries (Lerner 1969). They were increasing involved in trade unionism. As women entered the labor force in the early decades of that century, particularly working in the textile mills of New England, they engaged in efforts to organize for better working conditions. In 1869, the first women's trade union was founded in Massachusetts, the Daughters of St. Crispin. In the late 1860s, leaders of the women's rights movement made a short-lived attempt to organize working women as a new source of potential supporters. But the two groups had little in common. Union organizers focused on wages and hours, whereas women's rights activists tended to focus on issues such as property rights, suffrage, and education, privileges that most working women had not even considered. Although Susan B. Anthony began publishing her own weekly newspaper, *The Revolution*, at the end of the 1860s, she also "devoted considerable time and effort to helping such women organize" (Flexner 1974, 135).

By 1900, the composition of the female labor force began to change with the influx of immigrant women workers. Many activists in the suffrage movement came to adopt anti-immigrant rhetoric in their campaign for the vote either out of expediency or from a growing conservative belief system, which limited an alignment across classes for women's rights.

The suffrage movement had a strong link to the abolition movement, suggesting an ideology of racial equality among suffragists of at least some sort. But a linking of women's political rights and the political rights of Blacks came uncoupled after the Civil War. When suffrage was extended to former slaves but not to women with the passage of the 15th Amendment, much of the women's movement abandoned its alliance with Blacks. Suffragists also exhibited racism in their rhetoric and actions after they lost that campaign. From the late 1880s until the 19th Amendment was ratified, suffragists made many racist and nativist arguments for the vote (Marilley 1996, 161), some aggressively and enthusiastically and others defensively and reluctantly.

> Partly from belief—and partly as a tactic to win equally prejudiced male legislators, voters, and the business interest of the East and South—the NAWSA leaders often advocated limited suffrage for women during this period. They argued that the vote could be limited to all men and women who were educated and propertied, thus excluding most of the workers, immigrants, and blacks.
>
> (Deckard 1979, 282–283)

In the south in particular, suffragists hoped to gain the vote for White women at least in part as a counterbalance to what they perceived to be the threatening and corruptive nature of Black male voters (Alexander 1995). They supported the idea of White supremacy and advocated for "educated suffrage." Both northern and southern suffragists expressed indignation that their social inferiors (immigrants as well as Black men) had become their political superiors (Wheeler 1995, 38). In 1903, the NAWSA passed a resolution stating that there were more White native-born women who could read and write than all Black and foreign-born voters combined so that "the enfranchisement of such women would settle the vexed question of rule by literacy, whether of home grown or foreign-born production" (Terborg-Penn 1998, 110). Racism came to be a factor in suffrage ideology and strategy throughout the United States (Spruill 2002).

An expedient argument also contributed to suffrage organizations abandoning a more inclusive call for the vote. The national constitution strategy would first require the votes of some southern members of Congress and then at least some southern states voting for ratification to obtain the necessary three fourths of states voting for a constitutional amendment. Thus, the NAWSA adopted a strategy of systematically excluding Black suffragists from White-led suffrage organizations and meetings, as the suffragists sought to distance their movement from a historic association with advocacy for the rights of Black Americans (Spruill 2002). They were excluded from national campaign activities out of a worry that such visible involvement would "only exacerbate the latent antagonism of those politicians from Dixie and would thereby reinforce and guarantee their opposition to woman suffrage" (Alexander 1995, 80). It was expedient to ignore Black women when advocating for support in the South.

But what was the nature of the support and activism of Black women regarding suffrage? Black women were active in advocating for votes for women, even though they suffered many indignities from the NAWSA. They argued how much more they needed the vote than White women in order to protect themselves, being doubly victimized by both sexism and racism. They combined advocacy for the vote with a broader Black nationalist feminism regarding equality. Women's political empowerment would benefit the Black community as a whole, they argued (Alexander 1995). Black women worked with the mainstream suffragists on some levels, where they suffered indignities, but they also organized on local and national levels among themselves. They formed their own clubs. In 1896, they established the National Association of Colored Women (NACW), an organization that continues today. These organizations also brought their leaders into public view on local and national levels. Verifiably authentic Black women's voices emerged in the 1870s and 1880s (Terborg-Penn 1998).

Once women won the vote in 1920, what did they do with their new political voice? The dominant historical perspective has been that women's activism for a greater public voice entered into a period of "the doldrums" for approximately forty years, when a second wave of feminist awakening and activism emerged in the 1960s. More recent historical research has challenged this perspective, providing evidence of women's political activism in several domains rising and falling across the decades. Women's rights activists worked within the federal bureaucracy, and labor activism was especially notable. For example, beginning with World War II, millions of women fought against workplace discrimination on the basis of sex, race, age, and marital status, both seeking access to the better jobs men held and also enhancement of the light manufacturing, service, and clerical occupations in which the majority of them labored. They worked for equal pay, childcare, and the right to combine employment and motherhood. These labor feminists sought equal rights as well as special accommodations, like maternity leave, to make equality possible. "They would revalue housework and care work, whether performed for one's family or for a wage; indeed, the worth of the first was central" (Cobble 2004). The National Woman's Party also lobbied throughout this forty-year period for a constitutional Equal Rights Amendment (ERA).

Further, women's organizations were very active in national policy debates in the middle decades of the 20th century (Goss 2013). Women's groups worked in female-led and mixed coalitions, advocating not only for traditional concerns such as women's and children's well-being but also for emerging issues and those considered primarily the province of men.

> Far from retreating into some traditional apolitical "feminine" sphere after suffrage, women got to work, not only in the public spheres of their local communities but also at the highest levels of American government, the committee rooms of Congress. Women's groups worked in coalitions in numerous issue domains.
>
> (Goss 2013, 40)

A major group that grew out of the suffragist movement and that continues today is the League of Women Voters (LWV). Carrie Chapman Catt founded the league during the 1920 convention of the NAWSA. The league began as a "mighty political experiment" designed to help newly enfranchised women exercise their new responsibilities as voters. It encouraged women to use their new power to participate in shaping public policy (LWV. org). The LWV is officially nonpartisan, although in contemporary times, it has supported a variety of progressive public policy positions, including campaign finance reform, universal health care, abortion rights, climate change action, environmental regulation, and gun control. It opposes voter ID laws and joined in a lawsuit challenging them. In the 1970s and early 1980s, it was very active in the campaign for the Equal Rights Amendment and advocated for its passage. It has state and local affiliates across the country.

The Second Women's Rights Movement

A new wave of feminism arose in the 1960s, resulting in what has variously been called a second women's rights movement, a new feminist movement, or the women's liberation movement. It emerged from several different directions and changes in women's lives. Rather than having a single goal such as winning the vote as the suffragist movement did, the contemporary movement has worked to achieve a broad array of changes in women's lives in both the private and public spheres across classes and racial and ethnic groups and in cultural practices as well as legal and institutional changes. It emerged as a national force in part from the experience of primarily younger women who encountered sexism in the student rights, antiwar, civil rights, and new left movements. Their activism is often referred to as the liberation branch. A second branch was comprised mainly of professional women engaged in broad communications networks arising from organizations such as the President's Commission on the Status of Women, established by President Kennedy in 1961, state commissions, and groups such as the Business and Professional Women's Foundation. It is often referred to as the "older," more bureaucratic and rights-oriented segment of the second women's rights movement (Reger 2012).

The movement has been a collection of formal organizations, occupational caucuses, friendship circles, collectives, and interest groups at the national level and within local communities (Ferree and Hess 2000; Reger 2012). Women's rights advocates have engaged in a broad spectrum of activities from conscious-raising groups in which women gathered, often in small community groups, to discuss and rethink aspects of their lives that they had not previously questioned to conducting mass marches and demonstrations, lobbying, engaging in legal actions, and running for elective office. They have given their organizations such names as Feminist Majority, Redstockings, Bread and Roses, National Network to End Domestic Violence, National Center for Lesbian Rights, National Black Women's Health Network, and National Committee on Pay Equity, to name just a few of the many collectivities that have formed.

They have held festivals and conferences and established bookstores, women's health centers, rape crisis groups, lesbian feminist collectives, abortion rights organizations, domestic violence shelters, and other community-based direct-action groups (Staggenborg and Taylor 2005). Women's studies programs have also become areas of academic inquiry. The National Women's Studies Association was established in 1977. Currently, there are approximately two hundred women's studies majors or minors in American colleges and universities.

The Internet also abounds with cyberfeminist sites promoting a large number of actions and feminist identities. One set of ideas for change has centered on equality between the sexes and concrete changes that would make women's lives better. Other ideologies view women's rights from the perspective of "male dominance." Still others blame both capital-ism and male supremacy for the discrimination women faced.

In the early years of the new movement, women's rights activists formed the National Organization for Women (NOW) with the purpose of taking action "to bring women into full participation in the mainstream of American society now, exercising all the privileges and responsibilities thereof in truly equal partnership with men." It created a National Women's Political Caucus (NWPC), pledging to end "racism, sexism, institutional violence and poverty through the election and appointment of women to public office, party reform, and the support of women's issues and feminist candidates across party lines," as well as other organizations. These groups lobbied for a national Equal Rights Amendment and filed many legal cases against discrimination. Women's rights activists "achieved an unprec-edented amount of legislation designed to correct gender inequities" (Evans 2003, 62). U.S. Representative Bella Abzug, one of their leaders, described 1972 as "a watershed year. We put sex discrimination provisions into everything. There was no opposition. Who'd be against equal rights for women? So we just kept passing women's rights legislation" (quoted in Evans 2003, 67).

The initial years of the movement were a time in which, "armed with a new conscious-ness, feminists took to the streets with all kinds of protests designed to challenge public assumptions, alter cultural institutions, and create political change. It was a period when the movement was widespread, public, and contentious" (Staggenborg and Taylor 2005, 37). The movement also included many local socialist and radical feminist "women's libera-tion" groups. Although largely viewed historically as a middle-class White phenomenon in its formative years, the contemporary women's rights movement has evolved into a tremen-dous diversity of voices and actions across race, class, and ideologies. Black and Chicana feminist organizations actually formed simultaneously with White feminist movements. They have spearheaded a multiracial feminism linking class, race, and gender oppressions. They have worked with White-dominated feminist groups, formed women's caucuses in existing mixed-gender organizations, and developed autonomous Black, Latina, Native American, and Asian feminist organizations (Thompson 2002). Native American women formed Women of All Red Nations in 1974 primarily to fight sterilization in public health service hospitals. The National Black Feminist Organization was active for several years in the 1970s. It contributed to the founding of the Black feminist lesbian Combahee River Collective. The collective was named after a river in South Carolina where Harriet Tub-man had led an insurgent action that freed 750 slaves. They wrote the Combahee River Collective Statement that constructed an expansive idea of feminism that continues as an expansive model:

> Feminism is the political theory and practice to free all women: women of color, working-class women, poor women, physically challenged women, lesbians, old women, as well as white economically privileged heterosexual women. Anything less than this is not feminism, but merely female self-aggrandizement.
>
> (Thompson 2002, 340)

More than 1,200 union women formed the Coalition of Labor Union Women (CLUW) in 1974 to address sexism in unions and women's inequality in society more generally. It adopted four basic goals of action still central to its mission: to promote affirmative action in the workplace, to strengthen the role of women in unions, to organize the unorganized women, and to increase the involvement of women in the political and legislative process.

Observing and describing the organization of CLUW and its practice of politics directs us to the importance of *intersectionality* in the study of women's quest for equality. As

Picture 2.2 2014 Coalition of Labor Union Women Black Friday Rally
Courtesy of the Coalition of Labor Union Women.

the second women's rights movement became embedded in the nation's politics, critics began to challenge its seeming focus on White women joining the economic and political establishment of the country. Critics advocated for a movement that recognized the greater diversity of women's lives and positions in U.S. society—that is, their intersectionality. Intersectionality "is shorthand for the idea that it is impossible to separate social identities, or the discrimination that surrounds them. Gender, race, class and other identities overlap or intersect so intensely that focusing on one necessarily neglects another. A woman's gender, in this way of thinking, for example, cannot be considered separately from her race" (Roberts 2016) or place in the class system. Consider that in some ways women of color are disadvantaged as *women* of color and poor women are disadvantaged as poor *women* (Weldon 2006).

Intersectionality scholars ground their work in notions of marginalization and oppression. Intersectionality proponents challenge mainstream feminism as caring

> only for the concerns of the white, middle-class women who founded the movement and, because of their privileged race and socioeconomic status, have had more of an opportunity to shape it. Oftentimes, the policies that mainstream feminists put forth end up helping these white, middle-class women more than they help their non-white, lower income counterparts—or, by focusing solely on gender, these policies leave out issues important to groups marginalized in other ways.
>
> (Roberts 2016)

If one takes an intersectionality approach, then how gender intersects with race and with class position as well as with disability and sexual orientation provides a fuller perspective on one's place in society. Activists in the women's movement have become increasingly aware of the shortcomings of activism primarily centered on White women's quests for equity. Chapter 3 incorporates a focus on race and class as it traces the significance of increasing economic inequality on women's political equity.

Counter Movements

The campaign from 1972 through 1982 for ratification of the Equal Rights Amendment to the U.S. Constitution generated a massive coalition of organizations that undertook a variety of actions to promote its ratification by the requisite number of states. In the months immediately following Congressional approval, twenty-eight states ratified the amendment. But then it met growing grassroots opposition. In 1975, proponents formed ERAmerica as a nationwide bipartisan umbrella organization bringing together more than two hundred groups spearheaded by NOW, the League of Women Voters, and the National Federation of Business and Professional Women (BPW). ERA advocates engaged in an economic boycott of states that had not ratified the amendment, supported pro-ERA candidates for state legislative office, and sponsored a march on Washington, DC, that attracted more than one hundred thousand participants. Some groups engaged in acts of civil disobedience. For example, seventeen women chained themselves to the rotunda in the Illinois state capitol for four days during debate in that state's legislature over ratification. A thirty-seven-day fast also occurred during the ratification campaign in Illinois.

The pro-ERA campaign produced large-scale opposition primarily led by right-wing activist Phyllis Schafly and her Stop ERA campaign. She stimulated homemakers and other tradition-minded women to oppose ratification. Although ERAmerica was a national organization, the forces organized to oppose the ERA were better organized and more effective at the state level. In 1982, the time line Congress had mandated for ratification of the ERA ran out three states short of the necessary three quarters needed.

Conservative women's groups have also countered the activism of women's rights proponents throughout the decades since the emergence of the contemporary women's rights movement repudiating their social critiques, ideologies, and policy agendas (Goss 2013). Chronicler of conservative women's organizations Ronnee Schreiber notes that the conservative challenge has grown and become a substantial threat to the feminist movement. She describes these groups as being

> well organized, politically active, and have access to government institutions, political parties, and national media. . . . [They] vie with feminists over what women need and desire, they publicly contest definitions of women's interest an influence political debates and policy outcomes,
>
> (Schreiber 2012, 4)

Concerned Women for America (CWA) and the Independent Women's Forum (IWF) are the most prominent of the conservative women's groups. CWA is a socially conservative interest group mostly composed of evangelical Protestant women. It is concerned with public and private morality, opposes abortion and civil rights for homosexuals, and advocates for prayer in public schools. IWF is better described as an economic conservative group that advocates for individuals' self-sufficiency, limited federal social programs and business regulations, and increased private-sector involvement in the provision of public goods and services (Schreiber 2012, 5). Both groups see themselves as representing women.

In recent years, conservative women have achieved new heights of activism by vying for political leadership positions themselves, moving beyond lobbying against and countering feminist legislative proposals. Sarah Palin's nomination and campaign for vice president on the 2008 Republican ticket and her subsequent campaign to elect "mama grizzlies" to public office highlight these quests for political leadership.

Fifty Years Later: The Status of Feminism and the Women's Rights Movement

The contemporary women's rights movement has profoundly affected the social, economic, and political status of women in the United States, as the various chapters in this volume document. At the same time, news media and social commentators have reported the death of feminism and the contemporary women's movement many times over the course of its history. Scholar Jo Reger opens her 2014 essay on "Debating US Contemporary Feminism" with the statement that "one of the most common popular notions about contemporary feminism is that it is no longer viable or active in US society" (43). In 2004, Mary Hawkesworth counted eighty-six newspaper articles referring to the death of feminism between 1989 and 2001. In June 1998, *TIME* magazine's cover picturing suffragist Susan B. Anthony, second women's rights leaders Gloria Steinem and Betty Friedan, and actress Calista Flockhart, who played Ally McBeal, asked the question "Is Feminism Dead?" Some feminist scholars and activists, too, have asked what has happened to the women's movement and pronounced the demise of feminism (see, for example, Epstein 2001.) The *Time* cover story "Feminism: It's All About Me" accompanying the question raised on its cover in 1998 focused primarily on cultural aspects of feminism such as dress, sexuality, and entertainment (Bellefante 1998). Little commentary was spent on economic disparities, public policy issues, and political participation and empowerment.

Indeed, six years later, on April 25, 2004, feminist organizations mobilized one of the largest women's marches in U.S. history. Over a million women participated in the Washington, DC, March for Women's Lives, centering on reproductive freedom. Some 1,400 organizations cosponsored the event. The movement demonstrated its ability to generate highly visible, large-scale, newsworthy collective actions. As an article titled "Post-Feminism, R. I. P." argued, the march was important not only as a message to government officials but also "for networking, coordinating, strategizing, as well as morale boosting" as "women moved like a movement again" (*The Nation* 2004).

Then, in contrast to its 1998 piece, in its December 23, 2014, issue, *Time* columnist Charlotte Alter reported that "This May Have Been the Best Year for Women Since the Dawn of Time." She enumerated what she calls "victories" from the cinema, academia, the business world, the federal government, and perhaps most inspiring, seventeen-year-old Malala Yousafzai's award of the Nobel Peace Prize, the youngest person ever to receive this honor. But more importantly, she depicts the year positively for women as stemming from how hard and loud women fought for justice:

> 2014 was characterized by loud, frustrating, and often unresolved discussions about justice for women that reached an unprecedented volume. We didn't necessarily "win" any of these battles—and when it comes to debates over sexual assaults, domestic violence, and contraceptive coverage, it's hard to know what "winning" looks like—but we fought them harder and louder than ever before.

This 2014 article is only one informed commentator's perspective and not a cover story, as the 1998 *Time* piece was. Its emphasis on "battles" still being fought (note, for example, the political war against women described in Chapter 1) and questions still being asked about the movement's vitality and challenges to it from the conservative right suggest that the quest for equality and equity in public policy for women across classes and races still creates backlash, anger, and debates.

In the popular culture realm, contemporary social media sites popularize "women against feminism" messages. Tumblr and Facebook social media networking websites have pages titled "Women Against Feminism" in which women share selfies holding up pieces of paper with reasons written on them explaining why they do not need feminism, have rejected it, and believe the women's rights movement has become irrelevant. That Facebook page had nearly thirty thousand likes at the end of 2014.

In 2013, an academic group convened a panel at the American Political Science Association's annual meeting that asked the question, "Does the United States Still Need a Women's Movement?" The presenters at this panel, perhaps not surprisingly, recognized a continued need for such a movement (Goss 2014). But they also offered a variety of insights into what was needed for sustained relevance and how advocates for women might fruitfully direct their efforts as they go forward to achieve greater equity. Examples included giving more attention to accommodating women's group differences as well as their sameness when advancing policies that promote women's social, economic, and political inclusion (McDonagh 2014) and recognizing the importance of conservative women's activism. We must "distinguish between feminist and women's interests and representation as well as find any potential for collaboration among ideologically diverse women," Ronnee Schreiber argued (2014, 276). A "need to articulate more clearly what a feminist perspective offers to grassroots individuals and organizations that confront and seek to prevent sexual violence" was advanced as one perspective on the need for a continued women's movement (Corrigan 2014, 282). Lee Ann Banaszak (2014) reminded us of the "under the radar" work of feminist activists within governmental agencies in the construction of public policy. And Shauna Shames (2014) argued that we need a women's movement to recruit and support women as candidates for public office. Most especially, young and minority women must be stimulated to care about politics, get involved, and be inspired to run for elected office.

What do surveys tell us about support among the general public for feminism, the women's movement, and women's rights more generally in contemporary times? Several national polls have explored a variety of perceptions regarding aspects of gender equality in recent times. In a recent survey, the *New York Times* queried a national sample of Americans as to whether "all things considered in our society today do you think there are more advantages in being a man, or more advantages to being a woman, or that there are no more advantages in being one or the other?" Nearly half of the female respondents (48 percent) answered that it was more advantageous to be a man. Only 6 percent thought it was an advantage to be a woman, and 43 percent saw no more advantages to being either one. Among the men, 35 percent thought it was an advantage to be a man, 11 percent thought it was an advantage to be a woman, and more than half (52 percent) believed neither sex had an advantage.

Americans are split on whether women have about the right amount of influence in society today or too little, according to a 2016 ABC News/*Washington Post* survey. Nearly half (46 percent) said women have the right amount of influence, whereas 42 percent said women have too little influence. Only 10 percent said women have too much influence. The sexes were somewhat divided in their assessment of the influence of women; 46 percent of women believe women have too little influence compared with 39 percent of men (Holyk and Sinozich 2016).

Two other surveys have recently queried the American public about the extent to which they see themselves as feminists. In addition to giving us a sense of the public opinion on this matter, they also show the significance of how a question is worded and the response options presented in gauging public opinion. In 2014, a joint poll of the *Economist* and

YouGov asked a national sample of American adults, "Do you consider yourself to be a feminist or not?" In 2015, the *Washington Post* and Kaiser Family Foundation asked a national sample, "Do you consider yourself a strong feminist, a feminist, not a feminist, or an anti-feminist?" The first poll concluded that "most people don't want to call themselves feminists. Just one in four Americans—and one in three women—call themselves feminists today" (Frankovic 2014). However, and significantly, the *Economist*/YouGov poll found that when read a standard dictionary definition of feminism—someone who believes in the social, political, and economic equality of the sexes—identification increased dramatically: half of men and two thirds of women then said they were feminists.

Support was higher in the second poll in which respondents were given a greater range of options. In the *Washington Post*/Kaiser poll, "6 in 10 women and one-third of men call themselves a feminist (43%) or strong feminist (17%), with roughly 7 in 10 of each saying the movement is empowering." One third of men called themselves feminists (23 percent) or strong feminists (10 percent). A majority of women in all age groups in this study considered themselves feminists: 68 percent of women aged fifty to sixty-four, 63 percent of women aged eighteen to thirty-four, 58 percent of women sixty-five and older, and 51 percent of women aged thirty-five to forty-nine (Cai and Clement 2016).

The *Washington Post*/Kaiser survey also asked, "Do you think the feminist movement today is focused on changes you want, or not?" Forty-eight percent agreed, whereas 35 percent disagreed. Young women were the largest segment in agreement (58 percent). Seventy percent thought the word *empowering* described feminism, 43 percent did not think *angry* described feminism, and 66 percent said it was not "outdated." Women were split evenly as to whether "the choices women make themselves" (44 percent) or "discrimination against women" (44 percent) was a bigger factor in keeping women from achieving full equality with men (Weiyi Cai and Scott Clement 2016).

A 2010 Pew Global Attitudes Project Poll also found that the majority of men and women believed the United States needs to continue to make changes to give women equal rights with men (64 percent), whereas a third (33 percent) thought that the United States has made most of the changes needed to give women equal rights with men. A 2007 CBS national survey reported that 64 percent of its respondents agreed that the United States continued to need a strong women's movement to push for changes that benefit women.

In assessing the results of these polls, readers are urged to ponder and discuss the wording of the questions, the extent to which they think these polls measure what they purport to be describing, and to reflect on the surveys' assessments of the current state of public opinion concerning women's rights and gender equality. The chapters that follow explore the contemporary political activism of women as individuals and the work of women's rights organizations at the local, national, and international levels centering on a wide variety of equality issues in the public life of the nation and the political leadership of women. Chapter 3 first focuses on linking the quests for political equality and leadership with trends in economic inequality that have characterized contemporary decades.

Further Readings and Other Media Sources

The Suffrage Movement

Dubois, Carol. 1978. *Feminism and Suffrage: The Emergence of an Independent Women's Movement in America 1848–1869*. Ithaca, NY: Cornell University Press.

Flexner, Eleanor and Ellen Fitzpatrick. 1996. *Century of Struggle: The Women's Rights Movement in the United States*, enlarged edition. Cambridge, MA: Harvard University Press.

Kraditor, Aileen S. 1981. *Ideas of the Woman Suffrage Movement: 1890–1920*. New York, NY: W. W. Norton.

The Second Women's Rights Movement

Baumgardner, Jennifer and Amy Richards. 2000. *Manifesta: Young Women, Feminism and the Future*. New York, NY: Farrar, Straus, and Giroux.

Baxandall, Roxanne and Linda Gordon. 2000. *Dear Sisters: Dispatches from the Women's Liberation Movement*. New York, NY: Basic Books.

Cade, Toni. 1970. *The Black Woman: An Anthology*. New York, NY: Signet.

Collins, Patricia Hill. 2000. *Black Feminist Thought: Knowledge, Consciousness, and the Politics of Empowerment*. New York, NY: Routledge.

Evans, Sara. 1980. *Personal Politics: The Roots of Women's Liberation in the Civil Rights Movement and the New Left*. New York, NY: Vintage Books.

Freeman, Jo. 1975. *The Politics of Women's Liberation*. New York, NY: Longman.

Friedan, Betty. 1963. *The Feminine Mystique*. New York, NY: W. W. Norton.

Mansbridge, Jane. 1986. *Why We Lost the ERA*. Chicago, IL: University of Chicago Press.

O'Sullivan, Meg Devlin. 2007. "'We Worry about Survival': American Indian Women, Sovereignty, and the Right to Bear and Raise Children in the 1970s." Ph.D. Dissertation. University of North Carolina, Chapel Hill. https://cdr.lib.unc.edu/indexablecontent?id=uuid:7a462a63-5185-4140-8f3f-ad094b75f04d&ds=DATA_FILE.

Roth, Betina. 2004. *Separate Roads to Feminism: Black, Chicana, and White Feminist Movements in America's Second Wave*. New York,NY: Cambridge University Press.

Web Resources

National Women's History Museum, www.nwhm.org.
National Women's History Project, www.nwhp.org.

Women's Rights Organizations

American Association of University Women, www.aauw.org.
The Feminist Majority Foundation, www.feminist.org.
Feministing.org.
League of Women Voters, www.lwv.org.
MomsRising.org.
National Organization for Women, www.now.org.
National Women's Law Center, www.nwlc.org.
Planned Parenthood, www.plannedparenthood.org.
ThirdWaveFund.org.

Conservative Women's Advocacy Groups

Concerned Women for America, www.concernedwomen.org.
Independent Women's Forum, www.iwf.org.
SmartGirlPolitics.com.
Susan B. Anthony List, www.sba-list.org.

Films, Lectures, and Videos

"New Beginnings: Immigrant Women and the American Experience." www.youtube.com/watch?v=kQGx326u_9U&list=UUxTj7_3aVDR8RbeTGoyLTdQ.

Not for Ourselves Alone, PBS. www.pbs.org/kenburns/films/not-for-ourselves-alone.

Ruiz, Vicki. 2011. "Why Latino/a History Matters to U.S. History." *National Women's History Museum Sponsored Lecture at the Woodrow Wilson Center*. www.wilsoncenter.org/event/why-latinoa-history-matters-to-us-history-lecture-dr-vicki-ruiz.

"Standing Up for Change: Women and the Civil Rights Movement." www.youtube.com/watch?v=BlyI11DUAQw&list=UUxTj7_3aVDR8RbeTGoyLTdQ.

References

Alexander, Adele Logan. 1995. "Adele Hunt Logan, the Tuskegee Women's Club, and African Americans in the Suffrage Movement." In *Votes for Women: The Woman Suffrage Movement in Tennessee, the South and the Nation*, ed. Marjorie Spruill Wheeler. Knoxville, TN: University of Tennessee Press, 71–104.

Alter, Charlotte. 2014. "This May Have Been the Best Year for Women Since the Dawn of Time." *Time*, December 23, 2014. http://time.com/3639944/feminism-2014-womens-rights-ray-rice-bill-cosby/.

Baker, Paula. 1984. "The Domestication of Politics: Women and American Political Society, 1780–1920." *American Historical Review*, 89: 620–648.

Banaszak, Lee Ann. 2014. "The Hidden Women's Movement." *Politics & Gender*, 10, 2: 284–287.

Bellefante, Ginia. 1998. "Feminism: It's All about Me." *Time*, June 29.

Cai, Weiyi and Scott Clement. 2016. "What Americans Think about Feminism Today." *The Washington Post*, January 27. www.washingtonpost.com/graphics/national/feminism-project/poll/?tid=feminismseries.

Carpenter, David and Colin D. Moore. 2014. "When Canvassers Became Activists: Antislavery Petitioning and the Political Mobilization of American Women." *American Political Science Review*, 108, 3: 479–498.

Cobble, Dorothy Sue. 2004. *The Other Women's Movement*. Princeton, NJ: Princeton University Press.

Corrigan, Rose. 2014. "Why Feminist Theory Matters for Feminist Practice: The Case of Rape Response." *Politics & Gender*, 10, 2: 280–284.

Cox, Elizabeth M. 1996. *Women State and Territorial Legislators, 1895–1995*. Jefferson, NC: McFarland.

Deckard, Barbara Sinclair. 1979. *The Women's Movement*. New York, NY: Harper & Row.

Dorr, Rheta. 1928. *Susan B. Anthony: The Woman Who Changed the Mind of a Nation*. New York, NY: Frederick A. Stokes.

Epstein, Barbara. 2001. "What Happened to the Women's Movement?" *Monthly Review*, 53, 1. http://monthlyreview.org/2001/05/01/what-happened-to-the-womens-movement/.

Evans, Sara. 2003. *Tidal Wave: How Women Changed America at Century's End*. New York, NY: Free Press.

Ferree, Myra Marx and Beth B. Hess. 2000. *Controversy and Coalition: The New Feminist Movement across Four Decades of Change*. 3rd edition. New York, NY: Routledge.

Flexner, Eleanor. 1974. *Century of Struggle: The Women's Rights Movement in the United States*. New York, NY: Atheneum.

Ford, Linda. 2002. "Alice Paul and the Politics of Nonviolent Protest." In *Votes for Women: The Struggle for Suffrage Revisited*, ed. Jean H. Baker. New York, NY: Oxford University Press, 174–188.

Fowler, Robert Booth and Spencer Jones. 2002. "Carrie Chapman Catt and the Last Years of the Struggle for Woman Suffrage: 'The Winning Plan.'" In *Votes for Women: The Struggle for Suffrage Revisited*, ed. Jean H. Baker. New York, NY: Oxford University Press, 137.

Frankovic, Kathleen. 2014. "Feminism Today: What Does It Mean?" *Economist/YouGov Poll*, August 1. http://today.yougov.com/news/2014/08/01/feminism-today-what-does-it-mean/.

Goss, Kristin. 2013. *The Paradox of Gender Equality*. Ann Arbor, MI: University of Michigan Press.

Goss, Kristin. 2014. "Critical Perspectives on Gender and Politics: Does the United States Still Need a Women's Movement?" *Politics & Gender*, 10, 2 (June): 265–301.

Hawkesworth, Mary. 2004. "The Semiotics of Premature Burial: Feminism in the Post-Feminism Age." *Signs*, 29, 4 (Summer): 961–985.

Holyk, Gregory and Sofi Sinozich. 2016. "View on Race and Gender Mark Stark Divide Between Clinton, Trump Supporters." *ABC News*, September 28. http://abcnews.go.com/Politics/views-race-gender-mark-stark-divide-clinton-trump/story?id=42398850.

Hull, N. E. H. 2012. *The Woman Who Dared to Vote: The Trial of Susan B. Anthony*. Lawrence, KS: University of Kansas Press, 207.

Kraditor, Aileen. 1981. *The Ideas of the Woman Suffrage Movement/1890–1920*. New York, NY: W. W. Norton.

Lerner, Gerda. 1969. "The Lady and the Mill Girl: Changes in the Status of Women in the Age of Jackson." *Midcontinent American Studies Journal*, 10, 1 (Spring): 5–15.

Marilley, Suzanne. 1996. *Woman Suffrage and the Origins of Liberal Feminism in the United States, 1820–1920*. Cambridge, MA: Harvard University Press.

McCammon, Holly. 2003. "'Out of the Parlors and Into the Streets': The Changing Tactical Repertoire of the U.S. Women's Suffrage Movements." *Social Forces*, 81, 3 (March): 787–818.

McCammon, Holly and Karen Campbell. 2001. "Winning the Vote in the West: The Political Successes of the Women's Suffragist Movements, 1866–1919." *Gender and Society*, 15, 1 (February): 55–82.

McDonagh, Eileen. 2014. "Gender and the State: Accommodating Difference and Equality." *Politics & Gender*, 10, 2: 271–275.

Parker, Alison. 2002. "The Case for Reform Antecedents for the Women's Rights Movement." In *Votes for Women: The Struggle for Suffrage Revisited*, ed. Jean H. Baker. New York, NY: Oxford University Press, 21–41.

Reger, Jo. 2012. *Everywhere & Nowhere: Contemporary Feminism in the United States*. New York, NY: Oxford University Press.

Reger, Jo. 2014. "Debating US Contemporary Feminism." *Sociology Compass*, 8, 1: 43–51.

Roberts, Molly. 2016. "Hillary's Women Problem." *Politico Magazine*, February 12. http://www.politico.com/magazine/story/2016/02/hillary-clinton-2016-woman-problem-213621.

Schreiber, Ronnee. 2012. *Righting Feminism: Conservative Women & American Politics*. New York, NY: Oxford University Press.

Schreiber, Ronnee. 2014. "Understanding the Future of Feminism Requires Understanding Conservative Women." *Politics & Gender*, 10, 2: 276–280.

Shames, Shauna. 2014. "Making the Political Personal: A Challenge for Young Women." *Politics & Gender*, 10, 2: 287–291.

Simon, Rita J. and Gloria Danziger. 1991. *Women's Movements in America: Their Successes, Disappointments, and Aspirations*. New York, NY: Praeger.

Spruill, Marjorie Julian. 2002. "Race, Reform and Reaction at the Turn of the Century: Suffragists, the NAWSA, and the 'Southern Strategy' in Context." In *Votes for Women: The Struggle for Suffrage Revisited*, ed. Jean H. Baker. New York, NY: Oxford University Press, 102–117.

Staggenborg, Suzanne and Verta Taylor. 2005. "Whatever Happened to the Women's Movement?" *Mobilization: The International Journal of Research and Theory about Social Movements, Protest and Collective Behavior*, 10, 1: 37–52.

Stanton, Elizabeth Cady, Susan B. Anthony, and Mitilda Joselyn Gage. 1885. *History of Women's Suffrage*. Volume 3. New York, NY: Fowler and Wells.

Terborg-Penn, Rosalyn. 1998. *African American Women in the Struggle for the Vote, 1850–1920*. Bloomington, IN: Indiana University Press.

Thompson, Becky. 2002. "Multiracial Feminism: Recasting the Chronology of Second Wave Feminism." *Feminist Studies*, 28, 2 (Summer): 336–360.

Weldon, Laurel. 2006. "The Structure of Intersectionality: A Comparative Politics of Gender." *Politics & Gender*, 2: 235–248.

Wheeler, Marjorie Spruill. 1995. "The Woman Suffrage Movement in the Inhospitable South." In *Votes for Women: The Woman Suffrage Movement in Tennessee, the South and the Nation*, ed. Marjorie Spruill Wheeler. Knoxville, TN: University of Tennessee Press, 25–52.

3 Women's Political Voice and Economic Inequality

> Feminism had the misfortune of gaining ground in the period when the American economy suffered from its most severe shocks since the Great Depression. As a result, women entered the labor force in two "parallel streams," one highly educated and eager to seize new opportunities, the other forced into work by a declining economy and falling wages. The latter, of course, ended up in service jobs that were not particularly fulfilling.
>
> E. J. Dionne, *Why Americans Hate Politics* (1991, 105)

An age of increasing economic inequality has paralleled the era of the second women's rights movement, a time in which Americans have become "vastly richer and vastly more unequal" (Bartels 2008, 1). The Center for Budget and Policy Priorities summarizes the broad facts of the growth of income inequality over the past six decades in the following way:

> The years from the end of World War II into the 1970s were ones of substantial economic growth and broadly shared prosperity. Incomes grew rapidly and at roughly the same rate up and down the income ladder, roughly doubling in inflation-adjusted terms between the late 1940s and early 1970s. The income gap between those high up the income ladder and those on the middle and lower rungs—while substantial—did not change much during this period. Beginning in the 1970s, economic growth slowed and the income gap widened. Income growth for households in the middle and lower parts of the distribution slowed sharply, whereas incomes at the top continued to grow strongly. The concentration of income at the very top of the distribution rose to levels last seen more than 80 years ago (during the "Roaring Twenties").
>
> (Stone et al. 2014, 8)

Scholars have vividly characterized the contours of this economic transformation. For example, political scientists Jacob Hacker and Paul Pierson (2010, 3) describe the trend in the following way:

> Over the last generation, more and more of the rewards of growth have gone to the rich and superrich. The rest of America, from the poor through the upper middle class, has fallen further and further behind. . . . Consider the astonishing statistics. From 1979 until the eve of the Great Recession, the top one percent received 36 percent of all gains in household income—even after taking into account the value of employer-sponsored health insurance, all federal taxes, and all government benefits.

In a *New York Times* piece, Bill Keller (2013) states that

> the top 10 percent of Americans used to take in a third of the national income. Now they gobble up half. The typical corporate C.E.O. used to make 30 times as much as the average worker. Now the boss makes 270 times as much as the minion.

Nobel Laureate economist Paul Krugman (2007) called this period the Great Divergence era and described it in the following terms: "Average income has risen substantially, but that's mainly because a few people have gotten much, much richer. Median income, depending on which definition you use, has either risen modestly or actually declined" (125–126). Contemporary American inequality is the highest in the advanced industrial world (Hacker and Pierson 2010, 160). Figure 3.1 illustrates the trend in income inequality.

How do we know that rising inequality has characterized recent decades of American economic life? Federal agencies such as the Census Bureau, the Department of Education, and the Bureau of Labor Statistics conduct surveys of individuals, households, and businesses to gather information about people's salaries and other earnings. Most reports on national workforce participation, pay, and pay differences depend on data from the Current Population Survey (CPS) (www.census.gov/cps), the country's primary source of labor force statistics. The CPS is a monthly survey of about fifty thousand households conducted by the U.S. Census Bureau for the Bureau of Labor Statistics. The CPS dates from 1947. Respondents are asked which one of sixteen categories of income represents the total combined income of all members of their family during the past twelve months.

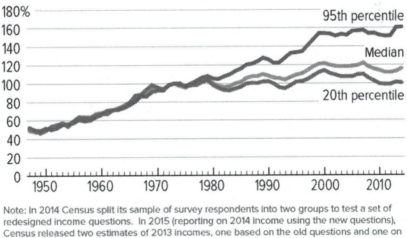

Income Gains Widely Shared in Early Postwar Decades — But Not Since Then

Real family income between 1947 and 2014, as a percentage of 1973 level

Note: In 2014 Census split its sample of survey respondents into two groups to test a set of redesigned income questions. In 2015 (reporting on 2014 income using the new questions), Census released two estimates of 2013 incomes, one based on the old questions and one on the new. The chart uses the estimate based on the old questions, based on CBPP's judgment that, due in part to sample size, it is likely more accurate for 2013.

Source: CBPP calculations based on U.S. Census Bureau Data

CENTER ON BUDGET AND POLICY PRIORITIES | CBPP.ORG

Figure 3.1 Trends in Income Inequality

They are told that this income figure includes money from jobs, net income from business, rent, pensions, dividends, interest, social security payments, and any other money income members of this family who are fifteen year of age or older receive. The Internal Revenue Service's (IRS) annual report of individual income tax returns is an additional set of data used to measure income inequality. The IRS compiles a Data Book for each federal fiscal year that provides this information.

The Great Recession that hit the U.S. economy beginning in 2007 and lasting through 2009 was followed by a slow recovery in the mid-teen years of the millennium and has not lessened the nation's economic inequality. Indeed, in 2013, the wealth gap between America's highest income groups and everyone else reached its greatest level on record, "with a clear trajectory of increasing wealth for the upper-income families and no wealth growth for the middle- and lower-income families" according to the Pew Research Center's economic analysis. In 2013, the median wealth of the nation's upper income families ($639,400) was nearly seven times the median wealth of middle-income families ($96,500), the widest wealth gap seen in thirty years since the Federal Reserve began collecting these data (Fry and Kochhar 2014).

Uneasiness about the negative effect of such inequality on participation and voice in the public life of the nation stimulated the American Political Science Association in 2002 to create the Task Force on Inequality and American Democracy. Its 2004 report titled *American Democracy in an Age of Rising Inequality* states that

> disparities of income, wealth, and access to opportunity are growing more sharply in the United States than in many other nations, and gaps between races and ethnic groups persist. Progress toward realizing American ideals of democracy may have stalled, and in some arenas reversed.
>
> (Task Force on Inequality and American Democracy, 2004, 651)

The task force expressed a troubled perspective over the possibility that "rising economic inequality will solidify longstanding disparities in political voice and influence, and perhaps exacerbate such disparities" (662). The gendered aspects of these phenomena are important in any study of women's political participation.

Women's involvement in the economic and public life of the nation changed dramatically during this time period. Indeed, economist Claudia Goldin (2014, 1091) describes the

> converging roles of men and women [as] among the grandest advances in society and the economy in the last century. . . . A narrowing has occurred between men and women in labor force participation, paid hours of work, hours of work at home, life-time labor force experience, occupations, college majors, and education, where there has been an overtaking by females.

This perspective, indeed, rightly captures an important perspective on the transformation of women's economic lives over the course of the last half-century.

E. J. Dionne's lens cited in this chapter's introduction captures a significant additional factor of gendered changes in the economic life of the nation. Activists within the women's rights movement have campaigned for pay equity, affirmative action policies to increase women's work opportunities, and the enactment of antidiscrimination legislation regarding women as workers. Women have made great strides in their occupational status. Yet men and women continue to work in different sectors of the economy, doing different kinds of work. Women continue to be relegated to the lowest paid, less prestigious jobs. In addition, a countertrend to women's occupational advance has been what has come to be known as the "feminization of poverty."

The authors of *Women Transforming Politics* (Cohen et al. 1997, 2–3) have starkly addressed these contradictions by asking,

> How do we explain the fact that many women's lives have significantly improved in the United States during the last two decades, and that all women have seen their legal status enhanced, whereas for many women daily life has become more tenuous and threatening? What kinds of political responses to these paradoxical effects of improved legal status and declining quality of life have different women undertaken?

This chapter describes the varied trends in women's educational and work and family lives since the beginning of the second women's rights movement, and paralleling those trends, it explores gendered aspects of the economic inequality that has characterized this same period. It examines the transformation both in terms of how the changes in women's lives have impacted the contours of economic inequality and how the "great divergence" has affected women's gains in economic equality. The chapter concludes with an examination of the gendered aspects of the Great Recession of the first decade of the 21st century and its "recovery" in its second decade. It explores the political response to that economic downturn in the form of the Tea Party and Occupy Wall Street movements, centering on the involvement of women in these movements.

Trends in Women's Economic Lives

Women are now nearly one half of the workforce, which is a remarkable transformation of the configuration of labor force participation in the United States. In the early 1960s, women comprised just over one third of all workers. The majority of women were not in the labor force. Marriage, and particularly motherhood, meant leaving paid work for women who could afford to do so. Women were less likely than men to have any formal education beyond high school (Hegewisch and Hartmann 2014) that would allow them to move into professional occupations. In the decades that followed, American women made extraordinary advances in education and employment. Women's rights policy advocacy during these decades stimulated the enactment of national legislation focused on educational and employment equity for women that positively impacted these trends.

In the second decade of the millennium, women make up nearly half the labor force and more than half of all college graduates and individuals with advanced degrees. Among younger age groups, women have surpassed their male counterparts in their educational attainment. Further, in nearly 65 percent of American families, mothers are either the single working parent or responsible for anywhere from a quarter to more than half of the total family income. They have little choice but to work through the life cycle (Chesler 2012). The trends represent absolute gains for women and gains relative to those of men. The relative gains have been achieved in part because of the advances women have made in educational attainment and in the workforce but also because of stagnation in men's economic position. But as this chapter will also show, more women than men are likely to be poor, and substantial job segregation continues to exist between the sexes, making the goal of equity difficult to obtain and negatively affecting economic equality.

Advances in Education

The most extraordinary change in women's lives has occurred in their educational attainment. In 1960, only 6 percent of women aged twenty-five and older had completed four or more years of college. In 2015, that percentage had risen to 33 percent compared with

32 percent for men. In the second decade of the millennium, women outperform men academically at all levels of schooling. They are more likely to obtain college degrees and enroll in graduate school than men (Diprete and Buchman 2013). In 1961, women made up 38 percent of the enrollees in postsecondary education institutions. In the 1980s, they began to exceed men in college enrollment. By 2012, they accounted for 57 percent of postsecondary students (National Center for Educational Statistics Table 303.10). Based on data from the American Community Survey, the Census Bureau titled its 2015 education report *Women Now at the Head of the Class, Lead Men in College Attainment* (Bauman and Ryan 2015).[1]

Since 1982, women have earned more bachelor's degrees than men; since 1987, they have earned more master's degrees; and since 2006, women have earned more doctorate degrees than men. In 2011, Census Bureau data showed that for the first time women had surpassed men in obtaining advanced college degrees as well as bachelor's degrees. For the class of 2011–2012, women earned 57.3 percent of bachelor's degrees, 59.9 percent of master's degrees, and 51.4 percent of doctorate degrees. For the class of 2010–2011, women earned 49.0 percent of professional degrees, including 48.4 percent of degrees in medicine, 61.8 percent of degrees in pharmacy, 77.4 percent of veterinary medicine degrees, and 47.1 percent of law degrees. On many educational fronts, women now surpass men by a large and growing margin, a profound transformation of women's lives. However, in engineering and computer sciences at the college level, women's share of degrees conferred in these fields is small (fewer than 20 percent) and has declined slightly over the last decade. Women received 19 percent of the bachelor's degrees in engineering in 2014 (a 1 percent decline from 2004), and they received 18 percent of computer science degrees (down from 23 percent in 2004) (National Student Clearing House 2015).

Race and ethnicity matter in higher educational attainment. Figure 3.2 compares the percentage of men and women across racial and ethnic groups who have obtained a bachelor's degree or greater based on 2014 census data. Within each group, women have higher levels of attainment than their male counterparts. Asian American females have the highest level of attainment of all, followed by their male counterparts.

Among White Americans, women surpassed men in obtaining bachelor's degrees for the first time in the mid-1980s, reversing a historical gender gap that had advantaged men. Black women have a much longer history of higher educational attainment than Black

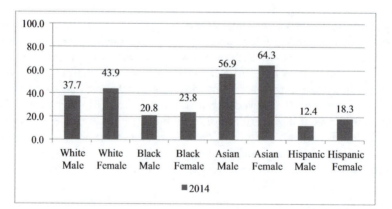

Figure 3.2 College Graduate or More, Persons Twenty-Five Years of Age or Older by Racial/Ethnic Groups and Sex, 2014

Compiled from the National Center for Educational Statistics, Table 104.20 (https://nces.ed.gov/programs/digest/d14/tables/dt14_104.20.asp).

men. "As early as 1954, when the great majority of Black college students were enrolled in historically black colleges and universities, women comprised 58 percent of the students enrolled in these institutions" (McDaniel et al. 2009, 6). At no point from 1940 on has a larger proportion of Black men completed college than Black women. In 2014, Hispanic women were also outpacing Hispanic men in obtaining bachelor's degrees.

In 1972, Congress passed Title IX of the Higher Education Amendments. Title IX stipulated that "no person in the United States shall, on the basis of sex, be excluded from participation in, be denied the benefits of, or be subjected to discrimination under any education program or activity receiving federal financial assistance." Whereas the enactment of Title IX was fairly noncontroversial, a battle ensued over the writing of regulations to implement it. Particularly controversial have been the regulations concerning athletics, which has continued for decades (McBride and Parry 2011). Chapter 9 describes the policies and politics involved in Title IX. The National Coalition for Women and Girls in Education, a feminist coalition of more than fifty groups and organizations experienced in legislative and administrative processes, formed in 1975 to lobby for the implementation of Title IX regulations. It continues to engage in public awareness campaigns, research, and advocacy regarding educational opportunities for women and girls.[2]

Labor Force Participation

Women are now nearly one half of the workforce. Increasing occupational equality and earnings equity with men, the elimination of barriers to workforce participation, and occupational advancement have been major goals of contemporary women's rights advocates. Women's participation in the world of work has changed significantly since 1960. Their labor force participation rate in 1960 was 35.5 percent. Men's participation rate was 83.3 percent. Women typically worked episodically. Once married, they identified primarily as homemakers with long stretches of time off for childrearing. Women's labor force participation increased significantly during the 1970s and 1980s, climbing to 57.5 percent in 1990. In 1999, women's participation rate reached a peak of 60 percent. Since then, however, labor force participation among women has declined (see Figure 3.3). In 2016, 56.8 percent of women were in the labor force, whereas the rate for men had fallen to 69.2 percent.[3] Women accounted for 47 percent of the workforce, nearly one half (U.S. Department of Labor).

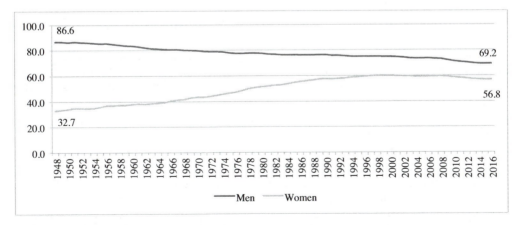

Figure 3.3 Male and Female Labor Force Participation Rates, 1948–2015

Compiled from the Bureau of Labor Statistics, Table A-1 Employment Status of the Civilian Population by Sex and Age (www.bls.gov/news.release/empsit.t01.htm).

Women of color have always been more likely than White women to work outside the home. The legacy of slavery and widespread poverty in the post–Civil War years led Black women's employment outside the home to be much higher than that of White women. Black women had worked intensively under slavery. That legacy affected norms and expectations about women's work among African Americans. The stigma attached to married women being employed outside the home that existed among Whites was not present among the African American population in the decades prior to World War II (Boustan and Collins 2013; Goldin 1977). In the latter decades of the 19th century, official government statistics estimated that about 40 percent of Black women were in the labor force, most likely a substantial underestimation of their workforce participation. White women's labor force participation was estimated at less than 15 percent, consisting primarily of unmarried women. The increase in the number of married workers drove the rise in White women's participation in the 20th century, whereas an increase in the number of unmarried workers accounts for much of the rise in Black women's participation, especially after 1970, when the share of married Black women fell sharply (Boustan and Collins 2013).

Between 1920 and 1950, the racial gap in women's labor force participation narrowed significantly from twenty-seven to fourteen percentage points as White women's participation increased, whereas the rate among Black women remained nearly constant. The rise among White women reflected both a shifting demand for clerical workers, as businesses and the federal government expanded and became more complex, and more White women obtaining a high school education. Black women, on the other hand, were generally barred from the expanding clerical sector, and relatively few had the opportunity to attend high school. They completed high school in large numbers a full generation after White women. Black women were also heavily concentrated in agriculture and domestic service until the latter part of the 20th century. Thus, Black women were not only far more likely to be in the labor force than White women but also far more likely to endure difficult working conditions once in the labor force. After 1950, both Black and White rates rose steeply, almost in parallel, until 1970. Over the next few decades, the overall gap narrowed again, and by 1990, was nearly eliminated (Boustan and Collins 2013).

The Gender Earnings Gap

Women's median earnings are lower than men's in nearly all occupations, whether they work in occupations in which women predominate, occupations in which men predominate, or in occupations with a more even mix of men and women (Hegewisch and DuMonthier 2016). The gender gap in earnings to women's disadvantage has been at the center of policy discussions and debates regarding women's role in the national economy for decades. The passage of the Equal Pay Act of 1963 and Title VII of the Civil Rights Act of 1964 made overt discrimination in pay and employment generally illegal. The Equal Pay Act was the first federal law to address sex discrimination. It prohibited employers from discriminating on the basis of sex by paying employees of one sex at a rate lower than they paid employees of the opposite sex for equal work on jobs requiring equal skill, effort, and responsibility and that were performed under similar working conditions. But at that time, women and men tended not to do equal work in the same professions. They were mainly employed in distinct occupations. No mandate existed that required the hiring of women. Thus, the Equal Pay Act was primarily symbolic rather than substantive at the time of its enactment. Male workers had little to fear that women would take their jobs because employers had little incentive to hire women if they had to pay them the same as their male employees.

Title VII of the 1964 Civil Rights Act addressed this weakness of the Equal Pay Act. It bars all discrimination in employment, including discrimination in hiring, firing, promotion, and wages on the basis of race, color, religion, sex, or national origin. Initially, the Equal Employment Opportunity Commission, which was created to enforce the Title VII provisions, did not take the ban on sex discrimination seriously. Members of states Commissions on the Status of Women who were frustrated with the commission's inaction founded the National Organization for Women (NOW) in 1966 to lobby for enforcement of Title VII.

The gender pay gap has long been expressed in terms of "cents to the dollar" as a way of representing women's wages relative to men's. In 1960, women made fifty-nine cents for every dollar that men made, thus "59 cents" became the rallying cry of the emerging women's rights movement.

In the decades that followed, the earnings gap between men and women narrowed substantially. Men and women experienced the strongest wage convergence in the 1980s. The gender pay gap in the United States fell dramatically from 1980 to 1989. Slower convergence has continued into the second decade of the millennium. Moreover, several other related trends also appear to have reached a plateau or slowed since the 1990s, including increases in female labor force participation rates and reductions in occupational segregation by sex (Blau and Kahn 2016). Figure 3.4 traces the trend in the gender gap in earnings from 1960

Picture 3.1 "59 Cents" Historical Equal Rights Button

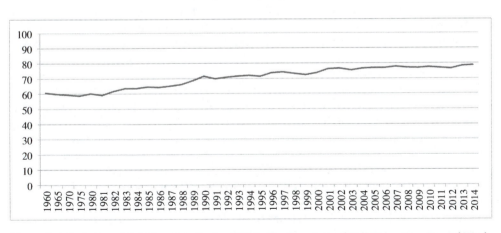

Figure 3.4 Female-to-Male Earnings Ratio and Median Earnings of Full-Time, Year-Round Workers Fifteen Years and Older by Sex, 1960–2015

Compiled from the U.S. Bureau of Labor Statistics, Income and Poverty in the United States, Report Number P60–256.

through 2015. In 2015, women's median annual earnings were $40,742, 80 percent of men's median annual earnings of $51,212,[4] a pay gap in actual dollars of $10,470, a substantial gain from the 59 percent figure of 1960 but still a significant pay gap.

Over the past half-century and more, women have made dramatic strides in their employment status. But within the age of increasing inequality and wage stagnation that has characterized the contemporary American economy, much of the progress toward women's pay equity has also come as a result of falling men's wages rather than as absolute improvements in the economic prospects of women and men. That is, gender pay gaps have gotten smaller but at a much lower level of pay than could have been possible if all wages had grown with productivity (Wilson 2016).

Income data come from government studies. Federal agencies such as the U.S. Census Bureau, the U.S. Department of Education, and the U.S. Bureau of Labor Statistics conduct surveys of individuals, households, and businesses to gather information about people's salaries and other earnings. The Census Bureau calculates annual earnings from surveys of U.S. households in the Current Population Survey's Annual Social and Economic Supplement (CPS ASEC), as described earlier, to show trends in the income inequality gap. Most reports on national workforce participation, pay, and pay differences depend on data from the CPS. The CPS is a monthly survey of a sample of one hundred thousand households jointly sponsored by the Census Bureau and the Bureau of Labor Statistics. This survey gathers information about earnings among full-time, year-round workers over the age of fifteen.

This information provides the basis for the current "80 cents to the dollar" pay gap figure. It is the result of dividing median female annual earnings cited earlier by median male annual earnings. The median value is the middle value, with equal numbers of full-time workers earning more and earning less. The median value is used rather than the mean value to prevent especially high salaries from skewing the results if one calculated the mean value instead.

Sometimes readers will see a smaller gender pay gap being cited. This comparison is based on weekly as opposed to annual earnings. This measure compares the base pay of women and men for the 60 percent of American workers, both full time and part time, who are paid by the hour as opposed to an annual salary. The annual earnings ratio includes only full-time workers, and time spent at work affects it; even among full-time workers, men put in more hours at work each week. This difference is why the annual pay gap is wider than the weekly or hourly pay gap (see Liner 2016). For 2015, the median gender earnings ratio for all full-time weekly workers was 81.1 percent, reflecting median weekly earnings for all female full-time workers of $726 compared with $895 per week for men (Hegewisch and DuMonthier 2016).

In general, the highest paid occupations have the biggest gender gaps, and the lowest paid occupations have the smallest gaps. The ten occupations with the largest gender wage gaps have earnings that are higher than median earnings for all workers; six of the ten occupations with the lowest wage gaps or with a gap in favor of women have earnings below the median for all workers (Hegewisch and DuMonthier 2016). Altogether, in only four occupations do women have slightly higher median earnings than men—wholesale and retail buyers (except farm products), police and sheriff's patrol officers, office clerks, and general and data entry keyers.

Various social and occupational factors have affected the size of the gender pay gap across groups. "The pay gap affects all women, but it doesn't affect all women equally" (American Association of University Women 2016, 10). Race and ethnicity affect the gender wage gap. In 2015, women of all major racial and ethnic groups had weekly and annual earnings less than men of the same racial and ethnic group, as Table 3.1 (weekly earnings)

Table 3.1 Weekly Earnings, All Full-Time Workers, by Race and Ethnicity, 2015

White Men	White Women	Black Men	Black Women	Asian Men	Asian Women	Hispanic Men	Hispanic Women
$1,005	$785	$680	$615	$1,129	$877	$631	$566

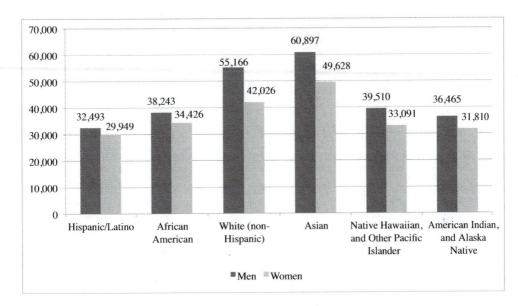

Figure 3.5 Median Annual Earnings by Race, Ethnicity, and Sex, 2015
Source: U.S. Census Bureau, 2015 American Community Survey.

and Figure 3.5 (yearly earnings) show. They also show that the pay gap varies across racial and ethnic groups. White women experience the biggest gap relative to White men. At the same time, they earn more than all other groups, except Asian women. Asian men are the highest earners overall, and Asian women are the highest female earners. It has been suggested that the earnings advantage of Japanese and Chinese workers is a result of changes in immigration laws that have advantaged highly skilled Asian workers (Snipp and Cheung 2016).

Educational attainment also has influenced the pay gap. The Institute for Women's Policy Research's *Status of Women in the States: 2015* report shows that

> education increases women's earnings but does not eliminate the gender wage gap. In the United States, women with a bachelor's degree earn, on average, more than twice the amount that women with less than a high school diploma earn. Yet, women who work full-time, year-round earn less than men at the same educational level, and at all but one level they earn the same as or less than men with lower educational qualifications. The gap in earnings is largest for those with the highest levels of educational attainment: women with a graduate degree earn only 69.1 percent of what comparable men earn, and women with a bachelor's degree earn 71.4 percent of the amount their male counterparts earn [see Figure 3.6]. These data indicate that women need more educational qualifications than men do to secure jobs that pay well.

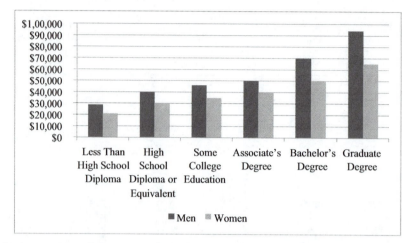

Figure 3.6 Median Annual Earnings and the Gender Earnings Ratio for Women and Men by Education, 2013

Adapted from Table 4.2, the Institute for Women's Policy Research's *Status of Women in the States: 2015*, 49.

The pay ratio has been shown to worsen as women moved from the early to middle stages of their careers. A woman in the early stages of her career currently makes ninety cents on the dollar today. Women in midcareer, however, earn only eighty-one cents on the dollar that midcareer men make. Some of the discrepancy is accounted for midcareer women having started work in an earlier, somewhat more difficult time period. However, the Economic Policy Institute reported in 2016 that the gap is widening straight out of college. Immediately upon graduation, women make four dollars less per hour than men—and the gap is getting wider, it reports, based on the Census CPS data (Kroeger and Gould 2016).

Much of the remaining discrepancy in pay can be attributed to the effects of marriage and childbirth. In 2014, women (regardless of age) who had never been married made 94 percent of what never-married men made on a weekly basis. Never-married women represent only 28 percent of women who work full time, however. In contrast, married women who work full time make just 79 percent of what married men who work full time make. Working mothers make 75 percent of what working fathers earned (regardless of marital status). Single mothers are affected disproportionately, and they face the added dilemma of paying for childcare or leaving their children unattended (Liner 2016).

Occupations and job segregation also account for the gender pay gap. Occupations with more female workers pay less than those with more male workers, by a ratio of eighty-three cents to the dollar. Men and women continue to work in different sectors of the economy, doing different kinds of work. The highest-paying jobs tend to have mostly male workers, whereas the lowest-paying jobs tend to have mostly female workers. An amazing 90 percent of those earning less than $15,000 annually and over two thirds of those making under $15,000 are women (Cobble 2007, 4). Chapter 6 describes how the large number of women and particularly minority women employed as domestic workers affects this gap.

Text Box 3.1 Women-Owned Businesses

The 2016 State of Women-Owned Businesses Report (Weeks 2016) estimates the following statistics.

- Between 2007 and 2016, while the total number of firms increased by 9 percent, the number of women-owned firms increased by 45 percent—a rate fully five times the national average.
- There are now 11.3 million women-owned businesses in the country, employing nearly nine million people and generating over $1.6 trillion in revenues.
- Women-owned businesses now comprise 38 percent of the business population, employ 8 percent of the country's private-sector workforce, and contribute 4 percent of the nation's business revenues.
- Since 2007, there have been 1,072 new women-owned firms launched each and every day.

Women-owned businesses span the individually owned or run local nail and hair salons to the Women's Presidents' Organization 2014 top three fastest growing women owned/led companies: Thirty-One Gifts, a Columbus, Ohio, based company Cindy Monroe started in her basement in 2003 with revenues growing to $760 million in 2013 and employing approximately 1,900 people; Kathy Mills's Louisville, Kentucky, based Strategic Communications, which provides technology services with revenues of $97.3 million in 2013; and Jennifer Maier, WDS, Inc., an international warehousing, distribution, and inventory management company with 2013 revenues of $155.8 million.

Women-owned businesses, however, are typically smaller than men-owned businesses, but they are continuing to diversify into all industries. The greatest number of women-owned businesses is found in health care and social assistance, including doctors and dentists, residential care facilities, and childcare providers. The industries with the highest concentration of women-owned firms are health care and social assistance (53 percent of firms in this sector are women owned compared to a 30 percent share overall), educational services (45 percent), other services (42 percent), and administrative support and waste management services (37 percent). The industries with the lowest concentration of women-owned firms (in industries contributing 2 percent or more of the business population) are construction (where just 7 percent of firms are women owned), transportation and warehousing (11 percent), wholesale trade (19 percent), and finance and insurance (20 percent).

According to the Women-Owned Businesses Report, the most remarkable trend over the past nine years has been the growth in the number of firms women of color have started. Their numbers have more than doubled since 2007, from 2.2 million to now nearly five million, comprising fully 44 percent of all women-owned firms.

Women of color-owned firms have seen faster growth in terms of total number of firms, employees, and revenue compared with all women-owned firms. The following graph adapted from the report compares the growth of minority-owned firms between 2007 and 2016 with that of all women-owned firms and nonminority firms.

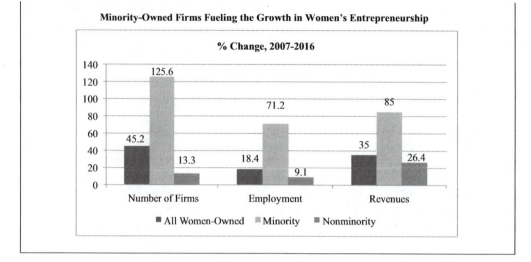

Minority-Owned Firms Fueling the Growth in Women's Entrepreneurship

Trends in women's occupational employment are complex. On the one hand, women have made remarkable advances at the professional level. In 1960, only 15 percent of managers were female; forty years later, women made up 38 percent of those in management jobs, and a higher proportion of women than men worked in managerial and

> **Sidebar 3.1 Women Chief Executive Officers**
>
> In 2016, twenty-one women (4.2 percent) were chief executive officers (CEOs) of Standard & Poor's Fortune 500 companies. One African American woman was the CEO of a Fortune 500 company, Ursula Burns of Xerox.

professional occupations (41.2 percent compared with 34.4 percent). Women's share of lawyers increased from 4 percent in 1972 to 32 percent in 2012; their share of physicians and surgeons rose from 10 to 34 percent, and for pharmacists, from 28 to 54 percent. Women comprised fewer than 10 percent of accounting majors at universities in the 1960s; by the mid-1980s, they were the majority of graduates in the field, and women are now more than 60 percent of the census occupational category of accountants and auditors.

Whereas racial and ethnic disparities continue to be characteristic of the labor market, women of color have seen significant improvement in job opportunities. In 1960, more than 40 percent of Black women were employed in just two census occupations—"personal service" and "housekeepers, maids, butlers, stewards and lodging quarter cleaners," and one in five Hispanic women worked in just two occupations in manufacturing—"machine operators, not elsewhere classified (n.e.c.)" and "other precision, apparel and fabric workers." Forty years later, more than one third of Black women (34 percent) and one quarter of Hispanic women (25 percent) worked in "management, professional and related occupations" (Hegewisch and Hartmann 2014). But as data from Bureau of Labor Statistics show, as reported earlier, their wages continue to fall substantially below that of White male workers.

Women's wages lag behind men's for a multitude of social reasons, but the disparity is mainly the effect of continued job segregation. "The difference in occupational distribution of men and women was largely responsible for the fact that in 1961 the earnings of women working full time averaged only about 60 percent of those of men working full time," the 1963 President's Commission on the Status of Women reported. The previous paragraphs have highlighted dramatic advances in women's economic work life since 1960. Yet gender segregation continues as a major feature of the labor market fifty years later. Significant change toward occupational integration of the sexes occurred in the 1980s and early 1990s but has stalled since then, as has movement toward pay equity.

What is the most common job for women today? According to *CNNMoney*, in 2013, it was the same as it was in 1950: secretary. About four million U.S. workers fell under the category of "secretaries and administrative assistants" between 2006 and 2010, and 96 percent of them were women, according to the U.S. Census (Kurtz 2013).

Trends in occupation segregation since the 1960s show that significant change occurred during the 1980s and early 1990s. But then progress in occupational integration stalled across the board for women and men with different levels of education, in different race/ethnic groups, and in different age cohorts (Hegewisch and Hartmann 2014). Gender segregation remains substantial in terms of the broad sectors where men and women work. For example, three in four workers in education and health services are women, whereas nine in ten workers in the construction industry and seven in ten workers in manufacturing are men (U.S. Bureau of Labor Statistics 2013). Measures of occupational segregation in the second decade of the millennium show that one half of women or men still have to change occupations for true sex parity to exist. Women are also more likely to work in occupations with other women, irrespective of their race, than they are to work with men of their own race or ethnicity. Research suggests that job segregation is a major contributor to the gender wage gap. The Institute for Women's Policy Research concludes that

> there is a clear penalty for working in female-dominated occupations, with women in each of the three broad skill categories earning less in female-dominated occupations than in integrated or male-dominated occupations. Men also suffer a wage penalty for working in female-dominated occupations compared to their earnings in male-dominated or integrated occupations at the same skill level.
>
> (Hegewisch and Hartmann 2014, 13)

Further, even within female-dominated occupations, males tend to earn more than their female counterparts, except in high-skill, female-dominated fields. A half-century after enactment of the Equal Pay Act in 1963, striking disparities in the wages paid to male and female workers in similar positions continue to be found. In a study sure to strongly affect the current pay equity debate, the *Journal of the American Medical Association* reported data from a study of more than 290,000 registered nurses, a field in which 90 percent of its workers are female, and found that the pay gap had not narrowed within workplace settings and specialties from 1988 to 2013. Male nurses make $5,100 more on average per year than female colleagues in similar positions. Even after the research team accounted for things such as location, hours worked per week, years of experience, and type of nursing degree, men still earned $5,148 more than women (Muench et al. 2015).

Examining pay ratios in occupations in general, women and men continue to take home different paychecks. Of 116 occupations, men out-earn women in 114 of them. In the occupation with the biggest discrepancy between men and women, male physicians and surgeons make $756 more than women on a weekly basis for an annualized difference of $39,312 (Liner 2016). Female lawyers earn 82 percent of what male lawyers earn. The gender wage gap is currently larger at the top of the wage distribution and has decreased more slowly at the top than at other points in the distribution. This remains the case even after accounting for measured characteristics (Blau and Kahn 2016).

Recent research has also suggested that when women enter fields in greater numbers, pay declines for the very same jobs that more men were doing before. Claire Miller (2016) provides several examples. First, in the field of recreation, working in parks or leading camps went from predominantly male to female from 1950 to 2000. Median hourly wages in this field declined fifty-seven percentage points, accounting for the change in the value of the dollar. The job of ticket agent also went from mainly male to female during this period, and wages dropped forty-three percentage points.

Second, the same thing happened when women in large numbers became designers (wages fell thirty-four percentage points), housekeepers (wages fell twenty-one percentage points), and biologists (wages fell eighteen percentage points). The reverse was true when a job attracted more men. Computer programming, for instance, used to be a relatively menial role done by women. But when male programmers began to outnumber female ones, the job began paying more and gained prestige (Miller 2016).

Beyond the gender gap in pay, wage inequality among women has also risen across these decades. The gap between the haves and the have-nots among women has increased. The ratio between women's wages among the top earners and those at the bottom of the wage scale has grown. E. J. Dionne, quoted in the introduction to this chapter, saw the onset of the age of rising economic inequality, resulting in a class war among women. When real wages stopped growing in the 1970s, families could no longer maintain a standard of living based on one income alone. Two parallel streams of women entered the workforce. "On the one side were well-educated women who commanded relatively high salaries—even if they generally made less than men in comparable jobs. On the other side were less-educated women who took whatever jobs the economy could provide" (Dionne 1991, 105). The class divide among women has not subsided. In *Feminism Seduced*, Hester Eisenstein (2009, 107) describes the changes in the workforce of these decades as resulting in

> an erosion in the availability of high paying working-class jobs and a rise of service McJobs with low wages and few or no benefits. As women with education and access climbed the corporate ladder, reaching near parity with male middle managers, uneducated, poor women crowded into the jobs offered by retail organizations such as Walmart, where much of the workforce was able to subsist only with the aid of food stamps, Medicaid, and section 8 housing.

Economists project job growth in coming decades to be concentrated in fields in which women dominate—health care, service, and education—but that often do not pay particularly well (Carmon 2012).

Women, Families, and Labor Force Participation

Trends in women's overall labor force participation rates are only one dimension of the substantial change in their economic lives in contemporary times. Women's role as family breadwinner has grown substantially, as women have increased their share of family earnings. Motherhood has become less of a factor in women's labor force participation, and women as single heads of households has risen sharply. In married couple families, women's contributions to the household economy have risen by nearly ten percentage points, from 26.6 percent of household income in 1970 to 37.3 percent in 2013 (BLS Reports 2015). At the end of World War II, only 10 percent of married women with children under the age of six held or were seeking jobs. In 2012, the labor force participation rate for mothers of children aged six years or younger was 64.7 percent, nearly two thirds of all such mothers. In 2015, 42 percent of mothers were sole or primary breadwinners, bringing in at least half of the family earnings. Nearly one quarter (22.4 percent) were co-breadwinners, bringing home from 25 percent to 49 percent of earnings (Glynn 2016).

One of the most profound changes in women's lives in the past half-century has been the rise of single motherhood. The change involves both the numbers of women raising children without a husband being present and the number of single mothers who have never been married. In 1960, of all single mothers, more than eight in ten (82 percent) were divorced, separated, or widowed. An additional 14 percent were married, but their spouses were not living in the household. Only 4 percent of all single mothers had never been married. By 2011, according to the Pew Research Center, the share of single mothers who had never been married had climbed to 44 percent (Wang et al. 2013).

Washington Post columnist Emily Badger (2014) characterizes the contemporary status of women and motherhood:

> More women are having their children later in life. Or they're doing so in less traditional ways: before marriage, without marriage, or with unmarried partners. Single motherhood has grown so common in America that demographers now believe half of all children will live with a single mom at some point before the age of 18.

The percent of women living in female-headed households intersects with race and ethnicity; 43 percent of Black women live in female-headed family households compared to 14 percent of non-Hispanic White women and 25 percent of Hispanic women.

Class and race also affect the likelihood of a child being born to a single mother. A Black child today is much more likely to be born to a single mother than a White child or the child of a mother with a college degree. More than 70 percent of all Black children today are born to an unmarried mother, a threefold increase in that rate since the 1960s. This percentage compares with 54 percent of children born to Hispanic mothers and 36 percent of births to White mothers (see Figure 3.7).

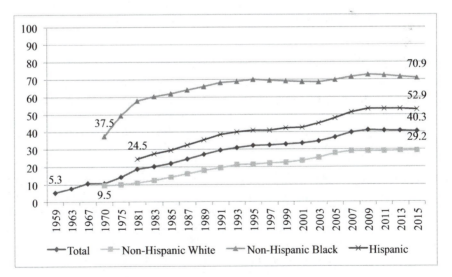

Figure 3.7 Unmarried Births by Race and Ethnicity, 1959–2015

Data adapted from the Centers for Disease Control and Prevention (https://www.childtrends.org/wp-content/uploads/2015/03/75_Births_to_Unmarried_Women.pdf).

Prior to 1969, Black denotes all non-Whites, including Asians and Native Americans; beginning in 1969, these data include Blacks only.

The Gendered Nature of Poverty

Scholar Dana Pearce coined the term the *feminization of poverty* in 1978 to describe a trend in women's and men's experiences of poverty. Whereas extraordinary gains in education, participation in the labor force, and professional advancement have characterized women's lives in the latter decades of the 20th century, rather paradoxically, in the same era, poverty had become "a female problem." Nearly two out of three of the fifteen million poor persons in the nation over eighteen were women, reported Pearce (1978, 28). Women were poor because they were women, she concluded. The percentage of female-headed households had increased substantially in the preceding decades, and the economic well-being of that group had especially eroded. Over 70 percent of the aged poor were women. The poverty imbalance has even been greater among certain groups. Black women, who were only 6.1 percent of the population in 1975, accounted for 17 percent of the poor at that time. Phyllis Palmer (1983) has written that the "'feminization of poverty' might be more truthfully labeled 'the racial feminization of poverty'" (5).

The gendered nature of poverty has continued. Since 1966, women in all age groups have been more likely to live in poverty (Cho 2014). What social and economic factors have accounted for poverty becoming a "women's problem"? Research has shown that the combination of increasing numbers of female-headed families and occupational segregation, which confined many women to lower wage jobs, appears to account for poverty becoming a gendered phenomenon. Women were concentrated in relatively few, low-paying occupations (Pearce 1978). Currently, two thirds of minimum wage workers are women. The proportion of children born to unwed mothers increased considerably since the 1950s, as noted earlier. Childbearing outside of marriage, coupled with a higher divorce rate, has translated into a significantly higher proportion of households headed by single women who are raising children on their own. Divorced and unmarried individuals with children have to balance the unpaid labor of raising children with paid labor, which is frequently inflexible and low paying (Thibos et al. 2007). In 2012, 40 percent of female-headed households lived in poverty (Cho 2014). Half of minimum-wage earners are single mothers.

In 2007, as the Great Recession started, 13.8 percent of women were poor compared to 11.1 percent of men. Experts declared the economy to be in "recovery" mode in 2009. (See the more detailed discussion in the next section.) But five years later, in 2014, according to U.S. Census data, the poverty rate among women had climbed to 16.1 percent. The comparative poverty rate for men was 13.4 percent. Women in the United States are also relatively further behind than women in other countries—the gap in poverty rates between men and women is wider in America than anywhere else in the Western world. Women continue to be poorer than men among all racial and ethnic groups. In 2012, 34.4 percent of Native American women were poor compared to 24.1 percent of Native American men; 25.1 percent of African American women were poor compared to 20.6 percent of African American men; 24.8 percent of Hispanic women were poor compared to 18.4 percent of Hispanic men; 11.5 percent of Asian women were poor compared to 10.6 percent of Asian men; and 10.3 percent of White women were poor compared to 7.7 percent of White men. Nearly 40 percent of women heading families (39.6 percent) fall below the poverty line (Cho 2014). More than two thirds (68.1 percent) of elderly poor were women. More than 40 percent of female-headed households with children lived in poverty.[5]

Gender, the Great Recession, and Economic Recovery

The term the *Great Recession* refers to the general economic decline that began in December 2007 and officially ended in June 2009 but continued to impact the economy throughout the second decade of the 21st century. More than eight million jobs were lost, the worst economic meltdown since the 1930s. More than thirteen million people were put out of work, nearly half of them for six months or more, the highest rate since World War II. The International Monetary Fund (2009) estimates it has been the worst global recession since World War II, with slow job growth characterizing the years of the recovery.

Although women have made major advances regarding their participation in the economic life of the nation—nearly one half of the labor force in 2007—we have seen that the contours of their economic life still differ from that of men's in economic areas such as job segregation, lower pay, and greater levels of poverty. These differences affected how women experienced the Great Recession relative to men and had important implications for public policy mechanisms to help achieve recovery. In 2007, at the onset of the recession, nearly eighty million women were in the labor force, comprising nearly one half of the workforce (46 percent). Their labor force participation rate was 59 percent. The unemployment rate for men and women was 5.1 and 4.9 percent, respectively. Among the unemployed were 3.5 million women (U.S. Department of Labor 2008).

Unemployment increased for both sexes over the course of the two years of the recession, but men's unemployment increased relative to women's. It peaked at 11.4 percent in October 2009; women's unemployment peaked at 8.8 percent. During the recession, men lost more than twice as many jobs as women; their job losses outnumbered those among women by 2.6 to 1. Men's job losses began before the recession was officially declared, whereas women's job losses began several months later, after the recession started. The Bureau of Labor Statistics data show steep drops in the number of jobs for men and women, especially in the fall of 2008 and early spring of 2009 for men.

The recession quickly took on a gendered focus. Gender affected the contour of job losses by industry in the Great Recession and the nature of governmental stimulus activities to reverse it. Commentators initially referred to the recession as a "mancession" (Rampell 2009) due to the negative impact of heavy layoffs in manufacturing and construction on men. Men experienced 82 percent of the job losses in the two years of the recession because of their high levels of employment in these distressed industries.

Feminist commentators, however, questioned the idea that the recession primarily negatively affected men. As Bryce Covert (2012) pointed out, women were also faring badly.

> Women may be over-represented in growing sectors, but those jobs pay poorly, offer few benefits, come with grudging work and provide little opportunity for advancement. The edge on wages experienced by young women evaporates as they progress in their careers. When women do get to middle management, they're paid less than men and they struggle to advance much further up the ladder. And women with children are left far behind.
>
> (Covert 2012)

Upon entering office in 2009, President Barack Obama initiated a federal stimulus plan, the American Recovery and Reinvestment Act, to help the country recover from the recession. The act sought to create 2.5 million jobs over the next two years, injecting over $800 billion in federal funds into the economy. The president's initial jobs' plan centered on "shovel-ready" jobs such as road and bridge maintenance, school repairs, and the creation of jobs that would reduce energy use and emissions that contribute to global warming. Efforts in support of state and local governments and education and health were a secondary focus of the stimulus plan.

Because few women worked in those targeted industrial sectors, they appeared to be left out of the recovery plan as initially conceived (Hirshman 2008). For example, just

2.7 percent of construction laborers, 1.9 percent of carpenters, 0.5 percent of highway workers, and 1.7 percent of electricians were women. The initial stimulus package did not include any affirmative action in the hiring for these positions that might have helped female workers. Cynthia Harrison of the National Council of Women's Organizations characterized the situation as follows (Seltzer 2011):

> We need federal aid and state support, not only for construction but for women in the public workforce. We need additional teachers, nurses and nurses' aides, as well as support for caregivers providing service in the home. And we also need to be sure that when we talk about shovel-ready projects . . . there's an opportunity for women to train for male-dominated jobs.

Women's groups' criticism of the initial focus of the stimulus plan led to health, education, and other human infrastructure components being added to the proposed act. In October 2010, the White House's Economic Council issued a *Jobs and Economic Security for America's Women* report highlighting implemented and proposed policies that "form a comprehensive plan to support women at all stages of their careers." Women in particular were hard hit by losses in government jobs because a greater share of women work in government jobs. In the second decade of the millennium, women comprised 56.8 percent of all government workers, 43 percent of federal government workers, 51.7 percent of state workers, and 64.1 percent of local government employees.

The Great Recession of 2007 to 2009, with its differential impact on women's and men's job loss and unemployment, provided a vivid illustration of the continued impact of gender segregation in employment (Hegewisch and Hartmann 2014). A comparison of the five years of the recovery on men's and women's employment is a tale of two parts. "Two Years of Economic Recovery: Women Lose Jobs, Men Find Them" is how the Pew Research Center titled its report regarding the recovery. From the end of the recession in June 2009 through May 2011, men gained 768,000 jobs and lowered their unemployment rate by 1.1 percentage points to 9.5 percent. Women, in contrast, lost 218,000 jobs during the same period, and their unemployment rate actually increased by 0.2 points to 8.5 percent (Bureau of Labor Statistics as reported by the Pew Research Center). Moreover, the Pew Research Center reported that men were making inroads into industries women had long dominated (Kochhar 2011).

According to Mimi Abramovitz (2012) in a piece titled "The Feminization of Austerity," the loss of public-sector jobs at a high rate and labor segregation that disproportionately locates women in industries and occupations that were cut at higher rates put many women in a double bind.

> Women represented just over half (57.2 percent) of the public workforce at the end of the recession, but they lost the majority (63.8 percent) of the 578,000 jobs cut in this sector between June 2009 and October 2011. The private sector picked up 1.6 million jobs over the course of the recovery, but women gained just one out of seven of these new jobs (252,000 jobs).

> (Abramovitz 2012, 37)

Abramovitz continues, "The stimulus package perpetuated sex segregation in employment by creating more 'shovel-ready' jobs that employ men than 'service-ready' jobs traditionally filled by women" (37).

According to the Economic Policy Institute's 2010 report, *The State of Working America*, women's poverty levels rose to their highest in seventeen years, and although they were regaining jobs at a higher rate than male workers, the jobs were more likely to be in low-wage industries and to pay poverty-level wages. Women were also less likely to receive unemployment insurance because of the nature of the jobs they were losing.

Re:Gender's 2014 report, *Gender Lens on Poverty*, noted that women, particularly since the 2008 recession, were increasingly occupying low-wage jobs. Women's "employment recovery" in terms of job growth had progressed at a greater rate than men's, but almost all the jobs had been at the lowest end of the pay scale. Women make up just under half of the national workforce, but about 60 percent of the minimum-wage workforce and 73 percent of tipped workers, the report stated (Cho 2014).

In 2015, three key indicators of well-being in the Census "moved decisively in the right direction," according to the Center on Budget and Policy Priorities. The number of uninsured Americans fell by four million from 2014 to 2015, on top of a drop of nearly nine million the year before. The typical household's income rose by 5.2 percent, or $2,798, after adjusting for inflation, the largest increase on record with data back to 1967. The poverty rate dropped from 14.8 percent to 13.5 percent, tying the largest improvement since 1968 (Greenstein 2016).

Eight years into the recovery and the election year of 2016, the Bureau of Labor Statistics reported that the unemployment rate had fallen from a high of 10 percent in October 2009 to 4.9 percent in July 2016. The July 2016 unemployment rate for men was 5 percent and for women in general it was 4.7 percent (Bureau of Labor Statistics, 2016). Black women's unemployment rate was 7 percent, however.

The problem of job segregation and women's access to good-paying jobs has taken a central place in the contemporary economic advocacy of women's rights groups. The Institute for Women's Policy Research, for example, asks, "Are Women Getting Left Out of the Growing Economy?" and graphically illustrates the problem for women as the economy moves forward. To overcome that problem, it has initiated the "Narrowing the Wage Gap by Improving Women's Access to Good Middle Skill Jobs" report and created the womenandgoodjobs.org website, which helps users identify pools of women workers who could be tapped to fill shortages. The website offers an interactive database to explore "on-ramp" occupations—those occupations dominated by women with many similar traits and duties as higher paying jobs dominated by men—and associated target occupations with higher earnings (see https://iwpr.org/publications/summer-2016-quarterly-newsletter/).

Political Response to the Great Recession

The recession and federal policy initiatives to reverse it generated fierce political criticism and activism from both the right and the left ends of the political spectrum. On the right, the Tea Party movement emerged in opposition to Obama administration proposals to alleviate the economic crisis of the recession. Expressing a high degree of government mistrust, their anger focused on the size and scope of the federal government and its regulation of the economy. Tea Party supporters were incensed over government spending and opposed tax increases and advocated lowering the national debt. They were particularly outraged by President Obama's health-care initiative and expressed great anger about immigration reform. They advocated a strict constructionist view of the Constitution, expressing a "widespread determination to restore twenty-first century U.S. government to the constitutional principles articulated by the eighteenth century Founding Fathers" (Skocpol and Williamson 2013, 48).

Only a small percentage of Americans identify with the Tea Party movement—18 percent, according to a 2012 CBS survey (Montopoli 2012)—but it has had outsized influence on the political process since its emergence as a political force. The Tea Party movement consists of a loose affiliation of national and local organizations that create their own platforms and agendas without central leadership. Individuals have formed local Tea Party groups and have engaged in national protests for lower taxes and less government spending and regulation. They gained notoriety particularly for their shout-outs to members of Congress at district meetings in 2009 over proposed health insurance reform. On September 12, 2009, approximately seventy-five thousand Tea Partiers took part in the Taxpayer March on Washington, DC. In 2010, they entered the electoral process, endorsing and working for candidates for public office.

According to researchers Skocpol and Williamson (2013, 84),

> There is not . . . a single Tea Party organization, not even a well-coordinated network. Instead, a gaggle of jostling and sometimes competing local and national organizations, none of them directly controlled by the institutional Republican Party are pushing to influence GOP officeholders, candidates and voters.

They identified more than eight hundred local Tea Party groups across the country by the fall of 2010 (Skocpol and Williamson 2013, 90). Self-appointed organizers who began as occasional protesters launched most of the local Tea Parties.

Tea Party supporters were initially characterized as tending to be Republican, White, male, married, and older than forty-five, based on a *New York Times* survey released in April 2010. The Pew Research Center for the People and the Press and the Pew Forum on Religion in Public Life 2010 survey found that 58.8 percent of Tea Party supporters were male compared with 42.1 percent of female supporters.

A very different picture of Tea Partiers emerges when the lens is focused on activists and leaders in the movement rather than on survey-identified supporters. From a gender perspective, Skocpol and Williamson's (2013, 43) study highlighted women dominating organizing efforts:

> Many of the men who tell pollsters that they sympathize with or generally support the Tea Party may be doing so from their armchairs in front of Fox News—or just sitting in the audience along with their wives at a Tea Party meeting or event. In the local Tea Party meetings we visited, women provided active leadership. Women leaders were at times the youngest people in the room.

Commentators, too, have cited the activism and leadership of women in organizing at the local level and their prominence at the national level. Politico.com columnist Kenneth Vogel (2010) highlighted, "The Face of the Tea Party Is Female," noting that "many of the tea party's most influential grass-roots and national leaders are women." Hanna Rosin (2010) has asked, "Is the Tea Party a Feminist Movement?" She stressed that to the extent the Tea Party has

> any legitimate national leadership . . . it is dominated by women. Of the eight board members of the Tea Party Patriots who serve as national coordinators for the movement, six are women. Fifteen of the 25 state coordinators are women. One of the three main sponsors of the Tax Day Tea Party that launched the movement is a group called Smart Girl Politics.

Smart Girl Politics started out as a mommy blog that turned into a mobilizing campaign that trains future activists and candidates. Jenny Beth Martin, thirty-nine at the time, cofounded and serves as the national coordinator of the Tea Party Patriots, an umbrella organization that claims 1,800 local affiliates with some fifteen million members. In 2010, she was named one of *Time* magazine's one hundred most influential leaders.

Political scientist Melissa Deckman (2016), who had interviewed Tea Party women, found that these women expressed a degree of animosity toward the Republican Party that was linked in part to their gender:

> Several activists I interviewed recounted attempts to influence their local or state Republican parties in a more conservative direction, only to encounter a hostile, good 'ole boys network. For example, Katrina Pierson, who co-founded the Garland Tea Party in Dallas, Texas in 2009, hails the Tea Party movement for allowing women to find their voices as a new generation of conservative leaders, telling me, "It used to be that men in the GOP or male leaders could take a woman's idea as their own—I have had this experience—but with social media women can be attributed, they can define their own brand, and define yourself and have your ideas heard. You don't have to go through the good old boys' club any longer and that has been huge for women." Women such as Pierson describe the Tea Party as a more appealing form of political activism for authentically conservative women than the GOP. Social media platforms, in particular, not only allow Tea Party women a chance to promote their political views, but also serve as launching pads for their own political careers. For instance, although Katrina Pierson failed in her challenge to Representative Pete Sessions in the 2014 GOP congressional primary in her home district in Texas, her high-profile involvement in the Tea Party led to her being hired as the national spokeswoman for the Trump presidential campaign.

Keli Carender is a prime example of female leadership in the movement. Carender, twenty-eight in 2009, whose youth is distinctive within the movement, is a teacher of math to adult learners and is credited with founding the first Tea Party protests in February 2009.

Picture 3.2 Female Tea Party Activists Cheering during a Tea Party Express Rally at Riverside Park in Grand Rapids, Michigan, April 10, 2010

AP photo

She initially organized what she called a "Porkulus Protest" in Seattle on Presidents' Day, February 16, the day before President Barack Obama signed the stimulus bill into law. Carender said she did it without support from outside groups or city officials. "I just got fed up and planned it." Carender reported 120 people as participating.

> Which is amazing for the bluest of blue cities I live in, and on only four days notice! This was due to me spending the entire four days calling and emailing every person, think tank, policy center, university professors (that were sympathetic), etc. in town, and not stopping until the day came.
>
> (Zerinke 2010)

Prominent women of the Tea Party movement are also national political figures, first and foremost being former Republican vice presidential candidate Sarah Palin and former U.S. representative, presidential candidate, and founder of the Congressional Tea Party Caucus, Michele Bachmann. Tea Party-supported candidates Debra Fischer of Nebraska and Joni Ernst of Iowa have been elected to the U.S. Senate. Entering the electoral arena as candidates for public office is only one, although the most prominent and possibly most powerful, means of creating political influence.

Women's organizing and leadership in the contemporary Tea Party movement is part of a long historical tradition of women's activism in American civic democracy. Chapter 2 noted how the suffrage movement emerged from women's engagement in a variety of reform movements, most notably abolitionism. U.S. voluntary associations have relied heavily on women's contributions historically, and as Skocpol and Williamson (2013)

Picture 3.3 Tea Party Activists at the U.S. Capitol on Election Night, 2010

Diana Reimer and Keli Carender hold flags during the Flag Ceremony during a Tea Party event on election night 2010 on the West Lawn of the U.S. Capitol.

Photo by Douglas Graham/Roll Call via Getty Images (CQ Roll Call via AP Images).

state, "American women built some of the most important moral and civic associations from the nineteenth through the mid-twentieth century" (44). Further, women's history scholar Melanie Gustafson suggests that "the tea party has provided a more direct way for conservative women to have influence than the Republican Party," where, she says, "women have always struggled for inclusion" (Vogel 2010). The surge of female activism in the Tea Parties, she suggests,

> is similar in some ways to the response to Theodore Roosevelt's Progressive Party in 1912 from women who couldn't vote, but who saw it as a moment where they could enter directly into politics, rather than by influencing their husbands. There's something happening here (in the tea party movement) in the same way which is bypassing the parties and I think women are comfortable with that type of organizing, because it's community organizing that revolves around family rituals.
>
> (Vogel 2010)

At the left end of the political spectrum, the Occupy Wall Street movement burst onto the political scene in the fall of 2011, first in Zuccotti Park in New York City two years after the emergence of the Tea Party. It then spread across the country. Income inequality is the main focus of Occupy Wall Street protests. They adopted the slogan "We are the 99%," which soon became infamous. The Occupy movement aimed to reduce corporate influence on politics, attain greater income equality, more and better jobs, banking system reform, student loan debt forgiveness, relief of the foreclosure situation, and stricter environmental standards. A Pew Research Center national survey taken shortly after the initial Occupy protest began in Zuccotti Park found about four in ten Americans (39 percent) expressed support for the movement, whereas 35 percent opposed it. In the same poll, 32 percent supported the Tea Party movement, whereas 44 percent were opposed to it (Pew Research Center 2011).

Locating in a public space, Zuccotti Park Occupy participants set up a camp as the center of their protest. In the weeks that followed, the encampment became quite established, with tents, desks, walkways, wireless Internet, a kitchen, and an extensive lending library. A sort of organization took shape, with people forming a seemingly endless array of working groups: structure, facilitation, sanitation, food, direct action, and safe spaces. A live-stream video feed was set up to follow their actions. To determine their strategies and tactics to achieve their goals, protesters acted on consensus-based decisions made in general assemblies. The assemblies emphasized direct action over petitioning authorities for redress, a type of leaderless democracy. Occupy groups used a consensus process in which anyone can join in the decision making and propose an idea. Proposers had to field questions, justify the hows and whys of their ideas, and engage a large-scale group discussion. Votes were then cast via an innovative system of hand signals, and proposals were revised until a nine-tenths majority approved. As one activist described it, "This is a leaderless movement without an official set of demands. There are no projected outcomes, no bottom lines and no talking heads. In the Occupy movement, *We are all leaders*" (Gautney 2011). The use of online social media tools was at the center of the spread of this movement. Whereas the Tea Party had adopted a specific set of goals and objectives in its "Contract from America," Occupy Wall Street had no centralized platform and attracts a variety of ideological perspectives under a broad call for change.

Two months later, police forced occupiers from Zuccotti Park. When they could not reoccupy the park, protesters focused on occupying banks, corporate headquarters, board meetings, foreclosed homes, and college and university campuses. The movement spread across cities and college campuses throughout the country. Both the Tea Party and the

Occupy Wall Street activists engaged in large protest demonstrations. The Occupy demonstrations, however, involved occupying both public and private spaces and clashing with police over encampments. On October 1, 2011, Occupy protesters set out to walk across the Brooklyn Bridge, which resulted in seven hundred arrests. After two years of encampments and demonstrations, nearly eight thousand Occupy protesters had been arrested.

In contrast to the Tea Party movement, Occupy Wall Street was very much, although certainly not totally, a younger person's movement. Media and academic observers' descriptions of the demographics of occupiers suggest that

> most of the demonstrators are in their teens or 20s, but plenty are older. Many are students. Many are jobless. A few are well-worn anarchists. Others have put their normal lives on pause to try out protesting and see how it feels.
>
> (Kleinfield and Buckley 2011)

According to Jocelyn Noveck in a *Long Island Press* (2011) report,

> As the protests have expanded and gained support from new sources, what began three weeks ago as a group of mostly young people camping out on the streets has morphed into something different: an umbrella movement for people of varying ages, life situations and grievances, some of them first-time protesters.

One survey of the protesters in Zuccotti Park found the average age to be thirty-three. "That means for every college student you have a mid-career professional in their 40s," the survey concluded. Those contributing financial donations were found to be "average, middle class donors."

Picture 3.4 Raging Grannies Occupy Protest
Courtesy of Shutterstock.

Picture 3.5 Women of the Occupy Wall Street Movement

Women were part of the occupation since its beginning. They were entrenched both in the day-to-day and in the long-term work of the Occupy movement. In a commentary reminiscent of the characterization of women in the Tea Party movement cited earlier, Sarah Seltzer (2011) titled her commentary on women and Occupy Wall Street in *The Nation*, "Where Are the Women at Occupy Wall Street? Everywhere—and They Are Not Going Away." They were instrumental in making its structure horizontal rather than hier-archical, according to Seltzer's accounting. Women were prominently captured in photos accompanying media reports of the movement and were often quoted in media coverage. They were among the arrestees and jailed individuals. Cicely McMillan, for one, was sentenced to three months in jail and five years of probation for elbowing a police officer when the protesters were being cleared out of Zuccotti Park. The police pepper-spraying eighty-four-year-old Dorli Rainey during a Seattle, Washington, protest made national headlines.

Women also challenged sexism in the movement and formed their own caucus, Women Occupying Wall Street (WOW), working for gender justice and the end to gender violence both within and outside the Occupy movement. A National Feminist General Assembly was also held in May 2012 in New York. WOW (http://interoccupy.net/womenoccupy/) grew out of the Occupy Wall Street movement with the mission

> to provide women across occupations with resources for creating safer spaces and feminist organizing. Building on the example of Occupy Wall Street, we will help to create and be a space for tools and shared best practices. A space for a conversation beyond local occupations, to allow activists to connect globally. To support the needs of women co-creating equal participation in the movement.

The sustainability of WomenOccupy.org is uncertain. Code Pink, a feminist peace organization that has been at the front of challenging U.S. militarism for over a decade, maintains Women Occupy's social media presence. Given the challenging and radical nature of the Occupy movement, establishing its impact on women's rights and women's political participation is more complicated than, for instance, examining the movement of Tea Party women into electoral office.

Public Policy and Gender Economic Equity

Women's rights activists continue to push for legislation to strengthen employment equity, close perceived loopholes in existing equal pay legislation, and address gender-related aspects of more general economic inequality. The most prominent of these legislative initiatives has been the Lilly Ledbetter Fair Pay Act and the Paycheck Fairness Act. The Lilly Ledbetter Fair Pay Act was successfully enacted into law in January 2009. The Paycheck Fairness Act has been introduced in several Congresses. Most recently, on September 15, 2014, the U.S. Senate failed in a cloture vote to open debate on a 52–40 vote. Sixty votes are needed in the Senate to end debate and to come to a final debate and vote on a proposed measure. Republican senators unanimously opposed the bill that Democratic Senator Barbara Mikulski had introduced. Each of these pieces of legislation have sought to update and strengthen the 1963 Equal Pay Act and Title VII of the 1964 Civil Rights Act to provide effective protection against sex-based pay discrimination.

The Lilly Ledbetter Fair Pay Act was introduced in Congress in response to the 2007 Supreme Court decision in *Ledbetter v. Goodyear Tire and Rubber Company*. In a 5–4 decision, the court ruled that Lilly Ledbetter, the only female supervisor in a tire plant in Gadsden, Alabama, did not file her lawsuit against Goodyear Tire within the time frame Title VII specified. The court interpreted Title VII to require that a lawsuit be filed within 180 days of the alleged unlawful employment act. But Ledbetter had no way of knowing that over the years of her employment she had received smaller raises than her male colleagues. She only realized that she had been the subject of pay discrimination when she received an anonymous note showing the salaries of her colleagues at the time of her retirement in 1999. The Ledbetter Fair Pay Act amends Title VII by stating that the 180-day statute of limitations for filing an equal pay lawsuit regarding pay discrimination resets with each new discriminatory paycheck.

A 2010 IWPR/Rockefeller national survey asked workers whether their workplaces had policies that discouraged or prohibited sharing information about pay. About one half of all workers (51 percent of women and 49 percent of men) reported that the discussion of wage and salary information was either discouraged or prohibited and/or could lead to punishment. The Paycheck Fairness Act aims to close the continuing pay gap by making wages more transparent, requiring that wage discrepancies be tied to legitimate business qualifications and not to sex and prohibiting companies from taking retaliatory action against employees who raise concerns about gender-based wage discrimination. Opponents of the Paycheck Fairness Act claim that revealing salary information violates privacy, that the wage gap (if it exists) is a product of women's choices, and that the legislation would encourage employers to just hire men in order to avoid lawsuits. The Paycheck Fairness Act has come up for a vote in one or the other houses of Congress on numerous occasions but has not yet received a positive legislative vote.[6]

Legislation raising the minimum wage would disproportionally positively affect women's wages, as women make up two thirds of minimum wage workers. The federal minimum wage is $7.25. More than 13.1 million women would see a wage increase from a minimum wage hike. The Fair Minimum Wage Act and the Minimum Wage Fairness Act (2014) would gradually raise the federal minimum wage to $10.10 per hour, increase the tipped minimum wage from $2.13 an hour to 70 percent of the minimum wage, and index these wages to keep pace with inflation. Women are two thirds of workers in tipped occupations. Women of color are disproportionately represented among minimum wage workers: 22 percent of minimum wage workers compared to less than 16 percent of workers overall. More than three quarters of women earning minimum wage are twenty years or older, and most do not have a spouse at home on whom to rely. It is estimated that raising the minimum wage would close the wage gap by 5 percent.[7] The biggest gap is between young men and young women. Among hourly workers ages twenty to twenty-four, some 10 percent of women made the federal minimum wage or less compared with 5.8 percent of men (Kronstad 2014).

Twenty-three states and the District of Columbia have higher minimum wages. Voters in four states—Alaska, Arkansas, Nebraska, and South Dakota—approved measures in the 2014 election to raise the minimum wage. Ten other states increased their minimum wage through bills passed in their legislatures. In April 2014, the Seattle city council raised its minimum wage to $15 an hour. Through an executive order, President Obama raised the minimum wage for federal contractors to $10.10 per hour in 2014. The National Economic Council, the Department of Labor, and others issued a report titled *The Impact of Raising the Minimum Wage on Women* (2014). The report argued that raising the minimum wage was especially important for women because:

- Women in the workforce are more highly concentrated in low-wage sectors such as personal care and health-care support occupations.
- Women account for more than half (55 percent) of all workers who would benefit from increasing the minimum wage to $10.10.
- Women also make up the majority of workers in predominantly tipped occupations. Under federal law, employers are allowed to pay a "tipped minimum wage" of $2.13 per hour to employees who regularly earn tips as long as their tips plus the tipped minimum wage meet or exceed $7.25 per hour.
- Women account for 72 percent of all workers in predominantly tipped occupations such as restaurant servers, bartenders, and hairstylists.
- Average hourly wages for workers in predominantly tipped occupations are nearly 40 percent lower than overall average hourly wages.
- Workers in predominantly tipped occupations are twice as likely as other workers to experience poverty, and servers are almost three times as likely to be in poverty.
- About half of all workers in predominantly tipped occupations would see their earnings increase as a result of the president's proposal.

Opponents of minimum-wage increases have argued that such measures will result in lost jobs, hurt small businesses and low-skilled workers, have little effect on reducing poverty, and might result in higher prices for consumers. For example, the CATO Institute, a conservative think tank, argues that

> there is no "free lunch" when the government mandates a minimum wage. If the government requires that certain workers be paid higher wages, then businesses make adjustments to pay for the added costs, such as reducing hiring, cutting employee work hours, reducing benefits, and charging higher prices.
>
> (Wilson 2012)

Several studies have challenged this perspective, providing evidence that increasing the minimum wage has not had a negative effect of the economy. For example, the Economic

Policy Institute 2012 report, *How Raising the Minimum Wage Would Help Working Families and Give the Economy a Boost*, argues that

> raising the minimum wage would help workers still reeling from the effects of the recession. The resulting impact on the overall economy would be demonstrably positive, as minimum-wage workers would spend their new earnings immediately, generating a positive impact on GDP and related modest employment growth.
>
> (Cooper and Hall 2012)

The Fair Labor Standards Act does not cover all workers. Particularly excluded have been domestic workers, the majority of whom are women. Activists are promoting public policy efforts to bring such workers into the minimum wage sector and improving their working conditions. Chapter 6 describes these efforts. The substantial numbers of low-income women in this part of the workforce certainly contribute to economic inequality in contemporary society.

Conclusion

This chapter has surveyed trends in women's increasing engagement in the economic life of the nation. It has puzzled over the ways in which changes in women's lives have impacted the rise in income inequality in this country and how the rise in income inequality has affected women's lives, working against gender equality. It has examined the intersection of race and class on women's economic status. Women's growing participation in the workforce and rising economic inequality among the populace is a complicated relationship. Has women's increase in economic participation mitigated the rise in income inequality or exacerbated it? Given the stagnation in men's wages, women's increased participation in the workforce and their growing numbers among professional workers mitigate the trend toward greater economic inequality. In an assessment of what has caused what he calls "the great divergence," Timothy Noah concludes that gender cannot be blamed for it. To contribute to the growth in income inequality over the past three decades, the income gaps between women and men would have to have grown. But they did not, as this chapter has shown. Indeed, women have swum against the tide of generally rising income inequality, with their earnings rising relative to men's (Goldin 1977), although the earnings gap has not been closed. At the same time, the decline in the family wage and lower marriage rates have seen women become the dominant low-wage workers, aggravating the economic gap and the majority of those living in poverty. Also of importance are not only the contours of an economic gender gap but also a rising inequality among women, as this chapter has described. Chapter 4 turns attention to women's participation in the political life of the nation.

Notes

1. In 2014, among the population twenty-five years of age and older, women for the first time were more likely than men to have bachelor's degrees (30.2 percent vs. 29.9 percent).
2. www.ncwge.org.
3. Persons aged sixteen years and older are surveyed in determinations of labor force participation. Thus, individuals going to school full time and retired persons account at least in part for labor force participation rates not being higher.
4. Two sets of figures are used to describe the size of the wage gap between the sexes. The data used to construct Figure 3.4 is based on annual earnings. In its *Highlights of Women's Earnings* series of reports, the Bureau of Labor Statistics present data based on "usual weekly earnings." Those

data show women earning 82.5 percent of male full-time wage and salary workers as opposed to the 78.6 percent figure based on annual earnings. The annual earnings data are used in Figure 3.4 because they allow for the presentation of a longer trend line. "Usual weekly earnings" data go back only to 1979.

5. The Census Bureau determines poverty status by comparing annual income to a set of dollar values called poverty thresholds that vary by family size, number of children, and age of householder. If a family's before-tax money income is less than the dollar value of their threshold, then that family and every individual in it are considered to be in poverty. For people not living in families, poverty status is determined by comparing the individual's income to his or her poverty threshold.

6. Republican U.S. Senator Kelly Ayotte has introduced an alternative to the Paycheck Fairness Act, the Gender Advancement in Pay Act (GAP Act). It is narrower in scope than the Paycheck Fairness Act. See, for example, Brynn Stylinski, 2015, "The Gender Advancement in Pay Act: The GAP Act Leaves Some Holes," http://uclawreview.org/2015/12/01/the-gender-advancement-in-pay-act-the-gap-act-leaves-some-holes/.

7. These data are based on Bureau of Labor Statistics, "Characteristics of Minimum Wage Workers," 2013, http://bls.gov/cps/minwage2013.pdf.

Further Readings and Web Resources

American Association of University Women. 2016. *The Simple Truth about the Gender Pay*, 2016 edition. Washington, DC: American Association of University Women.

Deckman, Melissa. 2016. *Tea Party Women: Mama Grizzlies, Grassroots Leaders, and the Changing Face of the American Right*. New York, NY: New York University Press.

Hegewisch, Ariane, Marc Bendick Jr., Barbara Gault, and Heidi Hartmann. 2016. *Pathways to Equity: Narrowing the Wage Gap by Improving Women's Access to Good Middle Skill Jobs*. Washington, DC: Institute for Women's Policy Research. www.jpmorganchase.com/corporate/Corporate-Responsibility/document/womens-wage-gap-middle-skills-jobs.pdf.

Institute for Policy Studies. 2015. "And Still I Rise: Black Women Labor Leaders' Voices/Power/Promises." www.and-still-I-rise.org.

Institute for Women's Policy Research. 2016. "Year in Review: IWPR's Top 10 Findings of 2016." https://femchat-iwpr.org/2016/12/30/year-in-review-iwprs-top-10-findings-of-2016/.

Web Resources

"2020 Vision: Mend the Gaps." *Network*. https://networklobby.org/2020vision.

"National Snapshot: Poverty Among Women & Families, 2015." *National Women's Law Center*. http://nwlc.org/resources/national-snapshot-poverty-among-women-families-2015/.

References

Abramovitz, Mini. 2012. "The Feminization of Austerity." *New Labor Forum*, 21, 1 (Winter): 32–41.

American Association of University Women. 2016. *The Simple Truth about the Pay Gap*. Washington, DC: AAUW.

Badger, Emily. 2014. "The Unbelievable Rise of Single Motherhood in America over the Last 50 Years." *The Washington Post*, December 18. www.washingtonpost.com/blogs/wonkblog/wp/2014/12/18/the-unbelievable-rise-of-single-motherhood-in-america-over-the-last-50-years/.

Bartels, Larry. 2008. *Unequal Democracy*. Princeton, NJ: Princeton University Press.

Bauman, Kurt and Camille Ryan. 2015. *Women Now at the Head of the Class, Lead Men in College Attainment*. Washington, DC: U.S. Census Bureau. www.census.gov/newsroom/blogs/random-samplings/2015/10/women-now-at-the-head-of-the-class-lead-men-in-college-attainment.html.

Blau, Francine D. and Lawrence M. Kahn. 2016. *The Gender Wage Gap: Extent, Trends, and Explanations*. Bonn, Germany: IZA.

BLS Reports. 2015. "Women in the Labor Force: A Databook." *U.S. Bureau of Labor Statistics.* www.bls.gov/opub/reports/womens-databook/archive/women-in-the-labor-force-a-databook-2015.pdf.

Boustan, Leah Platt and William J. Collins. 2013. "The Origins and Persistence of Black-White Differences in Women's Labor Force Participation." *Working Paper 19040.* National Bureau of Economic Research. www.nber.org/papers/w19040.

Bureau of Labor Statistics. 2016. "Labor Force Statistics from the Current Population Survey." https://www.bls.gov/web/empsit/cpseea10.htm.

Carmon, Irin. 2012. "Going for the Gold, Getting the Silver. Still." *National Journal*, March 9. www.theatlantic.com/business/archive/2012/03/going-for-the-gold-getting-the-silver-still/426354/.

Chesler, Ellen. 2012. "U.S. Women Poised for a Radical Tune-Up; Here's Why." http://womensenews.org/2012/09/us-women-poised-radical-tune-heres-why/.

Cho, Rosa. 2014. "Precarious Lives: Gender Lens on Low Wage Work." *Re:Gender.* www.icrw.org/wp-content/uploads/2016/11/precarious-lives.pdf.

Cobble, Dorothy Sue. 2007. "Introduction." In *The Sex of Class: Women Transforming American Labor*, ed. Dorothy Sue Cobble. Ithaca, NY: Cornell University Press.

Cohen, Cathy, Kathleen Thomas, and Joan Tronto. 1997. *Women Transforming Politics.* New York, NY: New York University Press.

Cooper, David and David Hall. 2012. *How Raising the Federal Minimum Wage Would Help Working Families and Give the Economy a Boost.* Washington, DC: Economic Policy Institute. www.epi.org/publication/ib341-raising-federal-minimum-wage/.

Covert, Bryce. 2012. "One Mancession Later, Are Women Really Victors in the New Economy?" February 27. www.thenation.com/article/166468/one-mancession-later-are-women-really-victors-new-economy.

Deckman, Melissa. 2016. "What Sarah Palin's Endorsement of Donald Trump May Say about Tea Party Women." *Presidential Gender Watch 2016.* http://presidentialgenderwatch.org/what-sarah-palins-endorsement-of-donald-trump-may-say-about-tea-party-women/.

Dionne, E. J. 1991. *Why Americans Hate Politics.* New York, NY: Simon & Schuster.

Diprete, Thomas and Claudia Buchman. 2013. *The Rise of Women: The Growing Gender Gap in Education and What It Means for American Schools.* Austin, TX: Council on Contemporary Families.

Eisenstein, Hester. 2009. *Feminism Seduced.* Boulder, CO: Paradigm.

Fry, Richard and Rakesh Kochhar. 2014. *America's Wealth Gap between Middle-Income and Upper-Income Families Is Widest on Record.* Washington, DC: Pew Research Center.

Gautney, Heather. 2011. "What Is Occupy Wall Street? The History of Leaderless Movements." *The Washington Post*, October 10. www.washingtonpost.com/national/on-leadership/what-is-occupy-wall-street-the-history-of-leaderless-movements/2011/10/10/gIQAwkFjaL_story.html.

Glynn, Sarah Jane. 2016. "Breadwinning Mothers Are Increasingly the Norm." Center for American Progress, December 19. www.americanprogress.org/issues/women/reports/2016/12/19/295203/breadwinning-mothers-are-increasingly-the-u-s-norm/.

Goldin, Claudia. 1977. "Female Labor Force Participation: The Origin of Black and White Differences, 1870 and 1880." *The Journal of Economic History*, 37, 1 (March): 87–108.

Goldin, Claudia. 2014. " A Grand Gender Convergence: Its Last Chapter." *American Economic Review*, 104, 4: 1091–1119.

Greenstein, Robert. 2016. "Commentary: Health Coverage, Income, and Poverty All Improved Decisively in 2015, with Historic Gains in Some Areas." Washington, DC: Center on Budget and Policy Priorities. www.cbpp.org/poverty-and-inequality/commentary-health-coverage-income-and-poverty-all-improved-decisively-in-2015.

Hacker, Jacob and Paul Pierson. 2010. *Winner-Take-All Politics: How Washington Made the Rich Richer and Turned Its Back on the Middle Class.* New York, NY: Simon & Schuster.

Hegewisch, Ariane and Asha DuMonthier. 2016. "The Wage Gap by Occupation 2015 and by Race and Ethnicity." *Institute for Women's Policy Research Fact Sheet #C440.* www.iwpr.org/publications/pubs/the-gender-wage-gap-by-occupation-2015-and-by-race-and-ethnicity.

Hegewisch, Ariane and Heidi Hartmann. 2014. *Occupational Segregation and the Gender Wage Gap: A Job Half Done*. Washington, DC: Institute for Women's Policy Research.

Hirshman, Linda. 2008. "Where Are the New Jobs for Women?" *The New York Times*, December 9. www.nytimes.com/2008/12/09/opinion/09hirshman.html?_r=0.

International Monetary Fund. 2009. "World Economic Outlook: Crisis and Recovery." Washington, DC: International Monetary Fund. www.imf.org/external/pubs/ft/weo/2009/01/pdf/text.pdf.

Keller, Bill. 2013. "Inequality for Dummies." *New York Times*, December 22.

Kleinfield, N. R. and Cara Buckley. 2011. "Wall Street Occupiers, Protesting Till Whenever." *New York Times*, September 20. www.nytimes.com/2011/10/01/nyregion/wall-street-occupiers-protesting-till-whenever.html.

Kochhar, Rakesh. 2011. "Two Years of Economic Recovery: Women Lose Jobs, Men Find Them." Washington, DC: Pew Research Center. www.pewsocialtrends.org/2011/07/06/two-years-of-economic-recovery-women-lose-jobs-men-find-them/.

Kroeger, Teresa and Elise Gould. 2016. "Straight Out of College, Women Make $4 less per hour than men – and the gap is getting wider." Economic Policy Institute, April 26. http://www.epi.org/publication/straight-out-of-college-women-make-4-less-per-hour-than-men-and-the-gap-is-getting-wider/.

Kronstad, Jens Manuel. 2014. "More Women Than Men Earn the Federal Minimum Wage." *Pew Research Center Fact Tank*. www.pewresearchcenter.org/fact-tank/2014//05/05/more-women-than-men-earn-the-federal-minimum-wage.

Krugman, Paul. 2007. *The Conscience of a Liberal*. New York, NY: W. W. Norton.

Kurtz, Annalyn. 2013. "Why Secretary Is Still the Top Job for Women." *CNNMoney*, January 13. http://money.cnn.com/2013/01/31/news/economy/secretary-women-jobs/index.html.

Liner, Emily. 2016. "A Dollar Short: What's Holding Women Back from Equal Pay?" March 16. www.afscmeinfocenter.org/blog/2016/03/a-dollar-short-whats-holding-women-back-from-equal-pay.htm#.VyjHyCHpeTk.

McBride, Dorothy E. and Janine A. Parry. 2011. *Women's Rights in the USA*, 4th edition. New York, NY: Routledge.

McDaniel, Anne, Thomas DiPrete, Claudia Buchmann, and Uri Shwed. 2009. "The Black Gender Gap in Educational Attainment: Historical Trends and Racial Comparisons." www.ssc.wisc.edu/soc/faculty/docs/diprete/Race%20Paper%2009232009.pdf.

Miller, Claire Cain. 2016. "As Women Take over a Male-Dominated Field, the Pay Drops." *The New York Times*, March 18. www.nytimes.com/2016/03/20/upshot/as-women-take-over-a-male-dominated-field-the-pay-drops.html?smtyp=cur&_r=0.

Montopoli, Brian. 2012. "Tea Party Supporters: Who They Are and What They Believe." *CBS News*, December 14. www.cbsnews.com/news/tea-party-supporters-who-they-are-and-what-they-believe/.

Muench, Ulrike, Jody Sindelar, Susan Busch, and Peter Buerhaus. 2015. "Salary Differences between Male and Female Registered Nurses in the United States." *Journal of the American Medical Association*, 313, 12: 1265–1267.

National Student Clearinghouse Research Center. 2015. "Snapshot Report-Degree Attainment." http://nscresearchcenter.org/snapshotreport-degreeattainment15/.

Noveck, Jocelyn. 2011. "Protesters Want World to Know They Are Just Like Us." http://web.archive.org/web/20120507064809/www.longislandpress.com/2011/10/10/protesters-want-world-to-know-theyre-just-like-us-2/.

Pearce, Diane. 1978. "Feminization of Poverty: Women, Work and Welfare." *The Urban & Social Change Review*, 11: 28–36.

Pew Research Center. 2011. "Public Divided Over Occupy Wall Street Movement." October 24. www.people-press.org/2011/10/24/public-divided-over-occupy-wall-street-movement/.

Rampell, Catherine. 2009. "The Mancession." *The New York Times*, August 10. http://economix.blogs.nytimes.com/2009/08/10/the-mancession/.

Rosin, Hanna. 2010. "Is the Tea Party a Feminist Movement?" *Slate*, May 12. www.slate.com/articles/double_x/doublex/2010/05/is_the_tea_party_a_feminist_movement.html.

Seltzer, Sarah. 2011. "Budget Cuts Most Likely to Affect Women: So Why Aren't There Any Women on the Budget-Slashing Committee?" *Alternet*, July 24. www.alternet.org/story/151057/

budget_cuts_most_likely_to_affect_women%3A_so_why_aren't_there_any_women_on_the_budget-slahsing_committee.

Skocpol, Theda and Vanessa Williamson. 2013. *The Tea Party and the Remaking of Republican Conservatism.* New York, NY: Oxford University Press.

Snipp, C. Matthews and Sin Yi Cheung. 2016. "Changes in Racial and Gender Inequality Since 1970." *Annals of the Academy of Political and Social Sciences,* 663 (January): 80–98.

Stone, Chad, Danilo Trisi, Arloc Sherman, and Brandon DeBot. 2014. "A Guide to Statistics on Historical Trends in Income Inequality." *Center for Budget and Policy Priorities.* www.cbpp.org/cms/index.cfm?fa=view&id=3629.

Task Force on Inequality and American Democracy. 2004. *American Democracy in an Age of Rising Inequality.* Washington, DC: American Political Science Association.

Thibos, Megan, Danielle Lavin-Loucks, and Marcus Martin. 2007. "The Feminization of Poverty." www.williamsoninstitute.org.

U.S. Bureau of Labor Statistics. 2013. "Current Population Survey Household Annual Averages." www.bls.gov/cps/cpsaat17.pdf.

U.S. Department of Labor. 2008. *Women in the Labor Force: A Databook (Report 1011).* Washington, DC: U.S. Department of Labor.

Vogel, Kenneth. 2010. "Face of the Tea Party Is Female." *Politico,* March 26. www.politico.com/news/stories/0310/35094_Page3.html.

Wang, Wendy, Kim Parker, and Paul Taylor. 2013. "Chapter 4 Single Mothers." *Bread Winner Moms,* Pew Research Center. www.pewsocialtrends.org/2013/05/29/breadwinner-moms/.

Weeks, Julie. 2016. "Women, Especially Women of Color, Are Fueling Business Startup Activity." http://about.americanexpress.com/news/docs/2016x/2016SWOB.pdf.

Wilson, Mark. 2012. "The Negative Effects of Minimum Wage Laws." Washington, DC: Cato Institute. www.downsizinggovernment.org/labor/negative-effects-minimum-wage-laws.

Wilson, Valerie. 2016. "State of Black Women in the American Economy." *Black Women in the United States 2016: Power of the Sister Vote.* Washington, DC: Black Women's Roundtable. https://bwrvoterguide2016.files.wordpress.com/2016/04/2final-black-women-in-the-us-2016-1.pdf.

Zerinke, Kate. 2010. "Unlikely Activist Who Got to the Tea Party Early." *The New York Times,* February 27. www.nytimes.com/2010/02/28/us/politics/28keli.html.

4 Gender, Voting, Electioneering, and Public Opinion

The concept of a gender gap became part of the U.S. political landscape during the 1980 presidential election. A voting gender gap was not a feature of political commentary prior to Ronald Reagan's election that year, nor were women viewed as a political force. It was not that men and women had never differed in their perspectives on public policy issues or voting behavior prior to this election, but rather, a group, the National Organization for Women (NOW), seeking change, noted a difference in the votes of men and women in 1980 postelection analyses. Seizing on those findings, it publicized this difference, thus making the gender gap a political story that became historical in significance.

Although Reagan handily won the 1980 election, that election experienced a difference of 8 percent in men's and women's votes for the winning candidate: 46 percent of women voted for Reagan compared with 54 percent of men. Women's votes had been noted during the campaign, but the idea of a women's bloc had primarily been ignored or dismissed. Adam Clymer was the first journalist to note the difference in Reagan's support between men and women, which he described in a *New York Times* postelection analysis piece. Clymer (1980, 18) reported that

> Mr. Reagan's long-standing difficulties in persuading women to vote for him . . . held down his percentages again Tuesday. . . . The [*New York Times* and *CBS News*] poll suggested that both fear about war and opposition to the Equal Rights Amendment handicapped Mr. Reagan's bid for their support.

As Kathy Bonk (1988, 85) recounts the story, Eleanor Smeal, president of NOW, recognized the political significance of Clymer's report. At that time, NOW and other women's rights organizations were discouraged over the failure of campaigns to get the Equal Rights Amendment ratified in the states. The gender gap in the 1980 election gave these groups a "hook" for media attention and ammunition to press politicians to vote for the amendment. Building on Clymer's story, NOW headlined its newspaper's December–January (1980–1981) issue with an article titled "Women Vote Differently Than Men, Feminist Bloc Emerges in 1980 Elections." The article stated that

> the NYT/CBS poll reported that 8 percent fewer women (46 percent) voted for Reagan than did men (54 percent). ABC's poll was similar. This difference calculated in actual votes, amounts to a net loss of 3.3 million female votes for Reagan.

(86)

NOW edited the article into op-ed pieces that it distributed to the news media. They were reprinted in both the *Chicago Sun Times* and the *Chicago Tribune* where the target audience was Illinois legislators who would be voting on the Equal Rights Amendment during the next fifteen months.

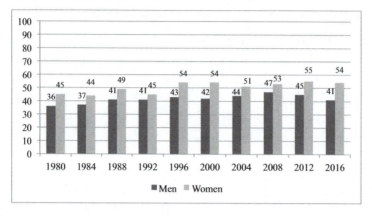

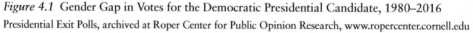

Figure 4.1 Gender Gap in Votes for the Democratic Presidential Candidate, 1980–2016
Presidential Exit Polls, archived at Roper Center for Public Opinion Research, www.ropercenter.cornell.edu

The term *gender gap* first appeared in the media in a Judy Mann piece in the *Washington Post* in 1981 (Smeal 1997). Since that time, gender has been the subject of much media commentary. Scholars of American politics have shown keen interest in its nature and extent, and activists have assumed the importance of the women's vote and sought to court it. A focus on gender in elections consists of several significant political features. First, we should examine turnout rates of men and women. Do men and women vote at the same rates? Women constitute more than half the population, so more women than men may vote. But what have been the trends in the percent of eligible female voters who turn out to vote compared to the percent of eligible male voters? Then, do women vote differently from men? Do they have the same policy preferences on political issues of the day? Third, how have political campaigns attempted to win women's votes? Figure 4.1 illustrates the gender gap in presidential voting preferences from 1980 through the 2016 election. The gender gap is measured by comparing women's votes for a candidate with men's votes. It is usually presented in terms of the votes for the Democratic candidate. To illustrate, in 2016, there was a thirteen-point gender gap in the vote for Hillary Clinton.

Historical Trends in Voter Turnout

When women finally obtained the vote in 1920 with ratification of the 19th Amendment, political speculation centered on the possibility that women would affect election outcomes with a large and distinctive vote. Feminists hoped, and some male politicians feared, that newly enfranchised female voters would back candidates supporting a wide range of "maternalist" social policies such as protective wage and hours laws, expansive health and housing policies, and other types of social provisions for indigent women and families. Such a vote, however, failed to materialize in elections following enfranchisement (Manza and Brooks 1998). Indeed, the conventional wisdom became that "women in general voted like their husbands if they voted at all" (Alpern and Baum 1985). Commentators suggested that perhaps suffrage was a failure.

It is not known how many women actually voted in the 1920 presidential election, as no official accounting of their votes in that election exists. In some states, residency requirements kept women from being able to register and vote until the next election. Jim Crow laws[1] also limited the ability of Black women as well as Black men to vote. It is estimated that about one third of the female electorate voted in the 1920 presidential election (Andersen 1996, 51). On average in the ten states that political scientists Kevin Corder and Christina Wolbrecht (2016) have studied, just 36 percent of women turned out to vote, but their turnout rates varied across the states related to the competitiveness of the presidential race in a state and state adoption of barriers to registering and voting.

The contours of the historical growth in women's voting participation are sketchy. It is only since 1964 when the U.S. Census Bureau began to collect survey data on turnout in presidential and midterm elections that the numbers of women voting and their rates of participation can be tracked and their turnout relative to that of men examined. In its 1964 November supplement, the U.S. Census Bureau Current Population Survey (CPS) first included questions about registration and voting in that year's presidential election. These questions have continued to be asked in all subsequent midterm and presidential election years, providing for a long trend analysis of overall turnout rates and who votes.[2] Figure 4.2 shows the trend in turnout rates for the two sexes since 1964 through the 2012 election.

Based on these surveys, we know that female voters exceeded male voters in each of the presidential and midterm congressional elections over the last five decades. Because of their larger numbers in the population, greater numbers of women voting does not necessarily mean that women turn out to vote at a higher rate than men. The turnout rate is based on the percent of citizens in a certain category eligible to vote who actually register and cast ballots. Between 1964 and 1976, the turnout rate of women was lower than men's turnout. In the 1980s, women's lagging as voters finally disappeared. Turnout rates have reversed to women's advantage.

According to the CPS in 1964, over 39 million women voted, 67 percent of those eligible, compared to nearly 37.5 million men, 71.9 percent of eligible male voters. The voting gender gap was particularly striking among older Americans. Fewer than 50 percent of women seventy-five years of age and older voted compared with two thirds of men of that age group in 1964. In 1980, the pivotal year in which gender became a political phenomenon, as noted in this chapter's introduction, 49.3 million women reported having cast a ballot, 59.4 percent of eligible female voters, compared to 43.8 million men, 59.1 percent of eligible male voters. In every presidential election since 1980, the proportion of female adults who voted have exceeded the proportion of made adults who voted. In the 2012 presidential election, nearly ten million more women voted than men, and they outvoted men by four percentage points.

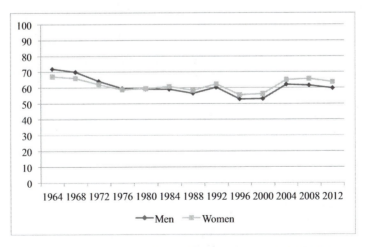

Figure 4.2 Voter Participation Rates, Presidential Elections by Sex, 1964–2012
Source: U.S. Census Bureau Current Population Survey.

Table 4.1 shows the participation rates for men and women in the presidential elections between 2000 and 2012 by various demographic groups. As Table 4.1 shows, women have outperformed men across these most contemporary elections within all levels of educational achievement and across all age groups, except among the oldest voters. Across all racial and ethnic groups, women now vote at higher levels than their male counterparts. Particularly striking is the participation rate of Black women. They had the highest turnout rate of all groups in three of these four elections.

Examining voting behavior in the 1950s throughout the 1970s, Sandra Baxter and Marjorie Lansing (1981) were struck by "the enigma of the Black woman voter." Given their disadvantaged status relative to White men and women and Black men, one would predict extremely low levels of political participation on the part of Black women. Yet, during this period, Black women increased their rate of voting faster than any of these other groups. Somehow, Baxter and Lansing concluded, the "double whammy" of sexism and

Table 4.1 Sex and Voter Turnout by Demographic Groups, 2000–2012 Presidential Elections

	2000	2004	2008	2012
White Men	59.2	64	62.4	60.5
White Women	63.8	66.7	66.3	63.8
Black Men	61.4	55.8	60.5	61.4
Black Women	70.1	63.3	68.1	70.1
Hispanic Men	46	44.8	47.9	46
Hispanic Women	49.8	49.4	51.8	49.8
Asian Men	46	41.9	47.6	46
Asian Women	48.5	46.2	47.5	48.5
Men 18–24	37.9	43.8	41	37.5
Women 18–24	44.5	49.7	47.7	43.4
Men 25–34	50.5	47.2	44	49.6
Women 25–34	53.6	59.1	52.9	57.3
Men 35–44	60.5	58.8	52.7	58.5
Women 35–44	62.1	66.4	57.6	63.7
Men 45–54	66.3	64.6	60.5	63.3
Women 45–54	67.9	70.4	64.7	70
Men 55–64	68.5	69.2	66.3	69.2
Women 55–64	70.5	73.5	69.7	72.1
Men 65–74	74.4	74.9	70.1	75.1
Women 65–74	72.7	71.8	70	73.5
Men 75+	73.6	72.8	70.3	74.3
Women 75+	67.6	65.8	62.9	67.6
Men < High School Diploma	37.9	38	37.7	35.5
Women < High School Diploma	38.9	40.1	40.9	40.4
Men: High School Graduate	49.7	53.3	51.8	49.8
Women: High School Graduate	54.8	59.1	57.8	55.4
Men: Some College	61.4	67.1	65.4	62.4
Women: High School Graduate	64.6	70.4	70.2	65.7
Men: Bachelor's Degree	74.3	77.1	76.2	74.5
Women: Bachelor's Degree	76.5	78	77.7	75.4
Men: Advanced Degree	81	83.1	82.5	80.2
Women: Advanced Degree	82.9	85.6	82.9	82.4

United States Census Bureau, Voting and Registration

racism propelled greater participation among this alienated group contrary to much political science research about the negative relationship of distrust, alienation, and involvement in a conventional political activity such as voting.

Women of color comprising all groups of women except non-Hispanic White women have become a key, emerging voting bloc and a growing force in American electoral politics. Women of color were just 6 percent of the overall population in 1964 and were one in twenty voters in that year's presidential election. By the 2012 election, women of color comprised 19 percent of the overall population. They made up 15 percent of the voting age population and were more than one in six voters (Baxter, Holmes, and Griffin 2015; Harris 2014).

In that election, 76 percent of African American women were registered to vote, whereas the registered share of all other eligible voters remained static at 71 percent. The historic surge in Black women's votes helped to account for President Obama winning the women's vote in 2012. Although he lost the White women's vote, he captured the votes of 96 percent of Black women, 76 percent of Latinas, and more than two thirds of Asian women to win the overall women's vote with 55 percent (Harris 2014). Black women are "the most potent political group in American politics," political guru Donna Brazile has attested. "It's not about our size, it's about our participation" (Owens 2015). Text Box 4.1 provides an example of Black female contemporary activism. Chapter 9 extends the turnout story to the 2016 presidential election.

Text Box 4.1 Black Girls Vote

In November 2015, Nykidra Robinson founded Black Girls Vote (BGV) in Baltimore after a man was shot and killed the previous summer in her neighborhood. Registering people to vote, especially young African American women, was central to her plan to change her northwest Baltimore neighborhood. BGV describes itself as a grassroots organization that seeks to uplift the Black community in Baltimore,

Maryland, by educating and inspiring voting age Black women to understand the policy decisions affecting their families and communities. Its goal is to "empower Black women to change policy through the electoral process." BGV engages in "pop-up" events at places such as hair salons, nail parlors, restaurants, and big box stores. They collect umbrellas to encourage people to vote, even if it is raining. They called day-care providers, urging them to stay open later on Election Day, and asked grandmothers to offer to babysit.

From a civic participation perspective centered on voting, women are now the preeminent democratic activists. A second significant aspect of gender in American elections revolves around its political implications. What does it matter that women have come to dominate at the polls? The story of the emergence of the gender gap as an electoral phenomenon that opened this chapter suggests policy consequences to women's voting as well as its civic effect. The attention paid to female voters in recent elections reinforces the contemporary importance of women's votes. The following section explores the trends in and consequences of the gender gap in the electoral process beyond voting.

Partisanship and Ideology

The two major parties have come to be viewed with distinct gender identities and references. From a policy perspective, the Democratic Party has been dubbed the "mommy party," concerned with health, nutrition, and welfare, and the Republican Party has been named "the daddy party," more concerned with national security and economic competition (Matthews 1991). Second, Americans' images of the political parties have taken on gendered characteristics so that Democrats are understood as the more feminine party (e.g., kind, gentle, compassionate) and Republicans as the more masculine party (e.g., statesmanlike, efficient, energetic) when Americans are asked what they like and dislike about each party (Winters 2010). Third, Democrats have been much more likely to believe that the Democratic Party does better regarding the interests of women (76 percent) than Republicans believe the Republican Party does better for women's interests (33 percent) (Grossman and Hopkins 2015). Then, too, media coverage of the gender gap and the recent war on women meme reinforces for the public the association of the Republican Party with men and the Democratic Party with women.

We would imagine that given the gender gap in votes for president that characterizes contemporary politics that a gender gap in men's and women's identification as Democrats and Republicans would follow. Party identification has principally been measured through response to the survey question "Do you consider yourself a Democrat, a Republican or an independent?" For more than seventy years, with few exceptions, more Americans have identified as Democrats than Republicans. The Pew Research Center 2016 polls show 34 percent of Americans identified as independents, 33 percent as Democrats, and 29 percent as Republicans.[3]

We would expect that given the gender gap in votes for president in recent elections that a gender gap in party identification would follow. The American National Election Studies (ANES) has asked Americans whether they usually think of themselves as a Republican, a Democrat, or an independent in their surveys from 1952 through 2012. If independent, respondents have been asked whether they think of themselves as closer to the Republican or Democratic Party. This set of studies allows for trends in men's and women's partisan attachments to be observed. Figures 4.3a to 4.3c present trends in party identification

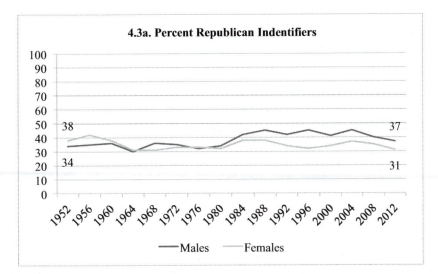

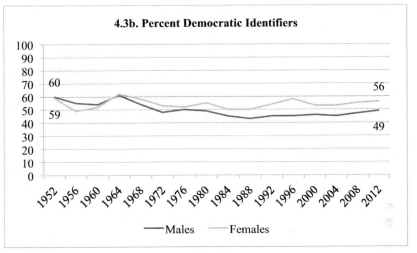

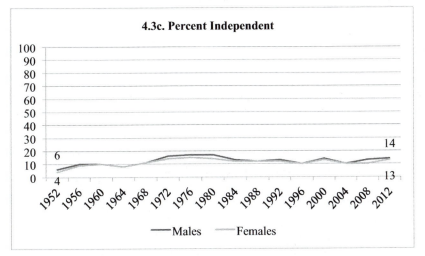

Figures 4.3a–c Party Identification by Sex, 1952–2012, American National Election Studies

among men and women based on the ANES surveys. The Democratic Party began the trend with a substantial advantage among both men and women, with little difference between the sexes. In 1952, at the time of the first ANES survey, 59 percent of women identified with or leaned toward the Democratic Party; in 2012, that number was 56 percent. No sharp dips or increases occurred at any point over these decades in women's identification with the Democratic Party; they have remained in the Democratic camp (Norrander 2008). Women's identification with the Republican Party dropped seven points from 38 percent to 31 percent over the course of these years. Women claiming pure independency climbed nine points across the time span. At the same time, men decreased their affiliation with the Democratic Party by eleven points and increased their support for the Republican Party in the 1980s and 1990s. It slipped back toward its starting point in 2012. The Pew Research Center described the gender gap as "Three decades Old, as Wide as Ever" in 2012 in terms of presidential candidate support (Pew Research Center 2012).

The Pew Research Center 2016 polls show a substantial gender gap, with 40 percent of women identifying with the Democratic Party compared with 26 percent of men. Men were 8 percent more likely to identify as independents than women (38 percent to 30 percent). Thirty-two percent of men and 27 percent of women identified as Republicans (see Endnote 3). Millennial women in 2016 had the highest level of identification as Democrats (43 percent) and the lowest identification with Republicans (18 percent).

Simple measures of political ideology include self-identification as a liberal, moderate, or conservative. Figure 4.4 displays the distribution of female respondents' answers to the ANES question "When it comes to politics do you usually think of yourself as extremely liberal, liberal, slightly liberal, moderate or middle of the road, slightly conservative, extremely conservative, or haven't you thought much about this?" From 1972 through 2012, this question shows substantial consistency in the distribution of responses. Only a small minority of women has consistently viewed themselves as political liberals, even though they have expressed a more liberal propensity than men in their partisanship and presidential voting behavior. Somewhat larger percentages identify as moderates or conservatives. Women certainly have not been monolithic in their general ideological orientation.

Men and women have differed little in the percentages who considered themselves to be liberal or moderate over these elections, whereas men have been more likely to call themselves conservative than women (34 percent to 25 percent in 2012). Women have also

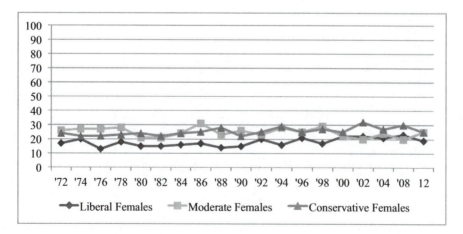

Figure 4.4 Women and Political Ideology, 1972–2012, American National Election Studies

been more likely to respond that they had not thought much about this question than men; in 2012, 28 percent of women and 19 percent of men would not place themselves on this scale, stating they had not thought much about it.

Electoral Involvement beyond Voting

Beyond voting, political science researchers have long noted women's lesser engagement in politics compared with that of men (see, for example, Campbell et al. 1960). Even in more contemporary times, they report women as being less knowledgeable about and interested in politics than men and expressing less confidence in their ability to affect the political process (Verba et al. 1997). The engagement of women in the electoral process and their involvement compared to that of men in the contemporary era merits attention.

The belief that one can understand politics and government and the belief that one's individual activities can influence political events (known as political efficacy) are central in affecting political participation. Internal political efficacy involves confidence in one's ability to understand politics and government and therefore affects one's likelihood of participating in politics. The ANES surveys have measured levels of what they call internal efficacy through agreement or disagreement with the statement "Sometimes politics and government seem so complicated that a person like me can't really understand what's going on." External political efficacy involves the belief that one's actions can influence what the government does. To measure external political efficacy, the ANES has asked respondents in their national surveys whether they agree or disagree with the following two statements: "People like me don't have any say about what the government does" and "I don't think public officials care much what people like me think." Trends in responses of both sexes to these questions allow us to measure women's sense of internal and external political efficacy and the extent of a gender gap over time in these orientations to politics.

Across time, women have expressed low levels of internal political efficacy as measured by their responses to the statement about politics and government being too complicated for them to understand. As Table 4.2 shows, two thirds to three quarters of female respondents have tended to answer this question affirmatively. Men also tended to have consistently low levels of internal political efficacy but to a lesser extent than women. Even in 2012, our most recent data point, women were thirteen points more likely to agree with this statement than men. At the same time, both men and women have tended to express higher levels of external political efficacy, yet those levels have declined across time for both sexes.

Political participation constitutes actions taken to influence government policies either directly by affecting the making or implementation of laws or indirectly by influencing the selection of people who make those policies (Burns et al. 2001, 4). A great variety of activities constitute political participation, from engaging in protests such as those the Occupy Wall Streeters have chosen to knocking on doors for a political party or candidate or seeking public office oneself. Beyond voting, substantial research has suggested that women are less likely to participate in other forms of electoral activity such as working for a candidate or party, contributing money, attending a political meeting or rally, trying to persuade someone else to vote, and wearing a campaign button or displaying a campaign sticker (e.g., Conway et al. 2005). Figures 4.5a–e show trends from the ANES surveys from 1952 through 2012 regarding men and women who have reported engaging in these activities. As the trend lines suggest, few men or women have participated in these activities; gender differences are minute, and participation has neither increased nor decreased

Table 4.2 Trends in Men's and Women's Sense of Political Efficacy

| | Internal Efficacy | | External Efficacy | | | |
| | Sometimes politics and government seem so complicated that a person like me cannot really understand what is going on: % agree | | Public officials don't care much what people like me think: % agree | | People like me don't have any say about what the government does: % agree | |
	Men	Women	Men	Women	Men	Women
1952	63	77	33	37	27	34
1956	56	69	27	26	24	32
1960	52	64	23	26	26	28
1964	61	72	37	36	28	31
1968	63	77	42	44	39	43
1972	67	79	48	50	38	42
1976	64	77	51	52	42	40
1980	61	77	53	52	37	41
1984	64	76	42	43	30	33
1988	61	77	52	53	40	43
1992	60	71	53	52	35	38
1996	56	68	66	57	53	53
2000	54	65	57	56	38	42
2004	NA	NA	48	52	40	45
2008	63	72	63	58	53	47
2012	47	60	63	59	47	48

Source: American National Election Study.

across time for either sex. The one exception is trying to influence others to vote, an activity in which men were substantially more likely to report engaging in the earlier years of these election studies, but in more recent elections, that gender gap has closed.

Few men or women among the general public reported donating money to political campaigns over the course of these elections, as Figure 4.5d indicates. At the same time, large sums of money have been contributed to candidates, political action committees, and the political parties to elect candidates in contemporary times. If we switch our focus from the general populace's monetary contributions to an exploration of the subpopulation of large campaign donors, then we can gain insight into the extent to which gender matters in financial contributions and trends in the financial political clout of men and women.

Contemporary federal law requires candidates for president and Congress to individually report all contributions of $200 or more to their campaigns. Using these reports, the Women's Campaign Forum (WCF) has tracked men's and women's giving in a number of *Vote with Your Purse* reports over the course of several election periods as part of its She Should Run (SSR) program. In conjunction with the Center for Responsive Politics (CRP), WCF examined men's and women's individual contributions of $200 or more to candidates for federal office.

Tracking the demographics of political giving at this financial level, the Vote with Your Purse and CRP projects reported a substantial gender gap in monetary donations in

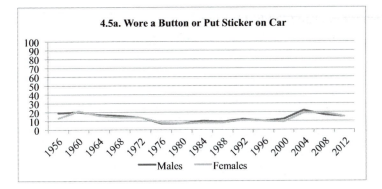

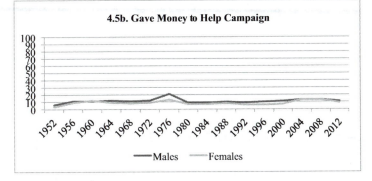

Not asked in 1952.

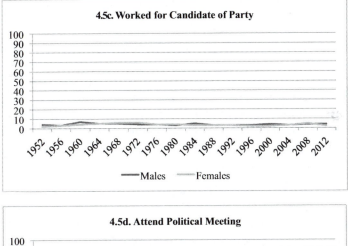

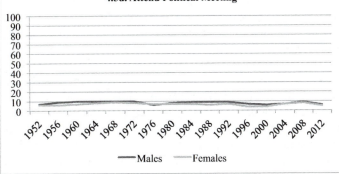

Figures 4.5a–e Trends in Participation in Campaign Activities by Sex, 1952–2012, American National Election Studies

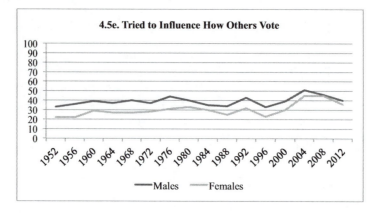

Figures 4.5a–e (Continued)

contemporary elections. Men have been the predominant large-dollar contributors. In an August 2011 "Women's Equality Day" press release, CRP reported that

> women have a long way to go until they see equality as political donors. At the federal level, men consistently give more than two-thirds of all donations reported in an itemized fashion to the Federal Election Commission, when measured by number of donors and amount of money contributed.
>
> (Beckel 2011)

She Should Run has put an important representational spin for women on this financial gap.

> Clearly money matters in politics, but women simply do not give enough. When women do not give, they do not have a voice. And without a voice, they cannot affect change. If all women—from different age groups, ethnicities, or economic backgrounds—vote with their purses in 2012, they will significantly increase women's political success.
>
> (SSR 2012, 1)

In its 2007 report, WCF contended that women could even "change the world for the price of a pair of shoes" (4).

The pool of donors contributing $200 or more to federal office-seeking campaigns is very small, fewer than 1 percent of the population. In the 2012 presidential election, for example, only 0.24 percent of adult females and 0.50 percent of adult males contributed $200 or more to the federal campaigns. Men were two thirds of the donors and gave 74 percent of contributions of $200 or more. Figure 4.6 presents the percent of women donors who gave $200 or more to federal campaigns from 1990 through 2016. Women's percent of all such donors grew slightly from approximately one fourth of the donors to one third over the course of these elections. Figure 4.7 shows the total amount of money in contributions of $200 or more that the sexes have invested in political campaigns. Men have clearly dominated as political donors through the 2016 presidential election.[4]

Partisanship matters in the donations of men and women. Just as we have seen that women are more likely to identify with the Democratic Party than men, they have been more likely to be large donors to Democratic candidates and more likely to give to female

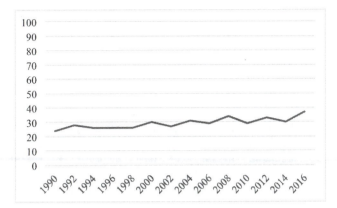

Figure 4.6 Women Donors as a Percent of Campaign Contributors

Based on Federal Election Commission reports of individual contributions of $200 or more.
Source: Center for Responsive Politics.

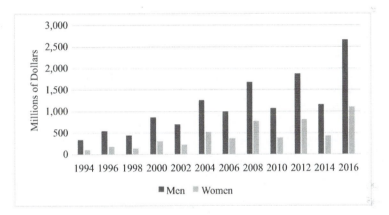

Figure 4.7 Amount of Money in Contributions of $200 or More in Federal Campaigns

Source: www.opensecrets.org

candidates and especially to female Democratic candidates (see Figure 4.8) (Bryner and Weber 2013). A consistent gender gap in giving to candidates of the two major parties has been present since 1990. In 2012, the gender gap was fourteen points; 47 percent of female contributions went to Democratic candidates compared with 33 percent of men's. Looking just at female donors, Crowdpac data show that the Democratic Party "has been far more effective in capturing new female donors" (see Figure 4.9). Their data show that "while both parties started off with 23,000 women donors in 1990, in 2016, Democrats have over five times more female donors than Republicans do: Democrats have 572,000 female donors, as compared to 102,000 for Republicans."[5] Further, the top five politicians who received the highest proportion of donations from female donors were all female Democrats. In 2015, Representative Jan Schakowsky of Illinois received 60 percent of her donations of $200 or more from women.[6]

Female donors have also become more polarized. In 1990, homemakers donated similarly to women who worked outside the home, but that gap has widened since then. In 2012, 56 percent of the donations from women who reported outside employment went

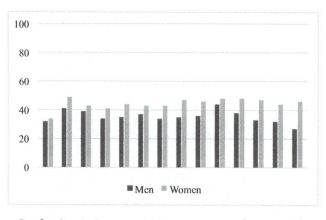

Figure 4.8 Partisan Gender Gap in Democratic Campaign Contributions of $200 or More

Based on giving to Democrats, Republicans, and Political Action Committees.
Source: www.opensecrets.org

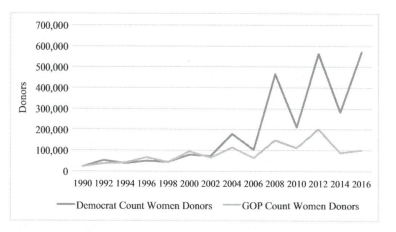

Figure 4.9 How Each Party's Female Donor Base Has Evolved

Recreated with permissions from Crowdpac.

to Democrats compared to 37 percent of the donations from women who self-identified as homemakers. Homemakers were a very small share of the overall pool of donors, however (Bryner and Weber 2013).

A recent study of small donors—that is, individuals giving contributions of less than $200 to federal candidates—provides another lens through which to view sex and financial giving and continuing partisan differences. This study of donors to presidential campaigns, including small donors, found women to be 46 percent and 47 percent of all donors in 2008 and 2012, respectively (Magleby et al. 2014). They were 52 percent of all donors making donations of less than $200 to the Obama and McCain campaigns in 2008, and 50 percent of such donors to the Obama and Romney campaigns in 2012. The study also found that women outnumbered men as donors to Barack Obama and the Democratic Party. Women comprised 55 percent of Obama donors. At the same time, Republican presidential donors in both elections were overwhelmingly male by more than two to one.

The financial gender gap may have lessened in 2016. "Women Build Political Clout as Big Donors," the *New York Times* headlined in a May 2016 report on women's giving.

> Women are bankrolling political campaigns this year more than ever, driven by their rising rank in the workplace, boosts in women's wealth, and networks set up to gather their donations and bolster their influence . . . transformation is occurring at every level of political giving and in both parties, from grass-roots supporters sending a few hundred dollars to the rarefied ranks of ultrawealthy donors who fund "super PACs."
>
> (Confessore 2016, A1)

Hillary Clinton's presidential campaigns have stimulated female financial giving. In 2008, women donated 50.9 percent of individual contributions to her campaign for the Democratic nomination for president (Palmer and Parti 2015; Schroeder 2015). Halfway through the 2016 election, more than 60 percent of her donors were women, with contributions totaling $70 million (Confessore 2016). Nearly half of Clinton's "bundlers"—the volunteers who solicit checks from friends and business associates—were women (Confessore 2016). EMILY's List (see Chapter 8) had bundled more than $37 million for candidate Clinton in the early stages of the 2016 presidential campaign.

Winning the Women's Vote

Contemporary presidential campaigns are very cognizant of the importance of winning the support of undecided women, given the partisan gender gap in voting and the higher turnout rate of female voters since 1980. They have created specific campaign strategies to win women's votes. One of the most prominent efforts in this domain of election tactics prior to 2016 was Republican George Bush's "W Stands for Women" bus tour in the last month of his 2000 presidential campaign. The theme was built around Bush's middle initial. With his opponent, Democrat Vice President Al Gore leading among women in preelection polls, Bush's campaign put his wife, mother, foreign policy adviser Condoleezza Rice, and Lynne Cheney, wife of his Republican running mate, Dick Cheney, on a bus with a huge "W Stands for Women" banner to travel across the battleground states, touting his record on such issues as education reform and tax cuts. They also made character a centerpiece of their message. One media report captured the effort:

> As polls show George W. Bush trailing among female voters, his wife and mother rolled through Pennsylvania yesterday on a bus that read "W Stands for Women," telling people that Bush was a decent, moral man who cared deeply about health care and education.
>
> (Ung 2000, A21)

The "W Stands for Women" mantra became an even more integrated and prominent aspect of the 2004 Bush reelection campaign.

A section devoted to policies that would distinctly affect and be of interest to women is a standard part of issue lists on campaign websites, and they often feature a "Women for . . ." section. Both the Romney and Obama campaigns had "Women for . . ." grassroots initiatives in the 2012 campaign. An independent "Black Women for Obama" grassroots organization was also organized. "Old White Women for Obama" created a blog in the 2008 campaign "for the growing community of white women between the ages of 50 and 90 who feel Senator Obama should be the next president of the United States."

It is not much of an exaggeration to say that the 2012 presidential election was very much about winning the votes of women and attracting different groups of women to the polls. The headlines of much media commentary illustrate this point. For example, Molly Ball (2012) in the *Atlantic* proclaimed, "This Election Will Be All About Women." The *Chicago Sun Times*' Lynn Sweet (2012) noted the "Election Could Come Down to What Women Want." In addition, Thomson-Deveaux (2012) asked in an online piece "Why the Young Women's Vote Will Matter in 2012," and CNN declared at the end of voting "How Women Ruled the 2012 Election." Democratic and Republican Party organizations engaged in multifaceted campaigns to win the votes of women (MacManus 2014). Voter registration drives targeted women. The political parties spotlighted women at their national conventions, sponsored TV and online video ads aimed at various groups of female voters, and used strong female surrogates, especially the candidates' wives, on the campaign trail advocating for the election of their party's nominee. Women were not viewed as a monolithic group; rather, sophisticated microtargeting techniques were employed to attract the attention of different demographic groups of women. The Obama campaign focused on young women, unmarried women, and women with professional degrees, whereas the Romney campaign targeted married women.

Feminist groups organized voter registration drives on college campuses aimed at female students such as the Feminist Majority Foundation's "Get Out Her Vote" groups and the American Association of University Women's Action Fund's "It's My Vote: I Will Be Heard" campaign. The Obama campaign had a "Women for Obama" operation, whereas

Picture 4.1 "Rosie" the National Federation of Republican Women's 2016 Campaign RV Touring the Country

Courtesy of the National Federation of Republican Women.

the Romney campaign's "Women for Mitt" operation hosted roundtables, forums, and town hall meetings and conducted extensive phone-banking outreach efforts (MacManus 2014, 101). In 2016, the National Federation of Republican Women toured the country in a red, white, and blue RV named "Rosie."

Obama's winning coalition of women voters consisted of Black and Latina women, unmarried women, and young women. Among young voters aged eighteen to twenty-nine, 66 percent of women voted to reelect President Obama compared with 53 percent of young men. Young Black women voted nearly unanimously for Obama, according to exit polls; 80 percent of young Black men voted for Obama. With the historic nomination of Hillary Clinton for president for the Democratic Party in 2016, women's electoral participation was even more central to the electoral process and received large amounts of media attention, as Chapter 9 chronicles.

The Clinton and Obama administrations also created units on women within the White House in efforts to engage women. In 1994, the midterm election was a disaster for Democrats and President Bill Clinton. Democrats lost fifty-four seats in the House of Representatives and control of the chamber to Republicans. EMILY's List, a major Democratic organization committed to electing more women to public office (see Chapter 8), conducted a turnout analysis in that election, seeking to determine what happened to the women's vote that had been so central to the Democrats' 1992 victory. Its research found that sixteen million women who had voted in 1992 did not participate in the 1994 election, 59 percent of the abstainers. These drop-off voters tended to be women who had not graduated from college. EMILY's List polls suggested that many female voters opted out in 1994 "because they felt no one was addressing the concerns they talk about over the kitchen table—concerns about their low wages, their children's safety and their danger of losing health care benefits." A lobbying effort ensued, urging the Clinton administration to adopt a focus on these concerns. Thus, the White House established the Office on Women's Initiatives and Outreach (OWIO) in June 1995 (Norton and Morris 2003). For the first time, the White House Office established a formally organized unit dedicated to women's issues in an effort to reach out to women's groups, stimulate women's turnout, and capture their vote in the 1996 national election. OWIO initiated a national networking effort called At the Table. This program involved sending female cabinet members and other presidential appointees to meetings around the country to gauge the policy concerns of women constituents and interest groups and to describe to women how their government could serve them (Mitchell 1996.) According to OWIO's website, the program aimed to promote communication among communities, women's groups, female appointees, and the president on the ways in which issues affect women, especially economic issues. OWIO was prominent in the run up to the 1996 election as an outreach effort to court female votes. President Clinton was successful in these efforts. But after the 1996 election, the OWIO lost the attention of the White House and ceased to make women's issues an important agenda item for the administration (Norton and Morris 2003).

After the 2008 elections, approximately fifty women's groups sent a letter to the new Obama administration asking the president to resurrect the OWIO. Responding to this recommendation, on March 11, 2009, President Obama signed an executive order establishing a White House Council on Women and Girls. The president said that the purpose of the new group "is to ensure that American women and girls are treated fairly in all matters of public policy. Our progress in these areas is an important measure of whether we are truly fulfilling the promise of our democracy for all our people." He listed these areas as economic security, a balance between work and family, violence against women, and women's health. The council would "provide a coordinated federal response to the challenges confronted by women and girls and to ensure that all Cabinet and Cabinet-level agencies consider how their policies and programs impact women and families." Valerie Jarrett, assistant to the president and senior advisor, was appointed chair. The council was made up of Cabinet secretaries and Cabinet-level advisers. Chapter 10 describes several of its initiatives as part of the policy-making process.

Women's and Men's Perspectives on Economic Inequality

Public opinion is an important element of political participation. Americans' opinions of many significant public policy questions as well as general approaches to politics such as ideology and efficacy examined earlier in this chapter have been the subject of many surveys. Differences in men's and women's attitudes, usually referred to as the gender gap, have attracted much research interest. Perspectives on various aspects of economic inequality have been the subject of many polls, which allow for the assessment of trends in men's and women's opinions on this significant aspect of contemporary American life.

The 2014 American Values Survey found that most Americans say they do not believe that major institutions—such as the overall economic system, business corporations, and government—were working for their benefit. Nearly two thirds (64 percent) of Americans believed the economic system in the country unfairly favored the wealthy compared to 34 percent who disagreed. Most Americans (53 percent) *did not* believe that business corporations generally strike a fair balance between making profits and serving the public interest, whereas 41 percent believed they did. Only one third (33 percent) of Americans agreed that government is run for the benefit of all the people, whereas nearly two thirds (64 percent) of Americans disagreed with that statement. Women were more likely than men to believe one of the big problems in the country was the lack of equal opportunity for all. Six in ten women (60 percent) said that one of the big problems in the country is that not everyone is given an equal chance in life, a view half (50 percent) of male respondents shared (Jones et al. 2014).

Pollsters have also asked about the division of the country into haves and have-nots, the fairness of the distribution of wealth, the role of government in reducing income differences, and the redistribution of wealth through taxes (Shaw and Gaffey 2012). Both sexes have seen the gap between the rich and everyone else in the United States as increasing (63 percent); 26 percent said it has stayed the same, and only 9 percent believe it has decreased, according to the Pew Research Center's January 2014 inequality report. Further, nearly three quarters of the female respondents (72 percent) and 65 percent of the male respondents said the government should do "a lot" or "some" to reduce the gap between the rich and everyone else.

The General Social Survey (GSS) has asked respondents about the role of government in reducing income differences. More female respondents have favored government intervention than have not. Approximately one half supported reducing differences, whereas about 30 percent opposed such intervention, with a bump in opposition in the mid-1990s (see Figure 4.10). Men were consistently somewhat less supportive than women of an active government role in reducing the gap. In 2014, 43 percent of men favored some government intervention, and 39 percent were opposed compared with 49 percent of women who favored at least some government intervention and 33 percent who were not in favor.

Shaw and Gaffey's (2012) report of trends in public opinion on income inequality tracked the Gallup Poll's questioning of the public on whether the distribution of wealth and income was fair or whether wealth should be more evenly distributed. They report that "results from 1990 to 2011 vary but do not show any clear longitudinal dynamism. Most often twice as many respondents called for a more even distribution than considered the status quo fair." In 2011, women were somewhat greater advocates of a more equal

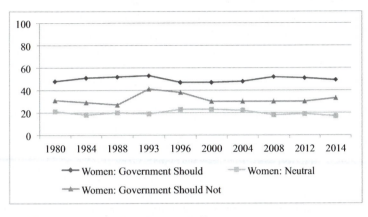

Figure 4.10 Should Government Reduce Income Differences?

Some people think the government in Washington ought to reduce the income differences between the rich and the poor, perhaps by raising the taxes of wealthy families or by giving income assistance to the poor. Others think the government should not concern itself with reducing this income difference between the rich and the poor. Here is a card with a scale from 1 to 7. Think of a score of 1 as meaning that the government ought to reduce the income differences between rich and poor and a score of 7 meaning that the government should not concern itself with reducing income differences. What score between 1 and 7 comes closest to the way you feel?

Responses 1–3 and 5–7 are combined.

General Social Survey (www.gss.norc.org).

distribution than men; 65 percent of women and 57 percent of men advocated for money and wealth to be more evenly distributed, whereas 29 percent of women and 41 percent of men believed the current distribution was fair.

Men and women have differed on a cluster of issues having to do with protecting the vulnerable—the aged, the sick, the poor, and the other "at-risk categories" (Fiorina 2011). Women have tended to have a more positive attitude toward government and government programs than men. Women have consistently told pollsters they favor a stronger role for government than men have. Women have expressed greater concern than men about the economy's future, and they have been more pessimistic than men in seeing signs of economic recovery. In part, this difference may be a consequence of the fact that women live longer and are, on average, less wealthy than men and that they bear more responsibility for the care of younger and older family members, who may depend on social security, Medicare, and other public programs. Women are also disproportionately employed in the public sector, particularly in health care and education. These structural differences in men's and women's economic positions mean that women as a group are more economically vulnerable and likely to be dependent on and supportive of the welfare state than are men (Box-Steffensmeier et al. 2004).

Public Opinion on Social Issues

In addition to economic issues, social issues have been prominent in public debates, particularly regarding abortion rights and gay rights. Perspectives on abortion have been remarkably stable in the decades since the Supreme Court ruled that women had the right to have an abortion. Over the same time, support for gay rights and most recently gay marriage has increased substantially. Few differences have been found between women and men on the issue of abortion, whereas on gay rights, women have led men in their support for ending discrimination based on sexual preference and for allowing gays to marry.

Abortion in particular has been one of the most contentious social issues in American politics since the Supreme Court's 1973 decision in *Roe v. Wade* declared that women's right to privacy included having an abortion. Opinions concerning abortion have changed little over the decades since the Supreme Court decision. Survey data show that public opinion about abortion has been quite stable, although different social and demographic groups vary considerably in support for abortion. Since 1980, opinions have become more polarized by party and political ideology (Hansen 2014). Since 1972, the GSS has asked respondents whether they would approve or disapprove of abortion under various conditions: serious birth defects, rape, risks to the mother's life or health, if she is married and does not want any more children, if the family could not afford to raise the child, and if the woman is not married and does not want to marry the man. The mean number of conditions approved in 1973 was 3.74. In 2014, the mean number was 3.67. The mean for women in 2014 was 3.54, and for men, it was 3.82.

Women's contemporary views on abortion can be further gauged from their responses to several other survey questions posed in a variety of formats. According to a Gallup 2014 survey, women are split on whether they consider themselves pro-choice or pro-life regarding abortion; 50 percent chose the pro-choice option, and 41 percent selected the pro-life option. Among men, 44 percent chose the pro-choice option, and 51 percent considered themselves to be pro-life.

The GSS has tracked approval of women obtaining a legal abortion since 1980 under a variety of circumstances. Figure 4.11 presents women's agreement that a woman should be able to have an abortion if she wants it for any reason. Approximately four out of ten women have taken this pro-choice response throughout this time period. (Men's opinions tended to track those of women.)

Over the past two decades, the Pew Research Center has asked respondents in a national survey whether they thought abortion should be legal in all or most cases or illegal in all or most cases. In its fall 2016 poll, a majority of the public said abortion should be legal in all or most cases (59 percent), whereas 37 percent said abortion should be illegal in at least most cases. This level of approval is the highest it has been over these decades. Support among Democratic women fueled the increase in approval; 85 percent of Democratic women believed abortion should be legal in all or most cases, an increase of eighteen points over an earlier 2016 survey. Seventy-one percent of Democratic men said abortion should be legal in at least most cases. In contrast, 36 percent of Republican

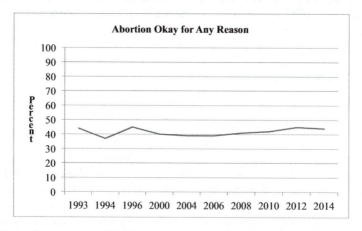

Figure 4.11 Women's Support for Obtaining a Legal Abortion for Any Reason

Source: General Social Survey (www.gss.norc.org).

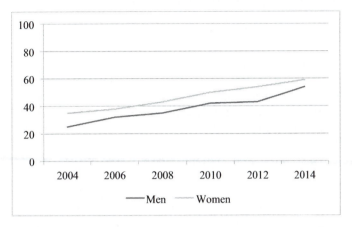

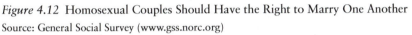

Figure 4.12 Homosexual Couples Should Have the Right to Marry One Another

Source: General Social Survey (www.gss.norc.org)

men and 32 percent of Republican women thought abortion should be legal in at least most cases (Fingerhut 2016).

As with abortion, laws and policies regarding homosexuality have been the subject of intense political debate and conflicting legal rulings over the last few decades. In the 1970s and 1980s, the public's views of homosexuality were overwhelmingly negative. GSS data show that in 1973, only 11 percent of respondents agreed that gay sex "is not wrong at all." In 2014, nearly 50 percent (49 percent) responded to the GSS study that gay sex "is not wrong at all," representing dramatic movement in a positive direction; 54 percent of women and 43 percent of men selected this response. At the same time, 44 percent of men and 37 percent of women believed it was "always wrong."

The rise in support for same-sex marriage over the past decade is among the largest changes in opinion on any policy issue over this time period, according to the Pew Research Center (2013). Since 2004, the GSS has queried respondents about homosexual couples' right to marry one another. Figure 4.12 shows the trend in support for gay marriage among men and women. Women have consistently been more supportive of gay rights than men, including marriage, as the figure shows. By 2014, a majority of both men and women agreed or agreed strongly that homosexual couples should have the right to marry; 60 percent of women agreed (35 percent strongly), whereas 29 percent disagreed. Among men, 54 percent agreed (28 percent strongly) and 35 percent disagreed.

Public Opinion on Issues of Force and Violence

Historically, survey researchers have found the greatest gender differences to be on opinions about the use of force and violence such as war and defense issues, capital punishment, and gun control. Having surveyed decades of public opinion polls, Poole and Zeigler reported in 1985 that

> women and men have always consistently differed on the use of force. In the aftermath of World War II, women were less favorable than men to the United States joining NATO, more opposed to a continuance of the draft, and more opposed to using the atomic bomb. Women were less supportive of the Korean and Vietnam wars and opposed handguns and the death penalty more than men did.

(53)

Shapiro and Mahajan (1986) have also reported that average gender difference in preferences toward policies dealing with the use of force and violence has consistently been moderately large between the 1960s and mid-1980s. Eichenberg (2003) concluded,

> To be sure, there is a general consensus that women are less likely than men to support policies that involve the use of force. Indeed, women are less likely to endorse any violent action than are men, and there is some evidence that they are less supportive of security policies more generally. But women have not been found to be uniformly pacifist, and men are not uniformly bellicose. Any difference is at the margins.

Gender gaps are also often seen in global surveys over the use of military force, with women far less likely than men to say that force is sometimes necessary in the pursuit of justice. The gender difference over drone strikes, a contemporary military tactic, is unusually large. In the United States, 70 percent of men compared with 53 percent of women approved of drone strikes, a signature antiterrorism tool of the Obama administration, in a 2013 Pew Research Center survey (Stokes 2013).

Public policy on gun ownership and control are among the most contentious in recent years as a consequence of a plethora of mass murders of school children, churchgoers, and other groups, including the 2011 shooting of U.S. Congresswoman Gabby Giffords. Gun rights groups and lobbyists have been particularly successful in opposing the enactment of laws focused on tightening the sale of weapons and ownership of guns, although support for stricter gun control laws has characterized public opinion.

Figures 4.13 and 4.14 show trends in perspectives on guns from two national polls. Perspectives on gun control have likely divided the sexes more than any other issue historically. In 1999, for example, 75 percent of female respondents in a Pew Research Center survey believed gun control was more important than protecting gun rights compared to only 48 percent of men, a twenty-eight-point difference. Belief in the greater importance of gun control dropped among women to 54 percent in the Pew Research Center's December 2014 survey, which is still a majority but shows a twenty-one-point decline.

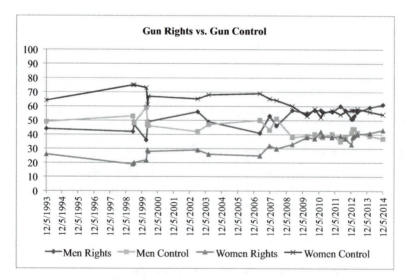

Figure 4.13 What Do You Think Is More Important—to Protect the Right of Americans to Own Guns, OR to Gun Control Ownership?

Source: Pew Research Center, December 7, 2014.

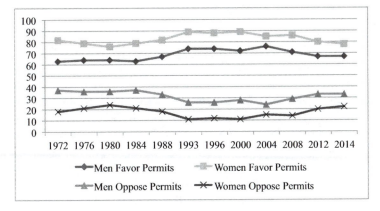

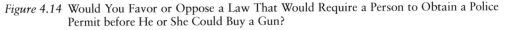

Figure 4.14 Would You Favor or Oppose a Law That Would Require a Person to Obtain a Police Permit before He or She Could Buy a Gun?

Source: General Social Survey (www.gss.norc.org).

Only 37 percent of men chose the gun control option in 2014, whereas 61 percent chose the gun rights option (see Figure 4.13). Among women, 43 percent chose the gun rights option at the end of 2014.

The GSS has been asking respondents since 1972 whether they would favor or oppose a law that would require a person to obtain a police permit before he or she could buy a gun. Figure 4.14 shows that a majority of both men and women have supported police permits to buy a gun throughout this time period, with women expressing overwhelming support; 82 percent were in favor of police permits when the question was first asked in 1972 compared with 63 percent of men. Support among women increased to 89 percent, and men's support rose to 72 percent in 2000. In the most recent survey in 2014, women's support declined slightly to 77 percent, whereas men's support stood at 66 percent.

While the National Rifle Association (NRA) has dominated policy debates on gun issues, pro-gun control groups have organized to challenge the NRA's dominance in the aftermath of mass shootings. Organizations based on gender are among these groups. Text Box 4.2 describes the emergence and strategies of one of these groups, Moms Demand Action. The formation of groups such as this one exemplifies a distinctive form of women's activism to affect public policy outside of partisan politics and traditional electoral behavior that is the center of Chapter 6. But first, Chapter 5 explores women's involvement in political party organizations.

Text Box 4.2 Moms Demand Action for Gun Sense in America

Groups have organized on both sides of the issue of gun control and engaged in highly charged debates and advocacy for legislative action in support of their positions. Most prominent by far is the National Rifle Association's demands for gun rights. Among the most active groups advocating for stronger gun control legislation on the other side is Moms Demand Action for Gun Sense in America. Immediately following the Sandy Hook Newtown school shooting, self-described stay-at-home mom Shannon Watts founded Moms Demand Action on December 15, 2012, in response. The group has since developed a chapter-based organization with chapters in all fifty states.

The group modeled itself after the Mothers Against Drunk Driving campaign. It has since joined a grand national coalition of gun control activists under the title Everytown for Gun Safety. It has launched a variety of campaigns to advocate for what it considers commonsense gun law. It undertakes traditional interest group activities of letter-writing campaigns and lobby days. An early action involved "stroller-jams" across the country at their senators' in-district offices and asking them to vote "yes" for new and stronger gun laws. When Congress then failed to enact background check legislation, they held lemonade stands across the country under the theme "When Congress Gives Moms Lemons, We Make Lemonade: Get Back to Work Gun Reform!"

Chapters have held "Whatever It Takes Day of Action"; created a "#NotAnAccident: Index and Interactive Map," a tracking of unintentional shootings by children; and "BeSmart," a public education campaign asking gun owners and non-gun owners alike to come together to reduce the number of unintentional shootings, suicides, and homicides that occur when firearms are not stored responsibly and children and teens get a hold of a gun. June 2, 2015, became the first National Gun Violence Awareness Day, followed by a "Backpacks, Not Bullets" campaign. The following is an ad the group created to dramatically illustrate the disparity between actions schools have taken to ban books while not enacting gun laws to protect children.

Notes

1. Jim Crow laws were racially discriminatory state and local laws that established barriers to the political, social, and economic involvement of Blacks in American life.
2. Surveys may overstate actual voter turnout. More people say they voted than who actually did vote.
3. www.people-press.org/2016/09/13/party-identification-trends-1992-2016/.
4. We should keep in mind that PACs, super PACS, and independent spending have become dominant ways of monetarily affecting the election process rather than direct giving to candidates. The gendered aspect of this giving deserves more research.
5. These data can be found at www.crowdpac.com/blog/women-donors3.
6. www.crowdpac.com/index.php/blog/female-donors.

Further Readings

Barnes, Tiffany and Erin Cassese. 2016. "American Party Women: A Look at the Gender Gap within Parties." Paper presented at the Southern Political Science Association Annual Meeting. www.academia.edu/24011708/American_Party_Women_A_Look_at_the_Gender_Gap_within_Parties.

Carroll, Susan and Richard Fox, editors. *Gender & Elections: Shaping the Future of American Politics*, 1st, 2nd, and 3rd editions. New York, NY: Cambridge University Press.

Hansen, Susan. 2014. *The Politics of Sex: Public Opinion, Parties, and Presidential Elections*. New York, NY: Routledge.

Whitaker, Lois Duke. 2008. *Voting the Gender Gap*. Urbana, IL: University of Illinois Press.

Web Resources

The League of Women Voters, www.lwv.org.

PresidentialGenderWatch.org.

The Voter Participation Center, www.voterparticipation.org.

References

Alpern, Sara and Dale Baum. 1985. "The Impact of the Nineteenth Amendment." *The Journal of Interdisciplinary History*, 16, 1 (Summer): 43–67.

Andersen, Kristi. 1996. *After Suffrage: Women in Partisan and Electoral Politics before the New Deal*. Chicago, IL: University of Chicago Press.

Ball, Molly. 2012. "The Election Will Be All about Women." *The Atlantic*, April.

Baxter, Emily, Katlin Holmes, and Robert Griffin. 2015. "The Importance of Women of Color Voters: Then and Now." *Center for American Progress*, August 26. www.americanprogress.org/issues/women/news/2015/08/26/120074/the-importance-of-women-of-color-voters-then-and-now/.

Baxter, Sandra and Marjorie Lansing. 1981. *Women and Politics: The Invisible Majority*. Ann Arbor, MI: University of Michigan Press.

Beckel, Michael. 2011. "Political Donors' Gender Disparity." www.opensecrets.org/news/2011/08/political-donors-gender-disparity.html.

Bonk, Kathy. 1988. "The Selling of the 'Gender Gap': The Role of Organized Feminism." In *The Politics of the Gender Gap: The Social Construction of Political Influence*, ed. Carol Mueller. Newbury Park, CA: Sage, 82–101.

Box-Steffensmeier, Janet, Suzanna de Boef, and Tse-Min Lin. 2004. "The Dynamics of the Partisan Gender Gap." *American Political Science Review*, 98: 515–528.

Bryner, Sarah and Doug Weber. 2013. "Sex, Money & Politics." *Center for Responsive Politics*. www.opensecrets.org/news/reports/gender.php.

Burns, Nancy, Kay Lehman Schlozman, and Sidney Verba. 2001. *The Private Roots of Public Action*. Cambridge, MA: Harvard University Press.

Campbell, Angus, Phillip Converse, Warren Miller, and Donald Stokes. 1960. *The American Voter*. Chicago, IL: University of Chicago Press.

Clymer, Adam. 1980. "Displeasure with Carter Turned Many to Reagan." *New York Times*, November 9.

Confessore, Nicholas. 2016. "Women Build Political Clout as Big Donors." *New York Times*, May 8: A1.

Conway, M. Margaret, David W. Ahern, and Gertrude A. Steuernagel. 2005. *Women and Public Policy: A Revolution in Progress*. Washington, DC: CQ Press.

Corder, Kevin and Christina Wolbrecht. 2016. *Counting Women's Ballots: Female Voters from Suffrage through the New Deal*. New York, NY: Cambridge University Press.

Eichenberg, Richard. 2003. "Gender Differences in Public Attitudes Toward the Use of Force by the United States, 1990–2002." *International Security*, 28, 1: 110–141.

Fingerhut, Hannah. 2016. "Women Drive Increase in Democratic Support for Legal Abortion." *Pew Fact Tank*. www.pewresearch.org/fact-tank/2016/11/03/women-drive-increase-in-democratic-support-for-legal-abortion/.

Fiorina, Morris. 2011. *Culture War? The Myth of a Polarized America*. Boston, MA: Longman.

Grossman, Matt and David A. Hopkins. 2015. "Ideological Republicans and Group Interest Democrats: The Asymmetry of American Party Politics." *Perspectives on Politics*, 13, 1 (March): 119–139.

Hansen, Susan B. 2014. *The Politics of Sex: Public Opinion, Parties, and Presidential Elections*. New York, NY: Routledge.

Harris, Maya. 2014. "Women of Color: A Growing Force in the American Electorate." Washington, DC: Center for American Progress. www.americanprogress.org/issues/race/report/2014/10/30/99962/women-of-color/.

Jones, Robert P., Daniel Cox, and Juhem Navarro-Rivera. 2014. *Economic Insecurity, Rising Inequality, and Doubts about the Future*. Washington, DC: Public Religion Research Institute.

MacManus, Susan. 2014. "Voter Participation and Turnout: The Political Generational Divide among Women Voters." In *Gender & Elections: Shaping the Future of American Politics*, 3rd edition, eds. Susan Carroll and Richard Fox. New York, NY: Cambridge University Press.

Magleby, David, Jay Goodliffe, and Joseph Olsen. 2014. "No Longer a Gender Gap among Democratic Presidential Donors: The Importance of Messenger, Message and Medium." Paper presented at the 2014 American Political Science Annual Meeting.

Manza, Jeff and Clem Brooks. 1998. "The Gender Gap in U.S. Presidential Elections: When? Why, Implications." *American Journal of Sociology*, 103, 5 (March): 1235–1266.

Matthews, Christopher. 1991. "Parenthood." *The New Republic*, May 23: 15–16.

Mitchell, Alison. 1996. "A Calculation in Tears." *New York Times*, April 12, A1.

Norrander, Barbara. 2008. "The History of the Gender Gap." In *Voting the Gender Gap*, ed. Lois Duke Whitaker. Urbana, IL: University of Illinois Press, 9–32.

Norton, Noelle and Barbara Morris. 2003. "Feminist Organizational Structure in the White House: The Office of Women's Initiatives and Outreach." *Political Research Quarterly*, 56, 4 (December): 477–487.

Owens, Donna M. 2015. "ESSENCE and Black Women's Roundtable Release Survey, 'The Power of the Sister Vote.'" *ESSENCE*, September 16. www.essence.com/2015/09/16/essence-and-black-womens-roundtable-release-survey-power-sister-vote.

Palmer, Anna and Tarin Parti. 2015. "Clinton Aims to Cash in with Women Donors." *Politico*, June 7. www.politico.com/story/2015/06/clinton-aims-to-cash-in-with-women-donors-118724.

Pew Research Center. 2012. "The Gender Gap: Three Decades Old, as Wide as Ever." www.people-press.org/2012/03/29/the-gender-gap-three-decades-old-as-wide-as-ever/.

Pew Research Center. 2013. "In Gay Marriage Debate, Both Supporters and Opponents See Legal Recognition as 'Inevitable.'" www.people-press.org/2013/06/06/in-gay-marriage-debate-both-supporters-and-opponents-see-legal-recognition-as-inevitable/.

Pew Research Center. 2014. "Most See Inequality Growing But Partisans Differ over Solutions." www.people-press.org/2014/01/23/most-see-inequality-growing-but-partisans-differ-over-solutions/.

Poole, Keith and L. Harmon Zeigler. 1985. *Women, Public Opinion and Politics*. New York, NY: Longman.

Schroeder, Robert. 2015. "Hillary Clinton Aims to Cash in with Women Donors." *MarketWatch*, June 8. www.marketwatch.com/story/hillary-clinton-aims-to-cash-in-with-women-donors-2015-06-08.

Shapiro, Robert and Harpreet Mahajan. 1986. "Gender Differences in Policy Preferences: A Summary of Trends from the 1960s to the 1980s." *Public Opinion Quarterly*, 50, 1: 42–61.

Shaw, Greg M. and Laura Gaffey. 2012. "American Public Opinion on Economic Inequality, Taxes and Mobility: 1990–2011." *Public Opinion Quarterly*, 76, 3 (Fall): 576–596.

She Should Run. 2012. "Lessons Learned: Women, Money, and Politics in the 2010 Election Cycle." www.sheshouldrun.org/vote_with_your_purse.

Smeal, Eleanor. 1997. "From Gender Gap to Gender Gulf: Abortion, Affirmative Action, and the Radical Right." *National Press Club Speech*, February 17. http://gos.sbc.edu/s/smeal.html.

Stokes, Bruce. 2013. "Big Gender Gap in Global Public Opinion about Use of Drones." *Pew Research Center*, July 25. www.pewresearch.org/fact-tank/2013/07/25/big-gender-gap-in-global-public-opinion-about-use-of-drones/.

Sweet, Lynn. 2012. "Election Could Come Down to Women." *Chicago Sun-Times*, October 13. www.realclearpolitics.com/2012/10/13/election_could_come_down_to_women_292965.html.

Thomson-DeVeaux, Amelia. 2012. "Why Young Women's Votes Will Matter in 2012." *Public Religion Research Institute*. http://publicreligion.org/2012/04/why-young-womens-votes-will-matter-in-2012/#.VQrv547K0xA.

Ung, Elisa. 2000. "Bush Women Encourage Female Voters in Phila." *The Philadelphia Inquirer*, October 20: A21.

Verba, Sidney, Kay Schlozman, and Henry Brady. 1997. *Voice and Equality: Civic Voluntarism in American Politics*. Cambridge, MA: Harvard University Press.

Winters, Nicholas T. J. 2010. "Masculine Republicans and Feminine Democrats: Gender and Americans' Explicit and Implicit Images of the Political Parties." *Political Behavior*, 32, 4 (December): 587–618.

Women's Campaign Forum. 2007. "Vote with Your Purse: Harnessing the Power of Women's Political Giving for the 2008 Election and Beyond." Washington, DC: Women's Campaign Forum Foundation. http://d3n8a8pro7vhmx.cloudfront.net/womenandpolitics/pages/50/attachments/original/1378712514/wcff-vote-with-your-purse-2007.pdf?1378712514.

5 Political Parties
Bringing Women into the Electoral Arena

Political parties are central to the democratic process. Indeed, the renowned political scientist E. E. Schattschneider has even written that "modern democracy is unthinkable save in terms of parties." Political parties especially have given those with no other resource than their numbers a say in who the governed will be through their votes. Political parties have also given individuals from diverse economic backgrounds the opportunity to become influential in the public realm. These statements may seem strange in today's polarized, high-priced campaigns for elected office, but they do have historical significance. Thus, in seeking a more equitable place in the public realm, women's rights activists have challenged the parties to advance women in their organizations, recruit them for elected positions and provide them with resources as political candidates in winnable elections, and speak to issues of particular concern to women.

The National Women's Political Caucus (NWPC), for instance, was established in 1971 to "help elect women and also men who declare themselves ready to fight for the needs and rights of women and all underrepresented groups." One of its goals was to reform party structures. It created Democratic and Republican task forces to work on that goal. Affecting the activities of the major parties continues to be a primary strategy of feminist activists seeking political leadership equity. Panelists in a June 2015 Federal Elections Commission public forum argued that

> political parties and organizations need to work much harder to recruit female candidates and ensure access to campaign cash to turn around the stubborn underrepresentation of women in elective office. . . . Political organizations as well as women officeholders can improve recruitment by better showcasing women's accomplishments and opportunities to influence policy. . . . Women really have to be recruited.
>
> (Beamish 2015)

This chapter chronicles the historical development of women's involvement in the major political party organizations, considers their emergence as leaders within those organizations, and provides an overview of trends and challenges in party efforts to elect women to national office. Suffragists and early women's rights activists struggled not only to win the vote but also to become players in these organizations. As noted in Chapter 1, women's efforts to become influential players within the parties have been characterized as entering the political house "a room at a time," passing through doors to the central rooms where the deals were made, the spoils were divided, and the candidates were chosen.

Party organizational dominance of political campaigns declined during the first decades of the second half of the 20th century, giving rise to candidate-centered campaigns as the principal organizational mechanisms would-be elected officials used to win elective office, especially national office positions. In recent decades, however, national party organizations have become reinvigorated and have reemerged as major players in electoral campaigns, assuming a more important role in the candidate-centered election system (Herrnson 2008; Jacobson 2013). They have been joined by other political organizations engaged in the electoral process, including women's groups that recruit and train candidates and provide financial and logistical support to their campaigns. A vibrant and complex organizational world characterizes contemporary electoral campaigns. This world has influenced women's quests for political leadership both within party organizations and as candidates for public office.

Women within the Parties: Historical Background

Beginning with the suffragists, women have a long and complex history of working within party organizations to become voters, attain political influence, and become party candidates for elected office. Table 5.1 presents a chronology of important dates in the history of parties, women's organizations, and women's candidacies for public office from suffrage to the contemporary period. Suffragists lobbied party organizations to include planks supporting the women's vote in their platforms. By their account, they undertook 277 such campaigns in the seventy-two-year effort to secure the right to vote (Kraditor 1965).

In the years immediately preceding the passage of the 19th Amendment, party leaders feared the entrance of women onto voter rolls. The major political parties worried that women, armed with the vote, might form their own parties and act independently in the political process, undermining the capacity of the major parties to control elections and the spoils of victory. The parties were concerned about the creation of a "petticoat hierarchy which may at will upset all orderly slates and commit undreamed of executions at the polls" and viewed the formation of the nonpartisan League of Women Voters as

Table 5.1 Important Dates in the History of Parties, Women's Organizations, and Women's Candidacies for Public Office

1918	Republican Women's National Executive Committee established.
1919	Democratic National Committee passes a resolution recommending that the Democratic State Committees "take such practical action as will provide the women of their respective states with representation, both as officers and as members thereof"; also passes a resolution calling for equal representation of the sexes on the Executive Committee of the Democratic National Committee.
	Republican National Committee urges state and country committees to select "one man and one woman member" as "the principle of representation."
1920	Delegates to the Democratic National Convention vote to double the size of their national committee and "one man and one woman hereafter should be selected from each state."
1924	Republican National Committee votes for one male and one female representative from each state.
1940	The Republican Party endorses an Equal Rights Amendment to the Constitution in its party platform for the first time.
1944	The Democratic Party includes a plank endorsing the Equal Rights Amendment in its platform for the first time.
1966	The National Organization for Women (NOW) is founded.
1971	The National Women's Political Caucus (NWPC) is founded, with the major aim of increasing the number of women in public office.

(Continued)

Table 5.1 (Continued)

1972	U.S. Representative Shirley Chisholm seeks the Democratic nomination for president.
	Frances "Sissy" Farenthold's name is placed in nomination for vice president at the Democratic National Convention. She receives 420 votes.
	Jean Westwood is appointed chair of the Democratic National Committee.
1974	The Women's Campaign Fund is founded, the first women's political action committee (PAC). Mary Louise Smith is appointed chair of the Republican National Committee.
1975	NOW forms a PAC to fund feminist candidates.
1976	Democrats mandate equal division between men and women in their national convention delegations, effective in 1980.
1977	The NWPC forms a PAC, the Campaign Support Committee.
1979	The NWPC forms a second PAC, the Victory Fund.
1980	The Republican Party removes support for the Equal Rights Amendment from its platform.
1984	Democrats nominate U.S. Representative Geraldine Ferraro for vice president.
	The National Political Congress of Black Women is founded.
1985	EMILY's List is founded on the principle that "Early Money Is Like Yeast (i.e., it makes the dough rise)."
1991	Former staffer Anita Hill accuses Clarence Thomas, a nominee for associate justice of the U.S. Supreme Court, of sexual harassment. Many women are disturbed by the absence of women senators and the dismissive attitude toward Hill during Thomas's confirmation hearings, and one result is a record number of women seeking office.
1992	Described as the "Year of the Woman" in American politics, as the number of female U.S. senators grew from two to six and the number of female U.S. representatives climbed from twenty-eight to forty-seven. The WISH List is founded.
	The NWPC sponsors the Showcase of Pro-Choice Republican Women Candidates at the Republican National Convention, with thirteen GOP candidates.
	NOW adopts the Elect Women for a Change campaign and raises about $500,000 for women candidates.
	NOW also initiates the formation of a national third party, the 21st Century Party.
1999	Elizabeth Dole enters the Republican race for president but drops out before the first caucuses and primaries.
2003	Former U.S Senator Carol Moseley Braun enters the Democratic race for president but drops out before the first caucuses and primaries.
2006	U.S. Representative Nancy Pelosi is chosen by her Democratic colleagues to be Speaker of the House, putting her second in line for the presidency and making her the highest female constitutional officer ever in the United States.
2007	U.S. Senator Hillary Clinton enters the Democratic primary for president of the United States.
2008	In June, at the end of the primary season, Hillary Clinton drops out, conceding the race to Barack Obama after putting "18 million cracks into the political glass ceiling."
	U.S. Senator John McCain, Republican nominee for president, chooses Alaska Governor Sarah Palin as his vice presidential running mate, making her the first Republican female nominee for that position.
2011	U.S. Representative Debbie Wasserman Schultz becomes chair of the Democratic National Committee.
2012	U.S. Representative Michele Bachmann enters the Republican race for president but drops out after several debates and primaries.
2016	The Democratic Party nominates Hillary Clinton for president.

Source: Compiled by author.

threatening to their hegemony in the electoral process (Chafe 1972). For these reasons, as Kristi Andersen (1996, 80–81) has noted,

> The national party organizations, sensitive to the demands and the potential influence of a new element in the electorate, responded to the imminent granting of suffrage with organizational changes designed to give women nominally equal roles in the party hierarchy and to allow for the efficient mobilization of women voters by women leaders.

Fearing the independence of women voters, the parties undertook a dual effort, establishing distinct women-led organizations to work with women voters and integrating women into their leadership committees through expansion of those organizations. The Democratic Party acted first in 1916, creating a Women's Bureau to mobilize female voters in the western states, where they had already gained the right to vote. In 1917, the Democratic National Committee (DNC), the main governing body of the party, created a women's version of itself, staffed by appointed female members from the states that had already granted women full suffrage (Harvey 1998). In 1919, they adopted a plan for an Associate National Committee of Women. The DNC also agreed that year to appoint a woman associate member from each state based on the nomination of the state committeeman. In addition, the DNC recommended that Democratic state committees provide women with similar representation at the state and local levels and equal representation of men and women on the executive committee. At their 1920 national convention, delegates voted to double the size of their national committee and stipulated that "one man and one woman hereafter should be selected from each state" (Harvey 1998, 85).

In 1918, the Republicans created the Republican Women's National Executive Committee. The next year, they adopted a plan calling for state chairmen to appoint "a State Executive Committee of women numbering from five to fifteen members to act with the State Central Committee" and established a women's division. But in 1920, they rejected equal representation for women on the Republican National Committee (RNC), although eight women were appointed to its twenty-one-member Executive Committee. In 1924, Republican leaders agreed to enlarge the RNC and to elect male and female members from each state (Harvey 1998).

Women came to represent about 10 to15 percent of the delegates to the parties' national conventions in the years after they won the vote. Although they gained some measure of formal equality in the party organizations in those days, women activists struggled for many years to gain respect and influence within the parties, in part because women neither voted differently from men nor in large enough numbers to cause the party organizations to worry about their influence. By the latter part of the 1960s, women were still only marginally represented within party leadership ranks. Party organizations had not made any particular effort to promote women as candidates for public office. Women were encouraged to seek elected office primarily in situations where the party had little chance of winning.

The Democratic Party established the McGovern-Fraser Commission in the wake of the debacle of its 1968 Chicago national convention and its subsequent loss in the presidential election to spearhead a reform effort. The commission's 1971 report recommended that racial minorities, youths, and women be represented in state delegations "in reasonable relationship to their presence in the population of the state." The NWPC pushed the Democratic Party to interpret "reasonable representation" as meaning matching a group's proportion in a state's population. As a result, they succeeded in substantially increasing the percentage of female convention delegates. Prior to the reform effort, at the 1968 Democratic National Convention, only 13 percent of the delegates had been women; in

1972, women constituted 40 percent of the delegates. The push for greater representation of women among delegates continued throughout the 1970s. Since 1980, Democratic Party rules have mandated gender equity within all state delegations to its national conventions.

The Republicans have not followed the Democrats in mandating equal numbers of men and women in convention delegations, but in the 1970s, under pressure from delegates, the GOP adopted affirmative steps to encourage state parties to elect more women as convention delegates. The percentage of female Republican delegates increased from 17 percent in 1968 to 30 percent in 1972.

But both parties have wanted to appear as promoters of women in political leadership positions. Thus, in an example Freeman (1993) cites, the 1992 national conventions spotlighted women candidates and raising money to elect more women far more than discussing polarizing issues. Once venues for political power struggles and ideological battles with uncertain outcomes fought before the public on television, national party conventions have become staged media events to spotlight candidates and to promote a favorable impression of the party among the general public. Party platforms and party nominees have been decided before the convention convenes, requiring only formal ratification. In this new style of convention highlighting, party support for women in political leadership positions has emerged as a major function, presumably in an effort to attract the support of women voters. The parties' 2012 conventions illustrate this function. Media headlines noted "News Analysis: GOP convention underscores efforts to tap Hispanics, blacks and women" (Rusling 2012), "Republicans are parading their party's women, taking full advantage of these women's power with delegates and voters" (Lee 2012), and "Democrats Seek to Fire Up Female Voters: At the Democratic National Convention in Charlotte, every night is ladies' night" (Cook 2012).

The parties' main convention tactic to appeal to women in the electorate in 2012 was to heavily feature female speakers in their prime-time lineup. The percentage of female speakers at each convention was similar: 33 percent and 36 percent, respectively, at the Republican and Democratic conventions (MacManus 2014). A count of the sex breakdown of prime-time presentations between 7:00 and 11:00 p.m. eastern time showed that women made up a nearly equal proportion of the two parties' speakers. Women accounted for sixteen of the fifty-one prime-time individuals making remarks (31 percent) at the Republican National Convention and thirty-one of the eighty-eight (35 percent) prime-time Democratic National Convention speakers. The Democratic convention also featured U.S. Senator Barbara Mikulski, dean of female senators, as the longest-serving female senator leading eleven of the twelve female Democratic senators in a group presentation on Wednesday night. Senator Mikulski spoke for the group, highlighting the Obama administration's record on women's issues. At the end of her speech, they all joined hands, holding them over their heads to the tune of Katy Perry's "Firework."

Female speakers at both conventions were racially and ethnically diverse. But women-elected officials from key states were a larger proportion of Republican speakers, whereas the Democrats featured a noticeably larger number of new faces, often young pathbreakers, telling personal stories of how policies the Obama administration promoted helped them or Republican proposals hurt them (MacManus 2014).

Female governors were the most prominent women featured in the Republican Party, especially the two who were members of minority ethnic groups—South Carolina Governor Nikki Haley and New Mexico Governor Susana Martinez. Along with Governor Mary Fallin of Oklahoma, they were given prime-time speaking roles at the Republican convention. Former Secretary of State Condoleezza Rice also received a prominent slot. Marquee female Republican candidate, African American, and Mormon Mia Love, mayor of Saratoga Springs, Utah, who was mounting a very competitive challenge to Democratic

U.S. Representative Jim Matheson in Utah's fourth congressional district, also gave a prime-time address.

The Democrats showcased prominent members of the reproductive rights movement: Nancy Keenan, president of the National Abortion Rights Action League Pro-Choice America, Cecile Richards, president of Planned Parenthood, and Sandra Fluke, a Georgetown University law student and birth control advocate. She had made national headlines when conservative radio host Rush Limbaugh called her a "slut" after Republican members of the House Oversight Committee refused to allow her to speak at a committee hearing considering an Obama administration mandate that companies providing insurance coverage to individuals employed in religious institutions such as hospitals also offer contraceptive coverage. Only five men, all opposed to the mandate, were allowed to address the committee, leading Democratic Representative Carolyn Maloney to ask, "Where are the women?" She and two of her colleagues walked out of the hearing, which resulted in much media coverage and commentary.

In terms of convention officials, Congresswoman Cathy McMorris Rodgers served as the Republican's official convention host, speaking at the start of each night of the convention and introducing the theme of the speeches for that evening. It was a role created for her to enhance her status and visibility within the party (Spin Control 2012). On the Democratic side, as chair of the Democratic National Committee, Congresswoman Debbie Wasserman Schultz played a prime leadership role in organizing, opening, and managing the convention. Chapter 9 describes the gender aspects of the 2016 national conventions.

Partisan Recruitment of Female Candidates

Recruiting candidates is a major function of party organizations. The Democratic Party's distinct culture made it the site of early historical action to recruit and promote women (Freeman 1987). Feminists, as an accepted organized group within the party, had the attention of leadership and gained a sympathetic ear within the party's liberal wing. As early as 1974, the Democratic Party sponsored the Campaign Conference for Democratic Women aimed at electing more women to political office (Scott 1974). The 1,200 women who attended the workshop passed resolutions urging their party to do more for potential female candidates. Most of the female members of the U.S. House of Representatives in the 1970s were Democrats, including several who won their seats not because they were championed within their local party organizations but because they challenged local party structures and beat them.

The Republican Party did not initiate similar women's conferences until nearly a decade later. The Republicans' later start does not mean that their party has been less receptive to female candidacies, however. Indeed, at one time, the feminist leaders Eleanor Smeal, former chair of the National Organization for Women (NOW), and the former liberal congresswoman Bella Abzug argued just the opposite (Freeman 1989). Republican women in the 1980s tended to credit men for bringing them into the organization (Romney and Harrison 1988).

Wanting to appear supportive of women in the face of an emerging gender gap in the 1980s, the parties saw it as expedient to champion women candidates. Republican leaders, in particular, publicly acknowledged this fact. The Republican Senatorial Campaign Committee (RSCC) chair, Senator Richard Lugar (1983), issued a press statement in 1983 declaring

> a concerted drive by the Republican Party to stamp itself as the party of the woman elected official would serve our nation as well as it serves our own political interests. The full political participation of women is a moral imperative for our society and

intelligent political goal for the Republican Party. [He pledged to] commit the RSCC to the maximum legal funding and support for any Republican woman who is nominated next year, regardless of how Democratic the state or apparently formidable the Democratic candidate. I am prepared to consider direct assistance to women candidates even prior to their nomination, a sharp departure from our usual policy.

In 1984, the Democrats included a section in their party platform on political empowerment for minorities and women:

> We will recruit women and minorities to run for governorships and all state and local offices. The Democratic Party (through its campaign committees) will commit to spending maximum resources to elect women and minority candidates and offer these candidates in-kind services, including political organizing and strategic advice. And the bulk of all voter registration funds will be spent on targeted efforts to register minorities and women.

In 1988, both national party platforms included statements recommending support for women's candidacies. The Democrats endorsed "full and equal access of women and minorities to elective office and party endorsement," whereas the Republicans called for "strong support for the efforts of women in seeking an equal role in government and [commitment] to the vigorous recruitment, training and campaign support for women candidates at all levels." However, these pledges did not include any action plans for implementation. Prior to 1990, the calls for increasing the number of women candidates were only rhetoric, as there were few substantive actions to ensure that women were nominated in favorable electoral circumstances.

Then, for a variety of reasons, 1992 emerged as the "Year of the Woman" in American politics. With the end of the Cold War, attention was increasingly turning away from foreign policy and defense and toward domestic issues on which women were perceived to have more expertise. The confirmation hearings for Clarence Thomas's nomination to the U.S. Supreme Court shone a spotlight on the absence of women in the Senate and upset women who thought that Anita Hill's charges of sexual harassment against Thomas were trivialized. (Chapter 8 spotlights this event.) The reapportionment and redistricting process of that election resulted in more open seats than usual, creating new electoral opportunities. These forces stimulated the parties to direct a greater share of their recruitment activity toward women than in previous years. The leadership of both parties' congressional campaign committees made special efforts to seek out qualified female House candidates. The Democratic Senatorial Campaign Committee formed a women's council that raised approximately $1.5 million for Democratic women running for Senate. These affirmative steps did not, however, spur the parties to clear the field of primary competition for women or discourage anyone, male or female, from running against women (Biersack and Herrnson 1994).

Republican women have initiated specific efforts in their party to recruit and train women as political and public leaders that include the work of the National Federation of Republican Women (NFRW) and the Republican National Committee's Excellence in Public Service Series. The NFRW provides training for potential Republican women candidates. As early as 1976, it published the booklet *Consider Yourself for Public Office: Guidelines for Women Candidates*. It now offers campaign management schools that local groups can bring to their areas (see Picture 5.1).

The Excellence in Public Service Series is a political leadership development program offered to Republican women in several states. Most of the programs are named for

Picture 5.1 National Federation of Republican Women Campaign Training Session

National political consultant Joe Gaylord discusses his "Eight Concepts for Running a Successful Campaign" during a Campaign Management School in Nashville, Tennessee.

Courtesy of the National Federation of Republican Women.

prominent Republicans, such as former Senator Richard Lugar. The initial program was the Lugar Series started in 1989 in Indiana. Now nineteen additional states have such programs, although not all are offered every year. Typically, a yearlong series of programs, with eight monthly sessions and a three-day leadership seminar in Washington, DC, is offered to selected women willing to make a commitment to play an active role in the political arena. Classes are designed "to encourage, mentor and prepare women leaders to seek new levels of involvement in government and politics."

The congressional parties have established four campaign committees: the Democratic Congressional Campaign Committee (DCCC), the National Republican Congressional Committee (NRCC), the Democratic Senatorial Campaign Committee (DSCC), and the National Republican Senatorial Committee (NRSC). Their job is to provide financial resources to vulnerable incumbents in their reelection bids and to recruit and support candidates for open seats and as challengers to the other party's vulnerable incumbents. They play significant roles in the contemporary campaign era. They are also major sources of campaign money, services, and advice for congressional candidates (Herrnson 2008). In recent election cycles, both parties have promoted women into leadership positions within their campaign committees and have established subgroups to promote the candidacies of women. The trend has also been to include female contenders in their more general candidate support programs such as the House Democrats' Red to Blue and the Republicans' Young Guns programs.

Female lawmakers headed both of the Democratic campaign committees in the 107th Congress at the beginning of the new millennium (2001–2002). Representative Nita Lowey of New York chaired the Democratic Congressional Campaign Committee, and Senator Patty Murray of Washington State chaired the Democratic Senatorial Campaign Committee. Senator Murray returned as chair of the DSCC in the 112th Congress.

In 1999, Representative Lowey founded Women Lead, a fund-raising subsidiary of the DCCC to target women donors and contributors to women candidates. When Lowey became chair of the DCCC, she appointed Representative Jan Schakowsky of Illinois to head Women Lead. In the 2001–2002 election cycle, that committee raised approximately $25 million for women candidates. Lowey had admired Schakowsky's fund-raising prowess in her initial run for an open House seat in 1997. Schakowsky had approached all the female law partners in the greater Chicago area, asking for donations in what she called "an untapped constituency" of women contributors. "The strategy paid off. . . . Schakowsky raised 57 percent of her campaign funds from women donors that year—a higher percentage than any other congressional candidate in the 1998 election cycle" (Stevens 2002). In office, Representative Schakowsky annually hosts an "Ultimate Women's Power" luncheon at a downtown Chicago hotel, including a keynote speaker from the entertainment world or the political world, which has raised hundreds of thousands of dollars for female candidates. In the 2016 election cycle, Representatives Debbie Dingle and Lois Frankel headed the Women Lead program.

Prior to being appointed to chair the DSCC, Senator Murray had launched a program in 1999 called Women on the Road to the Senate, which helped elect four female senators in 2000. In 2002, the program, renamed the Women's Senate Network, then headed by Michigan Senator Debbie Stabenow, raised $1.3 million on top of some $2 million collected through separate events early in that election cycle. Fund-raising activities included $1,000-per-person issue conferences that showcased Senators Hillary Clinton, Dianne Feinstein, and other "prominent senators who happen to be women" in a series of seminar discussions on topics such as terrorism, national security, and the economy. Senator Stabenow commented that it irked her that her female colleagues are so rarely interviewed on such topics (Stolberg 2004). The Women's Senate Network continued as a DSCC program headed by Senator Kay Hagan in the 2012 election cycle. Its current activities are monthly policy luncheons held in Washington, DC, as fund-raising events.

Through the 108th Congress (2003–2004), no woman had chaired a corresponding Republican campaign committee, although Representative Anne Northup of Kentucky headed recruitment for the National Republican Congressional Committee. However, for the 109th Congress (2005–2006), Republicans elected Senator Elizabeth Dole of North Carolina to head the National Republican Senatorial Committee. She won the position by defeating Minnesota Senator Norman Coleman by one vote in the Senate Republican caucus. Dole had campaigned for the presidency in the early stages of the 2000 election before winning her Senate seat in 2002. She had also served in two cabinet positions in earlier Republican presidential administrations. Described as "about as close to a rock star as the Republican Senate has," she was considered a celebrity within the party (Dettmer 2004, 9). She had helped raise more than $16 million for the NRSC in the 2004 election cycle (Dolan 2004). In addition, "Dole's supporters argued that she would help Republicans win over female and minority voters by putting a 'different face on the party'" (Frommer 2004).

Dole's leadership of the NRSC proved otherwise. The committee fell $30 million behind the DSCC. Some of the losing Republican Senate candidates blamed Dole and her committee for a lack of support and for making bad decisions regarding advertising in support of their campaigns and against their opponents. The Associated Press reported that

> President Bush's low approval ratings, the unpopular war on Iraq, voter concern about corruption and Democratic fundraising all figured in the GOP loss of Senate control in last month's elections. But among Republicans, long-hidden tensions are spilling into view, with numerous critics venting their anger at the GOP Senate campaign committee headed by North Carolina Sen. Elizabeth Dole.
>
> (Espo 2006)

Other than Senator Dole's campaign to chair the NRSC, no female members appear to have sought these party leadership positions, but party leaders have tapped them to head up informal efforts to get more women to run as Republican candidates. In 2007, the NRCC chair Representative Tom Cole appointed Representative Candice Miller of Michigan to lead an effort to recruit women as candidates for the House (Blake 2007). Little appeared in the media after this announcement about any follow-up recruitment activities, and the minuscule number of Republican women who mounted candidacies for House seats in the 2008 election, especially in the twenty-six House districts vacated by Republican incumbents, suggests that this effort was anemic at best. Republicans have continued with informal efforts to recruit and support female candidates. In recent elections, Representative Cathy McMorris Rodgers was appointed to spearhead such efforts. In a *National Journal* interview in 2010, she offered the following advice to her party:

> If we want women to run for office, it's important that we're doing the outreach that we're talking with women and just encouraging them to run for office. There's a recognition . . . that we want to encourage a broader face for our party.
>
> (McPike 2010)

These party campaign committees are organizations of highly skilled professional staff run by executive directors in addition to the elected legislative chair. A recent account of their organizational structure reported that the two senate committees (DSCC and NRSC) each had over fifty staff members, whereas the DCCC employed over one hundred individuals, and the NRCC had approximately seventy-five staff members. The staff are responsible for administration, fund-raising, research, communications, and campaign activities (Herrnson 2008). Women's visibility as organizational leaders within these party committees has grown in recent election cycles. In 2012, the NRCC appointed Joanna Burgos to head its independent expenditures division. Burgos was the first woman and the first Hispanic to achieve such an appointment. She had moved up through the party organization. The first woman to head the DSCC independent expenditure unit, Martha McKenna was also appointed in 2012, and Anna Cu was hired as its policy director.

For the 2016 election cycle, women served in over one half of the executive and deputy director positions in the DCCC. Women served as executive and deputy executive directors of the DCCC (Kelly Ward and Missy Kurek, respectively). Jessica Johnson served as deputy executive of the NRCC. (Liesl Hickey was executive director in 2014.) Women were half of the eight senior staff of the NRSC and three of the five senior staff at the DSCC as the parties entered the 2016 presidential election.

A significant feature of women's increasing influence in the political world has been their movement into professional political organizational positions as well as elective office posts. Women began to fill senior campaign positions decades ago. In 1988, Susan Estrich became the first female presidential campaign manager in contemporary times. She headed the Michael Dukakis campaign. Women ran the campaigns of Al Gore, John Kerry, and Hillary Clinton in 2008. Beth Myers who was Mitt Romney's chief of staff when he was governor, ran his 2008 campaign, and vetted his vice presidential prospects that year (Bowman and Marsico 2012). Kellyanne Conway became the first woman to manage a successful presidential campaign in 2016 as manager of Donald Trump's campaign. Conway was Trump's third manager and took over the campaign in August. She is a lawyer and has run her own political company, the Polling Company Inc. It includes WomanTrend, a research and consulting division formed to better connect corporate America with female consumers. WomanTrend monitors female consumers as well as a multitude of current and prospective lifestyle, home, work, entertainment, technological, and generational trends affecting all consumers.[1] Women were also campaign managers for 2016 Republican presidential contenders John Kasich and Michael Huckabee.

Female managers ran more than half of the thirteen most competitive Senate campaigns on the Democratic side in 2012. Only one female manager worked on the top thirteen most competitive races on the Republican side (Shira 2012). In 2014, the *National Journal* reported that the Republicans did not have one female manager in battleground Senate races.[2] Advances into these organizational leadership positions are important for individual careers for female professionals. Women in these positions also serve as role models for political careers beyond running for public office for young women.

Contemporary Party Initiatives to Win Women Voters and Promote Women's Candidacies

Over the course of several elections, the Republican Party has noted its image problem with female voters and its deficiency in nominating and electing female candidates. Many of the efforts they launched to cure these problems never seem to be much more than rhetoric, producing little in the way of substance and concrete results. "They talk about recruiting more women to run, but those efforts tend to disintegrate. I've seen it so often. They all sort of fizzle out. I don't think there's a genuine will," former Republican U.S. Senator Olympia Snowe chastised her party in 2013 (Collins 2013, 39).

The problem became particularly acute after Democratic charges of a GOP war on women and Mitt Romney's loss of women by eleven percentage points in the 2012 election. Party leaders expressed a renewed will to recruit and promote more women. They initiated a new set of programs. In June 2013, six Republican committees held a press conference to announce the launching of "Women on the Right Unite," a joint project focusing "on various sectors including recruitment, messaging, polling, training for candidates, localized field events, fundraising, strong digital presence and harnessing the power of data to increase female voter participation." Each of the committees was to announce substantive plans to achieve this goal. The NRCC established Project Grow (Growing Republican Opportunities for Women), a female candidate recruitment program. Project Rise (Republicans Inspiring Success and Empowerment) was the creation of several veteran female Republican House members to help their freshmen colleagues raise money. "Our freshmen women are facing their first re-elections, which can often be tough, so I wanted to help them early—along with my colleagues—to put them in the strongest position for success," McMorris Rodgers said in a statement. Project Grow's mission was to provide mentors to candidates and to offer strategy and polling support. As Chapter 8 shows, these efforts have had few successes.

Republicans also began a series of sessions during the 2014 campaign season to teach their male candidates and incumbents how to talk to women. GOP aides reported multiple sessions having been held with aides to incumbents in which they were "schooled in 'messaging against women opponents' . . . some of these guys have a lot to learn." Even Speaker John Boehner said that "some of our members are not as sensitive as they ought to be" (Palmer and Bresnahan 2013).

Democrats, too, have launched several initiatives to maintain and expand their support among women and to counteract the Republican efforts. In 2012, the DSCC created a series of joint fund-raising committees titled "Women on the Road to the Senate: 12 and Counting." Each committee was designated to a particular city such as Washington, DC, New York, and Boston and included a subset of the twelve candidates. As part of this fund-raising effort, for example, in early March, four West Coast fund-raisers were organized under the Women on the Road banner. The swing included a lunch in Denver, a dinner in Los Angeles, a brunch in San Francisco, and a dinner in Seattle—the largest city in DSCC Chairwoman Patty Murray's home state of Washington (Shiner 2012).

In addition, as part of this campaign, the DSCC produced a video stressing "it is time to end the culture wars and get to work for the middle class." Each of the twelve female candidates was introduced, and the video ended with the tag line "if you don't like what the Republicans are doing, send a Democratic woman to the Senate. In fact, send them all." U.S. Senators Barbara Boxer and Kirsten Gillibrand joined this effort with their own fund-raising projects for female candidates. Senator Boxer created "WinwithWomen2012" as part of her leadership political action committee (PAC) endorsing all eleven Democratic female senate candidates and providing them with the maximum amount allowed in direct contributions.[3] A music video, "A Woman's Voice," promoted the program. Senator Gillibrand has created an Off the Sidelines PAC and empowerment program.[4] The Democratic female Senate contenders did very well in 2012. All the incumbents were reelected, and four women were newly elected. The Democratic female senate candidates were dubbed the stars of the 2012 election in the media (see, for example, Davis 2012). Whereas 2012 was a good year for Democrats, 2014 was very different, reflecting 2010. Republican women picked up two Senate seats, whereas two female Democratic incumbents lost their bids for reelection. Thus, women made no advances toward gender equity in that legislative body.

Facing a difficult political landscape in 2014, female Democratic representatives once again took to the road. On June 1, 2014, female Democratic U.S. representatives kicked off the "Women on a Roll" bus tour in Seneca Falls, New York, the site of the first women's rights convention in 1848. The representatives traveled to seven cities to talk with local women about their comprehensive women's economic agenda dubbed "When Women Succeed, America Succeeds," which included legislative proposals on guaranteed paid family and sick leave, equal pay legislation, a higher minimum wage, more broadly affordable childcare, and stronger workplace protections for pregnant women.

A big challenge to liberal feminist dominance of the world of women's campaign organizations since the 2008 election undoubtedly has been former Alaska governor and Republican vice presidential nominee Sarah Palin's campaign for "common sense conservative" female candidates in recent elections. Her rhetorical invocation of what she called "mama grizzlies" in the midst of the 2010 election challenged not only the liberal feminist establishment but also Republican mainstream organizations. In a speech at a Susan B. Anthony List fund-raiser in May 2010, she issued a clarion call to mama grizzlies to rise up, delivering a warning that a herd of "pink elephants" were stampeding to Washington with an "e.t.a of November 2. You don't want to mess with moms who are rising up. If you thought pit bulls were tough, you don't want to mess with mama grizzlies." Mama grizzly candidates became part of the Republican campaign landscape in that election, with Palin endorsements and characterizations of several of the female candidates as mama grizzlies, tough conservative women. "She brought to the Republican Party what some members had once complained did not exist: a concerted effort to tap female candidates for promotion and lift them out of obscurity," Anne Kornblut noted in the *Washington Post* (2010).

SarahPAC, her political action committee, produced a video highlighting the mama grizzly phenomenon to raise money for their campaigns. In addition to making direct contributions to thirteen Republican women running for House seats and five Republican female Senate candidates, Palin's endorsement provided a priceless boost to the momentum of many of these candidacies in 2010. According to OpenSecrets.org, SarahPAC gave money to a total of seventy-four U.S. House candidates totaling $349,000 and $110,000 to twenty-five Senate candidates. SarahPAC did not file any independent expenditures. There is no way of knowing how much additional money it bundled into its endorsed candidates' campaigns.

In her video and speeches, Sarah Palin explicitly invoked women's status as mothers as a central reason why they would be good political representatives. Palin argued that voters should support her mama grizzly candidates "because moms kind of just know when there's something wrong." Moreover, Palin argued that the mama grizzlies represented an emerging conservative feminist ideology that would bring important and underrepresented perspectives to the policy table.

In 2012, the number of mama grizzly candidates to endorse was rather limited. In that election, SarahPAC reported raising nearly $5 million. It made direct contributions totaling $134,500 to seven senate candidates (six men and one woman) and seventeen House candidates (ten men and seven women). In only one case did the endorsement come with reference to being a mama grizzly. In a thirty-second ad, Palin praised Sarah Steelman, who was running in the Republican primary to challenge U.S. Senator Claire McCaskill in Missouri, as a "conservative maverick" who will defend tax dollars "like a mama grizzly defending her cubs." Steelman lost the primary to Representative Todd Akin. In 2014, SarahPAC reported raising $2.8 million. Four female U.S. House candidates and three U.S. Senate candidates received contributions from the PAC. In 2016, the PAC raised $1.4 million and reported contributing $67,500 to forty-two U.S. House and eight Senate candidates, only one of whom was a woman (U.S. Representative Elise Stefanik).

Given the structure of American elections, these efforts can only modestly advance the quest for gender equity in political leadership. The national party organizations are also the source of substantial financial support to favored candidates. Research shows that female candidates for the U.S. House and Senate are not laggards nor are they shunned as contenders when the party committees allocate financial dollars, especially in the crucial final days of an election (Burrell 2014). The party committees can make unlimited expenditures (e.g., buying television ads supported by the party committee and shown "independently" of the candidates' campaigns). The independent expenditure aspect of federal campaign financing is of greatest consequence to campaigns for the U.S. House and Senate in recent elections. The national party committees now pour significant resources into the campaigns of female as well as male candidates. Candidate sex has not made a difference in expenditure of independent funds once other factors have been taken into account. This support has important implications not only for encouraging women to enter the electoral arena but also for increasing the likelihood of their success (Burrell 2014).

Conclusion

Long gone are the days when women candidates won party nominations primarily as "sacrificial lambs" in districts where a party had little prospect of winning. The parties have found it to their advantage to promote women candidates, and once women become nominees, they are as likely as male candidates to have access to party resources, particularly in highly competitive races in which they can often count on substantial support in the final days of the campaign. Women candidates, particularly those who are pro-choice, also have the advantage of access to women's PACs, which have become formidable players in campaigns, although conservative women are increasingly having access to special PAC money and training (see Chapter 8). A continuing problem for women candidates, however, is reaching the point of being a competitive candidate. Research suggests women are more hesitant to run for office, and the limited opportunity structure for newcomers in the form of open seats, competitive districts, and vulnerable incumbents has offered few opportunities for women to expand their numbers as national lawmakers (see Lawless and Fox 2010).

Although now commanding substantial resources, party organizations no longer control the nomination process in most states. Whereas they are involved in recruiting candidates, few make it a policy to recruit women candidates and to promote them over male candidates to increase women's numbers in elective office. Members of Congress and the campaign committees' staff do appear to encourage prospective candidates to run. As congressional scholar Paul Herrnson (2008) has observed,

> Armed with favorable polling figures and the promise of party assistance in the general election they search out local talent. Promising individuals are invited to meet with the members of Congress and party leaders in Washington and to attend campaign seminars.
> (47)

One contemporary project, Representation 2020, aims to change the structure of American elections to jump-start a move toward gender equity in elected office. Representation 2020 is a project of FairVote, a nonprofit, nonpartisan organization that advocates for structural changes to make elections more participatory and representative at every level of government. Advocating for change in the way in which the major U.S. parties operate is a large part of Representation 2020's strategy to achieve the goal of elected office gender parity. It operates under the premise that

> political parties in many states and localities play a significant role in the recruitment, financing, and election of candidates. If parties do not recruit and support women at the same rate as men (and at this point, most do not), women are unlikely to achieve equal representation in elected office.

The Representation 2020 program of action advocates the following changes in the way the parties operate:

- *A dialogue among party members.* At least twice a year, statewide party leaders should meet with two or more statewide organizations that train and recruit women for elective office to discuss strategies to recruit more female candidates.
- *Gender parity task forces.* State parties establish gender parity task forces to develop and execute plans to recruit and train female candidates. This task force may do its own recruiting and/or training or may contract with existing private groups that provide this service.
- *Internal accountability.* Statewide party leadership should prepare an annual report on the state of gender parity in its own leadership, in its elected representatives, and in political appointments of elected representatives; the number of female candidates, nominees, and general election winners in the most recent election; and its plans to recruit women for upcoming elections. Statewide party leadership will present this report to the national party.

- *Incentives to increase recruitment.* The fastest way for political parties to increase women's representation is to adopt measures that would incentivize the recruitment of more women candidates. State and local parties would set goals, based on the current state of women's representation in their area, for how many women they hope to recruit each election cycle. Under this system, local and state parties would set goals for how many women they would recruit to run in their primary elections and especially in primary elections for positions in which a nominee from the party would have a good chance of winning in the general election. That way, women who are recruited and win their parties' nominations will also be likely to enter office. National political parties would award "Gender Parity Grants," financed by donations from party members who care about increasing the number of women in elected office, to the state and local parties that met their goals.

But how does one get party leaders to engage in such programs? What incentives might they have to invest in these actions? Certainly, the Republican Party has become very cognizant of its gender problem, as noted in their rhetoric about the problem and announcement of initiatives over the course of the past few elections. These initiatives include their 2013 Growth and Opportunity Project, which includes a section on outreach efforts to women, a women2women tour of the Republican Mainstreet Partnership group to develop a policy agenda based on concerns and motivations of women they talked with on their tour, and Empowered Women, a platform for conservative women that Republican strategist Mindy Finn launched in 2015. These organizations and activities speak to that recognition, but it is outside that party's culture to move beyond talk and events to actually mandate policies to achieve gender equity. What about a Title IX for women candidates? That is what Representation 2020's Cynthia Terrell (2015) argues in *The Nation*:

> Without Title IX, women athletes would not have had the opportunities that they do today. We need a similar movement for women candidates. . . . Better still would be for state and local parties—along with the "kingmakers" and would-be "queenmakers" associated with them like unions and chambers of commerce—to set goals of how many women they expect to recruit each election cycle and adopt requirements that at least half of their donations in a cycle need to go to women candidates.

Notes

1. See www.pollingcompany.com/about.
2. www.nationaljournal.com/s/63082/republicans-dont-have-single-woman-running-battleground-senate-campaign.
3. www.winwithwomen2012.com.
4. www.offthesidelines.org.

References

Andersen, Kristi. 1996. *After Suffrage: Women in Partisan and Electoral Politics before the New Deal*. Chicago, IL: University of Chicago Press.

Beamish, Rita. 2015. "The Road to Parity for Women in Politics: Follow the Money." *The New York Times*, June 13. http://nytlive.nytimes.com/womenintheworld/2015/05/13/the-road-to-parity-for-women-in-politics-follow-the-money/.

Biersack, Robert and Paul S. Herrnson. 1994. "Political Parties and the Year of the Woman." In *The Year of the Woman: Myths and Realities*, eds. Elizabeth Adell Cook, Sue Thomas, and Clyde Wilcox. Boulder, CO: Westview Press.

Blake, Aaron. 2007. "House Republicans Aim for More Recruitment of Women in 2008." *The Hill*, January 22.

Bowman, Karlyn and Jennifer Marsico. 2012. "The Past, Present and Future of the Women's Vote." *American Enterprise Institute*, October 12. www.aei.org/publication/the-past-present-and-future-of-the-womens-vote/.

Burrell, Barbara. 2014. *Gender in Campaigns for the U.S. House of Representatives*. Ann Arbor, MI: University of Michigan Press.

Chafe, William. 1972. *The American Woman: Her Changing Social, Economic, and Political Roles, 1920–1970*. New York, NY: Oxford University Press.

Collins, Gail. 2013. "Running in Reverse." *The New York Times*, December 12.

Cook, Nancy. 2012. "Democrats Seek to Fire Up Female Voters." *National Journal*, September 4.

Davis, Susan. 2012. "Female Candidates for Congress on Upward Trend." *USA Today*, January 29.

Dettmer, Jamie. 2004. "Senator Dole Is Eyeing Leadership of Key Senate Committee, GOP Post." *New York Sun*, November 12.

Dolan, David. 2004. "Dole to Lead GOP Senate Efforts; N.C. Senator Will Raise Money for 2006 Campaigns, Recruit Candidates." *Herald-Sun*, November 18.

Espo, David. 2006. "In Wake of Senate Loss, Republicans Turn Anger on Campaign Committee Led by Elizabeth Dole." *Associated Press*, December 23.

Freeman, Jo. 1987. "Whom You Know versus Whom You Represent: Feminist Influence in the Democratic and Republican Parties." In *The Women's Movements of the United States and Western Europe, Consciousness, Political Opportunity and Public Policy*, eds. Mary Fainsod Katzenstein and Carol McClurg Mueller. Philadelphia, PA: Temple University Press, 21–244.

Freeman, Jo. 1989. "Feminist Activities at the Republican Convention." *PS: Political Science & Politics*, 22 (March): 39–47.

Freeman, Jo. 1993. "Feminism vs. Family Values: Women at the 1992 Democratic and Republican Conventions." *PS: Political Science & Politics*, 26 (March): 21–27.

Frommer, Frederic J. 2004. "Republicans Choose Elizabeth Dole to Head 2006 Senate Campaigns." *SFGATE*, November 17. www.sfgate.com.

Harvey, Anna. 1998. *Votes without Leverage: Women in American Electoral Politics, 1920–1970*. New York, NY: Cambridge University Press.

Herrnson, Paul. 2008. *Congressional Elections: Campaigning at Home and in Washington*. Washington, DC: CQ Press.

Jacobson, Gary. 2013. *The Politics of Congressional Elections*, 8th ed. Upper Saddle River, NJ: Pearson Education.

Kornblut, Anne E. 2010. "Primaries Push More Women into General Elections, But Most Fresh Faces Now Belong to Republican Party." *The Washington Post*, September 15. www.washingtonpost.com/wp-dyn/content/article/2010/09/15/AR2010091506408.html.

Kraditor, Aileen. 1965. *Ideas of the Woman Suffrage Movement, 1890–1920*. New York, NY: Columbia University Press.

Lawless, Jennifer and Richard Fox. 2010. *It Still Takes a Candidate: Why Women Don't Run for Office*. New York, NY: Cambridge University Press.

Lee, Barbara. 2012. "Democratic National Convention: Where Are the Women?" *Huntington Post*, August 16.

Lugar, Richard. 1983. "A Plan to Elect More GOP Women." *The Washington Post*, August 21.

MacManus, Susan A. 2014. "Voter Participation and Turnout: The Political Generational Divide among Women Voters." In *Gender & Elections: Shaping the Future of American Politics*, eds. Susan J. Carroll and Richard L. Fox. New York, NY: Cambridge University Press, 80–118.

McPike, Erin. 2010. "Women's Prospects Still Lackluster." *The National Journal*, May 12. www.highbeam.com/doc/1G1-227666647.html.

Palmer, Anna and John Bresnahan. 2013. "GOP Men Told How to Talk to Women." *Politico*, December 5. www.politico.com/story/2013/12/gop-men-tutored-in-running-against-women-100701.

Romney, Ronna and Beppie Harrison. 1988. *Momentum: Women in America Politics Now*. New York. NY: Crown.

Rusling, Matthew. 2012. "News Analysis: GOP Convention Underscores Efforts to Tap Hispanics, Blacks and Women." *Xinhua General News Service*, August 25.

Scott, Austin. 1974. "Democratic Women See Gains in 1974." *The Washington Post*, March 31.

Shiner, Meredith. 2012. "Female Lawmakers Are Raising Money and Political Stakes." Roll Call. April 19.

Shira, Toeplitz. 2012. "Women in the War Room." *Campaign and Elections Magazine*, July 23.

Spin Control. 2012. "McMorris Rodgers GOP Convention 'Host.'" *The Spokesman-Review*, August 27.

Stevens, Allison. 2002. "Both Parties Say Women's Wallets Ripe for Tapping." *Women's eNews*, January 14. http://womensenews.org/2002/01/both-parties-say-womens-wallets-ripe-tapping/.

Stolberg, Sheryl Gay. 2004. "Partisan Loyalties and the Senate Women's Caucus." *The New York Times*, April 28.

Terrell, Cynthia. 2015. "We Need to Do More Than Fix the Pipeline to Get Parity for Women in Office." *The Nation*, June 18.

6 "Doing Politics"

Women's Empowerment
and Community Activism

What also emerged was that Latina women play a very active political role, a finding that challenges the invisibility of Latina women as political actors so prevalent in current political science literature.

Hardy-Fanta (1993, ix)

The chapters in this section explore the process of politicization and demonstrate how women's community-based activism can also transform politics.

Naples (1998, 16)

Women's grassroots political action does constitute the "news that's fit to print." . . . These women defy the portrayal of working-class women so common in the popular press as passive, politically disinterested, unskilled or ineffectual.

Bookman and Morgen (1988, 3)

These quotes from research on working-class, marginalized, and immigrant women "doing politics" challenge conventional ideas of what constitutes political participation. Chapters 4 and 5 have surveyed our knowledge of the substance and trends in women's participation in two of the main areas of conventional politics: voting and political party organizing. Chapter 8 picks up this focus on conventional politics with an overview of the scholarly literature on women as political candidates and a survey of trends in their election to public office at the state and national levels. This chapter and Chapter 7 proceed along two different tracks regarding the political life of U.S. women. Chapter 7 moves from the local to the international arena, exploring U.S. women's NGOs working to promote equal rights and empowerment of women globally.

Women's community activism is this chapter's focus. Community activism is a form of political engagement often neglected in studies of political participation. Women's community-based struggles are "usually left out of our historical record" sociologist Nancy Naples (1998, 2) has contended. Surveying and theorizing about women's community activism also moves knowledge on political participation drawn primarily from the experiences of middle-class White women to that of working-class women and to experiences of women of color and diverse ethnic backgrounds. Their activism centers on challenging and resisting power structures, as the chapter's introductory quotes suggest.

This chapter's exploration of such activism broadens what is defined as political. Nancy Naples (1991), whose research is steeped in community studies, for example, defines "doing politics" as "any struggle to gain control over definitions of 'self' and 'community'; to augment personal and communal empowerment; to create alterative institutions and organizational processes; and to increase the power and resources of their community" (479). How working-class White women, women of color, and immigrant women do politics must be included in any work that seeks to provide an overview of women and the practice of politics.

The three anthologies—*Women Transforming Politics* (Cohen et al. 1997), *Women and the Politics of Empowerment* (Morgen and Bookman 1988), and *Community Activism and Feminism Politics: Organizing across Race, Class, and Gender* (Naples 1998) plus Carol Hardy-Fanta's *Latina Politics, Latino Politics: Gender, Culture, and Political Participation in Boston*—present case studies from the 1970s into the 1990s that challenge the traditional focus on conventional politics and expand actions defined as politics. They shed light on how working-class, immigrant, and minority women have gained political consciousness and undertaken actions to alter and resist power structures in their communities and workplaces.

In *Women and the Politics of Empowerment*, Morgen and Bookman (1988) contend that the political worlds of working-class women have been obscured by both the popular media and by much of academic literature. The women who are the central subjects of the studies in their anthology

> defy the portrayal of working-class women so common in the popular press as passive, politically disinterested, unskilled, or ineffectual. Instead, they actively seek to change the places where they work, the neighborhoods where they live, and the schools, social services, and health facilities that serve them and their families. . . . Although in recent years middle-class women have made inroads into the arena of electoral politics, most of the substantive reforms benefiting working-class women have emerged from battles waged in extra-electoral terrains—the office, the factory, the hospital, the church, or the streets. And legislative reforms have emerged, for the most part, in response to pressure from grassroots activity.
>
> (Morgen and Bookman 1988, 3, 4)

Based on her study of the political lives of Latina and Latino men in Boston in the 1980s, Carol Hardy-Fanta (1993) concludes that "the story of Latina women in politics in Boston is one that deserves to be told, if only because it challenges myths about their supposed passivity and submissiveness and because it counters their invisibility in mainstream political science" (188).

Empowerment, connectedness, grassroots politics, struggles, community organizing, political consciousness, and "becoming political" are all central concepts in examining working-class and low-income women's, immigrant women's, and women of color's politicization and challenges to general perceptions of their lack of political engagement. They have less access to various resources such as civic skills and recruitment networks and tend not to possess the means to influence public policy such as time and money, both traditionally considered as central to the exercise of political power. They have usually been thought of as being passive participants in the nation's political life. Viewing politics solely in terms of voting behavior, electoral office seeking, political party building, and interest group lobbying obscures the development of a political consciousness among these women. But scholars such as Michelle Kondo (2012), who has interviewed and observed the actions of women in this segment of society, has concluded that "women are significant actors within local-level politics and community organizing. However, a concern amongst political scholars is that community organizing and development work by immigrant women, lower-income women and women of color is often depicted as not real or serious" (113). Rather than viewing poor and working-class women, immigrant women, and racial and ethnic minority women as primarily passive participants in the political process, a view from the lens of community action and workplace struggles as shown in these works suggests a much more varied portrait of women's political activism emanating from distinctive experiences and ways of thinking.

Inclusion of stories of the extent to which and how women who lack traditional resources such as wealth and education to affect public policy have developed a political consciousness and come to practice politics is significant for a comprehensive assessment of women's political participation in the United States. Together, such stories illuminate an often missing side of women's political activism. Researchers who have questioned the dominant perceptions have found it significant both to study the *process* by which women with few resources become politicized and to call attention to their *practice of politics* and assessing the effects of their organizational efforts.

This chapter describes how women in this segment of the economy developed a political consciousness and provides examples from various works that have sought a corrective to the passive depiction of working-class women's relation to the world of politics. Such an inclusion is important in and of itself but is essential when the goal is to link women's quests for political equity to a time of growing economic disparity.

The following story is one such example. It focuses on learning English from a political perspective and not just as an assimilation focus. A Korean immigrant working as a maid in an expensive San Francisco hotel described why she wanted to learn English to community researchers studying the work of the Asian Immigrant Women Advocates: "So we can tell the boss to stop yelling at us. We are not machines but human beings who deserve some respect" (Chun et al. 2013, 926). By challenging employers' assumptions that workers with limited mastery of the English language will not talk back, make complaints, or file written grievances, Asian immigrant women workers were engaging in a step toward disentangling the nexus between language ability and workplace discrimination (Chun et al. 2013).

Learning English is one tool immigrant workers have used in gaining rights and challenging power structures. The Asian Immigrant Women Advocates (AIWA), a community organization founded in Oakland, California, in 1983, highlights this connection for immigrant women. Among other initiatives, AIWA established workplace literacy classes as part of its goal of developing the collective leadership of low-income immigrant women and youth to make positive changes in their living and working conditions.

AIWA was one of the first community organizations created to address the concerns of Asian immigrant women employed in low-paid manufacturing and service jobs in the San Francisco Bay Area (Chun et al. 2013). Through its community transformational organizing strategy, AIWA continues to provide opportunities for immigrant women workers to become active and visible leaders in movements for social and economic justice, regardless of their prior educational level, English-language ability, or position in the social, economic, and political orders. It has developed three major program areas to achieve its goals: education, leadership development, and collective action. It has organized several campaigns in its three decades of community organizing, including the Garment Workers Justice Campaign (1992–1998) in which it publicly shamed Jessica McClintock clothiers for refusing to take responsibility for sweatshop abuses. This campaign resulted in an agreement that included a historic phone hotline for workers to report labor violations and helped raise a national movement around corporate responsibility. The Community Equity Campaign in 1999 was critical in passing the California Underground Economy Bill (AB 633), requiring manufacturers to ensure that subcontractors pay their employees according to AIWA's website. In 2014, AIWA undertook a multicity film tour of its documentary, *Becoming Ourselves*, which tells the story of how immigrant women and youth transformed into leaders who successfully advocated for improved conditions in their workplaces, schools, and communities.

Picture 6.1 Asian Immigrant Women Advocates
Courtesy of Asian Immigrant Women Advocates (www.aiwa.org).

AIIWA is an illustration of women's public resistance seldom captured in surveys of women's political participation. AIWA is a prime example of a community organization that has developed training strategies that empower disadvantaged groups to engage in political activism and participation and to run leadership development programs that address specific obstacles to public activism for women, especially low-income women, immigrant women, and women of color.

The Trusted Advocates is a second contemporary organizational example of the empowerment process. The Trusted Advocates, a White Center, Washington State multiethnic advocacy organization formed in 1999, originally funded by the Annie E. Casey Foundation. It was not founded as a women's advocacy group, but men were noticeably absent from the organization. In interviews with researcher Michelle Kondo (2012), Trusted Advocate women described their concerns and motivations as emerging from their roles as mothers, caretakers, or community leaders and from their cultural backgrounds and experiences based on their ethnic, racial, immigrant, or class status. The Trusted Advocates' overall approach reflected an emphasis on families. Its female members were primarily involved with educational initiatives, although they were called on to become engaged in a broader local political issue in 2005.

Kondo (2012) recounts how the Trusted Advocates found themselves in the middle of a community battle over annexation in that year. In 2004, King County launched an Annexation Initiative and began actively pushing for incorporation or annexation of all urban unincorporated areas. Annexation became the stage for a fight to maintain the historic power structures and traditional social relationships in the area that pitted White homeowners, often elderly, against low-income, often immigrant, groups who were prominent users of local social services. The initial informational process regarding the various annexation issues primarily involved the established White families. Responding to criticism, King County asked neighborhood organizations such as the Trusted Advocates to help increase participation in a second phase of outreach. Beginning in 2005, the Trusted Advocates took part in an effort to challenge the portrayals of lower-income groups as not worthy that had dominated in the first informational sessions.

In a section titled "Characterizing Immigrant Women's Political Work," Kondo (2012) describes the Trusted Advocates response. First, they questioned the assigned political "legitimacy" of the North Highline Unincorporated Area Council (NHUAC) and its Governance Study. The group questioned the methods of the Governance Study planners and attempted to increase the number of immigrants attending public meetings on annexation. They spoke out at public meetings. They also hosted their own community summit, or alternative forum on annexation, with the attendance of approximately three hundred residents of a wide variety of ethnic backgrounds. Some members ran for seats on NHUAC. Four non-White individuals were elected, but as a minority on the council, their concerns were not taken into account. In this instance, the Trusted Advocates met significant political barriers and were not able to overcome the entrenched power structure in this particular struggle. But they continued to express their voices as the annexation process continued.

The activism of AIWA and the Trusted Advocates are examples of empowerment. Empowerment in the context of women's engagement in politics centers on the political work of women who often have had few resources to challenge local power structures, as Bookman and Morgen (1988) conceptualized it in their work on working-class women and grassroots activism. For these women, empowerment

> begins when they change their ideas about the causes of their powerlessness, when they recognize the systemic forces that oppress them, and when they act to change the conditions of their lives. . . . [Empowerment is] a process aimed at consolidating, maintaining, or changing the nature and distribution of power in a particular social context.
>
> (Bookman and Morgen 1988, 4)

Workplace activism and community engagement are central to gaining a say in decisions that most directly affect women's lives and the inequality of their economic position. Community activists have campaigned for social justice and economic security, and against abuse, in diverse settings and often under extremely adverse conditions. Along the way, they have challenged deeply rooted patriarchal and heterosexual traditions, confronted the limits of democracy in the United States, and in some instances, experienced sharp opposition from the power structures of their communities. They have fought against the abuse of women, corporate poisoning of their neighborhoods, and homophobia and racism. They have organized for people-centered economic development, immigrants' rights, educational equity, and adequate wages (Naples 1998, 1).

Sidebar 6.1 Women as Volunteers

In 2009, 30 percent of women volunteered compared to 23 percent of men. Women most frequently volunteered with religious organizations (34 percent of all female volunteers), followed by educational or youth service-related organizations (28 percent).

Becoming Political

How do these women become political activists? What are the main processes by which they become empowered? The process is as intriguing as the effect and the actual practices undertaken. Communities and neighborhoods are places that connect diverse groups across race and class to affect change and empower individuals and groups. Poor and working-class women have been shown to be especially active within their communities in order to protect and improve their own and their families' lives. They do not always view their actions as political. They tend more to describe their work as civic activism. Often, the personal has acted as a starting point for the political as they describe their activism, but it is a distinctive process from that which has been central to feminism awakenings and defined as "the personal is political."

The development of a political consciousness is central to the politicization of women in this domain. Political consciousness involves making a connection between one's personal situation and that of others, and making the connection between people to take action on a common problem (collectivity) is what shifts a personal (private) problem to the larger (public) domain. People must consciously make connections between their present conditions of living and the larger political events—local, national, and international.

Becoming political, developing a political conscience, as Hardy-Fanta (1993) has described it, is a process, for many a contemplative process, of political development in which consciousness emerges slowly from a questioning of the conditions of life and a search for alternatives within themselves and with others. For others, this process is a quick spark that ignites the first recognition that a change is needed. Making the initial connection between one's daily problems and larger political issues is the first step toward participation (Hardy-Fanta (1993, 143). For Latina women in Boston in the 1980s, the subjects of Hardy-Fanta's research on Latino politics, their becoming political developed out of actions begun within their traditional roles.

> Latina women's decisions to protest or take other forms of political action may first be stimulated by concerns for children and by family needs. The internal and collective processes that occur by participating in such activities, however, can themselves be politicizing. Within the context of community and connectedness, community empowerment is personal empowerment.
>
> (Hardy-Fanta 1993, 147)

A major theme that runs through the studies of women and community activism is how often the politicization of the female subjects of these studies emerged from their personal lives as mothers. *Activist mothering*, which breaks down assumed distinctions among caretaking practice, community work, and political activism, is the term Nancy Naples (1992) coined to describe the actions of community workers in New York City and Philadelphia whom she interviewed in the early 1990s. These community workers had been hired in antipoverty programs that the Economic Opportunity Act of 1964 funded.

> The concept of activist mothering captured the complex ways in which these community workers, primarily African-American and Latina, made sense of their work. These workers linked labor, politics, and mothering, three aspects of social life usually analyzed separately, in their narratives. They defined good mothering as comprising all actions, including social activism that addressed the needs of their children and community. Their community work was a logical result of these women's desire to improve the lives of their families and neighbors. They testified before public officials, participated in public protests and demonstrations for improved community services, increased resources and expansion of community control.
>
> (Naples 1992, 446)

A related example of the relationship between women's roles as mothers and the development of a political consciousness and politicization emerges from threats to their children and community. Moms Demand Action, the group described in Chapter 4 as organizing for stronger gun control laws, is such an example. In that instance, it is primarily middle-class women who have become politicized through a process originating from protecting their families.[1] Celene Krauss (1998) provides a similar example, here focusing on working-class women in "Challenging Power: Toxic Waste Protest and the Politicization of White, Working-Class Women" that shows how the environmental justice movement grew out of "the concrete, immediate, everyday experience of struggles around issues of survival" (29). Women have been the primary leaders of community-based movements against toxics (Gottlieb 2005). The threat that toxic waste posed to family health and community survival disrupted their daily lives, centering on home and family and "politicizing women who had never viewed themselves as activists. . . . Propelled into the public arena in defense of their children, they ultimately challenged government, corporations, experts, husbands and their own insecurities as working-class women" (Gottlieb 2005, 130).

> Women came to identify the toxic waste movement as a women's movement composed primarily of mothers. Through their toxic waste protests the women discovered the power they wield as mothers to bring moral issues to the public exposing the contradictions of a society that purports to value motherhood and family, yet creates social politics that undermine these values.
>
> (Gottlieb 2005, 142)

Feminists created and acted on the idea that the "personal is political." They called attention to the boundary between the public and the private that excluded certain issues such as rape, domestic abuse, and contraception. The personal for feminists centered principally on relations within the home and middle-class concerns and women becoming conscious of personal discrimination being rooted in social structures. The development of a political consciousness and activism in the public realm growing out of the initially private concerns of working-class women described in the case studies referenced in this chapter and the engagement in what Naples (1992) has called activist mothering is different and distinctive from the feminist idea that "the personal is political." The everyday struggle to survive and the changing of power relations is the source of the development of a political consciousness for working-class women as opposed to internal relations within families and in a patriarchal society. Community work derived from concern with children's and families' well-being and class positions. One outcome of that development of a political consciousness was often a greater sense of one's own second-class status in a patriarchal society related to feminists' "personal is political" connection but not as a stimulus for public action.

In *Women and the Politics of Empowerment*, Bookman and Morgen (1988) present several case studies that explore how working-class women came to challenge power structures, not always successfully but with some victories, in their workplaces and communities. Chapters in that volume describe the development of a political consciousness among women as factory, hospital, office, and domestic workers as well as street vendors primarily in the 1970s. The female vendors in Washington, DC, that Spalter-Roth (1988) interviewed viewed themselves as autonomous workers, working flexible hours and being able to start their own businesses with little capital. However, the main problem they faced was harassment from male customers and vendors and from the police. According to Spalter-Roth, these women learned to use a variety of survival strategies to deal with the daily problems of harassment. They engaged mainly in individual strategies but also in some cooperative strategies to protect their economic interests and personal safety. All these strategies, Spalter-Roth states, are political "in that they are power struggles over the right to work on public streets unmolested" (281). Strategies included making an effort to appear cool, distant, and unfriendly. Others learned to be aggressive, and others still modified their dress to never appear wearing anything that could be described as provocative. They tried to select a safe vending spot. A final strategy Spalter-Roth described was to give up the right to work on the streets unattended and to seek out male protection. As the city enacted new restrictions on street vending, the female street vendors were particularly challenged to be able to operate free of harassment. They were not particularly successful in challenging the power structure of the city, but they had enough self-awareness that they tried and resisted the local powers.

Hardy-Fanta's (1997) study of Latinas in Boston described how confronting community needs, "crushing problems such as decent housing, AIDS, and a high dropout rate for Latino public school children" (224) molded the activism of these women. In *Community Activism and Feminism Politics*, Nancy Naples (1998) has described women organizing in their communities to "fight against the abuse of women, against corporate poisoning of their neighborhoods, against homophobia and racism, and for people-centered economic development, immigrants' rights, educational equity, and adequate wages" (1).

Text Box 6.1 "How a Local New Jersey Latina Became Mayor, a Rising Political Star"

In 2008, Wilda Diaz, a bank employee, ran for mayor of Perth Amboy, New Jersey. She won, becoming the city's first-ever female mayor and the city's only Latina mayor. Her victory was so unexpected—she had zero previous political experience—that one national magazine dubbed her "The Accidental Politician." Diaz's Puerto Rican heritage led her to take on a leadership role in her community. In 2006, the city's mayor issued a controversial ordinance, putting limits on the city's growing Puerto Rican Day festival. Diaz was so angered by what she saw as abuse of the public trust that she successfully ran against the incumbent mayor. "And years later, a federal judge declared that the ordinance was unconstitutional," she said. "And they caused all that pain and waste of money and it validated what we were saying. You cannot impose an unconstitutional ordinance on anyone because, you know what, if they did it to the Puerto Ricans, what's to stop them from doing it to any other community?" After her election, Diaz cut her own salary in an effort to get Perth Amboy back on track. She hired more police and expanded programs for seniors and children.

She admits that nothing prepared her for what she found when she first assumed office. "I came in when the country was in such a recession, I guess the worst of depression, and then at the same time, we had a debt of the city, which was astronomical—over $250 million in debt," she said. "And then I knew at the time that I was going to make some very difficult, hard decisions that were going to affect the community. And it did. People didn't understand at the time; years later they understand, because we are in a better place than we were in 2008."

Diaz was solidly reelected in 2012, only to face her next test: cleaning up after Hurricane Sandy. "Coming into office, I never knew I would be faced with that kind of hurricane that would change so many lives in our city and cause such damage." Although Perth Amboy prepared for the "Superstorm," some areas were evacuated, and others were left without power for ten days.

Diaz credits her parents, who raised six daughters, for inspiring her interest in public service. She accepts her local renown as a by-product of her job. "A lot of these people I do know, a lot of them are residents and hey, you're the mayor, you become known," she said. "And I think that they see me everywhere in the city. They see me during the tough times and during the good times. Either way they see me, I am always there."

Adapted from Paul A. Reyes, NBC News, November 16, 2015, www.nbcnews.com/news/latino/nj-latina-her-citys-first-woman-mayor-n451586.

The Institute for Women's Policy Research's 2008 report, *The Challenge to Act*, adds a more recent investigation of women's community activism, one that seems very connected to Hardy-Fanta's (1997) conception of Latina politics in Boston in the 1980s. Progressive community groups across the country have developed innovative programs and strategies to bring women together, the authors note, generating female leadership and affecting American democracy. *The Challenge to Act* describes how progressive women activists are reframing American democracy. This study is based on in-depth interviews with 120-plus women activists involved in progressive movements for change in the first decade of the millennium (Caiazza et al. 2008).

The women interviewed lived and worked throughout the country. They came from every major racial and ethnic group. They were elected officials, priests and rabbis, community organizers, and former welfare recipients. They were viewed as

> winning crucial struggles for reform at the grassroots. They secure non-traditional job training for women, reserve units in low-income housing for single mothers, and reform provisions for juvenile justice. They build schools and houses, promote living wages and revamp city planning goals on behalf of those with low incomes. They promote voting rights for the disadvantaged, design leadership programs for immigrants, and create multicultural community centers that support families. They keep landmark sites in African American history from being demolished for development, and they provide services to abused women, prostitutes, the homeless, and drug addicts.
>
> (Caiazza et al. 2008, 2–3)

Reframing American democracy for these progressive activists meant making the nation more inclusive and inspiring a wide range of Americans. This new democracy, they argue, will more energetically seek to include all voices in public life by promoting innovative, promising strategies for building power together and by inspiring activism and engagement. The authors view women's activism historically as beginning within local communities, where women are responsible for pursuing their children's education and developing the networks that support their families (Caiazza et al. 2008), similar to the earlier works of Naples, Bookman and Morgen, and Hardy-Fanta. These progressive activist women's approaches to politics are valued based. These values center on community, family, equality, power, compassion, and balance. Power from this perspective means something that a wider range of people could share.

> Using this frame, participation would look remarkably different. It would be as easy as possible, inviting to the least enfranchised, and well-equipped not only to change outcomes but to set priorities and define basic terms—including such key concepts as our basic rights, the responsibilities of individuals and corporations, and the role of government.
>
> (Caiazza et al. 2008, 31–32)

Doing Politics

"What do you do politically?" Hardy-Fanta (1993) asked her respondents in the Latino community in Boston. So far in this chapter, reference has been made to some political actions working-class and immigrant women have engaged in to challenge local power structures, such as learning English as a step toward empowerment or female street vendors adopting the tactic of dressing carefully to avoid attracting unwanted sexual advances. The emphasis on empowerment described so far, however, has centered on the *process* by which these women, long viewed as passive participants in the political realm, have come to be political players. A more detailed accounting of what has constituted their political engagement has been minimally addressed. What have they done to confront and fight power structures? What comprises their "doing politics"?

Naples (1991) defines "doing politics" as "any struggle to gain control over definitions of 'self' and 'community'; to augment personal and communal empowerment; to create alterative institutions and organizational processes; and to increase the power and resources of their community" (479). Carol Hardy-Fanta (1993) notes that Latina women in Boston were hardly passive when it came to participation in areas of traditional politics, including running for office, promoting voter registration, acting as links between city officials and the community, and providing political education. They also made up the majority of the participants and activists at political events and protest marches. They focused on participation rather than on power (as opposed to Latino men) and on connecting people to other people to achieve change. "Making connections" was how Boston's Latinas did politics. They connected personal problems with public issues. Making connections developed a political awareness that resulted in a more participatory community in which these Latinas' distinctive voices could be heard in the political process.

The Daughters of Mother Jones, also known as the Family Auxiliary, participated in picketing, protested stockholders' meetings, blocked roads, took over buildings, and were sent to jail. This organization consisted of Appalachian wives, widows, mothers, daughters, and sisters of coal miners formed during the coal mining strike against the Pittston Coal Company in 1989–1990. As Virginia Seitz (1998, 213) recounts,

> In this historically specific moment and setting, these mostly white, working-class women constructed an understanding of class struggle from their particular standpoint as Appalachian women. Through consciousness-raising and public and private expressions of resistance, they challenged the coal company, the state, and eventually, working-class men.

A community research conversation-based strategy composed Susan Parkinson Stern's effort to engage parents in her daughter's school to challenge the administration's notions that Black children are inferior learners and cannot be pushed to higher levels of achievement, as described in Nancy Naples's *Community Activism and Feminist Politics* (1998). She took her own individual struggle to better the educational experience of her daughter, which was met negatively by teachers and the school principal, to the community level by first raising questions at PTA meetings and then challenging other parents to converse about their concerns. Such a participatory

Sidebar 6.2 Mother Jones: "Convictions and a Voice"

"I have never had a vote, and I have raised hell all over this country! You don't need a vote to raise hell! You need convictions and a voice!"
—Mother Jones

research project, which was combined with Stern's ability to incorporate social science research with the parents' conversations, raised the parents' ability to create knowledge-based community struggles against oppressive conditions. "The parents-in-conversation began, somewhat self-consciously, to work on developing a theory about the mechanisms responsible for reproducing inequality in [their] schools" (Naples 1998, 124). The parents primarily involved in the project were women. Eventually, they succeeded in having the principal removed and the curriculum revamped. These are two examples of the practice of community politics.

Organizations have also formed at the national level to advocate for vulnerable women workers and for social justice more broadly. Domestic workers are among the most vulnerable women workers. There are 2.5 million domestic workers in the United States, the vast majority of whom are women (95 percent) and nearly half are immigrants (46 percent) who work as nannies, caregivers, and house cleaners.

Many of the laws and policies that have been enacted to regulate wages and hours, health and safety, and the right to organize simply do not apply to domestic workers. Domestic workers are excluded from many of the basic protections of the Fair Labor Standards Act of 1938 guaranteed to most other workers in the United States such as a minimum wage, overtime, and sick and vacation pay. They are excluded from the protections of the Occupational Health and Safety Act. They primarily work inside other people's homes, not in offices. Thus, they are viewed as being invisible. The National Domestic Workers Alliance advocates on their behalf.

In 2013, President Obama announced new rules extending the Fair Labor Standards Act to include the eight hundred thousand to two million home health workers under the federal government's wage and hour protection. Implementation of these rules, however, has been stalled due to court challenges. Campaigns in six states—New York, Hawaii, California, Massachusetts, Oregon, and Connecticut—have resulted in the adoption of the Domestic Workers' Bill of Rights, which allows the full spectrum of domestic workers to benefit from the same gains as home health workers in the Obama rules.

The National Domestic Workers Alliance (NDWA), founded in 2007, is a group of workers who advocate for their own rights. It has grown from a single chapter in New York City to nationwide organizations with campaigns for worker rights in nineteen cities and eleven states. It undertakes campaigns at the local, state, and national levels. NDWA has created from-the-ground-up reports and analyses on the working conditions domestic workers face in the United States. It uses these data to confront business and state agencies. NDWA has used a Caring Across Generations campaign. The campaign seeks to ensure that seniors receive the health care they need from workers who receive a living wage. Launched in 2011, the coalition's broad range of member groups includes organized labor, seniors, faith-based groups, women's rights organizations, and antipoverty groups. The presentation of real people's stories is at the center of this campaign to create public sympathy and understanding. NDWA also works with employer groups that are willing to take a stand on behalf of their employees' right to fair pay and labor conditions. For example, NDWA works with Hand in Hand, a national association of caregiver employers who were willing to take a stand on behalf of their employees' right to fair pay and labor conditions (Dean 2013).

The California campaign for a domestic workers bill of rights, for example, involved a coalition of organizations focusing on different issues. Groups documented stories and surveyed the needs of domestic workers, conducted leadership training sessions and storytelling workshops, and prepared domestic workers to speak to the media and legislators. They organized rallies to allow people to show their support, with domestic workers marching alongside their employers and children holding signs saying "Support My Nanny" or "Support My Mother" (Bornstein 2015).

Picture 6.2 Atlanta, Georgia, Domestic Workers United Rally
www.flickr.com/photos/domesticworkers/
Courtesy of Domestic Workers United (www.domesticworkersunited.org).

A second national group of women, Nuns on the Bus, is a Catholic social justice lobbying group that emerged on the political scene in 2012 when it toured nine battleground states in a bus in that year's presidential election promoting equality, attracting much notoriety. They would stop at homeless shelters, food pantries, schools, and healing centers run by nuns to highlight their work with the nation's poor and disenfranchised. Their leader, Sister Simone Campbell, addressed the 2012 Democratic National Convention.

Nuns on the Bus is a project of NETWORK, whose goal calls for economic and social transformation. A group of forty-seven U.S. Catholic sisters founded NETWORK in 1971. The NETWORK now consists of eighty thousand members and supporters. The nuns continue to make bus tours across the country, espousing social justice issues. Their focus in 2012 was on Republican budget proposals that the group believed hurt the poor and the vulnerable. Since then, they have undertaken voter registration drives, promoted immigration reform, and campaigned against outside money in elections. The theme of their 2015 tour was "Bridge the Divide, Transform Politics."

The Catholic Church hierarchy rebuked the nuns, among other things, accusing them of being outspoken on social issues but silent on other issues the church considered crucial, most notably, abortion and gay marriage. The nuns lobbying on behalf of President Obama's health-care reform particularly angered Catholic bishops around the country. The Vatican then initiated an investigation into every community of American nuns. In 2012,

Picture 6.3 Nuns on the Bus
Courtesy of NETWORK, A National Catholic Justice Organization (www.networklobby.org).

it accused the Leadership Conference of Women Religious, the country's largest group of Catholic nuns, of sponsoring "certain radical feminist themes incompatible with the Catholic faith." But the probe ended in 2014 with a report full of praise and without any disciplinary measures or new controls (Allen 2014).

Symbolic Actions

The empowerment activism chronicled so far in this chapter has focused principally on economic concerns. Empowerment activism also involves gaining freedom from social control over people's lives, particularly control over their bodies. In this realm, groups of women have organized to challenge this social control. Activism in this realm ranges from individual challenges and organized campaigns to symbolic actions. Symbolic actions take the form of individual or mass groups engaging in public spectacles to call attention to a particular problem and awareness of it as a societal problem. It may not have as its goal the passage of a piece of particular legislation but a larger changing of political power. Two long-standing examples of such symbolic actions centering on violence against women are The Brides' March and Take Back the Night marches.

The Gladys Ricart and Victims of Domestic Violence Memorial Walk/Brides' March is an annual event that began in New York City in 2001 to remember Gladys Ricart, a Dominican woman from Washington Heights who was murdered in New Jersey on September 26, 1999, by her abusive former boyfriend on the day she was to wed her fiancé. The first march took place on September 26, 2001, the second anniversary of Gladys's murder. Josie Ashton, a young Dominican woman from Florida, originated the idea for the march. She was moved by the murder and outraged at the media and community's insensitive response to Gladys Ricart's killing. Ashton resigned from her job and spent more than three months walking in a wedding gown through several states, down the East Coast, and ending in her home state of Florida in order to draw attention to the horrors of domestic violence.

Several organizations in New York City, including the Dominican Women's Development Center, the Violence Intervention Program, the Northern Manhattan Improvement Corporation, the Dominican Women's Caucus, and the National Latino Alliance for the Elimination of Domestic Violence, helped Ashton organize the first march, which served as a sendoff for her 1,600-mile journey. They organized supporters in the New York metropolitan area, including Gladys's family and friends, to join Ashton on the first leg of her walk from Gladys's home in New Jersey to the church in Queens where Gladys was to marry on September 26, 1999. The marches continue. To date, thousands of women, men, and youth, among them members of the Ricart family and other families affected by domestic violence, elected officials, civic leaders, clergy, students, and scores of domestic violence advocates and survivors, gather every September 26 to memorialize Gladys Ricart and other victims who have lost their lives to domestic violence and to raise awareness of domestic violence.

Take Back the Night, a second symbolic action, started in the 1970s as a college and community collaboration to bring awareness and draw attention to sexual assault and sexual violence. The first documented Take Back the Night event in the United States took place in October 1975 in Philadelphia, Pennsylvania. Citizens rallied together after a stranger stabbed to death a young microbiologist, Susan Alexander Speeth, as she was walking alone a block away from her home. For over thirty-five years in the United States, Take Back the Night has focused on eliminating sexual violence in all forms, and colleges, universities, women's centers, and rape crisis centers have sponsored events all over the country. Take Back the Night has become internationally known as a way to take a stand against sexual violence and to speak out against these horrible crimes. Hundreds of events are held in more than thirty countries annually.

Its symbolic actions to call attention to rape and other forms of sexual and domestic violence include marches, rallies, and vigils. Events typically consist of a rally followed by

Picture 6.4 Take Back the Night Rally, University of Oregon, 2016

The growing group, Mujeres, gather together holding the Take Back the Night sign. They painted their faces with half-skulls to represent those who have and have not survived experiences with sexual assault. The ASUO Women's Center and Sexual Assault Support Services of Lane County present Take Back the Night in Eugene, Oregon, on Thursday, April 28, 2016.

Courtesy of Amanda Shigeoka/Emerald.

a march and often a speak-out or candlelight vigil on violence against women. College campuses are popular venues for these actions. Katie Huskey, a campus victim advocate at the University of Wisconsin–Oshkosh, describes her university's participation: "We gather one night a year to use our voices. Our voices are never silenced" (Dickmann 2015).

In 2001, a group of women who had participated in the earliest Take Back the Night marches came together to form the Take Back the Night Foundation in support of the events throughout the United States and the world. Many of the early marches were deliberately women-only events to symbolize women's individual walk through darkness and to demonstrate that women united can resist fear and violence. Events now encourage men to participate. The foundation lists that more than six hundred events have taken place since the founding of the movement.

The Black Lives Matter movement is a prominent contemporary social challenge involving both women in leadership positions and a refocusing of attention to how repressive governmental actions affect women as well as men. In the summer of 2013, three female community organizers—Alicia Garza, a domestic worker rights organizer in Oakland, California, Patrisse Cullors, an antipolice violence organizer in Los Angeles, California, and Opal Tometi, an immigration rights organizer in Phoenix, Arizona—founded the social justice movement Black Lives Matter in cyberspace as a sociopolitical media forum, with the creation of the hashtag #BlackLivesMatter (Ruffin 2017). The acquittal of George Zimmerman in Florida in the shooting death of African American teen Trayvon Martin served as the catalyst for their social media initiative and the first protests of this movement. "We gave tongue to something that we all knew was happening," Tometi has stated. "We were courageous enough to call it what it was. But more than that, to offer an alternative. An aspirational message: Black lives matter" (Meyerson 2016).

Police shootings of other Black men under questionable situations that followed further stimulated Black Lives Matter protests and demonstrations. Black Lives Matter expanded into a national network of more than thirty local chapters and a global rights movement between 2014 and 2016. It works as a primarily decentralized network with no formal hierarchy. It has engaged in a diversity of tactics to raise awareness of its issues and to affect public policy: street demonstrations including die-ins, freedom rides, college campus protests, disruptions of presidential campaign events and challenges to the candidates, and demonstrations at malls and department stores across the country on Black Friday 2014 to disrupt holiday shopping. It has rallied to call on Black men to join the fight to stop violence against transgender women in the country and organized rallies across the country to spotlight the murders of Black transgender women. Black Lives Matter's website describes itself as

> a unique contribution that goes beyond extrajudicial killings of black people by police and vigilantes . . . [and] affirms the lives of black queer and trans folks, disabled folks, black undocumented folks, folks with records, women and all black lives along the gender spectrum.

Queer and transgender women have been prominent in the Black Lives Matter movement nationwide.

Alex Altman (2015), in his profile of the movement as a contender for *Time* magazine's 2015 Person of the Year award, described it as growing in 2015

> from a protest cry into a genuine political force. Groups that embraced the slogan hounded police chiefs from their jobs, won landmark prosecutions and turned college campuses into cauldrons of social ferment. At the University of Missouri, a hunger strike incited a boycott by the football team that drove the president out of office.

Picture 6.5 Black Lives Matter Rally
Protesters march against police shootings during a rally in Washington, DC, on December 13, 2014.
Photo by Rena Schild/Shutterstock.com.

The movement's challenging "unapologetic message," in the words of Black Lives Matter leader Brittany Packnett (2016), executive director of Teach for America, is that "until our laws and their enforcers treat black Americans equitably and with full respect, until police officers stop killing us, we will not continue business as usual."

Challenged to develop specific policy proposals, the Black Lives Matter movement created Campaign Zero with a ten-point plan for police reform. Its set of proposals includes recommendations at the local, state, and federal levels. The ten points centered on ending broken windows policing, community oversight, limiting the use of force, independent investigation and prosecution, community representation, filming the police, training, ending for-profit policing, demilitarization, and fair police union contracts. In addition, responding to the outcry about police brutality, in 2014, President Obama created the White House Task Force on 21st Century Policing. It issued its final report in May 2015.[2] Building trust between law enforcement officials and community members was at the core of the committee's charge.

Further, the female initiators of the Black Lives Matter movement, along with other female activists, created a feminist presence within the movement and demanded that more attention be given to Black women's experiences with police. To this end, the African American Policy Forum (AAPF) launched the #SayHerName campaign in 2015. Its website describes the campaign "as a resource to help ensure that Black women's stories are integrated into demands for justice, policy responses to police violence, and media representations of victims and survivors of police brutality."[3] TheSayHer Name campaign emphasizes gender-specific ways in which police brutality and anti-Black violence disproportionally affect Black women, especially Black lesbian and Black transgendered women.

Little systematic data on police brutality toward Black women have been collected.[4] Its 2015 report, *Say Her Name: Resisting Police Brutality Against Black Women*, calls attention to this problem, beginning a documentation and analysis of Black women's experiences of police

Sidebar 6.3 Say Her Name

#SayHerName: Black women are outnumbered by White women 5:1 in the United States yet are killed by police in nearly the same numbers.

violence. The report presents numerous stories to illustrate the ways in which gender, race, and sexuality operate to inform police abuse of Black women.[5] It particularly describes how the criminalization of poverty intersects with race and sex in police encounters.

Conclusion

The examples presented in this chapter show how women's grassroots organizing redefines politics. The term *grassroots politics* is often used to reflect a more community-focused type of politics that involves greater opportunities for self-government and self-direction and that increases participation by connecting private problems to public issues. Political activism emerges from more than self-interest and has been the basis of much scholarship on political participation. Making connections and networks suggest that women do not particularly enter the public arena solely as individuals. Networks and community associations develop from women's responses to issues that confront them, not as isolated individuals but as members of households, and more importantly, as members of the communities in which those households are embedded (Ackelsberg 1988). Political action viewed from this lens challenges limited constructions of feminism and political action that derive solely from White, middle-class women's experiences.

Naples's and Bookman and Morgen's anthologies and Hardy-Fanta's Latina study have provided the most comprehensive and theoretical studies about the empowerment of working-class women and immigrant women. Data for these studies were collected from the 1970s to the 1990s and centered on women challenging local economic and political power structures. The various authors principally employed ethnographic methods involved in case studies, which were qualitative in nature. The authors were concerned with describing the processes by which these women became political and understanding the constraints on the development of a political self as well as their collective efforts to change power structures. They are the main investigations that have put working-class White, minority, and immigrant women at the center of a political analysis, providing for a more comprehensive picture of the political life of American women. This chapter has also presented several more recent examples of local and national campaigns that women at the bottom of the economic and social structure have undertaken to improve their economic and social positions and to influence the democratic system more generally.

But incorporating activism as practiced by women other than predominantly White middle-class and elite women has not found a more central place in scholarly studies of women's political participation. The selection of cases for study limits the extent to which one can generalize quantitatively about the extent and effectiveness of working-class and minority women's activism. They call attention to the deficiencies of mainstream political studies of women's political activism. They challenge us to use their case studies as launching pads, so to speak, and to build on them for a more systematic study of their significance in political opposition struggles. They invite some intriguing queries of a more holistic and systematic nature regarding the process of becoming political and doing politics on the part of American women.

Notes

1. On Mothers Day 2000, a Million Moms March was held in Washington, DC, in response to earlier school shootings. Although it received much attention, it was not able to move the policy process in the direction of more gun control.
2. The final report can be found at www.cops.usdoj.gov/pdf/taskforce/taskforce_finalreport.pdf.
3. www.aapf.org/sayhername.
4. One exception is an Associated Press 2015 report after a yearlong study that "Hundreds of Officers Lose Licenses over Sex Misconduct," http://bigstory.ap.org/article/fd1d4d05e561462a85abe 50e7eaed4ec/ap-hundreds-officers-lose-licenses-over-sex-misconduct.
5. Crenshaw, Kimberle and Andrea Ritchie. 2015. *Say Her Name: Resisting Police Brutality against Black Women*. New York, NY: African American Policy Forum and Center for Intersectionality and Social Policy Studies. http://static1.squarespace.com/static/53f20d90e4b0b80451158d8c/t/ 560c068ee4b0af26f72741df/1443628686535/AAPF_SMN_Brief_Full_singles-min.pdf.

Further Readings and Other Resources

DVD: *Mother Jones: America's Most Dangerous Woman*. www.motherjonesmuseum.org/#.
Network. "Nuns on the Bus 2016." https://networklobby.org/bus2016/.
Lecture: Michel, Sonya. "Doing Well by Doing Good: American Women's Long Tradition of Reform." Woodrow Wilson International Center for Scholars. https://www.youtube.com/watch?v=FuF9rhWetMI.
Piven, Frances Fox and Richard Cloward. 1979. *Poor People's Movements: How They Succeed, How They Fail*. New York, NY: Vintage Books.
Video: "Standing Up for Change: Women and the Civil Rights Movement." www.youtube.com/wat ch?v=BlyI11DUAQw&list=UUxTj7_3aVDR8RbeTGoyLTdQ.
Voices. Votes. Leadership. The Status of Black Women in American Politics. A report by the Center for American Women and Politics for Higher Heights Leadership Fund. 2015. www.cawp.rutgers. edu/sites/default/files/resources/hh2015.pdf.

References

Ackelsberg, Martha A. 1988. "Communities, Resistance, and Women's Activism: Some Implications for a Democratic Polity." In *Community Activism and Feminism Politics: Organizing Across Race, Class and Gender*, eds. Ann Bookman and Sandra Morgen. New York, NY: Routledge, 297–313.
Allen, John L. 1014. "Vatican Probe Ends with an Olive Branch for American Nuns." *CRUX*, December 16. www.cruxnow.com/church/2014/12/16/vatican-probe-ends-with-an-olive-branch-for-american-nuns/.
Altman, Alex. 2015. "Black Lives Matter: A New Civil Rights Movement Is Turning a Protest Cry into a Political Force." *Time*. http://time.com/time-person-of-the-year-2015-runner-up-black-lives-matter/.
Bookman, Ann and Sandra Morgen. 1988. *Women and the Politics of Empowerment*. Philadelphia, PA: Temple University Press.
Bornstein, David. 2015. "A Living Wage for Caregivers." *The New York Times*, July 10. http:// opinionator.blogs.nytimes.com/2015/07/10/organizing-for-the-right-to-care/?_r=0.
Caiazza, Amy, Cynthia Hess, Casey Clevenger, and Angela Carlberg. 2008. *The Challenge to Act: How Progressive Women Activists Reframe American Democracy*. Washington, DC: Institute for Women's Policy Research.
Chun, Jennifer Jihye, George Lipsitz, and Young Shin. 2013. "Intersectionality as a Social Movement Strategy: Asian Immigrant Women Advocates." *Signs*, 38, 4: 917–940.
Cohen, Cathy, Kathleen Thomas, and Joan Tronto. 1997. *Women Transforming Politics*. New York, NY: New York University Press.
Dean, Amy. 2013. "How Domestic Workers Won Their Rights: Five Big Lessons." *YES! Magazine*, October 9. www.yesmagazine.org/people-power/how-domestic-workers-won-their-rights-five-big-lessons.

Dickmann, Noell. 2015. "Take Back the Night Is Wednesday." *Oshkosh Northwestern Media*, October 5. www.thenorthwestern.com/story/news/local/2015/10/05/25th-annual-take-back-night/73202420/.

Gottlieb, Robert. 2005. *Forcing the Spring: The Transformation of the American Environmental Movement*. Washington, DC: Island Press.

Hardy-Fanta, Carol. 1993. *Latina Politics, Latino Politics: Gender, Culture, and Political Participation in Boston*. Philadelphia, PA: Temple University Press.

Hardy-Fanta, Carol. 1997. "Latina Women and Political Consciousness: La Chispa Que Prenda." In *Women Transforming Politics: An Alternative Reader*, eds. Cathy Cohen, Kathleen Jones, and Joan Tronto. New York, NY: New York University Press.

Kondo, Michelle. 2012. "Influences of Gender and Race on Immigrant Political Participation: The Case of the Trusted Advocates." *International Migration*, 50, 5: 113–129.

Krauss, Celene. 1998. "Challenging Power: Toxic Waste Protests and the Politicization of White, Working-Class Women." In *Community Activism and Feminism Politics: Organizing across Race, Class and Gender*, ed. Nancy Naples. New York, NY: Routledge, 129–150.

Meyerson, Collier. 2016. "The Founders of Black Lives Matter: 'We Gave Tongue to Something That We All Knew Was Happening.'" *Glamour*, November 1. www.glamour.com/story/women-of-the-year-black-lives-matter-founders.

Naples, Nancy. 1991. "'Just What Needed to Be Done': The Political Practice of Women Community Workers in Low-Income Neighborhoods." *Gender & Society*, 5, 4: 478–494.

Naples, Nancy. 1992. "Activist Mothering: Cross-Generational Continuity in the Community Work of Women from Low-Income Urban Neighborhoods." *Gender and Society*, 6, 3: 441–463.

Naples, Nancy. 1998. *Community Activism and Feminism Politics: Organizing across Race, Class and Gender*. New York, NY: Routledge.

Packnett, Brittany. 2016. "Black Lives Matter Isn't Just a Hashtag Anymore." *Politico Magazine*, September/October. www.politico.com/magazine/story/2016/09/black-lives-matter-movement-deray-hacknett-politics-protest-214226.

Ruffin, Herbert. 2017. "Black Lives Matter: The Growth of a New Social Justice Movement." www.blackpast.org/perspectives/black-lives-matter-growth-new-social-justice-movement#sthash.oGleYooQ.dpuf.

Seitz, Virginia Rinaldo. 1998. "Class, Gender, and Resistance in the Appalachian Coalfields." In *Community Activism and Feminism Politics: Organizing across Race, Class and Gender*, ed. Nancy Naples. New York, NY: Routledge, 213–236.

Spalter-Roth, Roberta M. 1988. "Vending on the Streets: City Policy, Gentrification, and Public Patriarchy." In *Women and the Politics of Empowerment*, eds. Ann Bookman and Sandra Morgen. Philadelphia, PA: Temple University Press, 272–294.

7 Women's NGOs

Advocating for Global Women's Rights

In 1995, First Lady Hillary Clinton led the U.S. delegation to the Fourth World Conference on Women in Beijing, China. Speaking at the conference, she declared that "women's rights are human rights and human rights are women's rights." Her statement electrified the global women's rights movement that had struggled for decades to center women's rights in human rights campaigns. According to historian Karen Garner (2012), "Her speech and repetition of the slogan by feminists working inside and outside governments transformed the 'universe of political discourse' so that . . . new (feminist) issues [found] agenda access in the United States and throughout the UN system" (131).

Hillary Clinton's pronouncement was striking because of the historical struggle to move women's rights from the private sphere, such as violence against women in the home, into the public realm as part of the broader human rights movement. Charlotte Bunch, founder of the Center for Women's Global Leadership at Rutgers University, was instrumental in placing violence against women on the international human rights agenda. Her 1990 *Human Rights Quarterly* essay is credited with connecting women's rights to human rights within the academic community and advancing that vision in the public realm: "Despite a clear record of deaths and demonstrable abuse, women's rights are not commonly classified as human rights" (486). By the 21st century, embedding women's rights into the context of human rights had made great strides. For instance, eliminating violence against women is now widely seen as a question of fundamental human rights (Htun and Weldon 2012).

Americans have long been active in international efforts to advance the status of women. For example, Carrie Chapman Catt, president of the National American Woman Suffrage Association in the years just prior to victory in 1920, was also founder and president of the International Woman Suffrage Alliance, which campaigned for women's right to vote. As head of the U.S. United Nations delegation, Eleanor Roosevelt fought for the inclusion of sex in the Universal Declaration of Human Rights adopted by the United Nations in 1948. American feminists were prominent (some would say dominant) in the various UN conferences on women in the decades of the latter part of the 20th century. Leading U.S. feminists such as Gloria Steinem, Bella Abzug, and Robin Morgan founded organizations aimed at advancing the status of women globally.

At the same time, scholars and activists have questioned the involvement of the U.S. women's rights movement in transnational activism. They have suggested that the United States lagged in engagement in global women's rights activism. Margaret Snyder (2006), for example, has written, "In North America, the U.S. women's movement has long hesitated to identify with and support the global women's movement" (47). Participants at the 2010 twenty-year anniversary symposium of Rutgers University's Center for Global Women's Leadership advocated "engaging women in the U.S. to participate more actively in the global women's movement, given the influence of the U.S. in the world"[1] (Margi and Real 2010; see also Boles 2006; Gelb 2006.)

But several contemporary U.S. women's organizations have followed in the footsteps of Carrie Chapman Catt and Eleanor Roosevelt and are working to affect women's rights globally through multiple strategies and goals. Their activism is a distinctive aspect of U.S. women's political participation in general and a significant component of nongovernmental organizations' (NGOs) efforts to affect governmental policy. The United States has a vibrant civil society and is known as a nation of joiners (e.g., DeTocqueville 1969; Skocpol 1999;). In the political realm, interest groups are prolific and major players in affecting economic, social, and ideological values. This country also has substantial resources to contribute to human rights causes and a long history of its citizens engaging in and leading international human rights efforts. Its prominence, influence, and power on the world stage means that the engagement of women's NGOs whose aim is to advance women's rights matters. This chapter surveys the contemporary community of such U.S. women's NGOs, whose incentive for formation has been improving the lives of women in developing countries and the promotion of women's rights globally. Such activity is an important lens on women's political participation aimed at affecting women's status and rights and a significant link to questions of economic and social inequality. These groups engage in advocacy, service provision, training, and research in a wide variety of equal rights domains.

U.S. Global Women's Rights NGOs

This chapter describes the structure and activism of thirty-three contemporary global women's rights NGOs with U.S. leadership. The work of these groups provides a lens through which to view this collective action aspect of American women's political participation.[2] Global Rights for Women, an organization founded in 2014 in Minneapolis, Minnesota, is a good example of such groups. According to its mission statement, it "collaborates with partners around the world to promote women's human rights to *equality and freedom from violence* through legal reform and systems change" (emphasis added). The mission statements of these groups highlight the key words *empowerment, rights*, and *equality* within a global or regional context. They work "to prevent and end violence against women and children around the world" (Futures Without Violence); "to improve women's reproductive autonomy, choices, and health worldwide" (IBIS Reproductive); and "to provide small grants for grassroots projects that *empower women* and girls in developing countries" (Virginia Gildersleeve International Fund); these statements are just a few examples that illustrate their goals. Text Box 7.1 provides a list of key phrases from their mission statements that capture these organizations' essence as global women rights organizations, providing a comprehensive list of phrases that exemplify these organizations' global rights missions.

Text Box 7.1 Organizations and Their Mission Statements

The Alliance for International Women's Rights mission is to *support women's rights efforts* in developing countries.

Americans for UNFPA (Friends of UNFPA) mobilizes funds and actions for UNFPA's lifesaving work.

Captive Daughters has chosen to focus its efforts on combating sex trafficking, particularly as it affects women and girl children, and on *raising the issue of sex trafficking higher on national and international human rights agendas*.

The Centre for Development and Population Activities equips and mobilizes women and girls to *achieve gender equality.*

The Center for Health and Gender Equity's (Change) mission is to ensure that U.S. foreign policies and programs *promote women's and girls' sexual and reproductive health within a human rights framework.*

The Center for Reproductive Rights has used the law to advance reproductive freedom as a *fundamental human right* that all governments are legally obligated to protect, respect, and fulfill.

The Center for Women Policy Studies promotes *women's human rights* through enlightened public policy.

The Coalition Against Trafficking in Women's goal is to end human trafficking in our lifetime.

Equality Now seeks to achieve legal and systemic change that addresses violence and *discrimination against women and girls around the world.*

Futures Without Violence works to prevent and end violence against women and children around the world.

Gender Action's mission is to promote women's rights and gender equality and to ensure women and men equally participate in and benefit from International Financial Institution (IFI) investments in developing countries.

The Global Fund for Women is *advancing the rights of women and girls* worldwide by increasing the resources for and investing in women-led organizations and women's collective leadership for change.

The Global Justice Center works for peace, justice, and security by enforcing international laws that *protect human rights and promote gender equality.*

Global Rights for Women collaborates with partners around the world *to promote women's human rights to equality and to freedom from violence through legal reform and systems change.*

ICAN (International Civil Society Action Network) aims to *strengthen* civil society and *women's participation and influence* in conflict prevention, social justice, coexistence, and peace-building efforts.

The Institute for Inclusive Security works *to increase the participation of all stakeholders—particularly women—in preventing, resolving, and rebuilding after deadly conflicts.*

The International Center for Research on Women *empowers women, advances gender equality*, and *fights poverty* in the developing world in order to reduce global poverty by investing in the lives of women and girls.

The International Women's Democracy Center works to *strengthen women's global leadership* through training, education, networking, and research in all facets of democracy, with a particular focus on increasing the participation of women in policy, politics, and decision making within their own governments.

The International Women's Health Coalition promotes and protects the *sexual and reproductive rights* and health of women and young people, particularly adolescent girls, in Africa, Asia, Latin America, and the Middle East.

Ipas works around the world to increase women's ability to *exercise their sexual and reproductive rights*, especially the right to safe abortion.

The International Alliance for Women connects leading women's organizations worldwide to leverage their reach and resources, creating a global community of *economically empowered women.*

The U.S. National Committee for UN Women supports the mission of UN Women and *social, political, and economic equality* for women and girls around the world.

The Urgent Action Fund for Women's Human Rights supports women's rights defenders striving to create cultures of *justice, equality*, and *peace*.

The Virginia Gildersleeve International Fund provides small grants for grassroots projects that *empower women* and girls in developing countries.

Vital Voices identifies, invests in, and brings visibility to extraordinary women around the world by *unleashing their leadership potential* to transform lives and accelerate peace and prosperity in their communities.

Women for Women International helps women go from victim to survivor to *active citizen*.

Women Thrive Worldwide advocates for change at the U.S. and global levels so that women and men can *share equally* in the enjoyment of opportunities, economic prosperity, voice, and freedom from fear and violence. Their work is grounded in the realities of *women living in poverty*.

The Women's Environment and Development Organization *ensures that women's rights; social, economic and environmental justice*; and sustainable development principles, as well as the linkages among them, are at the heart of global and national policies, programs, and practices.

Women's Campaign International, in partnership with local communities, focuses on areas that are fundamental to *women's equality* through building skills that help women become effective agents of change.

The Women's Funding Network accelerates *women's leadership* and invests in solving critical social issues—from poverty to global security—by bringing together the financial power, influence, and voices of women's funds.

The Women's Global Education Project empowers young people in rural areas of sub-Saharan Africa, particularly women and girls, through education to build better lives and foster equitable communities.

Whereas these groups share a similar overarching purpose of affecting women's rights and status transnationally, the focus and action repertoires they have created to achieve their missions vary. They advocate, train, educate, and provide services. Partners for Women's Equality, for instance, focuses its work on programs aimed at directly improving marginalized women's lives, particularly indigenous women such as Mayan women in Guatemala, within a women's rights framework. On the other hand, Gender Action's focus is on international financial institutions such as the World Bank and the International Monetary Fund, prodding them to promote gender justice and women's rights in their financial programs. The targets of their activism vary, including affecting U.S. foreign policy, working with particular developing countries (note Partners for Women's Equality), and advocating for global changes in women's rights.

Organizational Structures

The organizational nature of civic engagement in the United States used to consist primarily of large membership associations often organized across class lines. In contemporary society, an explosion of advocacy groups has reoriented American civic life. As political scientist Theda Skocpol (1999) has described it, "Privileged and well-educated citizens have led the way in reshaping the associational universe, withdrawing from cross-class

Table 7.1 Nongovernmental Organization Characteristics

Organization	Year Founded	Headquarters	Assets (USD)	Staff
Alliance for International Women's Rights	2005	East Chatham, New York	24,453	0
Americans for UNFPA (Friends of UNFPA)*	1998	New York	3,445,838	12
Captive Daughters*	1997	Los Angeles	1,432	N/A
Center for Development and Population Activities (CEDPA)	1975	Washington, DC	4,120,900	16
Center for Health and Gender Equity (CHANGE)	1994	Washington, DC	1,480,652	16
Center for Reproductive Rights	1992	New York	33,638,421	125
Center for Women Policy Studies	1972	Washington, DC	187,723	2
Coalition Against Trafficking in Women*	1988	New York	480,081	8
Equality Now*	1992	New York	4,808,985	16
Futures Without Violence	1993	San Francisco	37,250,255	43
Gender Action	2002	Washington, DC	35,658	N/A
Global Fund for Women	1987	San Francisco	21,300,951	72
Global Justice Center	2007	New York	636,462	8
Global Rights for Women	2014	Minneapolis, Minnesota	164,871	3
Global Women's Education Project	2003	Chicago	79,176	4
IBIS Reproductive Health	2002	Cambridge, Massachusetts	2,035,166	20
ICAN (International Civil Society Action Network)	2006	Washington, DC	1,281,254	5
Institute for Inclusive Security**	NA	Washington, DC		29
International Center for Research on Women	1976	Washington, DC	7,240,664	62
International Women's Health Coalition*	1994	New York	5,714,851	26
International Women's Democracy Center*	1995	Washington, DC	45,503	0
IPAS (International Pregnancy Advisory Services)	1973	Chapel Hill, North Carolina	116,387,275	171
The International Alliance for Women*	1980	Washington, DC	88,796	
Urgent Action Fund for Women's Human Rights	1997	San Francisco	1,427,632	10
US National Committee for UN Women	1983	Arlington, Virginia	235,555	1
Virginia Gildersleeve International Fund	1969	New York	16,463,338	7
Vital Voices*	1997	Washington, DC	7,425,969	67
Women for Women International	1993	Washington, DC	15,639,088	112
Women Thrive Worldwide	1998	Washington, DC	709,700	17
Women's Campaign International	1998	Philadelphia, Pennsylvania	419,871	7
Women's Environment and Development Organization (WEDO)	1990	New York	36,943	7
Women's Funding Network	1985	San Francisco	1,924,829	13
Women's Global Education Project	2003	Chicago	79,176	4

* = United Nations Economic and Social Council advisory status

** Institute for Inclusive Security is a program of Hunt Alternatives and does not list a separate set of assets.

membership federations and redirecting leadership and support to staff-led organizations" (462). Contemporary civic life, according to Skocpol, is better characterized as advocacy groups without members, with thousands of new advocacy groups having set up national headquarters made up of professional staff.

Most of these women's rights NGOs fit this new model of civic life. Table 7.1 lists all the organizations and their major structural features. The majority are headquartered in the New York or Washington, DC, areas, with a smaller contingent located elsewhere around the country. Only the U.S. National Committee for UN Women is a chapter-based NGO. It currently has sixteen chapters organized at the state, college campus, and city levels. These organizations tend to operate under a board of directors and have a formal staff structure that varies from zero to 171 individuals.[3]

At one end of the organizational spectrum is the Alliance of International Women's Rights, which operates with a founder/director and several volunteer professionals focusing on developing women's leadership, primarily in Afghanistan. As its web page describes, the alliance's long-distance Empowerment Programs use free Internet-based communication technology to help open the world to women in developing countries through long-distance volunteers. Its volunteers use Skype and e-mail to converse with women and girls in developing countries to, as described on its website, "provide individual tutoring and mentoring. The exchanges that occur through this process help move women and girls toward their personal education or employment goals while also helping to bridge worlds and improve understanding between different cultures." Finding safe places in Afghanistan with adequate Internet connections is a major challenge of the alliance. It operates with assets of less than $25,000.

At the other end of the organizational spectrum is Vital Voice Global Partnership. Although neither the largest in terms of staff or assets nor having the longest tenure among the U.S. women's rights NGOs, Vital Voices Global Partnership is one of the most prominent of these organizations. It grew out of the U.S. government's Vital Voices Democracy Initiative that First Lady Hillary Clinton and Secretary of State Madeleine Albright created following the Beijing conference to promote the advancement of women as a U.S. foreign policy goal. The first Vital Voices Democracy Conference, titled "Vital Voices: Women in Democracy," was held in 1997 in Vienna, which U.S. Ambassador to Austria Swanee Hunt conceived and hosted. Vital Voice Global Partnership was created in 1999. Think about the phrase *vital voices*. The overall theme of the conference was

> to promote women's equality through their involvement in the governing of their societies in influential, decision-making ways, with the underlying assumption that "women" were a democratizing force. . . . This theme, that women were necessary political actors in democratic societies, became one conceptual frame of the 1997 Vital Voices Conference and for all that followed.
>
> (Garner 2012, 135)

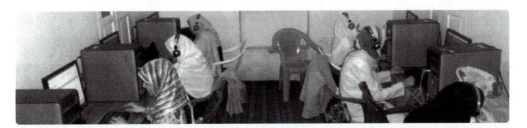

Picture 7.1 Afghan Women Participate in Alliance for International Women's Rights English Program

Nearly two decades since its founding, Vital Voices assesses its outreach in the following terms:

> Our international staff and team of over 1,000 partners, pro bono experts and leaders, including senior government, corporate and NGO executives, have trained and mentored more than 14,000 emerging women leaders from over 144 countries in Africa, Asia, Eurasia, Latin America, the Caribbean, and the Middle East since 1997. These women have returned home to train and mentor more than 500,000 additional women and girls in their communities. They are the Vital Voices of our time.

It has initiatives in three areas to achieve its mission: human rights, economic empowerment development, and political and public leadership.

Six of the organizations have regional offices outside the United States. Eight of the organizations have advisory status in the United Nations Economic and Social Council (ECOSOC). ECOSOC is the main UN body that provides a framework for NGO participation in UN activities. The granting of ECOSOC advisory status in the United Nations gives an organization a heightened presence in the international arena and a forum to advance its goals. NGOs apply for consultative status, which ECOSOC grants. The Virginia Gildersleeve International Fund describes its status in the following way: "As an organization in consultative status, VGIF may designate authorized representatives to sit as observers at public meetings of ECOSOC and its subsidiary bodies, and may, within guidelines, submit or make oral statements relevant to the work of ECOSOC."

Groups within this set of NGOs vary in the extent to which their work combines both a domestic and an international focus. Some work to improve the lives of women and girls both within the United States and in other countries. Some work to raise awareness in the United States, include the United States as a problem area, or advocate for women in U.S. foreign policy, whereas others have constructed programs to substantively improve the lives of women in developing countries. They also vary in terms of having a regional programmatic focus, such as the Alliance for International Women's Rights with its focus of working with Afghan women, or a more global reach based on a broad human rights perspective, such as the work of the Global Justice Center. They vary, too, in the extent to which they work as solitary organizations or are embedded in partnerships and transnational networks.

Aims: Policy Domains and Missions

The Fourth World Conference Report, the *Beijing Declaration and Platform of Action*, named twelve "areas of particular urgency that stand out as priorities for action" for the advancement and empowerment of women. Within each area, the report lists a set of strategic objectives.[4] The action platform variously charged governments, multilateral financial and development institutions and women's groups to take action on the strategic objectives presented. The platform's twelve areas of critical concern serve to categorize the policy action domains of these NGOs.

Overlap exists among the platform's areas. For example, actions regarding violence are prominent in several of the domains, but one critical area (area D) specifically focuses on violence. Table 7.2 provides a survey of the primary and secondary policy domains of these NGOs relative to the platform of action's critical areas. In some cases, organizational names signify the primary policy domain of the NGO. For example, violence is clearly the focus of the Coalition Against Trafficking in Women and Futures Without

Violence NGOs. In other cases, domain categorization is a matter of emphasis and stress in explaining an organization's reason for being rather than highlighting a distinct critical area. In some cases, mission statements highlight multiple areas of concern of equal importance aligned with the platform's critical areas, such as Vital Voices described earlier. Some groups have an overarching area of concern but implementing that concern involves programs targeting the platform's other critical areas. Such a focus is listed as a secondary policy domain in Table 7.2.[5]

As Table 7.2 shows, a diverse set of policy domains has stimulated the activism of these feminist U.S. NGOs. They organize to increase awareness of and lessen violence against women, advocate for women's reproductive health and rights, and enhance economic and political empowerment and legal equality. Some groups also promote women's voices in peace processes and create awareness of the special problems of women in conflict situations. Nine of the twelve Beijing areas of critical concern are included as either primary or secondary mission foci of NGOs in this accounting. No one area dominates, although five areas are the foci of ten or more of the groups, as indicated in the last row of Table 7.2.

Whereas poverty is listed as the first critical area in the platform of action and lessening the poverty of women and girls has been the overarching area of concern in UN work, only four of these organizations (International Center for Research on Women, Virginia Gildersleeve International Fund, Women Thrive Worldwide, and Women's Funding Network) explicitly describe the lessening of poverty among women and children as the primary stimulus driving their work. However, reducing poverty is an implicit aim of much of the activism across these NGOs, especially that which is aimed at advancing equity in educational and economic opportunities for women.

Listing human rights as a critical area of concern distinct from the other eleven areas rather than being an encompassing aspect of these NGOs' work may seem puzzling. How is it distinct as a critical area of concern? Is it not the overarching concern driving the mission of all these groups? The Beijing Platform's distinct critical Human Rights of Women (area I) lists three strategic objectives: (1) incorporating women and girls into all the UN conventions concerning human rights, (2) implementing equality and nondiscrimination in nations' laws, and (3) achieving legal literacy among all of a nation's people. The distinct emphasis as a critical area is on formal processes of governmental conventions, constitutions, and laws.

Thus, coding an NGO as having human rights as a distinct primary policy domain relies first on specific reference to altering laws and constitutions in its mission. For example, the Center for Reproductive Rights' mission statement focuses on using "the law to advance reproductive freedom as a fundamental human right that all governments are legally obligated to protect, respect, and fulfill." Equality Now describes itself as "an organization that advocates for the human rights of women and girls around the world" and lists discrimination in law as an area of focus. The Global Justice Center "works for peace, justice, and security by *enforcing international laws* that protect human rights and promote gender equality." A second group of NGOs was also coded as having human rights as a policy domain based on a more general mission statement emphasis. Illustrative of this point is the Alliance for International Women's Rights, whose mission "is to support women's rights efforts in developing countries." It seeks to achieve this goal "by developing a network of professionals . . . who are willing to use their skills and experience to help promote women's rights."

The girl child critical area of concern was not a primary or secondary critical area in any of the thirty-one groups' mission statements aligned with it as a critical area in the Beijing

Table 7.2 Policy Domains of Nongovernmental Organizations

NGO	Poverty	Education	Health	Violence	Armed Conflict	Economy	Power and Decision Making	Advance Women	Human Rights	Media	Environment	Girl Child
Alliance for Women's Rights	1st						1st		1st			
Americans for UNFPA			1st						2nd			X
Captive Daughters				1st								X
CEDPA		1st	1st				1st					X
CHANGE			1st									X
Center for Reproductive Rights			1st						1st			X
Center for Women Policy Studies				1st	2nd	2nd			2nd			
Coalition Against Trafficking in Women				1st								X
Equality Now				1st					1st			X
Futures Without Violence				1st								X
Gender Action	2nd		2nd	2nd		1st					2nd	
Global Fund for Women		1st	1st			1st	1st		1st		1st	X
Global Justice Center									1st			
Global Rights for Women				1st								
Global Women's Education Project												X
ICAN					1st							
Institute for Inclusive Security					1st							
International Center for Research on Women	1st		2nd									
International Women's Democracy Center			2nd				1st					
International Women's Health Coalition			1st									X

Organization										
Ipas	1st					2nd				X
Partners for Women's Equality		1st		1st						X
Peace X Peace				1st						
The International Alliance for Women			1st							
Urgent Action Fund for Women's Human Rights		1st	1st			1st				
US National Committee for UN Women			1st	2nd	1st					X
Virginia Gildersleeve International Fund	2nd	2nd			2nd	2nd			2nd	X
Vital Voices			2nd	1st	2nd					X
Women for Women International		2nd	2nd		2nd					
Women Thrive Worldwide	2nd		2nd		2nd	2nd				X
Women's Campaign International				2nd	1st					
WEDO		1st			2nd	1st		1st		
Women's Funding Network	2nd	2nd	2nd	1st	2nd	2nd	2nd	1st	2nd	X
Total - Primary	4	4	8	7	4	5	7	—	2	—
Total - Primary and Secondary	5	7	13	12	7	10	12	10	12	3

1st = Primary Domain, 2nd = Secondary Domain

Platform. In the girl child critical area L, the platform singles out discrimination that girls face from birth, including female infanticide, education, training, nutrition and health, violence against them, their rights, and economic exploitation of their labor.

These NGOs do not ignore these problems but rather incorporate them in a focus on *women and girls*. The final column in Table 7.2 includes a check for the girl child critical area when mission statements included girls as well as women in their reasons for being. For instance, the Center for Health and Gender Equity (CHANGE) states that its mission "is to ensure that U.S. foreign policies and programs promote women's *and girls'* sexual and reproductive health within a human rights framework" (emphasis added). Sixteen of the thirty-three NGOs cite girls as well as women in their program descriptions.

Practices: "What We Do"

Some NGOs include a "What We Do" section on their websites to describe their types of actions. For example, the International Women's Health Coalition states that it engages in "advocating," "empowering," "mobilizing," and "informing." In a "How We Do It" section, the U.S. National Committee for UN Women states that it "advocates," "educates and fundraises," and "collaborates." They help construct a list of political practices in which these NGOs engage to accomplish their goals.[6] They provide a sense of the methods and approaches U.S.-led, women's-focused NGOs have undertaken to affect the various critical areas of concern within the global women's rights movement.

Their activism takes multiple forms and includes a diverse set of formal programs. Women for Women International, for example, runs a Become an Ambassador program among its many endeavors, in which individuals commit to a year of working locally to support women survivors of war and to raising funds and awareness for its programs and the countries in which it works.

Text Box 7.2 lists these organizations' programs. The NGOs also give on-the-ground examples and write about success stories. As their titles indicate, these programs represent endeavors undertaken through diverse mediums; some are short-term efforts such as programs bringing women leaders from several countries to the United States for trainings and exchanges lasting from a few days to several weeks to yearlong on-the-ground formal programs.

Text Box 7.2　List of Formal Programs

Poverty

Thrive Institute for Advocacy (Women Thrive Worldwide)

Education

Better Life Options and Opportunities Model (BLOOM) (CEDPA)
Kenya Girls for Change (Partners for Women's Equality)

Health

International Initiative on Maternal Mortality and Human Rights (CRR)
Advocacy in Practice: Engaging New Leaders in International Policy (IWHC)

Violence

Beyond Title IX: Guidelines for Prevention and Responding to Gender-Based Violence in Higher Education (Futures Without Violence)
Enhancing Judicial Skills in Domestic Violence Cases (EJS) (Futures Without Violence)
Adolescent Girls' Legal Defense Fund (Equality Now)
Bridge to Change for Indigenous Women (Partners for Women's Equality)

Economy

The English Program—Opening the World to Afghan Women (AIWR)
Entrepreneurship Program (TIAW)
Microcredit Program (TIAW)
Partnership for Women's Prosperity (Women's Funding Network)
Gender Toolkit for International Financial Watchers (Gender Action)
Daughters e-Mentoring Program (TIAW)
Entrepreneurship Program (TIAW)
Microcredit Program (TIAW)
Making the Case (Women's Funding Network)

Armed Conflict

Connection Point (Peace X Peace)
Rapid Response Grantmaking Program (Urgent Action Fund)
Advocacy and Alliance-Building Program (Urgent Action Fund)

Power and Decision Making

The Mentor Program—Providing International Mentoring (AIW R)

The Community Advocate Mentor Program (CAMP), International Women's Democracy Center

Emerging Pacific Women's Leadership Program (Vital Voices)
African First Ladies Strategic Initiative (Women's Campaign International)

Human Rights

Foreign Policy Institute for State Legislators (Center for Women Policy Studies)
The Geneva Initiative (Global Justice Center)

Based on their antiglobalization feminist activism study, Catherine Eschle and Bice Maiguashca (2010) classify what antiglobalization feminists do into six political practices: protest, advocacy, knowledge production, service provision, popular education, and movement building. The political practices of American NGOs both fit into these categories and expand beyond them. The extent to which their practices align with and diverge from these larger world practices provides a distinctive perspective on their contributions to the global women's rights movement.

In Eschle and Maiguashca's (2010) study, groups across national sites used protest as a political practice. But leading or participating in protests is not a practice of these U.S.

NGOs. These NGOs tend not to engage in protests themselves or to train women outside the United States to mobilize around protest politics challenging government policies. Only one instance of leading a protest was found in reading their websites. The Coalition Against Trafficking in Women describes leading a protest in 2010 at Craigslist's corporate headquarters in San Francisco, holding it responsible for facilitating sex trafficking in North America and internationally. Funding source requirements may limit engagement in this type of activity as well as conventional rather than radical philosophies about change on the part of professional NGO organizers.

Three of the other practices—advocacy, knowledge production, and popular education—however, are prevalent actions of these NGOs. Movement building in the form of engagement in networks is also a common practice, as will be described later in this chapter. Service production is "not a particularly prevalent practice among feminist antiglobalization activists," according to Eschle and Maiguashca (2010, 141), and neither is it a prominent practice of the U.S. NGOs. The activities of these U.S. NGOs include four additional distinctive types of practices: public awareness campaigns, fund-raising and grant giving, training programs, and litigation strategies. Altogether, the practices of these U.S. NGOs can be grouped into seven principal types, as shown in row 1 of Table 7.3. Such practices are undertaken in a variety of contexts: domestically (both in terms of impacting women's lives in the United States and in terms of affecting American foreign policy), in specific developing countries, at the United Nations, or globally. These seven overarching types are further divided into thirteen more distinct activities in Table 7.3 to more specifically describe these NGOs' programs of action.

Public awareness campaigns, lobbying/advocacy, and trainings are the most frequent practices these NGOs use to achieve their goals. These actions are undertaken in many different ways across the groups. Some public awareness campaigns are focused on building support domestically within the United States, others within targeted countries. Education efforts include both informal and formal programs centered on academic learning as part of elementary and secondary school curricula. They differ from training programs that focus on adult skill development.

Some of the types of action may appear to be quite similar in nature but differ in terms of strategy. Mobilization, for instance, is distinguished from public awareness in that the latter involves a more diffuse effort to educate the general public, with an indirect goal of stirring it to action, whereas mobilization strategies aim to not only make a target group aware of the problem and supportive of solutions to it but also to directly stimulate it to action as part of "what we do." The International Women's Health Coalition is illustrative. It states, "We mobilize women and young people, enabling them to take action to secure their rights, health, and well-being. We have helped to build and sustain 75 organizations in 10 countries and create broad and powerful alliances." Captive Daughters, on the other hand, stresses that its aim is to educate the public about sex trafficking using its website and other social networking sites to achieve that goal. It is a recent recipient of a $150,000 grant from the Bill & Melinda Gates Foundation to produce a documentary film about the trafficking of Nepalese girls into Indian brothels.

These NGOs employ from one to five action strategies. Strategies are somewhat related to the policy domain of the NGOs, as Table 7.4 shows. For instance, among the twelve NGOs that have eliminating violence against women as their primary or secondary reason for being, nearly all (nine of the ten) have public awareness and advocacy campaigns, whereas training programs are the main endeavor constructed to increase women's running for political leadership positions.

Table 7.3 Political Practices

NGOs	Public Awareness			Advocacy	Service Provision	Popular Education			Fund-Raising	Project Grants/Funding	Knowledge Production	Litigation
	Public Awareness	Public Awareness Affected Group	Mobilization	Lobbying/Advocacy	Service Programs	Training Programs	Academic Education Programs	Tutoring/Mentoring				
Alliance for International Women's Rights						X	X	X				
Americans for UNFPA	X								X			
Captive Daughters	X		X									
CEPDA	X			X		X	X			X		
CHANGE	X			X		X			X		X	X
Center for Reproductive Rights				X		X		X				
Center for Women Policy Studies		X		X							X	X
Coalition Against Trafficking in Women	X				X	X	X					
Equality Now	X	X		X								
Futures Without Violence	X	X		X		X						
Gender Action				X		X					X	X
Global Fund for Women										X		
Global Justice Center				X				X				
Global Rights for Women	X			X		X						
Global Women's Education Project							X					
IBIS	X			X							X	
ICAN	X			X		X						
Institute for Inclusive Security				X		X					X	X

(Continued)

Table 7.3 (Continued)

NGOs	Public Awareness			Advocacy	Service Provision	Popular Education			Fund-Raising	Project Grants/ Funding	Knowledge Production	Litigation
	Public Awareness	Public Awareness Affected Group	Mobiliza-tion	Lobbying/ Advocacy	Service Programs	Training Programs	Academic Education Programs	Tutoring/ Mentoring				
International Center for Research on Women	X		X	X		X					X	X
International Women's Democracy Center		X		X		X				X	X	X
International Women's Health Coalition						X						
IPAS					X	X					X	X
Partners for Women's Equality	X					X				X		
The International Alliance for Women						X			X			
Urgent Action Fund for Women's Human Rights	X			X					X	X	X	X
U.S. National Committee for UN Women	X			X					X			
Virginia Gildersleeve International Fund	X			X						X		
Vital Voices		X				X		X				
Women for Women International		X				X				X		
Women Thrive Worldwide		X				X						
Women's Campaign International						X						
WEDO						X				X		
Women's Funding Network						X			X	X		
Total	13	7	2	16	2	22	3	5	6	9	8	8

Table 7.4 Actions and Policy Domains

Actions	Poverty (5)	Education (7)	Health (11)	Violence (12)	Armed Conflict (7)	Economy (10)	Power and Decision Making (10)	Human Rights (11)	Environment (3)
Public Awareness (1)	2	3	5	7	2	2	3	3	1
Public Awareness (2)	1	1	1	5	1	3	3	2	0
Lobbying/Advocacy	3	2	7	7	6	4	4	6	1
Mobilization	0	1	1	0	0	0	1	0	1
Training Programs	3	5	8	7	5	5	7	4	1
Service Programs	0	0	1	1	0	0	0	1	0
Academic Educational Programs	0	2	1	1	0	0	2	0	0
Tutoring/Mentoring	0	1	1	2	1	1	2	3	0
Fund-Raising	1	1	2	3	0	2	2	4	0
Project Grants/Funding	1	1	4	3	1	4	2	4	1
Research/Publications	2	0	5	4	2	2	0	3	0
Litigation Strategies	0	0	1	1	0	0	0	3	0

Numbers in parentheses are the number of organizations with the policy domain as a primary or secondary focus.

The final feminist antiglobalization practice—movement building—involves establishing and running feminist antiglobalization groups and creating alliances among these groups. A key aspect of the vibrancy of NGOs working in the domain of women's rights is the extent to which they develop partnerships and networks or join with other NGOs to achieve their aims. On their websites, these NGOs describe making connections, collaborating, coalition building, sharing, exchange, and dialogue facilitation as part of their practices central to achieving their missions. They tend not to work on their own to affect women's rights. Rather, they include partnerships and networks as important aspects of their work. Five of these NGOs define their organizations in their titles as a "Coalition," "Alliance," or "Network" that speaks for itself in framing the transnational nature of some of these groups. Overall, these thirty-three NGOs describe a variety of partnerships and networks in which they embed their action repertoires.

Partnerships are of two types. One involves collaborating with a specific set of other organizations, either other national or international NGOs working in the same area on specific programs. A second type are partnerships with local groups on the ground in a targeted area, those whose lives and status these groups aim to better.[7] Networks involve efforts to generate a broad coalition of groups working to achieve a particular goal such as ending violence against women. Networks are forms of organization characterized by voluntary, reciprocal, and horizontal patterns of communication and exchange (Keck and Sikkink 1998, 1999). Transnational networks are structures organized above the national level that unite groups around a common agenda (Moghadam 2005).[8]

Figure 7.1 quantifies the types of partnerships and networks these NGOs describe engaging in on their webpage. CHANGE, which focuses on affecting U.S. policies regarding the sexual and reproductive health and human rights of women and girls globally, describes developing a domestic network of supporters. In the organization's words, in recent years, it has begun building and mobilizing "a significant base of U.S. supporters, drawing from and building bridges among diverse U.S. constituencies such as students, reproductive justice advocates, faith-based organizations, HIV/AIDS groups, and women's organizations." Sixteen NGOs list involvement in international networks, some of which they initiated. Equality Now, for example, describes founding "the Equality Action Network for international advocacy with a membership of over 35,000 groups and individuals in over 160 countries who call on governments to guarantee women's rights."

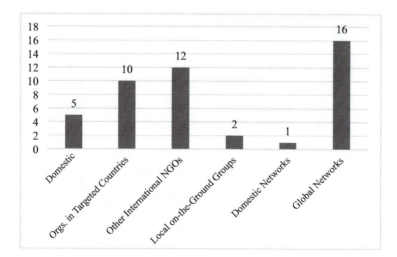

Figure 7.1 Partnerships and Networks

The Institute for Inclusive Security includes the creation of a Women Waging Peace Network in its "What We Do" website section that it states is a "network of more than 2,000 women peacemakers from conflict areas around the world." The International Women's Health Coalition credits itself as a founding member of Realizing Sexual and Reproductive Justice, "an international alliance of feminist activists seeking full implementation of international commitments to secure all women's and young people's sexual and reproductive rights and health by 2015." ICAN is a founding member of the U.S. Civil Society Working Group on Women, Peace and Security and is a program partner of the global Network of Women Peacebuilders. The UN's NGO Working Group on Women, Peace and Security also lists the Global Justice Center and the Institute for Inclusive Security as members.

The majority of the NGOs cite partnerships with other international organizations or NGOs in targeted countries in describing how they work. Illustrative of this approach is the Alliance for International Women's Rights, which operates the English Program—Opening the World to Afghan Women in partnership with the Kandahar Institute of Modern Studies, Justice for All, and Gawharshad Institute of Higher Education in Kabul. Partners for Women's Equality lists and describes four partner organizations in Brazil. WEDO, which in other work is described as a network itself (Moghadam 2005), lists twenty-three partner organizations, some of which are other NGOs in the database for this research.

Accomplishments

As the preceding section has described, these NGOs have adopted a variety of practices to improve diverse aspects of women's lives across the globe. What have been their achievements? Organizations may be interested in highlighting their successes or producing an annual report to raise additional funds and demonstrate a level of accountability to their donors. Highlighting what they consider to be achievements is a way to demonstrate to donors how the funds they provide are being used and to assess whether they are meeting their stated missions and goals (Najam 1996).

Eight of the NGOs provide no information on what they would consider their successes or accomplishments. Other websites, in contrast, include sections on "impact," in which they present "successes," "accomplishments," or "achievements" or provide links to annual reports. These presentations are primarily given in storytelling format rather than any outlining of systematic criteria to assess outcomes or descriptions of built-in assessment measurements in their projects. They principally take the form of a listing of activities (not outcomes), case studies (stories), testimonies, and implicit connections between outcomes and actions. Some do present statistics on the number of people trained and amount of dollars raised and spent. CEDPA, for example, reports "training more than 5,400 women, men and youth who are now leading change for women and girls in countries from Albania to Zambia." The International Women's Health Coalition states that since its founding, it has "helped build and strengthen nearly 80 organizations in Africa, Asia, Latin America, and the Middle East . . . provid[ing] mentorship and more than $19 million in grants to women and youth advocates across these regions."

Three NGOs have constructed metrics to measure the outcomes of their programs: International Center for Research on Women, Global Fund for Women (GFW), and Women's Funding Network. GFW has developed a navigation tool, "Mapping Our Movement Building." Using data from twenty-four years of grant making, it has identified nineteen indicators to measure the relationship between Global Fund's grants, grantees, partners, and advisors. The indicators were weighted "based on the extent to which they were relevant to efforts to build strong networks and collective power in the pursuit of common goals." For example, GFW's support to a grantee network, or to grantees that bring together a diverse population, is weighed more heavily than the length of time GFW has supported a specific grantee. It uses visualization technology to display geographically the results of it analysis.

Given its research emphasis, the International Center for Research on Women focuses its work with partners to "conduct empirical research, build capacity and advocate for evidence-based practical ways to change policies and programs." Thus, its website includes "Measurement and Evaluation" and "Research and Analysis" sections in which it describes designing gender-responsive evaluation programs. Further, the Women's Funding Network has created an assessment tool, Making the Case, to evaluate and measure social change. Gender Action has a Gender Toolkit for International Finance-Watchers.

Global feminism

> seeks to reduce and ultimately eliminate the complex inequities and inequalities characteristic of race- and gender-based oppression. . . . Toward that end, it envisions an expanded state provision to create adequate health care, education, welfare, employment, personal security, and a range of equity policies that redress gender- and race-based injustices. . . . Nongovernmental organizations have proliferated, creating a vibrant feminist civil society.
>
> (Hawkesworth 2006, 149–151)

A search for contemporary U.S.-led NGOs whose catalyst for their formation has centered on impacting the rights of women globally produced thirty-three such organizations active in the second decade of the millennium, including both singular U.S.-led groups and transnational organizations encompassing U.S. leadership and initiative. Ending violence against women and girls; enhancing women's voices in peace processes; improving their health, reproductive rights, and economic status; advancing their legal rights; and empowering women in the political realm stimulated individuals to found these various NGOs. Their strategies for achieving their goals are varied, spanning public awareness campaigns, government lobbying, funding grants, and providing services and trainings principally in developing countries. Their activism has centered on influencing American foreign policy, working within particular countries with local groups, and affecting women's rights globally. They have combined assets of nearly $116 million. They present themselves as not only being concerned with improving the condition of women but also as advocates for the transformation of women's position in society from a human rights perspective. Their websites present a public face of organizations dedicated to that transformation and to a challenging of conventional power structures. Whether the work of these groups constitutes a vibrant and robust U.S. feminist presence in transnational women's rights activism contrary to the perspective of a lagging U.S. activism that some women's rights advocates have cited remains to be determined.

In addition, a normative assessment should address critiques that Western activist domination has imposed its economic and cultural ideas on third-world women (see Eisenstein 2009; Tripp 2006). Several of these groups at least seem to be aware of this criticism. They highlight in their "Who We Are" and "What We Do" sections their concerns about learning from and consulting with those they seek to help in the development of their programs of action.

The International Center for Research on Women illustrates this awareness. It states that it "talks to women. We help their voices be heard." The Virginia Gildersleeve International Fund "believes that women know best what will help improve and enrich life in their own communities and they are the only ones equipped to empower themselves." The Urgent Action Fund supports "long-term change efforts by supporting the vision, creativity, and agency of local activists—and not telling them what they should be doing." These statements are just a few of the examples from the websites of the NGOs described in this chapter. The creation of U.S. NGOs focused on global women's rights is a significant domain of women's political participation growing out of the contemporary women's movement. Further research assessing their effectiveness is certainly in order. Their work joins the other chapters in this book that have surveyed the myriad ways in which women have increased their engagement both in general civic activities and as proponents of gender equity in the practice of politics. The final section of this text centers on women's elective leadership and public policy making. Text Box 7.3 provides an example of women's leadership in public policy making regarding women's issues and globalization.

Text Box 7.3 Women, Peace, and Security Act of 2016

On November 15, 2016, the U.S. House of Representatives passed the Women, Peace, and Security Act on a voice vote. This bipartisan legislation would require the United States to develop a government-wide strategy, including new efforts to train its personnel, consult with stakeholders on the ground, and coordinate with partners, in order to increase women's participation in peace and security processes. In the 114th Congress, the Senate did not act on this legislation, and therefore it must be reintroduced in the 115th Congress. The bill "expresses the sense of Congress that the United States should be a global leader in promoting the meaningful participation of women in conflict prevention, management, and resolution and post-conflict relief and recovery efforts," according to its official summary. Research has shown that an agreement is 35 percent more likely to last for fifteen years if women participate in its creation (Stone 2014).

The act would, among other things,

- turn a national strategy into law, built on the U.S. National Action Plan on Women, Peace, and Security, launched in 2011;
- require the president to provide reports to Congress that evaluate U.S. diplomatic and foreign assistance vis-à-vis women's participation;
- make an official statement that it is U.S. policy to promote the meaningful participation of women in all aspects of conflict prevention, management, and resolution;
- mandate training for U.S. defense, diplomatic, and development personnel on the value of women's inclusion and strategies for achieving it; and
- require the secretary of State and USAID administrator to establish guidelines for overseas personnel to ensure women's meaningful participation in consultations with key stakeholders on preventing and resolving conflict.

Reference

Stone, Laurel. 2014. "Women Transforming Conflict: A Quantitative Analysis of Female Peacemaking." https://papers.ssrn.com/sol3/papers.cfm?abstract_id=2485242.

Notes

1. Aili Tripp also argues that U.S. feminists have not focused enough on demanding that its government engage in action against abuses of women at home (see Tripp 2006).
2. The list of these thirty-three organizations was constructed through a search of several sources for what could be described as U.S.-based women's advocacy NGOs. We searched the United Nations' ECOSOC list of NGOs having consultative status for U.S. organizations, USAID's listing of private voluntary organizations (PVOs, academic and research group sources such as Duke University Library's search engine that provide lists of women's NGOs, the Global Women's Network, and women's rights news media sources). Listings such as Guidestar.org, Idealist.org, and GreatNonprofits.org, which are information services that catalog nonprofit groups, were also searched using key terms such as "women's employment," "women's economic empowerment," "women's health," "women and violence," "women's reproductive health," and "women's international" to identify groups meeting our criteria. Finally, relevant aid organizations covered in a special edition of *USA Today* (March 2010) completed the search for the type of women's-centered NGOs under investigation in this research project. In some cases, information gathered about one organization led to the identification of other organizations working in a particular domain. Whereas these search engines and sources may not represent an absolutely exhaustive search of contemporary U.S.-based NGOs specifically designed to address women's lives in the developing world and women's rights globally, the overlap and multiple listings found among these sources indicate the comprehensiveness of our search.
3. Some of the large staff include employees in countries being served as well as U.S.-based staff. Wherever available, only U.S. staff are enumerated.
4. The twelve critical areas of concern are (1) women and poverty, (2) education and training of women, (3) women and health, (4) violence against women, (5) women and armed conflict, (6) women and the economy, (7) women in power and decision making, (8) institutional mechanisms for the advancement of women, (9) human rights of women, (10) women and the media, (11) women and the environment, and (12) the girl child.
5. The statements used to assign principal and secondary policy domains are available in a codebook upon request for transparency purposes.
6. We borrow the term *political practice* from Catherine Eschle and Bice Maiguashca's *Making Feminist Sense of the Global Justice Movement* (2010).
7. Many of the organizations also describe corporations and large-scale public philanthropies as partners. These types of partnerships are not included in this assessment.
8. As Moghadam (2005) describes them, TNFs "create, activate, or join global networks to mobilize pressure outside states; participate in multilateral and intergovernmental arenas; act and agitate within states to enhance public awareness and participation" (13–14).

Further Readings and Web Resources

Chesler, Ellen and Terry McGowen, eds. 2015. *Women and Girls Rising*. New York, NY: Routledge.

Fraser, Arvonne S. and Irene Tinker, eds. 2004. *Developing Power: How Women Transformed International Development*. New York, NY: The Feminist Press.

Garner, Karen. 2013. *Gender & Foreign Policy in the Clinton Administration*. Boulder, CO: Lynne Reiner.

Nelson, Alyse. 2012. *Vital Voices. The Power of Women Leading Change around the World*. New York, NY: John Wiley and Sons.

O'Reilly, Marie, Andrea Ó. Súilleabháin, and Thania Paffenholz. 2015. *Reimagining Peacemaking: Women's Roles in Peace Processes*. New York, NY: International Peace Institute.

Peters, Allison. 2016. "Time for Congress to Take the Lead on Inclusive Security." *The Hill*, March 23. http://thehill.com/blogs/congress-blog/foreign-policy/273587-time-for-congress-to-take-the-lead-on-inclusive-security.

Web Resources

"Timeline: Gender Equality 2016 Year in Review." *UNWomen.* http://interactive.unwomen.org/multimedia/timeline/yearinreview/2016/en/index.html.
"Toward a More Feminist United Nations: A 100 Day Agenda for the New Secretary General." *International Center for Research on Women,* December 2016. www.icrw.org/wp-content/uploads/2016/12/ICRW_100DayAgenda_WebReady_v6.pdf.
"U.S. National Action Plan on Women, Peace, and Security." *U.S. Department of State 2012.* www.state.gov/documents/organization/196726.pdf.

Film

"Girls Rising." *Girls Rising* is a film that follows the life stories of nine girls from the developing world who struggle for freedom, education, and a voice in their own countries. www.girlsrising.com.
"The Hunting Ground." 2015. This documentary explores the issue of sexual assault on college campuses across the country. http://thehuntinggroundfilm.com/.

References

Boles, Janet. 2006. "A Social Movement Transformed: The U.S. Women's Rights Movement and Global Feminism." Paper presented at the 2000 Annual Meeting of the American Political Science Association.

Bunch, Charlotte. 1990. "Women's Rights as Human Rights: Toward a Re-Vision of Human Rights." *Human Rights Quarterly,* 12: 486–498.

Eisenstein, Hester. 2009. *Feminism Seduced: How Global Elites Use Women's Labor and Ideas to Exploit the World.* Boulder, CO: Paradigm.

Eschle, Catherine and Bice Maiguashca. 2010. *Making Feminist Sense of the Global Justice Movement.* Lanham, MD: Rowman & Littlefield.

Garner, Karen. 2012. "Global Gender Policy in the1990s: Incorporating the 'Vital Voices' of Women." *Journal of Women's History,* 24, 4 (Winter): 121–148.

Gelb, Joyce. 2006. "Trends and Transformations in Women's Movements in Japan and the United States." In *The U.S. Women's Movement in Global Perspective,* ed. Lee Ann Banaszak. Lanham, MD: Rowman & Littlefield, 177–196.

Hawkesworth, Mary. 2006. *Globalization & Feminist Activism.* Lanham, MD: Rowman & Littlefield.

Htun, Mala and S. Laurel Weldon. 2012. "The Civic Origins of Progressive Policy Change: Combating Violence against Women in Global Perspective, 1975–2005." *American Political Science Review,* 106, 3: 548–569.

Keck, Margaret and Kathryn Sikkink. 1998. *Activists across Borders: Advocacy Networks in International Politics.* Ithaca, NY: Cornell University Press.

Keck, Margaret and Kathryn Sikkink. 1999. "Transnational Advocacy Networks in International and Regional Politics." http://isites.harvard.edu/fs/docs/icb.topic446176.files/Week_7/Keck_and_Sikkink_Transnational_Advocacy.pdf.

Margi, Nathalie and Mary Jane Real. 2010. *Body, Economy and Movement: The Global Women's Movement at the Beijing +15 Review, A Report on the 20th Anniversary of Symposium of the Center for Global Women's Leadership.* New Brunswick, NJ: Rutgers University.

Moghadam, Valentine. 2005. *Globalizing Women.* Baltimore, MD: The Johns Hopkins University Press.

Najam, Adil. 1996. "NGO Accountability: A Conceptual Framework." *Development Policy Review,* 14: 339–353.

Skocpol, Theda. 1999. "Advocates without Members: The Recent Transformation of American Civic Life." In *Civic Engagement in American Democracy,* eds. Theda Skocpol and Morris P. Fiorina. Washington, DC: The Brookings Institution, 461–510.

Snyder, Margaret. 2006. "Unlikely Godmother: The UN and the Global Women's Movement." In *Global Feminism: Transnational Women's Activism, Organizing and Women's Rights*, eds. Myra Karx Ferree and Aili Mari Tripp. New York, NY: New York University Press, 24–50.

Tocqueville, Alexis De. 1969. *Democracy in America*, ed. J. P. Mayer, trans. George Lawrence. Garden City, NY: Anchor Books.

Tripp, Aili Mari. 2006. "Challengers in Transnational Feminist Mobilization." In *Global Feminism: Transnational Women's Activism, Organizing and Women's Rights*, eds. Myra Marx Ferree and Aili Mari Tripp. New York, NY: New York University Press, 296–312.

8 Women's Candidacies for Elected Office

Running for and getting elected to public office is the ultimate political activity in democratic societies. In the United States, women have been only 2 percent of the membership of the national legislature since the first Congress convened in 1789 to the swearing in of members to the 114th Congress in 2015; *only 2 percent* over the entire course of U.S. history (see Figure 8.1). Never over that same time period had either of the two major parties nominated a woman for president. This chapter traces the electoral history of female candidacies for and election to public office. It explores why so few women have been elected and the efforts to change that dynamic. Chapter 9 then chronicles the historical candidacy of Hillary Clinton for the U.S. presidency in the 2016 election.

In examining women's quests for elected office, it is important to reflect on the following question: What does it matter to have women in political leadership? Consider the following anecdote. On October 8, 1991, female members of the U.S. House of Representatives took to the House floor, and in the words of then-U.S. Representative Barbara Boxer, "stood up and spoke their minds" during the House's traditional one-minute speech time allotted members. The allegation of sexual harassment on the part of Supreme Court nominee Clarence Thomas against former assistant Anita Hill and the refusal of U.S. senators to hear those charges during Judge Thomas's nomination hearings were on their minds. Then seven female House members marched to the Capitol Room in the U.S. Senate where Democratic senators were holding their regular Tuesday caucus to "give them our view of what was going on in the country and to let them know that we believed that the charges were serious—and in need of investigation" (Boxer 1994, 30). *New York Times* columnist Maureen Dowd picks up the story.

> They knocked on the door, hoping to give their colleagues in the room, all men except for Barbara Mikulski of Maryland, "the woman's point of view," as Representative Louise Slaughter of upstate New York put it. They wanted to state their case about why the vote on Judge Clarence Thomas should be delayed to give a thorough airing to Prof. Anita Hill's accusations of sexual harassment.
>
> But they were told they could not come in. "Nobody ever gets in." They knocked again. They were told again that they could not come in. They waited in the hall, looking chagrined and angry. Finally an aide to Senator George J. Mitchell, the Senate majority leader, told the women Mr. Mitchell would meet with them for a few moments in his office around the corner. "We were told that nobody ever gets in there," said a disgusted Slaughter as she strode from the caucus room to Mr. Mitchell's office, adding sarcastically "certainly not women from the House. There's no monolithic way that women respond to this," she said. "But we are the people who write the laws of the land. Good lord, she should have some recourse here."
>
> (Dowd 1991, A1)

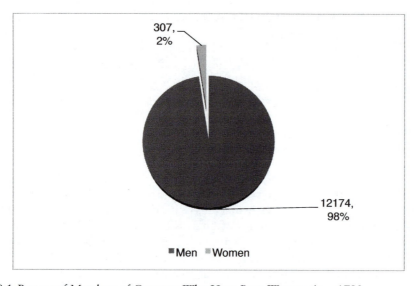

Figure 8.1 Percent of Members of Congress Who Have Been Women since 1789
Adapted from the Center for American Women and Politics, as of March 2015.

What if no women had been lawmakers in the U.S. House of Representatives to demand a hearing? President George H. W. Bush had nominated Clarence Thomas in July 1991 to be an associate judge on the U.S. Supreme Court to succeed Thurgood Marshall. Justice Marshall had been the only African American justice on the court. Thomas is also an African American. He had served as chair of the Equal Employment Opportunity Commission. In 1990, President Bush had nominated him for a seat on the U.S. Court of Appeals for the District of Columbia Circuit.

Toward the end of Justice Thomas's confirmation hearings, National Public Radio journalist Nina Totenberg reported confidential information that Oklahoma University law professor Anita Hill had given closed-door testimony to the Senate Judiciary Committee accusing Thomas of sexual harassment and that the Judiciary Committee had chosen not to pursue her charges. Hill, an African American attorney, had worked for Thomas at the Department of Education. She subsequently moved with him to the Equal Employment Opportunity Commission. After the leak, due to tremendous pressure from women's rights groups and the female lawmakers just described, the Judiciary Committee reversed its decision and agreed to extend the confirmation hearings, calling Hill to testify. In televised sessions, she testified that Thomas had sexually harassed her during the time the two worked together. Hill claimed that Thomas had asked her to go out with him, discussed pornography with her, and made inappropriate remarks about her body. Several senators aggressively questioned and challenged her. Eventually, the Senate voted 52–48 to accept the president's appointment of Thomas to the Supreme Court.

These hearings pitted a Black woman against a Black man. Surveys showed that large majorities of Black women, Black men, and White men all disbelieved Hill (Mansbridge and Tate 1992). White women seemed somewhat more likely to believe Hill, but in general, public opinion was decidedly against her. Thomas impassionedly contended in his testimony that the proceedings were "a high-tech lynching for uppity Blacks" and that "these are charges that play into racist, bigoted stereotypes." His statement heightened racial salience and lessened gender salience (Mansbridge and Tate 1992). Hill had waited ten years to bring her charges forward. She had not left her job but continued to work with Thomas, which made it difficult to organize on her behalf and against Thomas.

But some Black women did take a public stand in support of Anita Hill. A campaign named African American Women in Defense of Ourselves was initiated immediately after her testimony. Among other things, they raised $50,000 to publish an open letter in the *New York Times* on November 17, 1991, and in six Black newspapers, which included the names of 1,603 Black women. It denounced the racist and sexist treatment to which Anita Hill had been subjected. That action has received little attention in historical accounts of Thomas's nomination. The letter appears in Text Box 8.1.

Text Box 8.1 Letter to the *New York Times*: African American Women in Defense of Ourselves

We are particularly outraged by the racist and sexist treatment of Professor Anita Hill, an African American woman who was maligned and castigated for daring to speak publicly of her own experience of sexual abuse. The malicious defamation of Professor Hill insulted all women of African descent and sent a dangerous message to any woman who might contemplate a sexual harassment complaint.

We speak here because we recognize that the media are now portraying the Black community as prepared to tolerate both the dismantling of affirmative action and the evil of sexual harassment in order to have any Black man on the Supreme Court. We want to make clear that the media have ignored or distorted many African American voices. We will not be silenced.

Many have erroneously portrayed the allegations against Clarence Thomas as an issue of either gender or race. As women of African descent, we understand sexual harassment as both. We further understand that Clarence Thomas outrageously manipulated the legacy of lynching in order to shelter himself from Anita Hill's allegations. To deflect attention away from the reality of sexual abuse in African American women's lives, he trivialized and misrepresented this painful part of African American people's history. This country, which has a long legacy of racism and sexism, has never taken the sexual abuse of black women seriously. Throughout U.S. history black women have been sexually stereotyped as immoral, insatiable, perverse, the initiators in all sexual contacts—abusive or otherwise. The common assumption in legal proceedings as well as in the larger society has been that black women cannot be raped or otherwise sexually abused. As Anita Hill's experience demonstrates, Black women who speak of these matters are not likely to be believed.

In 1991, we cannot tolerate this type of dismissal of any one Black woman's experience or this attack upon our collective character without protest, outrage and resistance.

We pledge ourselves to continue to speak out in defense of one another, in defense of the African American community and against those who are hostile to social justice, no matter what color they are. No one will speak for us but ourselves.

Although the polls did not suggest a public outcry in support of Hill, these events significantly affected the electoral process. This spectacle ignited a host of women's rights issues and helped to propel attention to women's lack of political influence. The hearings highlighted the importance of having women in political leadership positions. Only two women were members of the U.S. Senate at that time. Neither served on the Judiciary

Committee that was empowered to hold hearings and to provide an initial vote on Supreme Court nominees. Had there not been a contingent of female U.S. representatives demanding that the harassment charges be heard, they would have been ignored. The hearings further spotlighted the issue of sexual harassment in a graphic fashion, bringing it into public discourse with more women publicly stating their concerns and demanding changes in behavior (Palley and Palley 1992). They energized several women to run for public office and generated momentum for campaign fund-raising to support those candidates.

Display Ad 28 -- No Title
New York Times (1923-Current file); Oct 25, 1991; ProQuest Historical Newspapers: The New York Times
pg. B16

What if 14 women, instead of 14 men, had sat on the Senate Judiciary Committee during the confirmation hearings of Clarence Thomas?

Sound unfair? Just as unfair as fourteen men and no women.

What if even half the Senators had been women? Women are, after all, more than half the population. Maybe, just maybe, women's voices would have been heard. Maybe the experiences and concerns of women would not have been so quickly dismissed or ridiculed. And maybe all of America would have benefited.

The behavior and performance of the United States Senate during the Clarence Thomas confirmation hearings demonstrated a stark truth: women are tragically under-represented politically. As long as men make up 98% of the U.S. Senate and 93% of the U.S. House of Representatives, women's voices can be ignored, their experiences and concerns trivialized.

The need for women in public office has never been more obvious. Or essential.

Men control the White House, the Congress, the courthouse and the statehouse. Men have political power over women's lives. It's time that women help make the rules, create the policies, and pass the laws about sexual harassment, day care, affordable health care, and hundreds of decisions that affect American families every day.

The National Women's Political Caucus is determined to even

the odds. To hear the voices of women echo in the halls of power.

If you're angry about what you've witnessed in the United States Senate, don't just raise your fist, raise your pen. Join us. The goal of the National Women's Political Caucus is to increase the number of women elected and appointed to public office. We're the only national bi-partisan grassroots organization working across this country to recruit, train and elect women into office at all levels of government.

Turn your anger into action. Join us.

Count me in. I want to help the National Women's Political Caucus increase the number of women elected and appointed to public office. Enclosed is my check payable to NWPC Inc. for:
( )$250 ( )$100 ( )$50 ( )$35 OTHER $____
Name ____
Address ____
City/State/Zip ____
Please bill my ( ) Mastercard ( ) Visa   Amount $____
Account Number ____   Expiration Date ____
Signature ____   Date ____
Contributions to NWPC are not tax deductible.
National Women's Political Caucus
1275 K Street, N.W., Suite 750, Washington, D.C. 20005

Paid for by the National Women's Political Caucus

Picture 8.1 National Women's Political Caucus "What If?" Ad, 1991

Ellen Malcolm, president of EMILY's List (a group dedicated to electing pro-choice Democratic women to national offices described in more depth later in the chapter), saw the hearings as creating a "very hot market for fundraising for women candidates" (Ifill 1991, 137). On October 25, the National Women's Political Caucus ran an advertisement in the *New York Times* featuring a drawing of the Senate Judiciary Committee grilling Justice Thomas under the title "What If? What if 14 women, instead of 14 men, had sat on the Judiciary Committee during the confirmation hearing of Clarence Thomas? Sound unfair? Just as unfair as 14 men and no women." In the accompanying caricature, all the committee senators were women (see Picture 8.1).

The Clarence Thomas confirmation hearing thus was one of several factors that contributed to 1992 becoming known as the "Year of the Woman" in American political folklore. The number of women in the U.S. Senate tripled, going from two to six, and twenty-four new women were elected to the U.S. House of Representatives, enlarging their membership from twenty-nine to forty-seven out of 435 members. The 1992 election was not the first time an election cycle was projected to be a "Year of the Woman," in which women had the potential to win a substantial number of elections and to increase their presence in political leadership positions. "Since the mid-1970s, journalists [had] written of a possible 'year of the woman' in which record numbers of women would be elected to public office" (Wilcox 1994, 1), but each election ended in unfulfilled hopes until 1992.

Several other features of the 1992 election cycle converged to ultimately make it a historic election for women in addition to the catalyst of the Thomas Supreme Court nomination. A wave of public sentiment against incumbents, along with reapportionment, created a substantial number of open and winnable seats in the U.S. House of Representatives for newcomers. The U.S. Census is taken every ten years, and subsequently, congressional boundaries are redrawn to maintain equal voting representation across districts. Some states gain seats, and some states lose seats. Some members running for reelection are put in a new district where their incumbency advantage is lessened. Some incumbents also were vulnerable in 1992 because of their involvement in scandals; fifty-two members retired. Retirements and the creation of new districts based on the census resulted in ninety-one of the 435 U.S. House districts being open in the 1992 general election, creating substantial opportunities for newcomers.

Record numbers of women took advantage of these opportunities to run for seats in the U.S. House and Senate in 1992. Several factors helped. In the previous decade, women's membership in local and state legislatures had grown, advancing the "political pipeline" for viable congressional candidacies (Elder 2008). In 1992, the political parties were aggressive in their efforts to recruit women candidates. Women's political action committees (PACs) were particularly active in recruiting women candidates and providing them with resources to run well-funded campaigns.

Election of Women to the U.S. Congress

Although women made substantial gains in winning election to national offices in 1992, they were still far from parity with men in elective office. As a result of the 1992 election, women made up just 6 percent of the U.S. Senate and 11.3 percent of the U.S. House of Representatives in the 103rd Congress (1993–1994). In the 115th Congress beginning in 2017, twelve elections after the 1992 "Year of the Woman" phenomenon, the number of female senators had grown from six to twenty-one of its one hundred members and increased to eighty-three members of the U.S. House, 19.1 percent of the its 435 members. In addition, five women were governors of their states, and three of the nine Supreme Court justices were women.[1] These figures represent progress but also show that women are a long way from parity with men in political leadership positions.

Figures 8.2 and 8.3 show the trends in the number of women elected to the U.S. House and Senate since the emergence of the contemporary women's rights movement in the latter half of the 1960s. As the trend lines depict, since the historic 1992 election, each subsequent election has produced modest increases at best in women's membership in the national legislature. Their numbers in the U.S. House actually declined as a result of the 2010 election but bounced back in 2012, crept upward again in the 2014 election, and then declined by one in the 2016 election. The election of women to the U.S House since the 1992 election has been a story of incremental increases, status quo elections, and slight setbacks.

Figure 8.2 also depicts a growing partisan gap in female representation in the U.S. House in contemporary elections. For most of the 20th century, Republican and Democratic female representatives progressed in roughly parallel numbers in obtaining membership in Congress. In the 1990s, this equal representation started to change. The number of Democratic women winning seats began to significantly outpace the number of Republican

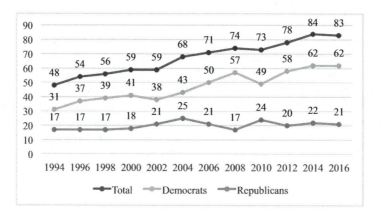

Figure 8.2 Number of Women Elected to the U.S. House of Representatives, 1966–2016

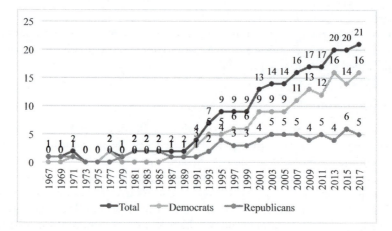

Figure 8.3 Number of Women Elected/Appointed to the U.S. Senate, 1967–2015

women. Indeed, it may be more accurate to call 1992 the "Year of the Democratic Woman" instead of the "Year of the Woman." Nearly all the women newly elected to the U.S. House and all the women elected to the U.S. Senate were Democrats.[2] In each following election, Democratic women continued to outpace their Republican female counterparts in gaining election to the U.S. House, with the exception of the 2010 election, in which nine Republican women were newly elected and several female Democratic incumbents (along with their male colleagues) lost their seats. That decline was reversed in the 2012 election when twenty-four women were newly elected as U.S representatives, bringing their representation to a record 18.4 percent in the House. Twenty of the twenty-four new female members were Democrats. The 2014 election resulted in an incremental increase of four female members in the U.S. House, 19.3 percent of the legislature. Democrats made up 73 percent of the female membership. The 2016 election resulted in a decrease of one Republican female member, whereas the Democrats maintained their status quo. Democrats were 75 percent of the female House members in the 115th Congress and account for 76 percent of all women in the Senate in the 115th Congress of 2017–2018.

Several factors help to account for the emergence and growth of this partisan gap in women's representation in the U.S. Congress. Chapter 4 described the increasing affinity of women in the general public with the Democratic Party and its candidates in the past few decades. This greater affinity among women for the Democratic Party might broadly impact the relative supply of women candidates in each party. The partisan gap among women in Congress, however, far surpasses that among women in the electorate. Whereas Democratic women have comprised between two thirds and three fourths of the women in Congress since the 1990s, the partisan gap among female voters has ranged only from about 3 percent to 16 percent in presidential elections during this time.

Researchers have pointed to several other factors that explain the increase in female Democratic membership in the national legislature and the minuscule rise in the number of female Republican members. First, the congressional pipeline cited earlier in this chapter centers on state legislative experience as the single most common stepping-stone to Congress. As described in more detail next, Democratic women have come to dramatically outnumber their Republican counterparts as state legislators, generating a growing partisan imbalance in the female congressional pipeline. In addition, Democratic women are also more likely to be lawyers, educators, and activists, the pool from which candidacies are most likely to be drawn. Fewer female Republicans enter contests for statewide and national office and tend to lag somewhat behind female Democrats in winning primary and general elections, seriously limiting opportunities for expanding their numbers as elected officials. For example, in the 2014 midterm election, the Center for American Women and Politics (CAWP) reported that Republicans continued to nominate fewer women than Democrats for congressional and statewide offices. Among those women who did enter primary contests, over twice as many Democratic women won their party's nomination for U.S. senator and representative. Among nonincumbent candidates, Republican women won primaries at a lower rate than their Democratic counterparts at nearly all levels of office seeking that year (CAWP 2014).

An additional contributing factor to the partisan gap is the regional realignment of the parties in the House of Representatives and Senate. Laurel Elder's research shows that

> over the last several decades, the regional bases of the two parties have undergone a significant shift. Since the 1950s Democrats have lost congressional seats in the South, the region they once dominated, while making gains in all other regions of the country. In contrast, Republicans have been making great gains in the South while losing seats in all other regions of the country. The South has been the region of the country least

hospitable to women's candidacies. Democrats have made gains in regions such as the Northeast and the West that are more welcoming to women's candidacies and representation.

(Elder 2008, 8)

Women of color have played a significant role in advancing descriptive representation of people of color and of women in the United States, concluded Hardy-Fanta et al. (2006), based on their extensive date collection effort of the presence of men and women of color in elected office from the local to the national levels. At the congressional level, a third factor contributing to the partisan gap in female representation is the comparatively larger gains women of color have made in obtaining congressional seats, almost exclusively within the Democratic Party. Over the past twenty years, minority women have become an increasing proportion of the women in Congress, growing from only 8 percent in 1987 to 37 percent in 2017. Of the 104 women serving in the 115th U.S. Congress, thirty-eight were women of color, thirty-four of whom were U.S. representatives. Three women of color were elected to the U.S. Senate, Catherine Cortez Masto from Nevada, who is a Latina, Tammy Duckworth from Illinois, who is Asian-Pacific Islander, and Kamala Harris from California, who is Black and South Asian. They join Asian American Mazie Hirono from Hawaii, who was elected to the Senate after having served as a U.S. representative. They are all Democrats. All but one of the female minority members of the U.S. House were Democrats in the 115th Congress. Mia Love of Idaho is the lone minority female Republican in the House, first elected in 2014.

**Text Box 8.2 U.S. Representative Elise Stefanik Being Sworn
              into Congress**

Elise Stefanik was elected to the U.S. Congress as a Republican in November 2014 to represent the 21st district of New York. At age thirty, she is the youngest woman ever elected. Representative Stefanik is an honors graduate of Harvard University, where she was awarded the Women's Leadership Award. After graduating from Harvard at twenty-one years old, she joined the administration of President George W. Bush, working on the Domestic Policy Council and the office of the White House Chief of Staff. She has worked as communications director for the Foreign Policy Initiative, as the policy director for Tim Pawlenty during his 2012 presidential campaign, and then for Paul Ryan in the general election. She then returned to New York to work in her family's business. Businesswoman is the occupation she listed on her campaign website. Running for Congress was her first attempt at seeking an electoral office.

In a Political Parity interview, Representative Stefanik was asked, "When you were running in your campaign, and even before, do you think your age was an asset, or is it something you had to convince people that you were up to this task?"

She responded, "This was a very big strategic decision that I made. When I was first talking to leaders in the district about running for Congress, they were quite surprised at my age, and I don't look like, I don't sound, like a typical Congressional candidate. At the time, I was a twenty-nine-year-old professional woman, which is not the typical snapshot if you look at Congress today. But I made the decision early on instead of running away from those attributes, I decided to make them a strength and own them and talk about my youth. Talk about my energy, talk about fresh perspective, and that stayed something that I focused [on] and was a very central theme

Picture Courtesy of *Watertown Daily*

to the campaign from the day I announced to the day I won. I also think about that as I am serving in Congress.

I really owned that as part of the rationale for my candidacy. Even such basic decisions such as my campaign slogan. A lot of candidates will use their last name, so a typical way would be to use 'Stefanik for Congress.' But instead, I wanted to own my youth, own the fact that I am accessible and very energetic. So my slogan was 'Elise for Congress.' It seems like a minor decision but it was really a very strategic decision early on that I think helped me get across the finish line." Available at www.politicalparity.org/congresswoman-elise-stefanik-podcast/.

Asian American Patsy Mink, elected to the U.S. House in 1964 from the state of Hawaii, was the first woman of color to become a member of Congress. She was the first Asian American woman to practice law in Hawaii and to serve in the Hawaii Territorial House before Hawaii became a state. Shirley Chisholm, from Brooklyn, New York, made history in 1968 as the first Black woman elected to the U.S. House. Carol Moseley Braun of Illinois, elected in 1992 and defeated for reelection in 1998, is the only Black woman to have served in the U.S. Senate prior to the 2016 election. Figure 8.4 shows the number of Black women elected to Congress through the 114th Congress. In addition, nine Latinas have been elected to the U.S. House.

In general, women of color comprise a larger proportion of U.S. representatives of their respective racial groups than White women. In the 114th Congress, eighteen of the Black representatives were female, 39 percent of all Black representatives. Latinas (nine) made up 26 percent of Latino representatives, and women (six) made up 46 percent of Asian American representatives. At the same time, White women (fifty-one) comprised 15 percent of White representatives.

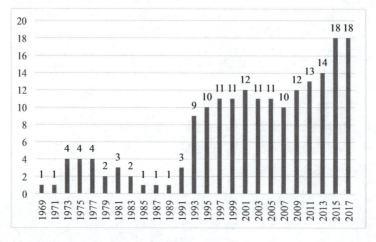

Figure 8.4 Black Women in Congress, 1970–2015

Figures compiled from the Center for American Women and Politics.

Election of Women to State Legislatures

A slow, steady increase characterizes the presence of women in the U.S. Congress over the past quarter century. One would also expect that either the same incremental process would describe women's presence as state legislators or that an even steeper and quicker rise would characterize the trend in their membership. But Figures 8.5 and 8.6 show a somewhat different trend line. Women's presence in state legislatures has been lagging since the mid-1990s after a period of modest steady increase with each election. Women's presence as state legislators has increased from less than 5 percent as the contemporary women's rights movement got under way in the 1960s to nearly one quarter of state legislators after the 2014 election. But as the figures also show, the progression slowed to a trickle after the 1992 election, and the numbers and proportions of women officeholders have stagnated since the millennium, increasing by only two percentage points from 22.5 percent to 24.2 percent from 2000 to 2014. It declined slightly following the 2010 elections before inching slightly upward as a result of the 2012 elections and then dropping slightly after the 2014 elections (CAWP 2015).

Female state legislators' contingents vary greatly across the states. In Vermont, women were 41.1 percent of its legislators in 2015, the largest contingent of female state legislators, whereas in Louisiana, only 12.5 percent were female, the smallest percentage across the states. Women in 2015 were 30 percent or more of the membership in eleven states, whereas in thirteen states, they were less than 20 percent of the membership of their legislatures.

The 2008 election resulted in a notable first in the history of female state legislators: women became the majority of the New Hampshire State Senate, the first time such a majority has occurred in any legislature. On a negative note, in 2005, when South Carolina had the lowest percentage of female legislators of all the states—fewer than 10 percent—feminist activists in the state had a billboard erected on Highway 85 shaming the state, highlighting its high level of violence against women and its low level of women elected in public office. It got worse. The 2008 election resulted in *no* women serving in the South Carolina State Senate. However, in 2010, Republican State Representative Nikki Haley was elected governor of the state. She was reelected in 2014, winning 56 percent of the vote.

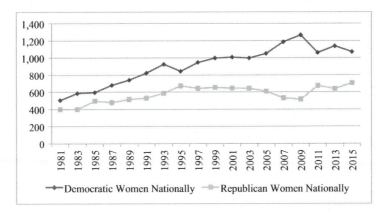

Figure 8.5 Number of Women Elected to State Legislatures by Party, 1981–2015

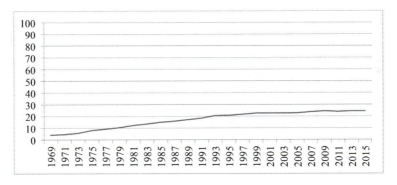

Figure 8.6 Women as a Percentage of State Legislators, 1969–2015

Picture 8.2 South Carolina Billboard

States vary in their cultures, the professionalization of their legislatures, and the strength of their party organizations. Women have made less office-holding progress in states with traditional cultures and strong, male-dominated party organizations. Research has shown that female legislators have a stronger presence in states with more liberal electorates and more women in nontraditional social positions. Women are more likely to run for office in such settings, and party leaders, voters, and interest groups are more willing to support them. Women also have a greater presence in "citizen" legislatures that meet infrequently and pay low stipends to their part-time, nonprofessional officeholders (see Reingold 2012).

Similar to trends in the U.S. Congress, state legislatures have experienced a substantial partisan gap among their female members. Democrats, as Figure 8.5 illustrates, have driven the gains women have made at the state legislative level, with some recent fluctuations. In 2015, Democratic women made up nearly 60 percent of all women in the state legislatures; prior to the 2010 election, they comprised 70 percent. Whereas Democrats tended to dominate in state legislatures in the early decades of the contemporary women's rights movement, during the 1990s and first decade and a half of the 21st century, Republicans gained strength and numbers in these legislatures, moving from the minority to the majority in many states. But women did not share proportionately in that success. Recent elections have been missed opportunities for Republican women in light of that party's dramatic gains and the fact that the Republican Party has largely controlled the legislative redistricting process in the states (Sanbonmatsu 2014). They have not been gaining as a proportion of Republican legislators.

Similar to findings at the congressional level, the election of women of color as state legislators is a significant factor in the rise of the partisan gap. As Carroll and Sanbonmatsu (2013) have summarized, "To a great extent, the rise of women Democrats is about the rise of women of color . . . one of the most notable changes in women's office holding since the 1980s," (99, 121). Women of color represent approximately one third of the all Democratic female state legislators. Overall, women of color accounted for 22 percent of female state legislators in 2015. They tend to represent districts that have substantial, if not majority-minority, populations. Few have been elected in predominately White districts.

Research has suggested that the rightward trend ideologically of the Republican Party provides an additional political explanation for the shortfall in female Republican state legislators in recent elections., According to Carroll and Sanbomatsu's (2013, 79) research, most Republican women reach office with party support, and because Republican women legislators tend to come from the moderate wing of the Republican Party, the increasing difficulty that moderate Republicans face in reaching office has disproportionately affected women. A conservative ideological bias in the selection process has made it more difficult for moderate female Republicans to win primary elections, argue Carroll and Sanbomatsu.

Election of Women to Statewide Office

Only thirty-seven women have served as governor of their states, twenty-two Democrats and fifteen Republicans. Women served as governors as early as 1925 when Nellie Taylor Ross won a special election to succeed her husband, William Ross, upon his death. She was defeated for reelection in 1927.[3] Not until 1974, when Congresswoman Ella Grasso was elected governor of Connecticut, did a woman win a gubernatorial election through her own credentials and political support. She was reelected in 1978, winning 59 percent of the vote. Twelve, or approximately one third, of these female governors gained that position either by succeeding their husbands for a variety of reasons, standing in as an interim governor, or finishing their predecessor's terms. Women have been governors of twenty-seven states that span all regions of the country. The highest number of women governing states at the same time has been nine, which occurred in 2004 and 2007. In 2017, as noted earlier, four women serve as governors, two Democrats and two Republicans.

Contrary to the partisan gap that categorizes female representation in Congress and state legislatures, a somewhat greater partisan balance is present among female governors, although Democrats have outpaced Republicans in nominating and electing female governors. Since 1992, a substantially larger number of female Democrats has received their party's nomination than female Republicans. The numbers were identical for both parties, however, in 2006 and 2010. The 2010 election was a historic one for Republican female gubernatorial candidates; four were elected, a historic high. In addition, two of the four were women of color, Latina Susana Martinez in New Mexico and Asian American Nikki Haley in South Carolina, who was thirty-eight at the time of her election. They all were reelected in 2014.

In 2012, only one woman was a major party nominee for governor, New Hampshire Democrat Maggie Hassan, who won her election. Six Democrats and three Republicans won nominations for governor in 2014; four were incumbents, all of whom were reelected. In addition, Democrat Gina Raimondo won an open seat in Rhode Island. In February 2015, Kate Brown, treasurer of the state of Oregon, assumed the state's governorship after Governor Kitzhaber resigned amid myriad criminal and ethical investigations. She won a full term in 2016.

Women assuming governorships as a result of male governors being removed due to scandals is a quirky factor in their political history and one that spans that history. It includes the colorful story of Mariam "Ma" Ferguson, who won election as governor of Texas in 1924 several years after the impeachment and removal of her husband, "Pa" Ferguson, from the governorship and who was ruled ineligible to hold office under Texas jurisdiction. Consequently, he entered his wife, Mariam, in the Democratic primary for governor in 1924. She told voters she would follow the advice of her husband and that Texas would get "two governors for the price of one." A popular campaign slogan was "Me for Ma, and I Ain't Got a Durned Thing Against Pa." Against the odds, Ma Ferguson was elected governor, becoming the first female chief executive of Texas. Former Governor Ferguson actually managed much of the state's business during his wife's tenure, and the scandals of his earlier administration continued to harm her time in office. Mariam Ferguson was primarily a figurehead as governor. Ma Ferguson was defeated in the Democratic Party primary in 1926 but was elected for a second term in 1932.

Since 2000, twenty women have been appointed (four) or elected (sixteen) as governors of their states, including Sarah Palin, who, while serving as governor of Alaska, was chosen by John McCain to be the Republican vice presidential nominee in 2008. All these women were experienced politicians at the time they assumed the governorship of their states, having served as state legislators, state attorney generals, treasurers and insurance commissioners, lieutenant governors, or mayors, in Governor Palin's case. Whereas Democratic women have historically outnumbered Republican women as governors, if we widen our lens to consider all statewide elected executive positions such as lieutenant governor, secretary of state, and attorney, then female Republicans held more of these positions than female Democrats in 2015 (forty-two to thirty-six). However, in eight of the fourteen elections since 2000, more Democratic women than Republican women have won election to these executive positions.

Because of the small number of female governors, it is difficult to determine whether women bring distinctive characteristics to this office and whether they govern in a distinct manner compared with male governors. Female governors do appear to appoint more women to office (Riccucci and Saidel 2001) but do not appear to have significant policy differences from male governors (Ferrara 2012). Recent female governors appear to be neither more nor less popular in their states than their male counterparts (see Cohen 2013).

With the election of Republican Joni Ernst of Iowa to the U.S. Senate in 2014, Mississippi remains the only state in the nation that has not elected a woman to either represent it in the U.S. Congress or to serve as its governor. The 2012 election resulted in women holding all of New Hampshire's congressional delegation seats—Senate and House—and its governorship. Four states have had women as both of their U.S. senators—Maine, New Hampshire, Washington, and California. Women have become visible and commonplace as political leaders across the country, although parity in elected office holding is a long way off.

Female Office-Holding Pioneers

The United States elected its first woman mayor in 1887 in the small Quaker village of Argonia, Kansas. Kansas women had recently won the right to vote in cities of a certain size.

Susanna Salter was a twenty-seven-year old housewife and an active member of the Women's Christian Temperance Union (WCTU), which endorsed an all-male slate of candidates for local office that year.

This activist group's bold act annoyed some of Argonia's male residents, who devised a plan to make the WCTU look silly, discredit its endorsements, and, they hoped, drive the group to disband in shame.

> They published a fake WCTU endorsement list, exactly like the real one except that Salter was named as the group's choice for mayor. The idea was that Salter would get only a couple of votes and the people of Argonia would see that the WCTU (and, by extension, all women) had no power in politics and no place trying to grub some up. The plan backfired spectacularly when Salter was elected, becoming the first female mayor in the U.S. and one of the first women elected to any kind of American political office.
>
> (Koerth-Baker 2016)

Jeannette Rankin was the first woman elected to the U.S. Congress. She was elected as a Republican in Montana in 1916.[4] She served only one term, choosing to run for a seat in the U.S. Senate in 1918 but was defeated in the Republican primary. Over twenty years later, she was elected a second time to the U.S. House in 1940, again serving only one term. Her two terms in Congress coincided with U.S. entry into both world wars. A lifelong pacifist, she was one of fifty-six members of Congress who voted against entry into World War I in 1917, stating, "I felt the first time the first woman had a chance to say no to war, she should say it." In her second term, she was the only member of Congress to vote against declaring war on Japan after the attack on Pearl Harbor in 1941, declaring, "As a woman I can't go to war and I refuse to send anyone else." Needless to say, this stand was extremely unpopular, leading her to decide not to run for reelection in 1942, knowing she would most likely have been defeated. She continued her antiwar efforts throughout her life. Among other actions, she protested against the Vietnam War in the 1960s. In January 1968, the Jeannette Rankin Brigade, a coalition of women's peace groups, organized an antiwar march in Washington, DC—the largest march by women since the 1913 woman suffrage parade. Rankin led the five thousand participants from Union Station to the steps of the Capitol Building, where they presented a peace petition to then-House Speaker John McCormack of Massachusetts.

During the 19th and early 20th centuries, women ran for and won office in both suffrage and nonsuffrage states. These offices were almost uniformly related to the governance of school systems. In the 1860s and 1870s, for example, a few women were elected to school committees in Massachusetts, even though women could not vote in these elections. In 1906, eighteen women were elected county school superintendents (out of fifty-three) in South Dakota (Andersen 1996, 112–113). The first female state legislators were three women elected to the Colorado General Assembly in 1894. Two years later, Utah elected

Picture 8.3　Jeannette Rankin Campaigning
AP photo

the first woman to a state senate. By the turn of the century, sixteen women had served in the state legislatures of Colorado, Idaho, and Utah (Cox 1996).

Of the few women who were members of the U.S. House of Representatives in the decade after suffrage, many were widows initially elected to complete their deceased husbands' unexpired terms. The majority of women who ran for congressional office were "sacrificial lambs" nominated by the state's or district's minority party. As India Edwards, vice chair of the Democratic National Committee in the years following the suffrage victory, put it, "If the party backs a woman you can be pretty sure they do it because they think it is a lost cause but they know they to have *some* candidate" (Deckard 1979, 309).

The first woman to serve in the U.S. Senate, Rebecca Latimer Felton, a Democrat from Georgia, held office for only one day in 1922. Governor Thomas Hardwick appointed her to fill the vacant seat of Senator Thomas Watson, who had died in September. The senator's death created both a special election to complete the current term and a general election for senator in the next Congress. Governor Hardwick, who was a candidate for the Senate seat in the special election and general election, appointed Felton, knowing she would not be a candidate in the special election to fill the vacant seat until the election and as a way to secure the vote of new women voters whom he had alienated by his opposition to the 19th Amendment. Hardwick pointed out that his appointee would not actually "serve" because Congress was not in session when Watson died, and the next session would not begin until the following year after the general election. However, Congress did reconvene on November 21, and Walter George instead of Governor Hardwick won both the special and the general elections. George then allowed Felton to be sworn in rather than taking the seat immediately after bowing to a campaign by Georgian women for seating her. Felton thus became the first woman seated in the Senate and served until George took office on November 22, 1922, one day later. She had been an ardent suffragist but also a White supremacist.

Although women had occasionally served in state legislatures before the suffrage amendment was ratified, the number of women running for and winning state legislative seats increased substantially during the 1920s. By 1931, only Louisiana had never elected a female legislator (Andersen 1996, 116).

Contemporary Women Elected to the U.S. House of Representatives

The concept of representation is central to electoral politics and political leadership. A significant aspect of representation as described in the preceding paragraphs is its descriptive nature. Who leads and how they get there are among the most significant political questions we ask. The backgrounds of political candidates are theoretically important because they are related to success in the political sphere, illustrate the degree of openness in the political system, and may affect interests and behaviors in public office, although these latter empirical relationships are complex (Burrell 1994, 58). In addition to a wider diversity of demographic characteristics, the distinctive backgrounds and experiences of the female winners could contribute to a more expansive approach to agenda setting, lawmaking, and contemporary descriptive representation. Scholars, therefore, have asked: how similar or different are the pathways men and women have taken into national elected office? The following anecdote from the 2010 election provides a political perspective on this aspect of representation.

Nine Republican women were newly elected to the U.S. House in the 2010 elections. The Republican Party was quick to capitalize on their success, given the problems the party has had in increasing its female contingent of national legislators and its perception of being an antiwoman party, as Chapter 4 discussed. Immediately following the election, ten Republican female members of the U.S. House issued a press release trumpeting 2010 as the "year of the Republican woman." They highlighted the record-breaking number of Republican women who had mounted campaigns for the House, their successes, varied backgrounds, and areas of the country from which they came. The press release noted,

> These are the stories that made 2010 the year of the Republican woman. They're about farmers, attorneys, teachers, nurses, doctors, small-business owners, law enforcement officials, entrepreneurs, wives and mothers. They're the stories of the dynamic and driven women who will be sworn in as members of the 112th Congress.
> (Women Members of the House GOP Caucus 2010)

This press release highlights the political importance attached to descriptive characteristics of elected officials. In the elections since the 1992 "Year of the Woman" election and throughout the 2014 election, 750 individuals were newly elected to the U.S. House; 133 (18 percent) were women. Their mere presence, in addition to the number of women of color who have been elected, as described earlier, represent a growing diversity among its members, although the national legislature remains a predominantly White male institution. The 2014 election was distinctive in having the youngest woman ever elected, thirty-year-old Elise Stefanik of New York. Text Box 8.2 highlights aspects of her biography.

Among other things, rather than perceiving her youth as a challenge, Representative Stefanik promoted it as an asset in her campaign. At the other end of the ideological and age spectrum, Text Box 8.3 highlights the campaign of Nancy Jo Kemper.

Text Box 8.3 Nancy Jo Kemper Announces for Congress

Occasionally, one finds exceptions to the strategic nature of a candidacy of national office among contemporary female politicians. Democrat Nancy Jo Kemper, a sixty-five-year-old United Church of Christ minister is one such example from the 2016 congressional election. In announcing her candidacy to oppose second-term U.S. Representative Andy Barr in Kentucky's district, she describes how she came to be a candidate. "It started as a wild idea," she said, but as she thought about it more, she concluded that in this year that has brought success to other political outsiders, voters just might give a nonpolitician like her a chance. "I'm rooted with a lot of passion and a lot of energy. I didn't see anyone stand up, so I said, 'Why not.'"

"The idea of a woman—a grandmother who doesn't have deep pockets and who is living basically on Social Security; someone who knows how to be a single mother; someone who understands that Washington has some severe broken places; and someone who is intent on reaching out to try to find ways to heal the divide that keeps people from working together with dignity—is very appealing to our voters," she said.

Eli Yokley, Roll Call January 22, 2016, http://atr.rollcall.com/kentucky-andy-barr-challenger-wont-shy-away-obama-policies/?dcz=emailalert.

See also Claire Zillman, 2017, "As Trump Inspires More Women to Run, This Mayor Explains How She 'Googled' Her Way into Office," *Fortune*, January 24, http://fortune.com/2017/01/24/trump-women-politics-sonoma-mayor/.

Representative Stefanik is also distinctive in that running for a seat in the U.S. Congress was her first campaign for elected office. Possessing prior electoral credentials is more characteristic of female newcomers to national office holding in the current era (1994–2014) than their male counterparts. Nearly 75 percent of women had held an elective office compared with 63 percent of men prior to being elected to the U.S. House of Representatives. This gender gap may be one of the few remaining pieces of evidence suggesting that women must be better to win or at least perceive that they have to be better.

Republican male representatives primarily account for the gender gap in prior office-holding experience in the contemporary era. They are the largest contingent not to have won some other office before running for a seat in the U.S. House; 41 percent of them were first-time candidates compared with 31 percent of the newly elected Democratic males, 24 percent of their Democratic female counterparts, and 26 percent of the female Republicans. A majority of the first-term female members (51 percent) had had state legislative office experience, as did 41 percent of the men. Regarding prior executive office experience, a few of both sexes had been mayors (3 percent of each), whereas nearly twice as many of the men (9 percent) had held some type of statewide elected office as women (5 percent).

Contemporary male and female newcomers have very similar educational credentials. Only one member elected since 1992 had not completed high school.[5] More than 90 percent of both sexes had college degrees, and the female members were nearly as likely to have law degrees (33 percent) as the male members (36 percent).

Family factors have long been central in considerations of women's political careers. Women's disproportionate responsibility for raising their children in particular has accounted for delays in their undertaking candidacies, especially for elected positions that would take them away from their communities. A female Republican state party leader's comment in Political Parity's 2015 *Right the Ratio* report illustrates the problem.

> What frustrates me is that people say, "She has kids. Can she manage this?" A lot of men have kids at home and it doesn't cross their mind. This whole "Can she manage being a wife, mother and an elected official?" We never care about men in that way.
>
> (Shames 2015, 30)

The constraint of traditional sex role perceptions about women running and serving in high elected positions while having young children may be changing, however. Lyndsey Layton's 2007 *Washington Post* article on women in the U.S. House and Senate titled "Moms in the House, with Kids at Home," nicely illustrates this change. Layton characterized these women, ten of them raising children under thirteen, as a select group. The article focused on how they balanced motherhood with politicking and lawmaking. Little mention was made in the article of their encountering criticism along the campaign trail or having had to face and overcome discrimination in seeking such a high-powered position while caring for young children. Although such an article would not have been a news piece for a comparable set of male representatives and senators, it set a positive tone while highlighting gender roles. The article centered on these female lawmakers' coping mechanisms and the support they have given to one another.

> They reside on a shaky high wire, balancing motherhood with politicking, lawmaking, fundraising and the constant shuttle between Washington and their home states. . . . And they all live with a reality possibly even more difficult: The public will scrutinize and judge the mothering choices these politicians make. It is this that sets them apart from other professional women and their male counterparts in Congress, and the

10 in the group are keenly sensitive to it. If they have private moments in which they question the work-life balance, most are reluctant to reveal them. Instead, they say their kids benefit from the special opportunities—picnics at the White House and VIP tours of landmarks—and get early exposure to public service. One boasted that her daughter, when she was 11, could rattle off an explanation of the Medicare "doughnut hole."

(Layton 2007, A01)

Several of these representatives and senators expressed determination to show that a woman can raise a family while serving in Congress. Nearly all said they felt compelled to use their own positions as the tiny minority of working mothers in Congress to represent the 70 percent of mothers who have school-age children and jobs outside the home. The number of female U.S. representatives with young children has continued to expand in recent Congresses.

Giving birth while serving in the national legislature is no longer a media phenomenon. Nine women have had babies while serving as a U.S. representative. Seven babies have been born to female members since 2007. The 111th Congress experienced a new first in this regard. Linda Sanchez, forty, gave birth in May 2009. What made her experience unique was that she was the first female representative to be openly pregnant out of wedlock. She and her boyfriend subsequently married prior to her giving birth. Whereas her experience received much media attention, little consternation was expressed in the mainstream print media, and she won reelection in 2010 with 64 percent of the vote. Representative McMorris Rodgers has given birth to three children since becoming a U.S. representative and serving in the Republican House leadership.

The female members newly elected since 1992 were less likely to be married (66 percent compared to 87 percent) and more likely to be divorced than their male counterparts (15 percent to 3 percent). Profile data do not tell us whether a member has been divorced and then remarried, only their marital status at the time of their elections. It may be that the male members are more likely to have been divorced and remarried, whereas female members who have been divorced have not entered into a second marriage. The sexes do not differ in the number who have never been married, about 10 percent of both sexes. Nine of the contemporary female members are widows, and one of the male members is a widower. Gays and lesbians have been elected to the U.S. Congress. Tammy Baldwin, a Democrat from Wisconsin, broke the lesbian barrier when she was elected to the U.S. House in 1998. In 2012, she was elected to the U.S. Senate.

Public service/politics, business, and law are the most frequent occupations U.S. House members in the 114th Congress cited in describing their precongressional careers. Education is a distant fourth profession (Manning 2015). Although a particular subset of professions may dominate among this elected elite group of individuals, many members of Congress have eclectic career paths. Whether the women elected are similar to their male colleagues in their career backgrounds or tend to take distinctive paths to national office is an important representational question. Note the diverse backgrounds highlighted in the 2010 Republican press release cited earlier touting their newly elected Republican female members as one illustration of that distinctiveness.

Elise Stefanik, the youngest woman elected to the U.S. House in 2014, pursued a public service and political career immediately upon graduating from college and then entered her family's business to establish a local connection to run for Congress. At the other end of the age spectrum, sixty-eight-year-old Alma Adams was elected to represent the 12th district of North Carolina in 2014. She has had a long career in politics, having served as a North Carolina state representative since 1994 and a member of the Greensboro School Board prior to election as a state representative. She has a PhD in art education/multicultural education from Ohio State University. In addition to her professional career in politics, Representative Adams has been a professor of art at Bennett College in Greensboro and director of the Steel Hall Art Gallery. In 1990, she helped cofound, with Eva Hamlin Miller, the African American Atelier, an organization established to advance awareness of and appreciation for visual arts and cultures of African Americans.[6]

Further illustrating distinctive career paths are the two women elected as part of the California delegation, one a Republican and one a Democrat, to the U.S. House in 2014. Republican Mimi Walters, age fifty-two, lists her profession as stockbroker. Her biography states that she possesses a background in business, finance, and local government. Her professional career has included serving as an investment executive for seven years at a major investment banking firm. Her political career includes election to the Laguna, California, city council, mayor of Laguna, state representative, and state senator. Thus, she has combined business and public service careers. Democrat Norma Torres, age forty-nine when elected to the U.S. House, was born in Guatemala and immigrated to Los Angeles at age five. She lists her profession as police dispatcher and has long been active in her union. Although their professional careers are quite dissimilar, Representative Walters's and Representative Torres's political careers have been similar. Representative Torres's political career includes election to the city council, service as mayor of Pomona, California, and election to the California State Senate.

The 114th Congress had three female representatives who were military veterans: Tammy Duckworth, a helicopter pilot during the Iraq War, had been shot down and lost her legs; Tulsi Gabbard is a captain in the Hawaii National Guard and has served two tours of duty in Iraq, where she was awarded the Meritorious Service Medal; and Martha McSally, a retired air force colonel and the first woman to command a U.S. Air Force fighter squadron. U.S. Senator Joni Ernst (R-IA) is a retired Lt. Colonel in the Iowa National Guard.

A rough grouping of these contemporary members into Congressional Research Service's four major profile occupational categories finds some slight differences between the sexes. The female members were more likely to have business occupations (56 percent to 44 percent) and less likely to have had law occupations (26 percent to 32 percent). Similar proportions had careers in public service/politics. Nine percent of the female representatives and 7 percent of the male representatives had had educational occupations. Perhaps what is most striking, however, is the great diversity of careers the female (as well as the male) representatives have brought to the U.S. House. They have engaged in a great variety of occupations prior to their elections to Congress, ranging from a Mary Kay Cosmetics saleswoman (Democrat Debbie Halverson) to ambassador to Luxembourg (Representative Ann Wagner).

Political Ambition

"Ambition lies at the heart of politics. Politics thrives on the hope of preferment and the drive for office," the preeminent scholar of political ambition, Joseph Schlesinger (1966), has told us. He argues that individuals climb the political career ladder and gain higher office when the opportunity presents itself. Political actors inherently possess a progressive political ambition that leads them to further their political careers by seeking higher level office.

Studies of political careers center on the ambitious politician. According to political ambition theory, long-standing interest in public life precedes office holding. The decision to enter a given electoral contest is understood as an individual, rational calculus in which a politician assesses the relative costs and benefits of running for a given office and the probability of winning. Studies of political ambition have centered on nascent political ambition—that is, interest in first becoming a political candidate and progressive ambition and the decision to seek higher office, often risking or giving up one's current elected office. But how does one form a politically ambitious persona? Do women acquire nascent political ambition and progressive ambition similarly to men? Do the same factors affect both nascent and progressive political ambition among women and men?

Women as a group tend to be less politically ambitious than men. Scholars have long noted this gender gap in political ambition. The notable studies of Jennifer Lawless and Richard Fox (2015a, b) in the first decade of the 21st century have found contemporary evidence in support of lesser ambition on the part of women. Their studies of well-educated, well-credentialed professional men and women found that women are less likely than men to consider running for public office, are less likely to run for office, and are less likely than men to express interest in running for office in the future (Lawless and Fox 2010, 164).

Studies of the subset of women who have actually run for and been elected to public office offer two divergent takes on the role of political ambition in their careers. At the national level of office holding, political scientist Irwin Gertzog (2002) has described contemporary female members of Congress as ambitious, experienced, rational, and skillful. They tend to be similar to men in their electability and in their campaign strategies and techniques. As strategic candidates, they carefully consider the chances of securing their party's nomination. Their entry into a race is based on the likelihood of success.

> They calculate how victory or defeat will affect their careers, and more often than not, they wait for an incumbent to retire or otherwise leave an office before seeking the office. Political decisions, particularly those about whether to run and which office to seek, are made dispassionately, only after the advantages and drawbacks of each course of action are subject to rational calculation.
>
> (Gertzog 2002, 103)

Text Box 8.4 describes the work of a recently created organization that promotes Black women's political leadership.

Text Box 8.4 Higher Heights for America

Higher Heights for America and its sister organization, Higher Heights Leadership Fund, is a national organization founded in 2012 to promote Black women's leadership. Its goals according to its statement of purpose include the following:

- Reconfigure the makeup of decision-making tables to include Black women from across the socioeconomic spectrums at all levels.
- Elevate Black women's voices to shape and advance progressive policies and politics.
- Foster creative collaboration across constituencies and issues, ensuring that race/gender equity and inclusion are incorporated into ongoing progressive-based building efforts, issue-based advocacy campaigns, and voter engagement campaigns and electoral strategies.

Higher Heights runs three programs to advance its goals.

- **SISTER TO SISTER SALON CONVERSATIONS**

  Sister to Sister Salon Conversations are gatherings in which Black women come together to share their views, concerns, and opinions about their political power and leadership potential. Black women are encouraged to host salons in their communities and are provided toolkits.

- **SUNDAY BRUNCH WITH HIGHER HEIGHTS**

  Sunday Brunch with Higher Heights is bringing the power of talking and brunching into the 21st century. A joint program from Higher Heights for America and Higher Heights Leadership Fund, this monthly social media-driven series seeks to encourage Black women to become part of national conversations on trending political and current events affecting their communities.

- **SISTAS TO WATCH**

  When looking at politics and government, our representation remains mostly White and mostly male. Look closer, and you can see eighteen Black women serving in Congress. Look even closer, and you see 250 Black women legislators serving in forty-four states.

Higher Heights has issued three reports: *Black Women's Response to the War on Women*; *Voices, Votes, Leadership: 2015 Status of Black Women in American Politics*; and the *Status of Black Women in American Politics*. It runs its own PAC, Higher Heights for America PAC, which raised $15,000 for federal election candidates.

Further information about Higher Heights for America is available at www.higherheightsforamerica.org.

At state and local levels, however, research suggests that women make the decision to run differently from their male counterparts. They use a different cost-benefit calculus to determine whether it is worth the risk. The research of Carroll and Sanbonmatsu (2013) suggests that instead of pure ambition driving the decision to enter a race, women's candidacies are initiated more through the recruitment and encouragement of others than men's decisions in the context of a specific political opportunity, even in the absence of prior ambition, what they call a "relationally embedded process." Candidacy may be equally or even more dependent on the consequences of that candidacy for others than on the personal costs and benefits to the candidate (Carroll and Sanbonmatsu 2013, 61). A majority of the female state legislators they surveyed responded that they had never thought seriously about running until someone else suggested it. The encouragement of other people plays a greater role in women's decisions than in men's at this level. Based on his interviews with male and female governors, Jason Windett suggests, too, that women will often become motivated to run for elective office for different reasons than their male counterparts:

> They will generally become involved in a form of political participation other than seeking office prior to running for their first elective position. For many female potential candidates, this type of political participation will often take the form of lobbying or promoting specific causes. Women will become active in political movements, which will eventually give them confidence or allow them to interact with individuals who influence them to later run for office. In addition, women who have been active on the campaigns of others develop ambition to run for office themselves at higher rates than women who do not have campaign experience.

(Windett 2014, 291)

Because women's decisions more often are relationally embedded than men's, recruitment, support, and encouragement from political parties, political organizations, and friends and family, from all kinds of sources, are critically important. Also, sprinkled throughout this text are examples of women initiating their own campaigns for elected office. This chapter's conclusion addresses efforts to enhance women's political ambition and to build the capacity of women to run for elected office.

Campaigning for Elected Office

For many years, women were believed to be disadvantaged relative to male candidates when running for public office. Conventional wisdom held that voters were less likely to vote for them than for male candidates, party leaders did not recruit them for winnable seats, and women were less capable than men of raising money to fund their campaigns. Media coverage of their campaigns stereotyped female candidates by emphasizing feminine traits and issues and giving them less coverage. But that conventional wisdom is no longer an accurate representation of women's quests for political leadership. Female candidates now raise as much money to fund their campaigns as male candidates. They are ambitious, experienced, rational, and skillful. Research has shown them to be similar to men in their electability and in their campaign strategies and techniques.

Political commentators have come to characterize female congressional candidates as being "fierce and well-financed competitors in a large number of the country's hottest and nastiest races" (Leonard 2000, A37). In the 2004 election cycle, they were described as "the most capable group of women candidates yet" (Chaddock 2004, 1). In this same article, Karen White of EMILY's List states,

> The women who are running this year are tough as nails. These are women who know how to raise money, put together the campaign operation, and have the political and constituent bases. . . . In the early 1980s, women were the anomaly, the underdog. These are leading candidates.
>
> (Chaddock 2004, 1)

The phrase "when women run, women win" has become the new summary wisdom based on much research comparing the campaigns of men and women for national office. What this phrase means is that voters are as likely to vote for a female candidate as a male candidate and that female candidates equal male candidates in the credentials they bring to a campaign and the resources, especially financial ones, they acquire to support their campaigns. Yet activists and scholars continue to suggest that although female candidates may be as likely as men to win, when they run, they still have to *work harder* and *be better* than their male counterparts to win and be reelected and to spend more time and effort building financial war chests. But little empirical evidence supports this new caveat about women's campaigns.

A main obstacle to wider descriptive representation based on sex at all levels of political office in the United States is that most incumbents are men. In most electoral settings, incumbents easily win reelection, limiting opportunities for new office seekers to win seats in a legislative body or an executive office. Incumbency advantage is the primary factor accounting for the glacial pace at which women have increased their numbers in elected office. Most incumbents in the national legislature, for example, run for reelection. Typically, more than 90 percent of them are reelected. In the 2014 election, for instance, 390 of the 435 members of the U.S. House of Representatives ran for reelection; four were defeated in a primary election, and only thirteen lost in the general election. Overall, 96 percent were victorious. Since running for political office has long been something that only men did, their numbers as incumbents have limited women's strategic possibilities of winning either state or national elective office.

The challenge of incumbency advantage is shown in the nature of contemporary U.S. House of Representatives' freshmen classes. All the newly elected female U.S. House members elected in the 1992 "Year of the Woman" election won open seats—that is, seats in which an incumbent was not running. In the elections since then through the 2014 contests, 18 percent (132) of the 747 individuals elected to the U.S. House for the first time have been women. Seventy percent of the newly elected women and 68 percent of the newly elected men won open seats. Thus, the problem regarding increasing female representation as national lawmakers has been in the first instance that so few seats have offered the opportunity of contests not involving incumbents. Further, in each election, some female incumbents decide not to seek reelection, some decide to run for the U.S. Senate, and a few suffer defeat when seeking reelection. Thus, just to maintain the numerical status quo, in addition to expanding their representation, is a continuing challenge for would-be female legislators.

Commonplace in contemporary election seasons is commentary on whether it would be another year of the woman, a record year for female candidacies, or a decline in their numbers while pondering the positives and negatives for such candidacies. Every election season since 1996, CAWP has tracked and reported on the number of women running for Congress, issuing a press release at the end of the primary season, such as the 2012 release titled "Women Surpass House, Senate Candidate Records as Final November Slates Are Set" (CAWP 2012). Drawing on these reports, pundits have chronicled the ebbs and flows in the number of women candidates across these elections as a measure of women's ambition for political leadership and as an assessment of a particular election's environment for women's candidacies. For example, when *Politico*'s John Fortier (2008) wrote about the promise of the 2008 environment for female candidates, he looked at the early CAWP numbers of women who had become congressional candidates in that year's election, observing that,

> in Congress, where the number of women has increased each election for the past 30 years, that rise may come to a halt in November. . . . 2008 does not look like a banner year for women. Fewer women are running in primaries, and there are fewer likely female nominees. In 2006, 211 House women filed for primaries. That number will drop below 200 this year.

(He turned out to be wrong.)

The 2016 election was no different in this media speculation, as the following two examples illustrate. "If 2016 has been the year of Trump in politics, it may also end up being a new Year of the Woman, if Democrats get their way" (Werner 2016). Ann Friedman (2016) wrote in the *Huffington Post*,

> In 2016 we could see a record-breaking number of women elected to the Senate. There are nine pro-choice Democratic women running for Senate this year, most of whom have a good shot at election. Compare that to the supposedly watershed "Year of the Woman" in 1992, which only saw four women senators elected. And, this year, four of the nine contenders are women of color, which is huge because only two women of color have *ever*, in history, been elected to the Senate.

CAWP's 2016 tracking of women's candidacies concluded at the end of the primary season that

> the prospects for women in races for the U.S. Senate and House of Representatives point to a year of moderate to minimal change, with a few historic landmarks likely. Republican women, who secured fewer nominations this year than in the past, are

likely to see their numbers dip further. The number of women who will serve in the 115 Congress will depend heavily on how the parties fare overall, but the number of Republican women will likely decline from the current 22 to 21, based on current election ratings.

Figure 8.7 shows the number of female Democrats and Republicans who have entered different types of primaries for a seat in the U.S. House between 1993 and 2016. Few women in either party have challenged their party's incumbent representatives in a primary election. The largest contingent of female candidates in both parties has been women who entered a primary in the out-party to challenge the other party's sitting representative. The number of female Democratic incumbents running to keep their seats accumulates over the elections to far surpass female Republican incumbent quests for reelection. What is most significant for growing the numbers of female U.S. Representatives and reaching gender equity in the national legislature is the presence of women as open-seat contenders. The following paragraphs examine the trends and factors affecting women's candidacies in open seats.

Tracking the overall number of female entrants in congressional elections is important, but assessing women's presence requires taking context into account, including partisanship, electoral swings, opportunity structures, and issue contexts of the various election cycles under examination, as they appear to affect women's candidacies. These factors are all important ingredients in any analysis of women's candidacies as indicators and measures of equity gains in the political process.

Although they have vastly increased their presence as candidates, women still lag behind men in entering opportune contests for newcomers, which are primarily open-seat elections not involving an incumbent. Over the course of open-seat contests from 1994 through 2014, women have accounted for 24 percent and 26 percent, respectively, of the Republican and Democratic primary candidates for these seats. But it is not just a matter of entering any open-seat primary. Although open seats are the prime opportunities for newcomers, they vary in how opportune they are for any particular candidate, depending

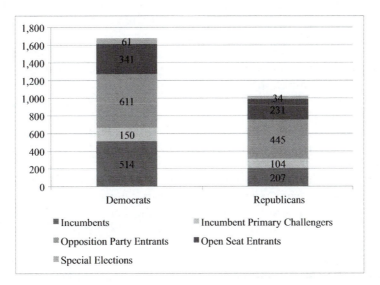

Figure 8.7 Number and Type of Female Candidacies for the U.S. House of Representatives, 1993–2016

on party affiliation and the strength of one's party in a district. The Democratic Party dominates some districts, some districts are competitive, and in some districts, Republicans dominate. Throughout these contemporary elections, at least one Democratic woman has run in her party's primary in 72 percent of the Democratic-dominated districts, and at least one Republican woman was a candidate in 45 percent of the Republican-dominated districts. A woman candidate has been as likely to win an open-seat primary as a male candidate (see Burrell 2014).

Gender Stereotyping

What do Americans think about women as candidates for elected office and as political leaders? Voters have been thought to view and evaluate female candidates differently from their male counterparts, attributing distinctive skills and capabilities to each sex affecting the vote-getting potential of female candidates. For much of our political history, conventional wisdom suggested that voters were biased against female candidates engaging in quests for political leadership in what would be described as voter sexism. Women were thought to be too emotional for politics, and their family life roles precluded them from active participation in public roles.

Regarding personality traits, early studies showed that female candidates were thought to be more compassionate and honest than men, whereas men were viewed as stronger leaders and better decision makers. Female politicians, too, were perceived as having distinctive policy concerns and positions, such as being more liberal and more interested in issues that affect women, children, education, and health and less focused on such issues as business, the economy, and foreign affairs. These distinctive perspectives of men and women are called gender stereotypes. A stereotype involves ascribing attributes to a group based on its demographic characteristics, such as race and sex, and not necessarily related to actual behavior. Stereotypes allow people to quickly and efficiently, if not accurately, make assumptions about the likely characteristics and behaviors of people. Gender stereotypes in the political realm seem to cause voters to have distinctive views of men and women and thus to evaluate them differently as political leaders. But as with so much else in the political world regarding women and political leadership, those stereotypes are waning. Public attitudes about the political leadership of women have shifted toward similarity with perspectives regarding male leaders.

Consider first that, for more than thirty years, the General Social Survey has asked a national sample of respondents whether men are better suited emotionally for politics than most women. Figure 8.8 tracks men's and women's responses to this question. In 1991, just before the "Year of the Woman" election, 72 percent of men and 70 percent of women disagreed with this statement that men were better suited emotionally for politics than most women. By 2014, 80 percent of both sexes disagreed that men were better suited emotionally for politics than most women. Chapter 1 showed that the public had also come to support the idea of a woman as president at least in response to a general survey question. "Americans believe women have the right stuff to be political leaders," the Pew Research Center concluded in 2008 after surveying a national sample of men and women (Taylor 2008). In a follow-up study in 2014, they reported, "According to the majority of Americans women are every bit as capable of being good political leaders as men" (Parker 2015).

The 2008 Pew Research Center survey respondents were asked whether a set of leadership traits such as honesty and intelligence were truer of men or women. Sixty-nine percent said men and women make equally good leaders, 6 percent said women make better leaders, and 21 percent said men. The survey also asked respondents to assess whether

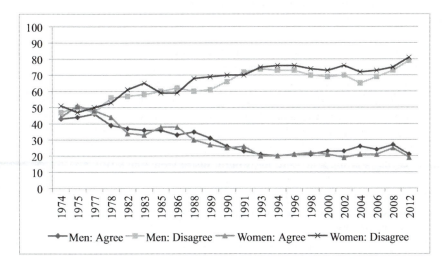

Figure 8.8 Men Better Suited Emotionally for Politics
Source: General Social Survey (www.gss.norc.org).

men or women in public office were better at handling a range of policy matters and job performance challenges. On the policy front, women were widely judged to be better than men at dealing with social issues such as health care and education, whereas men had a big edge over women in the public's perception of the way they deal with crime, public safety, defense, and national security. As for job performance skills, women got higher marks than men in all the measures tested: standing up for one's principles in the face of political pressure, being able to work out compromises, keeping government honest, and representing the interests of "people like you." The Pew Research Center's 2014 survey confirmed these findings; notably, 78 percent of women said that more women in leadership would improve the quality of life for all women: 38 percent said "a lot," and 40 percent said "some." Among the male respondents, 19 percent said "a lot," and 43 percent said "some."

In the 2010 election, Kathleen Dolan surveyed voters regarding whether they thought eight characteristics better described male or female candidates or whether they did not think there was a difference. The characteristics were intelligent, honest, decisive, compassionate, can build consensus, can change the way government works, leadership, and has political experience. On each of these traits, large majorities saw no difference. For most of the issues, respondents holding stereotypes held them in the expected direction: women as more compassionate and men as more decisive. Two exceptions were found: women and men were equally likely to be able to build consensus, and women were seen as more intelligent than men (Dolan 2014, 64). Further, majorities of respondents believed that there should be more women in elected office than was currently the case and that more women in office would be positive for our system. Abstract gender stereotypes had relatively limited influence on specific candidate evaluations. Instead, what mattered most in people's evaluations of candidates, women or men, were traditional political considerations such as political party, incumbency, and campaign spending.

In addition, based on several large, representative national experiments, political scientist Deborah J. Brooks (2013) found little evidence that voters penalize women candidates due to gender stereotypes. For example, Brooks failed to find gender bias in her experiments when examining voter response to news stories about candidate experience and candidate displays of anger, crying, toughness, lack of empathy, and knowledge gaffes. She concludes that

> women candidates do not face a tougher road to winning over the American public than their male counterparts, as many have long feared was the case. Women do not need to be "twice as good" as men to do well in politics. Women do not start on more tenuous ground, and they are not more likely to alienate the public with missteps along the way. This research should give them more confidence that their first slip-up is unlikely to be their last; or at the very least, that their slip-ups and imperfections would be similarly damaging for their male counterparts. None of the behaviors tested in this study—crying, getting angry, acting tough, displaying a lack of empathy, or engaging in knowledge gaffes—hurt female candidates significantly more than male candidates. The public appears to be receptive to the idea of female political leadership, and that is very good news, indeed. . . . It appears that women leaders are judged more as leaders than as ladies by most people.
>
> (Brooks 2013, 164–165)

The 2016 election was historical for women candidates not only because Hillary Clinton won the Democratic Party nomination for president but also because thirty-year-old Misty Snow became the first openly transgender person to receive a major party nomination for the U.S. Senate, winning the Democratic primary in Utah to face incumbent Republican Mike Lee in the general election. Misty Plowright, also a transgender woman, won the Democratic nomination in Colorado's 5th congressional district to face Republican incumbent Douglas Lamborn. Both women lost their elections.

Financing Election Campaigns

When considering a campaign for elected office, especially for national office, the question of the amount of money it will take to run a credible campaign and the potential likelihood of an individual being able to raise those dollars is among the most prominent one potential candidates face. The cost of winning a congressional election doubled in 2012 dollars over the last two decades (Ornstein et al. 2013). In 2012, the average cost of winning a U.S. House seat was $1.6 million, and the price tag for a successful U.S. Senate bid averaged $10.35 million. As the cost of campaigns has risen, so, too, has outside campaign spending. From 1992 to 2012, nonparty independent expenditures have increased nearly fifty-fold in U.S. House races and nearly one hundred-fold in U.S. Senate contests (Ornstein et al. 2013). Congressional candidates running in the 2013–2014 election cycle raised $1.7 billion and spent $1.6 billion in the twenty-four-month period, according to campaign finance reports filed with the Federal Election Commission that cover activity from January 1, 2013, through December 31, 2014.

Most any discussion and research on women's quests for political leadership at some point highlight the issue of raising money to finance those campaigns. The one perspective that has been especially difficult to overcome is the idea that women have a harder time acquiring campaign war chests to compete on an equal basis with male candidates, even though much contemporary research has shown either no difference between the sexes in raising money or female candidates being advantaged (Burrell 2014).

Figure 8.9 shows the average amount of money male and female general election candidates for the U.S. House of Representatives facing major party competitors have received in elections from 1994 through 2014. Female candidates as a group raised more money than their male counterparts in eight of the eleven elections. Further, if one controls for

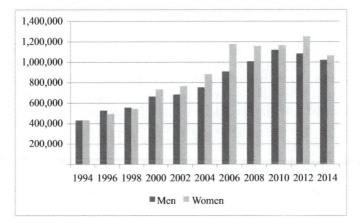

Figure 8.9 Mean Receipts, General Election Candidates by Sex, U.S. House of Representatives, 1994–2014

Only candidates with a major party opponent are included in this analysis.

candidate status—that is, whether a candidate is an incumbent, an incumbent challenger in the general election, or an open-seat candidate—and comparing Republican women with Republican men and Democratic women with Democratic men within these candidate status categories, research has found little to suggest a gender bias in acquiring the financial resources for an electoral campaign (Burrell 2014). Women are now as formidable fundraisers as men and in some instances have surpassed male candidates in the dollars they have raised to finance their campaigns.

But the amounts of money individual candidates raise are increasingly dwarfed by the enormous amounts of money today's super PACs inject into campaigns and their effect on the tenor of campaigns. Super PACs are a new kind of political action committee created in July 2010 following the outcome of federal court case *SpeechNow.org v. Federal Election Commission*. Technically known as independent expenditure-only committees, super PACs can raise unlimited sums of money from corporations, unions, associations, and individuals and then spend unlimited sums to advocate for or against political candidates. Super PACs must, however, report their donors to the Federal Election Commission on a monthly or quarterly basis, just as a traditional PAC would. Unlike traditional PACs, super PACs are prohibited from donating money directly to political candidates. According to OpenSecrets. org, as of November 28, 2016, 2,398 groups organized as super PACs reported total receipts of $1,575,391,894 and total independent expenditures of $1,117,599,467 in the 2016 cycle.[7]

Increasingly over the years, women's political organizations have become major actors in the campaign finance world, raising money as political action committees to make female candidates competitive with male candidates in this fast-changing money chase. Women's PACs that raise money primarily or exclusively for female candidates stand "at the nexus of political change and politics as usual: bringing women into positions of power by mastering the political money game" (Day and Hadley 2005). They have encouraged women to run, trained them in campaign tactics and strategy, raised vital early money to launch their campaigns, and provided a network of supportive organizations that can sustain a campaign during the final weeks of an election.

The National Women's Political Caucus (NWPC) founded in 1971, as noted in Chapter 5, was the first organization to recruit and train female candidates and to provide resources for their campaigns. In 1974, it conducted its first Win With Women campaign to recruit, train, and support feminist women candidates for local, state, and congressional office. The Women's Campaign Fund (WCF) joined NWPC that year. It was the first group to establish a PAC to provide resources for female candidates. These two groups are bipartisan, supporting both Democratic and Republican candidates who are pro-choice. However, the vast majority of their money has gone to Democratic candidates who are more likely to support reproductive rights, an important litmus test for these organizations. Indeed, at the federal level in 2012, all the candidates the NWPC endorsed were Democrats, and all but one of the WCF-supported candidates were Democrats. Representative Judy Biggert of Illinois was the only WCF-endorsed Republican. (These two PACs did not endorse any federal candidates in 2016.)

The emergence and growth of the Democratic Party's EMILY's List has come to dwarf the influence and financial clout of these two bipartisan organizations. The initial impetus for EMILY's List, now considered the "grand dame" of women's PACs, was that female candidates needed access to early money to overcome negative stereotypes about their fund-raising abilities. Its acronym, EMILY, stands for "Early Money Is Like Yeast (i.e., it makes the dough rise)." In 1984, EMILY's List was expressly created to construct a network of female donors who would provide early funding to competitive, progressive, female Democratic congressional candidates. Its mission was to build "a progressive America by electing pro-choice Democratic women to office." It has become *the* preeminent campaign organization dedicated to electing female candidates, legendary for the resources it has acquired to achieve its goal and influence the campaign world. Its political muscle has brought awe, dismay, and complaints from political foes (see Burrell 2014). The amount of money EMILY's List has raised to fund the campaigns of the female candidates it has endorsed over the course of its existence is shown in Figure 8.10.

The financial resources EMILY's List brings to the campaigns of female Democratic candidates goes beyond these Federal Election Commission financial figures. EMILY's List created the idea of "bundling" and made it into a political art. Bundling involves an organization collecting checks from individuals written to a specific candidate the group has endorsed and bundling them together to give to the candidate in one package (or perhaps several packages over the course of a campaign). The organization gets credit from the candidate for this infusion of cash to her campaign, but because the checks are written directly to the candidate's campaign and are from individual donors and not the PAC, they

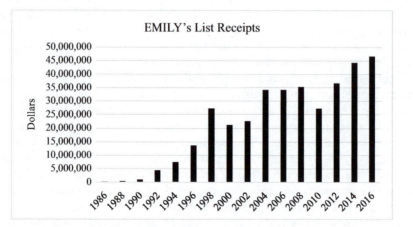

Figure 8.10 EMILY's List Receipts, 1986–2016

do not violate Federal Election Commission rules on the amount a PAC can contribute directly to a campaign—nor are they included in Figure 8.10 data. While PACs themselves are limited to a total of $10,000 in direct contributions to candidates for national office, bundling greatly expands a PAC's clout by allowing it to deliver larger sums made up of individual contributions—for example, a $20,000 package consisting of two hundred $100 checks written directly to the candidate.

For several election cycles, EMILY's List was joined by the Wish List on the Republican side. EMILY's List founder Ellen Malcolm even advised the organizers of the Wish List. The Wish List provided support to pro-choice female Republican candidates. However, the number of such candidates has so dwindled in recent election cycles that the Wish List has ceased to exist as a separate organization and PAC in the most recent elections.

EMILY's List has come to wield considerable power within Democratic Party circles due to its accumulated financial clout and campaign expertise. It is classified as a "heavy hitter" among PACs. In recent elections, it has been among the leading PACs (not just women's PACs) in the amount of money raised. "Heavy hitter" is a designation the Center for Responsive Politics, which runs the OpenSecrets.org website, gives to the highest-funded PACs. In the 2012 election cycle, EMILY's List ranked sixth among the heavy hitters. Indeed, one scholar suggests that Democratic Party efforts to recruit women candidates have become virtually indistinguishable from the candidate recruitment strategies of EMILY's List (Cooperman 2001). It also created a super PAC in 2012, WOMEN VOTE! It quickly became the dominant super PAC supporting women's campaigns. It reported $7.9 million in independent expenditures for that election and over $12 million in the 2014 election cycle. As a super PAC, at the end of October 2016, it had reported having raised $29,441,246 and expending $28,446,646 (ranking eleventh among super PACs in expenditures).

The absence of a comparable entity on the Republican side is considered a serious structural deficit for female Republican candidates (Shames 2014). Republicans are increasingly seeing the importance of exercising financial muscle on behalf of female candidates. Several PACs dedicated to underwriting conservative Republican female candidates have been created, although they lag far behind the clout of EMILY's List. Republicans fault themselves for not developing a coordinated effort. Although they credit themselves with engaging in earnest attempts to elect more Republican women, support has been fragmented (Shames 2015).

Four PACs have been established in recent elections on the conservative side to promote female candidates. View PAC (Value in Electing Women), founded in 1997, is the oldest of these PACs. Female members of Congress and professional women organized it to provide financial support to Republican women running for a seat in the U.S. House and Senate. Its website states that it has directly contributed and helped to raise over $2,750,000 to candidates since its inception. At the end of the October reporting cycle in 2016, it had raised a reported $400,000 and contributed $199,000 to twenty-three U.S. House candidates and three Senate candidates.

Maggie's List, founded in 2010, is a political committee that works to elect conservative women who espouse a fiscally conservative vision. Maggie's List is named after former Republican U.S. Senator Margaret Chase Smith. Maggie's List provides training and get-out-the-vote programs as well as financial support for female candidates for the U.S. House of Representatives and the U.S. Senate. In the 2016 election cycle, it reported raising $178,000 and had contributed $26,650 to fifteen U.S. House candidates.

She-PAC was created in 2012 as both a traditional political action committee that gives directly to campaigns and a super PAC planning "to pour millions of dollars into the campaigns of conservative women running for state and federal office." However, it lasted only two election cycles. According to its mission, it had a twofold purpose: to make contributions directly to the campaigns of principled conservative women running for federal office and to make expenditures on behalf of principled conservative women running for federal and statewide office. "She" stood for "support," "honor," and "elect." Its aim for 2012 was to raise $25 million. Condoleezza Rice served as the group's star attraction at fund-raising events. At the end of the 2012 election cycle, it reported having raised $154,860 for five candidates: two Senate candidates, Deb Fischer and Heather Wilson, and three U.S. House candidates, Karen Harrington, Mia Love, and Kim Vann. As a super PAC, it must be considered a failure. It reported only $430 in independent expenditures. In 2014, it reported contributing less than $4,000 to eight federal candidates before shutting down.

In an additional effort, in 2014, Republicans launched the RightNOW Women's PAC with the particular goal of getting young women involved in the Republican Party. Its founders described the effort as a "low-fund, high-involvement" movement that will mobilize female voters and encourage young women to consider running for office. It raised $87,000 in that election cycle, contributing $44,000 to twelve female U.S. House candidates and four Senate candidates. In 2016, the October reporting period showed it had raised $216,000 and contributed $102,500 to twenty U.S. House candidates and three U.S. Senate candidates.

Building Women's Capacity as Elected Officials: "Don't Get Mad, Get Elected"

Beyond providing financial resources, contemporary groups engage in a multitude of other efforts to encourage women to see themselves as political leaders and potential political leaders and to provide them with the skills to be effective campaigners for elected office and effective office holders. These efforts have become a central focus of existing women's rights groups. Comparative politics researchers Pippa Norris and Mona Krook (2011) call this movement "capacity building." Under the auspices of the Organization for Security and Cooperation in Europe (OSCE), Norris and Krook developed a six-step action plan involving a series of fast-track strategic interventions to contribute to the attainment of gender equality in elected office. Capacity building is one of the six interventions they advocate to achieve this goal, and they describe a range of activities as capacity-building exercises.

> A diverse range of initiatives are designed to build the capacity of the pool of potential women leaders in the pipeline, to strengthen the skills, experience, and knowledge of women once they enter elected office, as well as to address broader issues of institutional capacity-building. These interventions can be categorized in terms of three distinct but overlapping threads: *equal opportunity initiatives* (candidate training, recruitment initiatives, and knowledge networks), *initiatives to combat stereotypes and raise awareness* (media campaigns and citizen education), and *political party initiatives* (women's sections, fundraising, and women's parties).
>
> (Norris and Krook 2011, 8)

Capacity-building programs have been a popular strategy among advocates of increased female political leadership in the United States, especially since institutional changes such as the adoption of quota systems or movement to a proportional representation system, parts of Norris and Krook's (2011) six-step plan, are unlikely even to be considered, let alone adopted in the United States. U.S. programs have focused on girls and young women as well as women old enough to run for office and even older women. They have been organized at the state and national levels. They are both partisan and nonpartisan in nature, with a variety of colorful names such as Running Start, Emerge America, and Elect Her! A significant diversity of women's groups engaged in the political process, such as the American Association of University Women (AAUW) and the National Federation of Republican Women, as well as EMILY's List and various university programs, have undertaken efforts to build the capacity of women running for elected office and to improve their confidence and effectiveness. The Girl Scouts of the USA even developed a Ms. President Patch Program in cooperation with the former White House Project. This program has been a participation project as opposed to the traditional badges girl scouts work to earn. Girls had to participate in at least one project centered on learning about women in leadership positions historically, get involved in a school election campaign, look for female leaders in their communities, and write about and follow them to obtain a Ms. President patch.

CAWP provides an interactive website listing all the campaign and leadership trainings aimed specifically at potential female candidates and future female political leaders. In 2016, it listed twelve such national programs; eight were nonpartisan, two were Democratic Party affiliated groups, and two were Republican groups. Five additional nonpartisan programs involved leadership training. The website also shows the various state-run programs.

CAWP itself engages in such an activity with its Ready to Run campaign training. Held annually, Ready to Run is a bipartisan program for women who want to run for office, work on campaigns, get appointed to office, become community leaders, or learn more about the political system. EMILY's List launched the Political Opportunity Program (POP) after the 2000 election. POP is a training and support program for pro-choice Democratic women seeking state legislative, constitutional, and key local offices. In addition, EMILY's List held 180 trainings in 36 states, training more than 6,300 people between 2001 and 2010. In July 2007, the Women's Campaign Forum launched the Ask a Woman to Run campaign. By September 2008, more than one hundred thousand women had been nominated to run by having their names submitted to an online database the Women's Campaign Forum had constructed.

A variety of capacity-building programs provide young women with political leadership skills. AAUW's and Running Start's collaborative effort Elect Her: Campus Women Win program is one such example. This program encourages and trains college women to run for student government and future political office. The daylong Elect Her! training teaches college women why more women are needed in student government and provides them with the skills to run successful student body campaigns. Students learn how to create campaign messages and to communicate them effectively as well as how to reach out and mobilize voters on campus. Fifty colleges and universities ran Elect Her! programs in 2014. Text Box 8.5 provides an example of an organized effort to stimulate the political involvement of young women.

**Text Box 8.5 Elect Her! These Campus Women Won:
Hear Their Voices**

"I would advise other young women running for student office to approach campaigning, elections, and governing with confidence, grace, and tenacity. Ultimately, if you don't believe in you, no one else will. Decide you will run, decide you will win, decide you will govern to your best ability."

—Kathleen Hunt, George Washington University,
undergraduate senator

"My advice to other young women running for office on campus is to do your research, decide on a strategy based on the voters, and plan how you will execute it."
—Shontol Harris, University of West Indies, Mona,
Jamaica, deputy hall chair

"Elect Her! really helped me realize how much a hand shake and a short conversation can help a campaign. We knocked on every single door that we could. People want to see a friendly face, they want to shake your hand, and they want you to ask them what you can do for them."
—Lindsey Lieck and Elizabeth Dow, Northern Michigan University,
student body president and vice president

"My biggest takeaway from the Elect Her! training was [the reminder] that I have a network of women behind me who want me to succeed, and that it is important to encourage other women to do the same."
—Alyssa Weakley, George Washington University, business school
undergraduate senator

"I love taking initiative and helping out students. I thought about the most profound way that I can voice the thoughts and opinions of students, and I realized that running for class presidency would achieve just that."
—Amy Lyons, University of Maine, class president

American Association of University Women (www.aauw.org/2015/06/26/these-campus-women-won/).

In addition to the efforts of these programs specifically aimed at recruiting, training, and supporting female candidates, other groups have formed with the aim of altering the public culture regarding women and political leadership. They include Political Parity, She Should Run, Representation 2020, Women's Media Center, and the Barbara Lee Family Foundation. They challenge the campaign process and promote gender equity more broadly through research, advocacy of structural reforms, and media watches. Notable is Political Parity's Name It, Change It campaign that calls out examples of media sexism toward female candidates. Individuals are urged to report sexist incidents in the media, which are then highlighted throughout social media. Negative awards are given for the most sexist media coverage of female candidates and politicians. Representation 2020 "works to raise awareness of the under-representation of women in elected office, to strengthen coalitions supportive of measures to increase women's representation, and to highlight the often overlooked structural barriers to achieving gender parity in American elections." Representation 2020 has created a Gender Parity Index measuring how well women are represented in each state's elected offices. The index scores and ranks each state and can be found at its website: www.representation2020.com. The Women's Media Center launched Who Talks?, a project to analyze and publicize the gender balance of analysts on the highest-rated morning and cable shows during the 2016 presidential election campaign. The Barbara Lee Family Foundation also seeks to "advance women's equality and representation in American politics" through the research they have sponsored centered on women's candidacies. Their research reports include *Keys to Elected Office: The Essential Guide for Women, Change the Channel: Ads That Work for Women Candidates*, and *Pitch Perfect: Winning Strategies for Women Candidates*.

These capacity-building efforts are certainly good news in the quest for gender equity in political leadership, especially those programs aimed at young women. Unfortunately, they encounter a strong headwind against growing a political interest among young people. Young Americans are growing up in an era of political polarization, systemic dysfunction, and disillusion with public officials. Partisan antipathy is deeper and more extensive than at any point in the past few decades; for example, over a quarter of Democrats (27 percent) view the Republican Party as a threat to the nation's well-being, and more than one third of Republicans (37 percent) have the same view of Democrats (Pew Research Center 2014). A career in politics is held in disdain. After surveying and interviewing thousands of young people, scholars Jennifer Lawless and Richard Fox (2015a) concluded that young people "see politics as pointless and unpleasant. They see political leaders as corrupt and selfish. They have no interest in entering the political arena. Ever" (4). Disinterest in running for public office characterizes young people across the board. Black or White, rich or poor, liberal or conservative, northeastern or southern, the next generation is turned off to politics, Lawless and Fox assert.

The young women highlighted in Text Box 8.5 in the Elect Her! program are a distinct minority. We also do not know the extent to which their political leadership on their campuses will stimulate a political career later in life. In Lawless and Fox's (2015a) study of college students, young women were less likely than young men to have ever considered running for office, to express interest in a candidacy at some point in the future, or to think of elective office as a desirable profession. Asked whether they have ever thought when they are older they might want to run for public office, 63 percent of the women responded that they had never thought about it compared to 43 percent of the men. Fourteen percent of the men surveyed and only 7 percent of the women reported that they definitely plan to run for office sometime in the future. Asked to choose from among four professions if they were paid the same amount of money, which one would they be most like to have, only 11 percent of the women compared with 20 percent of the men chose being a member of Congress.

Lawless and Fox (2015b) identify five factors that contribute to the gender gap in political ambition among these young people.

1. Young men are more likely than young women to be socialized by their parents to think about politics as a career path.
2. From their school experiences to their peer associations to their media habits, young women tend to be exposed to less political information and discussion than young men.
3. Young men are more likely than young women to have played organized sports and care about winning.
4. Young women are less likely than young men to receive encouragement to run for office—from anyone.
5. Young women are less likely than young men to think they will be qualified to run for office, even once they are established in their careers.

> The male and female students reported very different views when asked about the most effective way to bring about societal change. Female respondents were 50 percent more likely than male respondents to say that working for a charity is the best way to bring about change. Men, on the other hand, were nearly twice as likely as women to see running for elective office as the best way to bring about change (28% to 15%). Women and men both aspire to work to improve the world around them. But women are much less likely than men to see political leadership as a means to that end.
>
> (Lawless and Fox 2015b, 16)

She Should Run is another organization devoted to expanding the talent pool of future female elected leaders. Its most recent effort in this campaign is the creation of the book

See Joan Run. "This modern take on an iconic story, shows that women have an invaluable place in the political landscape if only they would run. By bridging the gender gap with humor, we're showcasing the critical need for more women in office" (Mallon 2016). The book, as Erin Cutrano, founder of She Should Run, describes it, is a "comical response to the not-so-comical lack of women in elected office" (Cutrano 2016). The fourteen-page book follows a woman called Joan in a world full of Dicks—Congressman Dick, Alderman Dick, City Council Representative Dick. Joan, a community leader and devoted mother, wants to get involved in government but is hesitant to do so. Her friends Bob and Sue encourage her to run. The book shows Joan running, winning, and encouraging other women to run. "See Joan Run," goes the story. "See Joan win. See Joan make a difference."[8]

If political ambition is low among these college students and particularly absent among female students, then it is highly likely that few young people not attending college have visions of becoming political leaders. Cynicism regarding creating a more equitable society is likely to be a prominent feature of their lives.

It is not just young people who are turned off to politics. Activists have noted that women generally find little of a positive nature in the political process. Government is

Picture 8.4 Cover Page of She Should Run's *See Joan Run*

not seen as a site for positive change. According to Marni Allen, director of Political Parity,

> Women select themselves out of the electoral process partly because they are turned off by today's combative landscape. . . . Women today look at the federal government and they see nastiness, gridlock. It doesn't look particularly appealing. Women choose to stay where they are.
>
> (Beamish 2015)

Longtime political consultant Kathleen Schafer (2012) makes the same assessment:

> The truth is that preparing women for the battle of politics is not the answer. Woman are not running for office because they are choosing to spend their time and energy in ways other than engaging in the senseless, and all too often futile, act of policy making in contemporary politics. No amount of preparation is going to change the pragmatic nature of women who will choose to focus their energy and attention on real world solutions, rather than engage in politics that rarely creates meaningful change and when it does at a very high personal cost to one's quality of life. In other words, politics is a very masculine game. Might makes right, the accumulation and wielding of power is rewarded and winners take all, hardly the environment to create meaningful solutions to societal challenges and enduring change for the betterment of the greater good. Which brings us full circle, as the literal and figurative "givers of life," women value the investment of their time and want to see that it has meaning.

CAWP's 2012 Project, a campaign to increase the number of women in Congress and state legislatures, adopted the slogan "Don't Get Mad, Get Elected" for its campaign seminars precisely to channel this negativity into a positive direction. Further, if the financing of campaigns is perceived as a major roadblock to more women entering politics, then a call to action is in order to raise voices to change the financial system. As Celinda Lake, one of the Democratic Party's leading political strategists, has explained,

> More women should *become* candidates themselves and make those necessary changes from within: Voters don't like it either, so run and change it. Run and pass campaign finance reform. You don't like raising the money? Voters don't like the way the money's being raised either. Run and change it. You can't change it from the sidelines.
>
> (Schnall 2015)

Finally, as one potential candidate reflected on the outcome of the 2016 presidential election, "We need regular people to run. We need people who care about these issues . . . you know what? Why *shouldn't* we run?" (Cauterucci 2017).

Notes

1. Donald Trump nominated South Carolina Governor Nikki Haley to be the U.S. representative to the United Nations, which reduced the number to four female governors.
2. Republican Kay Bailey Hutcheson of Texas was elected in a special election in 1993.
3. In 1933, Nellie Ross became the first female director of the U.S. Mint, a position she held until 1953.
4. Montana had granted women the right to vote in 1914.
5. Democrat Harry Teague of New Mexico is the only member elected during this time period without a high school degree. Representative Teague grew up in a family of sharecroppers.

6. Representative Adams is also well known for the many distinctive hats she wears.
7. www.opensecrets.org/pacs/superpacs.php?cycle=2016.
8. *See Joan Run* can be downloaded from She Should Run's website, www.sheshouldrun.org.

Further Readings and Other Resources

Burrell, Barbara. 2012. "Practicing Politics: Female Political Scientists as Candidates for Elective Office." *PS: Political Science & Politics*, 45, 1 (January): 83–86.
Gillibrand, Kirsten and Elizabeth Weil. 2014. *Off the Sidelines: Raise Your Voice, Change the World.* New York, NY: Ballentine Books.
Mikulski, Barbara, Kay Bailey Hutchison, Dianne Feinstein, Barbara Boxer, Patty Murray, Olympia Snowe, Susan Collins, Mary Landriew, and Blanche L. Lincoln. 2000. *Nine and Counting: The Women of the Senate.* New York, NY: William Morrow.
Shames, Shauna. 2017. *Out of the Running: Why Millennials Reject Political Careers and Why It Matters.* New York, NY: New York University Press.
Zillman, Claire. 2017. "As Trump Inspires More Women to Run, This Mayor Explains How She 'Googled' Her Way into Office." *Fortune*, January 24. http://fortune.com/2017/01/24/trump-women-politics-sonoma-mayor/.

National Organizations Training Women for Elected Office

Center for American Women and Politics: Ready to Run; Teach a Girl to Lead, www.cawp.rutgers.edu/education_training/ReadytoRun/.
Emerge America, www.emergeamerica.org.
EMILY's List: Political Opportunity Program, www.emilyslist.org/pages/entry/run-for-office.
National Federation of Republican Women: Campaign Management School, www.nfrw.org/cms.
Running Start, http://runningstartonline.org.
VoteRunLead, https://voterunlead.org.

Web Sources

Girl Scouts' Research Institute. "Running for a Change: Girls and Politics Pulse Poll." October 2014. www.girlscouts.org/content/dam/girlscouts-gsusa/forms-and-documents/about-girl-scouts/research/girls_and_politics.pdf.
"Money in Politics with a Gender Lens." www.icrw.org/publications/money-in-politics-with-a-gender-lens/.
"MsRepresentation." www.wcfonline.org/msrepresentation_signup.
Barbara Lee Family Foundation, www.barbaraleefoundation.org/.
Political Parity, www.politicalparity.org/.
Women's Media Center, www.womensmediacenter.com/.

Films

"Strong Women: Elected Women in Colorado." www.strongsisters.org.

References

Andersen, Kristi. 1996. *After Suffrage: Women in Partisan and Electoral Politics before the New Deal.* Chicago, IL: University of Chicago Press.
Beamish, Rita. 2015. "The Road to Parity for Women in Politics: Follow the Money." *The New York Times*, June 13. http://nytlive.nytimes.com/womenintheworld/2015/05/13/the-road-to-parity-for-women-in-politics-follow-the-money/.
Boxer, Barbara. 1994. *Strangers in the Senate*. Washington, DC: National Press Books.

Brooks, Deborah. 2013. *He Runs, She Runs: Why Gender Stereotypes Do Not Harm Women Candidates*. Princeton, NJ: Princeton University Press.

Burrell, Barbara. 1994. *Campaigning for Congress in the Feminist Era*. Ann Arbor, MI: University of Michigan Press.

Burrell, Barbara. 2014. *Gender in Campaigns for the U.S. House of Representatives*. Ann Arbor, MI: University of Michigan Press.

Carroll, Susan J. and Kira Sanbonmatsu. 2013. *More Women Can Run: Gender and Pathways to the State Legislatures*. New York, NY: Oxford University Press.

Cauterucci, Christina. 2017. "How Do You Inspire Women to Run? Elect Trump." *Slate*, January 16.www.slate.com/articles/news_and_politics/cover_story/2017/01/when_women_run_they_win_and_trump_s_election_is_inspiring_a_surge_of_new.html.

Center for American Women and Politics. 2012. "Women Surpass House, Senate Candidate Records as Final November Slates Are Set: Democrats Continue to Lead GOP in Nominating Women." https://news.rutgers.edu/news-releases/2012/09/women-surpass-house-20120913#.WT1rfTOZP64.

Center for American Women and Politics. 2014. "With Final November Slates Set, Democrats Continue to Lead GOP in Nominating Women." www.cawp.rutgers.edu/sites/default/files/resources/pressrelease_09-10-14_postprimary.pdf.

Center for American Women and Politics. 2015. "Women in State Legislatures 2015: Numbers Still Stuck." www.cawp.rutgers.edu/sites/default/files/resources/pressrelease_01-06-15_stleg.pdf.

Center for American Women and Politics. 2016. "Outlook for Women in Senate and House: Not Much Change in Numbers, Few Likely Landmarks, and Continuing Underrepresentation of GOP Women." http://www.cawp.rutgers.edu/sites/default/files/resources/pressrelease-senate-house-outlooks-2016.pdf.

Chaddock, Gail Russell. 2004. "The Rise of Women Candidates." *Christian Science Monitor*, 19 (October): 1.

Cohen, Micah. 2013. "Popular Governors, and Prospects for 2016." *FiveThirtyEight*, May 28. http://fivethirtyeight.blogs.nytimes.com/2013/05/28/popular-governors-and-prospects-for-2016/?_r=0.

Cooperman, Rosalyn. 2001. "Party Organizations and the Recruitment of Women Candidates to the U.S. House Since the Year of the Woman." Paper presented at the Annual Meeting of the American Political Science Association, San Francisco, CA.

Cox, Elizabeth M. 1996. *Women State and Territorial Legislators, 1895–1995*. Jefferson, NC: McFarland.

Cutrano, Erin. 2016. "Majority of Girls Believe This." *Huffington Post*, May 25. www.huffington-post.com/erin-loos-cutraro/majority-of-girls-believe_b_10132856.html.

Day, Christine L. and Charles D. Hadley. 2005. *Women's PACs: Abortion and Election*. Upper Saddle River, NJ: Prentice Hall.

Deckard, Barbara. 1979. *The Woman's Movement: Political, Socioeconomic, and Psychological Issues*. 2nd edition. New York, NY: Harper & Row.

Dolan, Kathleen. 2014. *When Does Gender Matter? Women Candidates & Gender Stereotypes in American Elections*. New York, NY: Oxford University Press.

Dowd, Maureen. 1991. "The Thomas Nomination: 7 Congresswomen March to Senate to Demand Delay in Thomas Vote." *New York Times*, October 9: A1.

Elder, Laurel. 2008. "Whither Republican Women: The Growing Partisan Gap among Women in Congress." *The Forum*, 6, 1, article 13. www.bepress.com/forum/vol6/iss1/art1www.bepress.com/forum/vol6/iss1/art13.

Ferrara, Barbara. 2012. "Gender and Governors' Policy Agendas." Paper presented at the 12th Annual State Politics and Policy Conference, Rice University and University of Houston, Houston, TX. http://2012sppconference.blogs.rice.edu/files/2012/02/Ferrara-paper-SPPC-2012.pdf.

Friedman, Ann. 2016. "If You Care about Electing Women, Don't Focus on Hillary." *Huffington Post*, March 30. www.huffingtonpost.com/thecut/if-you-care-about-electing-women-dont-focus-on-hillary-clinton_b_9576508.html.

Fortier, John. 2008. "2008 Will Not Be a Banner Year for Women." *Politico*, March 24.

Gertzog, Irwin. 2002. "Women's Changing Pathways to the U.S. House Representatives: Widows, Elites, and Strategic Politicians." In *Women Transforming Congress*, ed. Cindy Simon Rosenthal. Norman, OK: University of Oklahoma Press, 95–118.

Hardy-Fanta, Carol, Pei-te Lien, Dianne Pinderhughes, and Christine Marie Sierra. 2006. "Gender, Race and Descriptive Representation in the United States: Findings from the Gender and Multi-cultural Leadership Project." *Journal of Women, Politics and Policy*, 28: 9–41.

Ifill, Gwen. 1991. "Female Lawmakers Wrestle with New Public Attitude on 'Women's' Issues." *The New York Times*, November 18.

Koerth-Baker, Maggie. 2016. "Why We Don't Know How Much Sexism Is Hurting Clinton's Campaign." *FiveThirtyEight*, November 5. http://fivethirtyeight.com/features/why-we-dont-know-how-much-sexism-is-hurting-clintons-campaign/?ex_cid=2016-forecast.

Lawless, Jennifer and Richard Fox. 2010. *It Still Takes a Candidate: Why Women Don't Run for Office*. New York, NY: Cambridge University Press.

Lawless, Jennifer and Richard Fox. 2015a. *Running from Office: Why Young Americans Are Turned Off to Politics*. New York, NY: Oxford University Press.

Lawless, Jennifer and Richard Fox. 2015b. *Girls Just Wanna Not Run: The Gender Gap in Young Americans' Ambition*. Washington, DC: American University School of Public Affairs.

Layton, Lindsey. 2007. "Moms in the House, with Kids at Home." *The Washington Post*, July 19.

Leonard, Mary. 2000. "Women Candidates, Fierce, Financed." *Boston Globe*, November 5: A37.

Mallon, Maggie. "This Racy Book Is All About Getting More Women into Politics." *Glamour*, March 17.

Manning, Jennifer. 2015. *Membership of the 114th Congress: A Profile*. Washington, DC: Congressional Research Service.

Mansbridge, Jane and Katherine Tate. 1992. "Race Trumps Gender: The Thomas Hearings in the Black Community." *PS: Political Science & Politics*, 25, 3 (September): 488–492.

Norris, Pippa and Mona Lena Krook. 2011. "Gender Equality in Elected Office: A Six Step Plan." *OSCE Office for Democratic Institutions and Human Rights*. www.osce.org/odihr/78432.

OpenSecrets.org. 2016. "Super PACs." www.opensecrets.org/pacs/superpacs.php?cycle=2016.

Ornstein, Norman, Thomas E. Mann, Andrew Rugg, and Michael J. Malbin. 2013. *Vital Statistics on Congress*. Washington, DC: Brookings Institute.

Palley, Marian Lief and Howard Palley. 1992. "The Thomas Appointment Defeats and Victories for Women." *PS: Political Science & Politics*, 25, 3 (September): 588–591.

Parker, Kim. 2015. "Women and Leadership: Public Says Women Are Equally Qualified But Barriers Persist." *Pew Research Center*. www.pewsocialtrends.org/files/2015/01/2015-01-14_women-and-leadership.pdf.

Pew Research Center. 2014. "Most See Inequality Growing But Partisans Differ over Solutions." www.people-press.org/2014/01/23/most-see-inequality-growing-but-partisans-differ-over-solutions/.

Reingold, Beth. 2012. "The Uneven Presence of Women and Minorities in American State Legislatures—And Why It Matters." *Scholars Strategy Network*. http://thesocietypages.org/ssn/2012/11/12/minority-representation/.

Riccucci, Norma M. and Judith R. Saidel. 2001. "The Demographic of Gubernatorial Appointees: Toward an Explanation of Variation." *Policy Studies Journal*, 29: 11–22.

Sanbonmatsu, Kira. 2014. "Women's Election to Office in the Fifty States: Opportunities and Challenges." In *Gender & Elections: Shaping the Future of American Politics*, eds. Susan J. Carroll and Richard L. Fox. New York, NY: Cambridge University Press.

Schafer, Kathleen. 2012. "Parity in Politics—Why Women Don't Want It." www.govloop.com/community/blog/parity-in-politicswhy-women-dont-want-it/.

Schnall, Marianne. 2015. "She Talks Dirty: Money in Politics." Political Parity, August 18. www.politicalparity.org/she-talks-dirty-money-in-politics/.

Schlesinger, Joseph. 1966. *Ambition and Politics: Political Careers in the United States*. New York, NY: Rand McNally.

Shames, Shaun. 2014. "Making the Political Personal." *Politics & Gender*, 10, 2: 287–292.

Shames, Shauna. 2015. *Right the Ratio*. www.politicalparity.org/wp-content/uploads/2015/01/primary-hurdles-full-report.pdf.

Taylor, Paul. 2008. "A Paradox in Public Attitudes: Men or Women Who Is the Better Leader?" Washington, DC: Pew Research Center. www.pewsocialtrends.org/files/2010/10/gender-leadership.pdf.

Werner, Erica. 2016. "Dems Field Large Roster of Women in the Year of Trump." *Worcester Tele-gram & Gazette*, May 6.

Wilcox, Clyde. 1994. "Why Was 1992 the 'Year of the Woman'? Explaining Women's Gains in 1992." *The Year of the Woman: Myths & Realities*, eds. Elizabeth Adell Cook, Sue Thomas, and Clyde Wilcox. Boulder, CO: Westview Press, 1–24.

Windett, Jason. 2014. "Differing Paths to the Top: Gender, Ambition, and Running for Governor." *Journal of Women, Politics and Policy*, 35, 4: 287–314.

Women Members of the House GOP Caucus. 2010. "2010: The Year of GOP Women." *Politico*, December 15. www.politico.com/story/2010/12/2010-the-year-of-gop-women-046374?o=1.

Yokley, Eli. 2016. "In Kentucky, Andy Barr Challenger Won't Shy Away from Obama Policies." *Roll Call*, January 22. http://atr.rollcall.com/kentucky-andy-barr-challenger-wont-shy-away-obama-policies/?dcz=emailalert.

9 The 2016 Presidential Election and the First Woman President?

> To all the women, and especially the young women, who put their faith in this campaign and in me, I want you to know that nothing has made me prouder than to be your champion. To all of the little girls who are watching this, never doubt that you are valuable and powerful and deserving of every chance and opportunity in the world to pursue and achieve your own dreams.
>
> Hillary Clinton's Presidential Concession Speech,
> November 9, 2016

On April 12, 2015, former first lady, U.S. Senator, and Secretary of State Hillary Clinton officially launched her long-anticipated campaign to become the forty-fifth, and first woman, president of the United States. "I'm running for president. Everyday Americans need a champion, and I want to be that champion—so you can do more than just get by—you can get ahead. And stay ahead. Because when families are strong, America is strong. So I'm hitting the road to earn your vote, because it's your time. And I hope you'll join me on this journey," she exhorted the public as she introduced her campaign in a video presentation. She was the first Democrat to enter the race and the prohibitive favorite at that moment. Former Maryland Governor Martin O'Malley and Vermont independent U.S. Senator Bernie Sanders joined her as major contenders in the quest for the Democratic Party nomination. After long consideration, Vice President Joe Biden, another potentially strong contender for the Democratic Party nomination, decided against seeking it. Governor O'Malley dropped out of the nomination process early, whereas Senator Sanders gave Clinton a strong and long contest for the Democratic nomination. Clinton was not assured of the nomination until the final set of primaries in June 2016. The Republicans began their nomination quest with seventeen announced candidates, eventually settling on business tycoon Donald Trump as its nominee after a raucous nominating season, an outcome resulting in a historic roiling of the election process. The 2016 election was a long, nasty affair, spoiling the historical spectacle of a campaign to elect the first woman president regardless of one's support or opposition to Secretary Clinton's election. In the end, in an amazing upset, Donald Trump won the election. Although Clinton won the popular vote by more than two million votes, Trump won the Electoral College vote, 290 to 232. Thus, the one-hundred-year anniversary of the 19th Amendment granting women the right to vote will occur in 2020 without that ultimate political glass ceiling of winning the presidency having been broken.

With her April 12, 2015, announcement, Hillary Clinton began her second attempt to win the Democratic Party nomination for president, and when she was formally nominated sixteen months later at the Democratic National Convention in Philadelphia, it was a historic moment for female political leadership. Other women had sought the presidency of the United States over the course of American history, beginning with Victoria Claflin Woodhull, a women's rights advocate. In 1872, the Equal Rights Party nominated her as

Cartoon 9.1 Women's Rights from Seneca Falls to the White House?

Signe Wilkinson Editorial Cartoon used with the permission of Signe Wilkinson, the Washington Post Writers Group, and the Cartoonist.

their presidential candidate. Thirty-four other women have been the presidential nominees of minor parties over the course of American history. Six women had sought a major party nomination prior to Hillary Clinton's campaign. Two women—Democrat Geraldine Ferraro in 1984 and Republican Sarah Palin in 2008—had won major party nominations for vice president but failed to win that office.

Clinton had been prominently mentioned as a presidential contender in the run up to the 2004 presidential election while serving her first term in the U.S. Senate. She declined to seek the Democratic Party nomination in that election. Easily reelected to the Senate in 2006, she was again prominently mentioned as a potential nominee in the 2008 election, and for the first time, a woman entered the 2008 election season as the presumed frontrunner for a major party nomination. However, she went on to lose the nomination to U.S. Senator Barack Obama. The nomination campaign between the potentially first Black president and the potentially first woman president was historic. In conceding the nomination to Obama, Clinton stated, "Although we weren't able to shatter that highest, hardest glass ceiling this time, thanks to you, it's got about 18 million cracks in it, and the light is shining through like never before, filling us all with the hope and the sure knowledge that the path will be a little easier next time." Upon winning the presidency, Barack Obama appointed her secretary of state, a position she served in for the four years of his first administration.

Winning the 2016 Nomination

Following her April 2015 video announcement, Clinton embarked on a "listening tour" and then formally kicked off her nomination campaign June 15 on Roosevelt Island, New

York, invoking the legacies of Franklin and Eleanor Roosevelt. Her deputy communications director, Kristina Schake, described Clinton as having

> long been inspired by FDR's belief that America is stronger when we summon the work and talents of all Americans. Her fight, like his, is to work to ensure that everyday Americans can achieve not just a sense of economic stability, but lasting prosperity.
> (Collinson 2015)

In that speech, she addressed income inequality in the United States, called for universal prekindergarten, paid family leave, equal pay for women, college affordability, and incentives for companies that provide profit sharing to employees.

Winning the nomination became more of a challenge than expected at its commencement for Clinton. Senator Bernie Sanders quickly captured the imagination of many with his challenge to the wealthy 1 percent and condemnation of Wall Street. Preaching radical change and a revolution, he seemed to especially energize liberal millennials. Self-inflicted wounds also negatively affected Secretary Clinton, including the large speaking fees major corporations had given her in the time period after she left her position as secretary of state in 2013 and before she announced her candidacy. Her reluctance to release the texts of the speeches she gave to these groups further put her on the defensive, and her use of a private e-mail server while secretary of state was a constant challenge throughout the campaign. It especially flared up in the last weeks of the campaign, just as she started to outpace Trump. The Clinton Foundation, created by former President Bill Clinton, also came under fire. Donald Trump fanned the flames wildly, calling her out as "Crooked Hillary" and encouraging his supporters to "lock her up."

Picture 9.1 Democratic U.S. Presidential Candidate Hillary Clinton Speaks at Her Primary Night Victory Rally at the Brooklyn Navy Yard in New York

Courtesy of Shutterstock.com.

Clinton barely won the first in the nation Iowa caucuses in January 2016 and came in a distant second to Senator Sanders in the New Hampshire primary that immediately followed. She regained some momentum when she next won the South Carolina primary. Clinton and Sanders went on to exchange victories to the end of the nomination season. Clinton clinched the nomination with a thirteen-point victory over Sanders in California. In total, Hillary Clinton won 16,914,722 votes in the Democratic primaries compared with 13,206,428 for Bernie Sanders. Clinton won thirty-four contests, and Sanders won twenty-three. Sanders did better in states holding caucuses rather than in primaries to select convention delegates.

Clinton's advantage with superdelegates to the Democratic National Convention enhanced her nomination prospects. Superdelelegates are elected officials and party activists and officials who are automatically seated at the national convention because of their formal positions within the party. They are free to support any candidate for the presidential nomination. (The Republican Party does not have formal superdelegates.) They make up about 15 percent of the delegates. The Democratic Party set up the Hunt Commission, which created the system of superdelegates as part of the nomination process, starting with the 1984 election. Embedding superdelegates into the nomination process was an attempt to balance the involvement of activists, rank-and-file members, and outsider single-issue groups participating in caucuses and primaries with individuals invested in the party as a viable organization. The Hunt Commission saw "a need for there to be a voice for the establishment within the party to not necessarily overturn the will of the voters, but to nudge along a nominee who would be well equipped to win during the general election" (Roberts 1984). In the 2016 election, Bernie Sanders's supporters attacked the superdelegates as elites unrepresentative of the will of the participants in the caucuses and primaries. They started several online petitions, one calling for the elimination of superdelegates altogether and another asking superdelegates to align their choices with those of regular voters, not the party elite. The Clinton campaign was on the defensive about her reliance on superdelegates.

Young people were particularly attracted to the Bernie Sanders campaign. The Sanders campaign had chapters on college campuses across the nation and a seventy-point margin among young voters in the Iowa caucuses. But Clinton beat Sanders by twenty-three points among voters ages forty-five to sixty-four and by forty-three points among voters sixty-five and older, according to exit polls. At the same time, women of all generations favored Clinton more than men during the nomination process (Sides 2015). Gender was a factor in campaign divisions in the Democratic Party nomination campaign.

Among the Bernie Sanders's supporters were the "Bernie Bros," a pejorative term Robinson Myer (2015) first coined in an *Atlantic* piece in which he caricatured this group of Sanders supporters. Bernie Bros were characterized as young male supporters who questioned Clinton supporters on a spectrum that ranged from simply tone-deaf to outright misogynistic, primarily through social media but also in face-to-face confrontations.

> He's the smug-seeming young Sanders supporter who asked Clinton at a CNN town hall why young voters aren't enthusiastic about her candidacy, then suggested it was because she's dishonest. He's the guy who floods Internet comment boards accusing Clinton supporters of voting with their "vaginas." He's the idealistic young liberal who replies to any critique of Sanders on social media with a flood of crass terms and vitriol.
>
> (Alter 2016a)

Journalists writing columns critical of Senator Sanders received angry Twitter comments. Feminist supports of Clinton were frequent targets of Bernie Bros' vitriol. Sanders had to call them out. "I have heard about it. It's disgusting," Sanders said of the Bernie Bro phenomenon. "Look, we don't want that crap. We will do everything we can, and I think we have tried. . . . That is not what this campaign is about."

A generational clash among women also engulfed the Clinton campaign during the primary season. As former Secretary of State Madeleine Albright and feminist icon Gloria Steinem campaigned for Clinton, they "called on young women who supported Mr. Sanders to essentially grow up and get with the program," in the words of a *New York Times* reporter (Rappeport 2016). Albright inflamed the debate when she stated at a Clinton rally in New Hampshire that "there's a special place in hell for women who don't help each other! We can tell our story of how we climbed the ladder, and a lot of you younger women think it's done. It's not done," she said of the broader fight for women's equality. (Albright had long used that line in her many talks.)[1] In an interview, Steinem suggested that young women were backing Senator Sanders so that they could meet young men. "When you're young, you're thinking: 'Where are the boys? The boys are with Bernie,'" Ms. Steinem said. These remarks drew strong criticism and much backlash, as they seemed to be hectoring younger women into supporting Clinton. "Walk it back, Ms. Steinem, We aren't here for the boys," People for Bernie demanded in an online petition. "As students of your own powerful model of feminist activism in the media, we demand that you admit your mistake and apologize," they wrote. Modern campus feminists watching Albright and Steinem "see a group of older, privileged white women circling the wagons around one of their own. The problem they're solving is real, but it might not be the most important one anymore" (Roberts 2016).

Steinem did apologize, writing on her Facebook page,

> In a case of talk-show Interruptus, I misspoke on the Bill Maher show recently, and apologize for what's been misinterpreted as implying young women aren't serious in their politics. What I had just said on the same show was the opposite: young women are active, mad as hell about what's happening to them, graduating in debt, but averaging a million dollars less over their lifetimes to pay it back. Whether they gravitate to Bernie or Hillary, young women are activist and feminist in greater numbers than ever before.

Her posting, not surprisingly, received thousands of critical responses.

Commentary also noted mother-daughter debates about the Clinton campaign and its historical nature as taking place across the country "as women of varying ages and backgrounds confront the potential milestone implicit in Mrs. Clinton's bid very differently" (Chozick and Alcindor 2015). As her chances of becoming the first female major party nominee increased, many women were considering how much gender should play into their decisions of whether to embrace Clinton's candidacy.

In primaries and caucuses across the country, women made up a solid majority of the Democratic Party electorate. In none of the twenty-three states holding primaries through the end of April in which exit polls were conducted did women make up fewer than 54 percent of Democratic voters. In several of the states, they were more than 60 percent of the voters. In each of the states, Hillary Clinton experienced a substantial gender gap in her vote, with women in all cases more supportive of her than men. In twenty of the states, she received a majority of women's votes. In twelve states, Bernie Sanders won the support of a majority of men's votes. He won the majority of women's votes in three states (Vermont, New Hampshire, and Oklahoma).

Black women were among Clinton's strongest supporters in the primaries. In the early southern primaries, Clinton's support among Black women contributed significantly to her lead over Bernie Sanders. Clinton won 89 percent of Black women's votes in South

Carolina, a state where 78 percent of Black women voted for Obama in 2008. Clinton won 93 percent of Black women's votes in Alabama, the same state where she won just 18 percent of Black women's votes in 2008 against Obama. In Georgia, Clinton won 86 percent of Black women's votes on Super Tuesday compared to just 12 percent in 2008. She won 86 percent and 85 percent of Black women's votes in Texas and Virginia, respectively, on Super Tuesday, states where she won less than 20 percent of Black women's support eight years earlier (Dittmar and Carr 2016).

The Democratic Convention

Whereas the Democratic convention began with Bernie Sanders's supporters angrily expressing their dismay with how the Democratic National Committee had seemingly structured ("rigged") the nomination process to assure Hillary Clinton's nomination, over the course of four days, the party presented a united front in its historic nomination. Women at the Democratic convention celebrated the historic moment of Hillary Clinton's nomination.

> They put on temporary tattoos that said "Run like a girl" and "Pantsuit Up" and mugged for photos. They slapped stickers on their chests that read "A woman's place is in the White House" and "Women Can Stop Trump." They wore T-shirts featuring a donkey wearing red pumps and the words "It's time."
>
> (Milibank 2016)

The diversity of the speakers on the first night of the convention was notable. They were diverse in their gender identities, political leanings, religious and racial identities, and life experiences. They addressed racial injustice and the power of protest, equal pay and abortion rights, the dignity of workers, mental health, and smashing glass ceilings (Gray 2016). U.S. Senator Elizabeth Warren gave the keynote address, only the third woman in party history to do so, and First Lady Michelle Obama addressed the convention. Commentators widely viewed her performance as particularly powerful.

On the second night of the convention, almost twice as many women as men spoke from the podium; there was a segment for women in Congress and another for Mothers of the Movement—moms whose children were killed under questionable circumstances. When the speeches ended, women running for Congress took the stage while Beyonce's "Run the World" played. In total, women made up 50.4 percent of the 236 speakers at the Democratic convention. In comparison, women accounted for just 26.1 percent of the 111 speakers at the Republican convention (Dittmar 2016a).

In addition to traditional Democratic themes of equality, speakers emphasized patriotic themes, long hallmarks of Republican rhetoric: tributes to service, sacrifice, American leadership, and above all, a repeated reaffirmation of American exceptionalism. Democratic delegates chanted "USA! USA!" and military leaders celebrated America's power. Throughout the convention, Democratic speakers struck optimistic notes, emphasized patriotism and a muscular American presence in the world, messages that happen to have strong appeal for disaffected Republicans and independents (Gaouette 2016).

On the third night of the convention, delegates officially nominated Hillary Clinton as its presidential candidate. At the end of the poll of states, Senator Sanders moved to make Clinton's nomination unanimous. She then formally accepted the nomination the next night with a speech sprinkled with lines such as "We have the most powerful military. The most innovative entrepreneurs. The most enduring values—freedom and equality, justice and opportunity. We should be so proud that these words are associated with us.

That when people hear them, they hear America." She said the word "together" at least fifteen times. She blasted Donald Trump and reached out to Sanders's supporters with the words "I've heard you. Your cause is our cause." She presented herself as a dedicated and indefatigable fighter for children, the disabled, blue-collar workers, women, and the poor while promising a backbone of steel as she vowed to take out ISIS.

At the conclusion of the Democratic convention, the Pew Research Center issued its findings on "5 facts about Hillary Clinton's Candidacy." Highlights include the following (Oliphant 2016):

- More voters say they know a lot about where Clinton stands on important issues than say the same about Trump.
- Few voters think gender will hurt Clinton in the fall. Supporters and opponents see Clinton's political views differently. Over three quarters of Trump supporters (78 percent) say Clinton has predominantly liberal views, including 59 percent who say she is liberal on almost all issues.
- By contrast, Clinton's supporters are just as likely to say she has a mix of liberal and conservative views (42 percent) as to say her positions are predominantly liberal (42 percent). Just 9 percent say she's liberal on almost all issues.
- Many voters—including many of her supporters—doubt Clinton will change Washington much.
- Democrats feel warmly toward Clinton, while Republicans view her as very cold.

The Republican Convention

At the Republican National Convention in Cleveland, Ohio, on July 18, speakers and delegates gathered under a massive sign proclaiming "Make America Safe Again." Republicans spent more time calling out Hillary Clinton than talking about and promoting their nominee, Donald Trump. During the first three days of the convention, the event's prime-time speakers mentioned Clinton's name more than 135 times, nearly twice the number of times that Trump's own name was mentioned. The first night included a long segment on Benghazi, showing Clinton in the worst possible light. Speakers and delegates were unrelenting in their disparaging remarks and negative "callouts" about her. Night after night, convention speakers called for Clinton to be put in prison with chants of "Lock her up. Lock her up." Some even went so far as to say she should be shot for treason.

New Jersey governor Chris Christie led a mock prosecution of Clinton from the stage. In his speech to the convention, former Republican presidential contender Dr. Ben Carson linked Clinton to Satan through her association with Saul Alinsky, a community leader and writer who acknowledged Lucifer in his book *Rules for Radicals*. Sharon Day, cochair of the Republican National Committee, called out that Clinton had "viciously attacked the character of women who were sexually abused at the hands of [her] husband." One elected official declared that she should be "hanging from a tree"[2] (Weaver 2016).

In his acceptance speech, Trump declared that he was the voice of "the forgotten men and women of the country." He emphasized law-and-order themes. His speech took on dark "overtones with a mix of tough-talking rhetoric and an embrace of nationalism." Hillary Clinton's legacy, he intoned, was "death, destruction, terrorism, and weakness." He painted her as a corrupt puppet of the political elite eager to maintain the status quo in America. He suggested she was personally responsible for many recent "humiliations" in the world, including the 2012 attack of the U.S. Consulate in Libya, the Muslim Brotherhood's rise to power in Egypt, and the Iran nuclear agreement (Bluestein and Hallerman

Picture 9.2 Women Dressed in Hillary Clinton Inmate Costumes Stand Outside a Trump Rally
Courtesy of Shutterstock.com.

2016). He would be the law-and-order president. He alone had the leadership strength to secure the homeland and to rejuvenate the economy (Farenthold and Rucker 2016).

The General Election

On November 8, the day the United States might elect its first female president, over a thousand people lined up at the New York grave site of suffrage leader Susan B. Anthony to pay their respects and to place their "I Voted Today" stickers on her tombstone. This action was an Election Day tradition but with additional meaning in 2016 in anticipation of the first woman being elected to the highest office in the country. Because of the anticipated long lines, local officials extended the hours the grave site was open until the end of voting. A live camera documented the daylong event. During the campaign season, many feminists had encouraged others to visit the graves of Anthony and those of other influential women, using the hashtag #VisitASuffragist as a "calming reminder of the long view during a presidential election seething with toxic gender politics" (Onion 2016).

Clinton had numerous advantages in the general election. The most dramatic advantage during the campaign was her opponent's derogatory behavior toward many groups and individuals. Donald Trump's crass comments and myriad allegations of sexual misconduct, mockery of a handicapped reporter, derisive comments about the Gold Star Khan family, and anti-immigrant rhetoric brought him immense criticism generally and sharp opposition even from leading Republicans, among them the former presidential Bush families. Former First Lady Barbara Bush even went so far as to say she was "sick of him" in a CNN interview. "He's said terrible things about women, terrible things about the military. I don't

Picture 9.3 Voting Stickers on Susan B. Anthony's Tombstone, November 8, 2016

understand why people are for him, for that reason" (Killough 2016). On CBS she stated, "I don't know how women can vote for Trump" (CBS 2016). Former president George H. W. Bush was quoted as saying he planned to vote for Clinton.

The Clinton campaign had a substantially larger financial war chest. Reports filed with the Federal Election Commission show that Clinton and her allies, including her joint committees with the Democratic Party and the super PACs backing her, raised more than $1.2 billion for the full cycle, whereas Trump and his allies collected approximately $600 million (Arnsdorf 2016). She was also touted as having a better and more extensive ground operation.[3] Her governmental knowledge and experience vastly outweighed her opponent's. She received an unprecedented number of news media endorsements.

In large part because of Trump's temperament and campaign tactics, the vast majority of news media outlets endorsed Clinton, some endorsing a Democrat for the first time ever and some endorsing a presidential candidate for the first time ever. For example, *USA TODAY*'s editorial board wrote,

> In the 34-year history of USA TODAY, the Editorial Board has never taken sides in the presidential race. We've never seen reason to alter our approach. Until now. This year, the choice isn't between two capable major party nominees who happen to have significant ideological differences. This year, one of the candidates is, by unanimous consensus of the Editorial Board, unfit for the presidency.

The *San Diego Union Tribune* endorsement of Secretary Clinton noted that "this paper has not endorsed a Democrat for president in its 148-year history. But we endorse Clinton. She's the safe choice for the U.S. and for the world, for Democrats and Republicans alike."

It cited a long list of negatives regarding Trump's candidacy. In its endorsement of Hillary Clinton, the *Birmingham News* of Alabama described Donald Trump as a

> narcissistic, childish bully who has mocked women, Americans with disabilities, veterans, Gold Star families, judges, immigrants, the working poor, people of faith, Muslim Americans, Jewish Americans, refugees, people with weight issues and any other group that challenges his inflated view of himself. A Trump presidency could send the Republican Party down a dark, exclusionary path that would be tough to recover from.

Not surprisingly, the traditional liberal newspapers unanimously endorsed Sectary Clinton, praising her in strong terms, as exemplified by the *New York Times* statement, "Our endorsement is rooted in respect for her intellect, experience, toughness and courage over a career of almost continuous public service, often as the first or only woman in the arena."

Numerous prominent Republicans, led by Colin Powell, endorsed her, and Republican women even formed a committee in support of her campaign, Republican Women for Hillary. One of its founders, Jennifer Pierotti Lim, spoke at the Democratic National Convention. On its website, Republican Women for Hillary characterized itself as a "volunteer grassroots group to provide Republican women a voice in the 2016 presidential election through leadership in the media, organizing networking events, and serving as a clearinghouse for broader GOTV efforts." Citing that Donald Trump was unfit to be commander in chief, PAC Republicans for Her was formed (Alter 2016b). It reported raising $75,000. All these pluses for Clinton were for naught in the end, however, when Donald Trump's message of change, "drain the swamp," and "make America great again" resonated with many Americans who felt they had been forgotten by the political elite.

The Likability Question

Candidate likability has played prominently in public opinion polling of presidential contenders and assessments of their candidacies, especially female contenders. Pollsters measure "likability" primarily by asking survey respondents how favorable they feel toward a candidate. *FiveThirtyEight* reported Clinton and Trump to be "historically disliked" (Enten April 2016; see Figure 9.1). A *USA TODAY* headline on the August 31

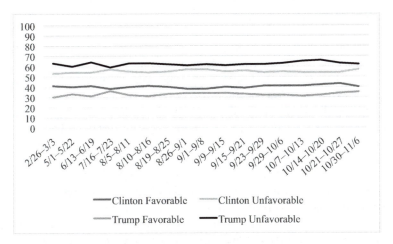

Figure 9.1 2016 Favorable Ratings of Clinton and Trump
Adapted from Gallup.com data.

edition declared, "Poll: Clinton, Trump Most Unfavorable Candidates Ever," based on an ABC/*Washington Post* poll showing that, among U.S. adults, Clinton had an unfavorable rating of 56 percent, whereas Trump's unfavorable rating was 63 percent. "Ever" referred to the life of ABC/*Washington Post* polls.

Hillary Clinton's low likability ratings were a particular problem from a women and politics perspective. Research by the Barbara Lee Foundation (2016) has shown that

> voters will support a male candidate they do not like but who they think is qualified. Men don't need to be liked to be elected. Voters are less likely to vote for a woman candidate they do not like. Women have to prove they are qualified. For men, their qualification is assumed. Women face the double bind of needing to show competence and likeability.

Similarly, according to the Center for American Women and Politics researcher Kelly Dittmar,

> Likability matters more for women candidates than for men. In other words, voters are much more comfortable voting for male candidates that they don't like, but think are qualified to serve. For women, likability and qualifications are tied together in voters' minds. They must demonstrate *both* traits to earn voter support. It's no surprise, then, that we seem to spend a lot more time worrying about how likable Hillary Clinton is than we do about whether or not we want to have a beer with Donald Trump.
>
> (quoted in Newton-Small 2016)

The Misogyny of Donald Trump

Gender aspects of the election would clearly be at the forefront of commentary, political discussion, and observation in the 2016 presidential election, given the historic nature of Hillary Clinton's candidacy. It could not be otherwise. In a *Dame* magazine post titled "I Am Voting with My Vagina," columnist Kate Harding (2015) poignantly stated the uniqueness of this quest for the presidency:

> There has never been a president who knows what it's like to menstruate, be pregnant, or give birth. There has never been a president who knows what it's like to be the target of subtle and categorically unsubtle sexism. There has never been a president who was criticized widely for his political ambition, or forced into a bake-off to prove he's not too career-oriented to cook for his family. There has never been a president who was forced to take his spouse's last name for appearances' sake. There has never been a president criticized for showing too much cleavage, or having "cankles," or wearing unflattering headbands or colorful pantsuits. There has never been a president who was presumed to be mentally and emotionally unstable because of naturally occurring hormones.

However, in the campaign, "gender" took a strange and ugly twist, as media accounts of Donald Trump's history of misogyny—defined as dislike of, contempt for, or ingrained prejudice against women—was broadcast. He had a long record of making degrading and insulting comments regarding women. His behavior in that regard during the campaign further inflamed the election. His derogatory comments about women, his crude disdain toward Hillary Clinton as a presidential candidate, and his history of brutish treatment of women turned what might have been a policy-focused campaign into a dark circus.

Feminist writer Rebecca Traister's (2016) description of Trump's behavior is representative of commentary about his campaign misogyny:

> During the presidential campaign, many Americans, notably those most likely to have voted for Hillary Clinton, were on the receiving end of torrents of vitriol coming from Donald Trump and his supporters. They were caricatured as rapists and criminals, bimbos, dogs, and pigs, and subjected to the humiliation of watching a man repeatedly accused of sexual assault run for president, advised by a cadre of racists adorably referred to as members of the "alt-right," all while our first black president and first woman nominee were regularly called crooks and threatened with imprisonment and execution.

Trump said women who have abortions deserved to be punished and women facing sexual harassment at work should "find another career."

Late in the campaign season, the *Washington Post* reported having obtained a tape of Trump bragging during a 2005 conversation with Billy Rush, then of *Access Hollywood*, in vulgar terms about kissing, groping, and trying to have sex with women. "When you are a star, they let you do it. I don't even wait," he bragged. "Grab them by the pussy. You can do anything." The tape continued with a graphic account of a failed attempt to seduce a married woman (Farenthold 2016). In response, Trump tried to brush it off. "This was locker-room banter, a private conversation that took place many years ago. Bill Clinton has said far worse to me on the golf course—not even close," Trump said in a statement. "I apologize if anyone was offended."

His misogynistic antics during the Republican primary and in the general election campaign were nearly a daily occurrence. He mocked the face of onetime GOP rival Carly Fiorina. He's retweeted an unflattering image of primary opponent Senator Ted Cruz's wife, Heidi, juxtaposed with a glamorous photo of his wife, Melania. He engaged in a long-running dispute with Megyn Kelly of Fox News in which he dismissed her as a "lightweight" and "bimbo" and described her at one point as having "blood coming out of her eyes, blood coming out of her wherever." More than a dozen women came forward, accusing him of sexual assault in previous years.

He renewed his attacks against former Miss Universe winner Alicia Machado, whose story resurfaced at the end of the first presidential debate when Clinton reminded viewers of his frequently crude remarks about women and their bodies. "One of the worst things he said was about a woman in a beauty contest. He loves beauty contests, supporting them and hanging around them," Clinton said as she slowly told the story. "And he called this woman 'Miss Piggy.' Then he called her 'Miss Housekeeping,' because she was Latina." Clinton paused. "Donald, she has a name: Her name is Alicia Machado. And she has become a US citizen and you can bet she is going to vote this November." In the following days, Trump went on a rant against Ms. Machado.

Clinton was the subject of unrelenting personal attacks. She was regularly referred to as "Crooked Hillary" and told she should be locked up. Trump's supporters wore T-shirts adorned with slogans such as "Trump That Bitch," "Proud to Be a Hillary Hater," "I Wish Hillary Had Married OJ," "She's a Cunt/Vote for Trump," and "KFC Hillary Special: 2 Fat Thighs, 2 Small Breasts . . . Left Wing." Merchandise on sale outside the Republican National Convention included pins with such slogans such as "Don't be a pussy, vote for Trump in 2016," "Trump 2016: Finally someone with balls," "Life's a Bitch: Don't Vote for One," and a white pin showing a boy urinating on the word HILLARY. T-shirts could be bought that read "Trump the Bitch" or "Hillary sucks but not like Monica." One could get a black T-shirt depicting Trump as a biker and Clinton falling off the motorcycle's back alongside the words "If you can read this, the bitch fell off" (Beinart 2016).

Picture 9.4 The Woman Card

Trump continually demeaned Clinton beyond the "crooked" line. She did not "look presidential." She was always "screaming." She lacked "strength and stamina." She was a "nasty woman." He made fun of her hair, noting that she had a new hairdo: "I tell you what, it really was shocking to see it because you're right it must be, it was massive. Her hair became massive" (Diamond 2015). He also even more directly attempted a gender attack on her. "Frankly, if Hillary Clinton were a man, I don't think she'd get 5 percent of the vote. The only thing she's got going is the women's card. And the beautiful thing is, women don't like her," he declared in April. Clinton responded, "Mr. Trump accused me of playing the 'woman card.' Well if fighting for women's health care and paid family leave and equal pay is playing the 'woman card,' then deal me in.'" The Clinton campaign quickly capitalized on the "woman card" theme as a fund-raising tactic. Supporters could get their own "woman card" similar to a credit card for a small donation to the campaign (see Picture 9.4).

In the final days of the campaign, Clinton's TV ads highlighted Trump's misogyny. One sixty-second spot featured clips of Trump saying that letting women work outside the home is dangerous, that he goes "through the roof" if dinner is not ready when he arrives home, and bragging about being able to grab women by their genitals because he is a celebrity. Trump was also seen in the ad talking about going into dressing rooms to look at underage girls as they changed.

Feminist columnist Katha Pollit (2016) summed up the election's outcome:

> It was supposed to be the election in which women rejected the candidate who hates women in favor of the candidate who is one. Trump and his followers have normalized the demeaning of women, even in its coarsest, crudest forms. You can say things about women in public you couldn't say before and suffer no consequences. You can call a woman in public life a bitch and demand that she be imprisoned—or even executed.

Clinton's campaign, on the other hand, generated a positive gender frame regarding her candidacy. After playing down women's issues in her 2008 campaign against Barack Obama, for this election, Clinton more readily embraced the historic nature of her candidacy and played up her roles as a grandmother and longtime advocate for women. She emphasized issues of special interest to female voters such as equal pay, health care, and paid family leave. Her economic plan promised to "lift up participation in the workforce—especially for women." She talked often of her own experiences in the workplace and in politics. She spoke frequently of breaking "that highest, hardest glass ceiling" of electing a female president, and she jokingly told audiences that after more than two hundred years and forty-four male presidents, "It's time" (DelReal and Gearan 2016). Women's issues were a key part of Clinton's closing argument. On her final day of campaign rallies, she called out, "If you believe women and girls should be treated with dignity and respect, and that women should be able to make our own health care decisions and that marriage equality should be protected, then you have to vote."

The gender script was actually "flipped" in the 2016 campaign, according to political scientist Kathleen Dolan (2016): "From the perspective of gender politics, one of the most amazing aspects of this campaign is that when we discuss personality traits and 'temperament' of the candidates, we do NOT hear the woman candidate being labeled as unfit to be president," as has historically been the case. Professor Dolan used Trump's performance in the first debate as primary evidence of the "gender flip."

> Since the first presidential debate last week, there has been a clear shift in the conversation about the personality traits of Clinton and Trump and their fitness to be president. Here, for the first time, we see a male candidate's "temperament" judged negatively. When Trump confidently declared that his temperament was probably his greatest strength as a potential president, the audience at the debate laughed out loud. In critiquing his debate performance, reporters and opinion writers have referred to aspects of his personality and behavioral traits in negative ways not generally associated with male leaders. Clinton, on the other hand, has been described in positive terms that are often seen as "masculine" or male strengths. A quick review of media articles published in the days following the debate reveals Trump described as "angry," "undisciplined," "sensitive," "impulsive," and being ready to "blow his top." These same writers called Clinton "measured," having given a "strong performance," and demonstrating "command," and a "sense of humor." While the sense that Clinton had "won" the debate and Trump did himself no favors was widely accepted outside of strong conservative and Republican circles, what is new and fascinating is the way in which the gender script on personality traits was flipped. Clinton, the woman, was determined to have appeared presidential, while Trump, the man, was widely thought to be anything but. When Trump tried to attack Clinton for not having the stamina to be president, commentators remarked on how he appeared "haggard" and "weaker" than Clinton. Several commentators even referred to the number of times she smiled without framing this as a negative, as too soft or feminine. Instead it was used as an illustration of her ability to stay steady and let Trump's provocations roll off her back (or shimmy off her shoulders). Media writers and commentators spent several days after the debate talking about Clinton's strengths in ways that almost seemed easy and obvious. But this conversation is anything but casual and common. For those who study gender politics, hearing a woman candidate described positively in terms usually reserved for men is a surprising, almost astounding, shift in tone.

Trump's poor performance in the two presidential debates that followed further challenged his presidential status. He was viewed as stalking Clinton in the second debate, the format of which involved interaction with members of the audience. Polls and commentary suggested Clinton won each of the three presidential debates.

Gender and the Vote in the 2016 Election

Preliminary analysis suggests that 59.2 percent of potential voters participated in the 2016 election compared with a turnout rate of 59.7 percent in 2012 (McDonald 2016). The most recent census data show there are 124.8 million women and 118.1 million men of voting age. According to the census, 67 percent of women are registered to vote, and 58.5 percent have voted in the past compared with 63.1 percent and 54.4 percent for men. The 2016 exit poll reports women as being 52 percent of the voters, a percentage similar to that of other recent elections.

The exit polls also tell us who voted and how they voted in the 2016 election. Table 9.1 breaks down the voting decision of various groups. The historic presidential candidacy

Table 9.1 The 2016 Exit Poll: The Demographics of the Presidential Election

2016 Exit Poll Results

	Percent of Electorate	*Clinton Percent*	*Trump Percent*
Sex			
Women	52	54	42
Men	48	41	53
Age			
18–29	19	55	37
30–44	25	50	32
45–64	40	44	53
65 and older	15	45	53
Race/Ethnicity			
White	70	37	58
Black	12	88	8
Latino	11	65	29
Asian	4	56	29
Race and Sex			
White Men	34	31	63
White Women	37	43	53
Black Men	5	80	13
Black Women	7	94	4
Latino Men	5	62	33
Latino Women	6	68	26
Education			
High School or Less	18	45	51
Some College	32	47	52
College Graduate	32	49	45
Postgraduate	18	58	37
Income			
Under $30,000	17	53	41
$30,000–49,999	19	51	42
$50,000–99,999	31	46	50
$100,000–199,999	24	47	48
$200,000–249,999	4	48	49
$250,000 or More	6	46	48
Marital Status by Sex			
Married Men	29	37	58
Married Women	30	49	47
Unmarried Men	19	46	45
Unmarried Women	23	62	33

of Hillary Clinton did not produce a larger gender gap than in other recent elections. As noted in Chapter 4, the gender gap was thirteen points, with 54 percent of women voting for Clinton compared to 41 percent of men. More specifically, the majority of women cast their ballots for Hillary Clinton in twenty-three of the twenty-eight states where exit polls are available. In fact, if only women voted, Trump's success in at least ten battleground states (Arizona, Florida, Georgia, Iowa, Michigan, North Carolina, Ohio, Pennsylvania, Texas, and Wisconsin) would have been reversed (Dittmar 2016b).

Clinton won voters forty-five and younger, whereas Trump won among older voters. But she underperformed Obama's 2012 share of the millennial vote. Among those between eighteen and twenty-nine, Clinton's vote percentage was five points less than Obama's (55 percent to 60 percent). Young women were strong Clinton supporters, however. She won women ages eighteen to twenty-nine 63 percent to 31 percent; support was more evenly split among men in the same age group, 46 percent for Clinton to 42 percent for Trump. Trump won White voters, whereas Clinton overwhelmingly won the votes of Blacks and decisively won the votes of Latinos and Asians. Yet she won a smaller percentage of the Black vote than President Obama did in 2012 (88 percent to 93 percent) and the Latino vote (65 percent to 71 percent). Clinton won 94 percent of Black women's votes. Black women were 8 percent and 7 percent of exit poll voters in 2012 and 2016.

In something of a contradiction, Clinton won the votes of college-educated citizens while losing the votes of those with less formal education while simultaneously winning the votes of the lowest-income individuals but quite evenly splitting the votes of higher income individuals with Trump. This seeming contradiction may be due to the confluence of race and income.

Clinton won married women by two points, the first Democratic candidate to do so in twenty years. Black women were her biggest supporters, winning 94 percent of their votes. Trump won the votes of White men decisively and White women marginally. Clinton did marginally win the votes of White female college graduates (51 percent to 45 percent). (Mitt Romney had a six-point advantage over Obama in 2012.) Although some commentary suggested otherwise, Kelly Dittmar (2016b) shows that, in examining the 2016 election from a historical perspective, "White women did not abandon Clinton."

Why did Hillary Clinton lose the election, an election she was predicted to win for so long, and what does her loss mean for women's political leadership? Commentators, political scientists, and campaign operatives, as well as feminist activists, will be providing assessments of her loss and debating these questions long into the future.

Several factors stand out as helping to explain her loss. The scandal over her use of her family's private e-mail server for official communications, rather than official state department e-mail accounts maintained on federal servers, and the reemergence of it as an issue at the end of the campaign, was the most prominently cited factor. During the campaign summer, the Gallup organization asked a national sample what they had recently heard or read about Hillary Clinton. The word *e-mail* drowned everything else out. Nearly one half of the responses mentioned some aspect of the e-mail affair. Few mentioned the substantive themes Clinton talked about on the campaign trail. Donald Trump was primarily associated with the word *immigration* (Newport et al. 2016).

Added to the e-mail scandal in undermining Clinton's campaign was the hacking of Democratic party e-mails that received intense media coverage and a seemingly badly run campaign organization that did not focus enough attention on the alienation so many people felt toward the "political elite." President Barack Obama faulted his party's campaign strategy in a December interview, arguing that Democrats suffered "stinging electoral losses in last month's vote because they failed to campaign in hard-hit rural areas" (Liptak 2016). She was accused of focusing too much on "identity politics," calling out explicitly to

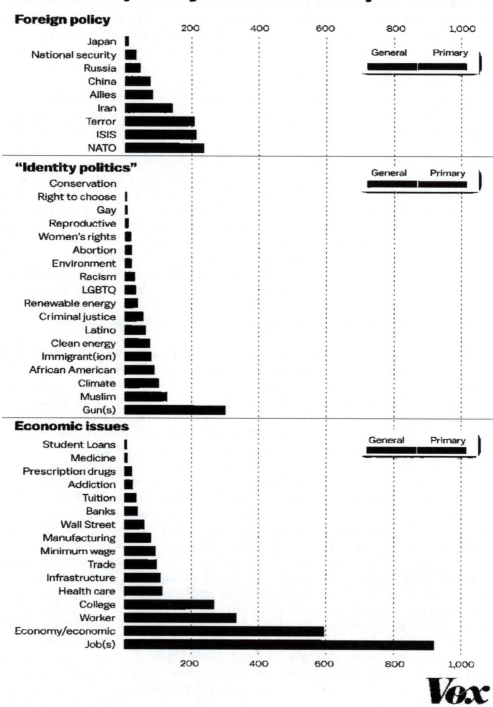

Figure 9.2 Word Frequency of Clinton's Speeches

David Roberts, 2016, "The Most Common Words in Hillary Clinton's Speeches, in One Chart," *Vox*, December 19, www.vox.com/policy-and-politics/2016/12/16/13972394/most-common-words-hillary-clinton-speech.

African American, Latino, LGBT, and women voters at every stop (Lilla 2016) rather than focusing on broader economic issues. However, after gathering all her campaign speeches (from both the primary and general campaigns) into one document and conducting a simple word-frequency analysis, David Roberts (2016; see Figure 9.2) concluded that the words she used in her speeches show she

> talked about jobs, workers, and the economy—more than anything else. They were the central focus of her public speeches . . . you cannot say she *didn't* talk about jobs, workers, and the economy. She talked about them all the time, more than anything else.

She was described as being an establishment candidate in a time when voters were anxious for change. The perception that she was an incredibly polarizing figure who was unable to generate enthusiasm among young women is also seen as a factor in her loss. But the fact that her positive debate performances and Trump's egregious behavior toward women and other groups did not propel her to victory will long be puzzled over in postmortems of the election. As one commentator summed it up, "Abhorrence of Trump failed to drive enough voters to the polls for Clinton" (Newton-Small 2016). The surge in female voters that the Clinton campaign had hoped for did not happen. But Clinton won nearly three million more votes than Trump. The question of whether voters would cast a ballot for a woman candidate for president, the subject of public opinion polls since the 1930s, was put to rest. But what effect would both her candidacy and her defeat have on women's political leadership?

Political scientists Christina Wolbrecht and David Campbell (2016) suggest from their research that what the effect will be first depends on the extent to which female politicians are portrayed as "unusual, pathbreaking and remarkable." They assert that most Americans view the Clinton campaign as indeed being pathbreaking. But second, they suggest that "it's not just what girls see or read that matters." It may also depend on whether the Clinton campaign spurred conversations about politics between parents and daughters at home. When the presence of female politicians leads parents and children to talk politics, girls become more interested in political participation. Thus, parents play an important role in ensuring that youth make the connection between the political world and their own lives. Ironically, such conversation means that even the disparaging rhetoric of the Trump rallies about Clinton may help to engage young girls. "If the unprecedented nature of Clinton's candidacy—highlighted by the candidate herself, her opponent and the media—means politics became a topic of conversation within America's homes, adolescent girls may become more engaged in politics as a result" (Wolbrecht and Campbell 2016).

Jennifer Lawless, director of American University's Women and Politics Institute, shares her perspective for the future:

> This was not your typical election cycle, and Hillary Clinton is not a typical female candidate. She's unique in so many ways, that I think the best piece of advice that we can give to young women is to say: "Look, this does not mean that women can't win elections. This does not mean that you should not fight the fight by running for office. When we look at all of these other levels of office, women are just as successful, and it's likely that one day we'll elect a female president as well."
>
> (Kamm 2016)

Several early indicators of women actually being energized to enter the political fray emerged in the weeks after the 2016 election. Emerge America, the Democratic Party state training programs for potential female candidates, reported a spike in interest from women who want to learn more about becoming candidates after the election. EMILY's List also touted an increase in donations and a rise in the number of women looking to run for office. The nonprofit, nonpartisan She Should Run organization described in Chapter 8 reported a record 2,700 women pledging to run for office, and 2,200 women joined the She Should Run Incubator, which provides practical, actionable guidance they'll need to launch their path to leadership (Gowland 2016). VoteRunLead, a nonpartisan organization that trains future female candidates, reported having 1,100 women sign up for their next webinar in a forty-eight-hour postelection period compared to the usual thirty to eighty applicants (Walters 2017). But what does it matter that women seek and hold elected office and engage in political leadership more generally? Chapter 10 addresses that question, exploring the policy consequences of women's political leadership.

Notes

1. The "special place in hell" quote has been memorialized on Starbucks coffee mugs.
2. The official later apologized for his comment.
3. Postelection analyses suggest that the ground game, however, did not work as anticipated. See, for example, Edward-Isaac Devere, 2016, "How Clinton Lost Michigan—and Blew the Election," *Politico*, December 14, www.politico.com/story/2016/12/michigan-hillary-clinton-trump-232547.

Suggested Readings and Presentations from the Campaign Trail

"Cracked But Not Shattered: 20 Women on Clinton's Run." 2016. *CNN*, November 10. www.cnn.com/2016/11/09/opinions/women-elex/index.html.
"The Politics of Gender: Women, Men and the 2016 Campaign." *The Atlantic Politics & Policy*. www.youtube.com/playlist?list=PLwj46yNDLyTVQu6ADiKvkh7Ad7lPzInBa.
Rebecca Traister. 2016. "Hillary Clinton vs. Herself: There's Nothing Simple about This Candidacy—Or Candidate." *New York Magazine*, May 30.
Women's Media Center, "#Who Talks—Cable/News Analysts & Gender in 2016 Presidential Debates." www.womensmediacenter.com/preview/pages/whotalks-cable-news-analysts-gender-in-2016-presidential-debates.

Women, the Presidency, and the Executive Office

Chisholm, Shirley. 1970. *Unbought and Unbossed*. New York, NY: Houghton Mifflin.
Cohen, Nancy. 2016. *Breakthrough: The Making of the First Woman President*. Berkeley, CA: Counterpoint Press.
Fitzpatrick, Ellen. 2016. *The Highest Glass Ceiling: Women's Quest for the American Presidency*. Cambridge, MA: Harvard University Press.
Jalalzai, Farida. 2013. *Shattered, Cracked or Firmly Intact? Women and the Executive Glass Ceiling Worldwide*. New York, NY: Oxford University Press.
Lawrence, Regina G. and Melody Rose. 2010. *Hillary Clinton's Race for the White House*. Boulder, CO: Lynne Rienner.
Traister, Rebecca. 2010. *Big Girls Don't Cry: The Election That Changed Everything for American Women*. New York, NY: Free Press.

Web Resources

Natalia Osipova, Megan Specia, and Carolyn Ryan. "Women at the Conventions." www.nytimes.com/video/us/politics/100000004547772/women-at-the-conventions.html.

References

Alter, Charlotte. 2016a. "The Spirit of BernieBro Lives On." *Time*, January 31. http://time.com/4201356/bernie-sanders-berniebro/.

Alter, Charlotte. 2016b. "Why This Republican Created a PAC to Elect Hillary Clinton." *Time*, June 8. http://time.com/4360519/hillary-clinton-republican-pac-craig-snyder/.

Arnsdorf, Isaac. 2016. "Trump Won with Half as Much Money as Clinton Raised." *Politico*, December 12. www.politico.com/story/2016/12/trump-clinton-campaign-fundraising-totals-232400.

Barbara Lee Family Foundation. 2016. "Politics Is Personal: Keys to Likeability and Electability for Women." http://oe9e345wags3x5qikp6dg012.wpengine.netdna-cdn.com/wp-content/uploads/BLFF-Likeability-Memo-FINAL.pdf.

Beinart, Peter. 2016. "Fear of a Female President." *The Atlantic*, October 15–17.

Bluestein, Greg and Tamar Hallerman. 2016. "Republican National Convention: 'I Am Your Voice.'" *The Atlantic Journal-Constitution*, July 22: A1.

CBS News. 2016. "Barbara Bush: 'I Don't Know How Women Can Vote' for Trump." www.cbsnews.com/videos/barbara-bush-i-dont-know-how-women-can-vote-for-donald-trump/.

Chozick, Amy and Yamiche Alcindor. 2015. "Mother and Daughters Debate Gender Factor in Hillary Clinton's Bid." *The New York Times*, December 12. www.nytimes.com/2015/12/13/us/politics/moms-and-daughters-debate-gender-factor-in-hillary-clintons-bid.html?action=click&contentCollection=Politics&module=RelatedCoverage&region=EndOfArticle&pgtype=article.

Collinson, Stephen. 2015. "Hillary Clinton Channels Roosevelts in First Campaign Rally." *CNN Wire*, June 12.

DelReal, Jose A. and Anne Gearan. 2016. "Trump: If Clinton 'Were a Man, I Don't Think She'd Get 5 Percent of the Vote.'" *The Washington Post*, April 27. www.washingtonpost.com/news/post-politics/wp/2016/04/27/trump-if-clinton-were-a-man-i-dont-think-shed-get-5-percent-of-the-vote/?utm_term=.67f8efa930b9.

Diamond, Jeremy. 2015. "Trump Talks Clinton's 'Massive' New Hairdo." *CNN Politics*, November 12. www.cnn.com/2015/11/12/politics/donald-trump-hillary-clinton-hair/.

Dittmar, Kelly. 2016a. "DNC Speakers by the Numbers." *Center for the American Woman and Politics Presidential Gender Watch*, August 2.

Dittmar, Kelly. 2016b. "2016 Election Analysis: Women Voters Did Not Abandon Clinton, Nor Did She Fail to Win Their Support." *Center for American Women and Politics Press Release*, November 11, 2016.

Dittmar, Kelly and Glynda Carr. 2016. "Black Women Voters: By the Numbers." *Huffington Post Politics*, March 25.

Dolan, Kathleen. 2016. "Flipping the Gender Script in Election 2016." *Presidential Gender Watch, Center for American Women and Politics*, October 4. http://presidentialgenderwatch.org/flipping-gender-script-election-2016/.

Enten, Harry. 2016. "Americans' Distaste for Both Trump and Clinton Is Record Breaking." *FiveThirtyEight*, May 5. http://fivethirtyeight.com/features/americans-distaste-for-both-trump-and-clinton-is-record-breaking/.

Farenthold, David A. 2016. "Trump Recorded Having Extremely Lewd Conversation about Women in 2005." *The Washington Post*, October 8.

Farenthold, David and Philip Rucker. 2016. "Strong Again." *Hartford Courant*, July 22: 1.

Gaouette, Nicole. 2016. "The Democrats' Republican Moment." *CNN Wire*, July 30. www.cnn.com/2016/07/29/politics/democratic-convention-gop-moment-national-security/index.html.

Gowland, Lelia. 2016. "She Should Run: This Nonprofit Incubator Is Launching Thousands of Women's Political Careers." *Forbes*, December 1. www.sheshouldrun.org/she_should_run_nonprofit_incubator_is_launching_thousands_of_womens_political_careers.

Gray, Emma. 2016. "Trump Is Right: He Doesn't Know What Is Going on with the Women." *Huffington Post*, July 26. www.huffingtonpost.com/entry/trump-is-right-he-doesnt-know-what-is-going-on-with-the-women-but-dems-do_us_5796e0e4e4b01180b5301295.

Harding, Kate. 2015. "I Am Voting with My Vagina: Hillary Clinton for President." *Dame*, April 14. www.damemagazine.com/2015/04/14/i-am-voting-my-vagina-hillary-clinton-president.

Kamm, Rebecca. 2016. "What Hillary Clinton's Loss Means for the Future of Women in Politics." *VICE*, November 15. https://broadly.vice.com/en_us/article/what-hillary-clintons-loss-means-for-the-future-of-women-in-politics.

Killough, Ashley. 2016. "Barbara Bush on Donald Trump: 'I'm Sick of Him.'" *CNN Politics*, February 6. www.cnn.com/2016/02/05/politics/barbara-bush-jeb-bush-donald-trump/index.html.

Lilla, Mark. 2016. "The End of Identity Liberalism." *The New York Times*, November 18. www.nytimes.com/2016/11/20/opinion/sunday/the-end-of-identity-liberalism.html?_r=1.

Liptak, Kevin. 2016. "Obama Says Democrats Lost By Not Showing Up." *CNN*, December 19. www.cnn.com/2016/12/19/politics/president-obama-npr-interview/index.html.

McDonald, Michael. 2016. "2016 November General Election Turnout Rates." www.electproject.org/2016g.

Meyer, Robinson. 2015. "Here Come the BernieBro." *Atlantic*, October 17. www.theatlantic.com/politics/archive/2015/10/here-comes-the-berniebro-bernie-sanders/411070/.

Milibank, Dana. 2016. "At the Democratic Convention, Women Seize Their Moment—And Momentum." *The Washington Post*, July 27. www.washingtonpost.com/politics/at-the-democratic-convention-women-seize-their-moment--and-momentum/2016/07/27/d6921634-5456-11e6-bbf5-957ad17b4385_story.html?utm_term=.018e75fa9ab5.

Newport, Frank, Lisa Singh, Stuart Soroka, Michael Traugott, and Andrew Dugan. 2016. "'Email' Dominates What Americans Have Heard about Clinton." September 2016. www.gallup.com/poll/195596/email-dominates-americans-heard-clinton.aspx.

Newton-Small, Jay. 2016. "Is Hillary Clinton Likable Enough?" *Time*, May 25. http://time.com/4347962/hillary-clinton-donald-trump-likability/.

Oliphant, Baxter. 2016. "5 Facts about Hillary Clinton's Campaign." *Pew Research Center Fact Tank*, July 27. www.pewresearch.org/fact-tank/2016/07/27/5-facts-about-hillary-clintons-candidacy/.

Onion, Rebecca. 2016. "Take the Long View of a Toxic Election with #VisitASuffragist." *Slate*, November 7. www.slate.com/blogs/xx_factor/2016/11/07/twitter_and_instagram_campaign_visitasuffragist.html.

Pollit, Katha. 2016. "An Unabashed Misogynist Is in Charge of Our Country. Now What?" *The Nation*, November 15. www.thenation.com/article/an-unabashed-misogynist-is-in-charge-of-our-country-now-what/.

Rappeport, Alan. 2016. "Gloria Steinem and Madeleine Albright Rebuke Young Women Backing Bernie Sanders." *New York Times*, February 7, https://www.nytimes.com/2016/02/08/us/politics/gloria-steinem-madeleine-albright-hillary-clinton-bernie-sanders.html.

Roberts, David. 2016. "The Most Common Words in Hillary Clinton's Speeches, in One Chart." *VOX*, December 16. www.vox.com/policy-and-politics/2016/12/16/13972394/most-common-words-hillary-clinton-speech.

Roberts, Molly. 2016. "Why Millennials Don't Care That Hillary Clinton Is a Woman." *Politico*, February 12. www.politico.com/magazine/story/2016/02/hillary-clinton-2016-young-women-gender-213620.

Roberts, Steven. 1984. "Rules of Party Playing Desired Role, Poll Finds." *The New York Times*, www.nytimes.com/1984/07/15/us/rules-of-party-playing-desired-role-poll-finds.html?pagewanted=all.

Sides, John. 2015. "Are Moms and Daughters Divided Over Hillary Clinton? Not So Fast." *The Washington Post*, December 22. www.washingtonpost.com/news/monkey-cage/wp/2015/12/22/are-moms-and-daughters-divided-over-hillary-clinton-not-so-fast/?utm_term=.cda7e62206b2.

Traister, Rebecca. 2016. "Blaming Clinton's Base for Her Lose Is the Ultimate Insult." *New York Magazine*, November 23. http://nymag.com/thecut/2016/11/blaming-clintons-base-for-her-loss-is-the-ultimate-insult.html.

Walters, Johanna. 2017. "Trump Victory Spurs Women to Run for Office across U.S.: Our Time Is Coming." *The Guardian*, January.

Weaver, Courtney. 2016. "Hillary Clinton: Unwitting Star of the Republican Convention." *Financial Times*, July 22. www.ft.com/content/2709b762-4fdd-11e6-8172-e39ecd3b86fc.

Wolbrecht, Christina and David Campbell. 2016. "Even in Defeat, Clinton's Campaign Could Still Inspire Young Women." *The Washington Post*, November 14.

10 Public Policy on Women's Rights and Equity Issues

Why, Women?

Political Parity

The "Women of the Senate" were awarded the 2014 Allegheny College Prize for Civility in Public Life. The twenty U.S. senators were honored for banding "together to help end the 2013 government shutdown, and in so doing helped to show the way toward a more civil climate in Washington, D.C.," the college stated in announcing the award. In presenting the award, college president James Mullen stated,

> This year we're going to honor a moment in time when 20 women in the Senate at a very difficult and challenging moment in American politics, a time when incivility was reigning, got together and said enough and set a wonderful example for us and particularly for young people. We've allowed sometimes a cynicism to set in about the possibilities of American politics. If that cynicism takes hold and people won't go into politics, that's dangerous for the nation, for democracy.

TIME magazine's Jay Newton-Small tells the story that led to the award. At one of the darkest moments of the government shutdown, with markets dipping and both ends of Pennsylvania Avenue hurling icy recriminations, Maine Republican Susan Collins went to the Senate floor to do two things that none of her colleagues had yet attempted. She refrained from partisan blame and proposed a plan to end the crisis. "I ask my Democratic and Republican colleagues to come together," Collins said on Oct. 8. "We can do it. We can legislate responsibly and in good faith."

Senate Appropriations Committee chair Barbara Mikulski, a Maryland Democrat, happened to be standing nearby, and she soon picked up a microphone and joined in. "Let's get to it. Let's get the job done," she said. "I am willing to negotiate. I am willing to compromise." Ten minutes later, a third Senator stood to speak. "I am pleased to stand with my friend from Maine, Senator Collins, as she has described a plan which I think is pretty reasonable," said Alaska Republican Lisa Murkowski. "I think it is pretty sensible."

As with most anything that happens on C-SPAN, the burst of bipartisan vibes was meant to send a message. But behind the scenes, the wheels really were turning. Most of the Senate's 20 women had gathered the previous night for pizza, salad and wine in the offices of New Hampshire Senator Jeanne Shaheen, a Democrat. All the buzz that night was about Collins' plan to reopen the government with some basic compromises. Senator Amy Klobuchar, a Minnesota Democrat, proposed adding the repeal of the

Picture 10.1 Senators Barbara Mikulski and Susan Collins Accept the 2014 Allegheny College Prize
for Civility in Public Life

unpopular medical-device tax. Senate Agriculture Committee chair Debbie Stabenow
suggested pulling revenue from her stalled farm bill. In policy terms, it was a potluck
dinner.

In the hours that followed, those discussions attracted more Senators, including
some men, and yielded a plan that would lead to genuine talks between Senate leaders
Harry Reid and Mitch McConnell to end the shutdown. The pieces were all there:
extending the debt ceiling and reopening the government with minor adjustments to
the implementation of Obamacare. No one doubted the origin. "The women are an
incredibly positive force because we like each other," Klobuchar boasted to TIME
as the negotiations continued. "We work together well, and we look for common
ground." An unspoken rule among what Collins calls "the sisterhood" holds that
the women refrain from publicly criticizing one another. And there is a deep sense
that more unites them personally than divides them politically. "One of the things we
do a bit better is listen," said North Dakota Democrat Heidi Heitkamp. "It is about
getting people in a room with different life experiences who will look at things a little
differently because they're moms, because they're daughters who've been taking care
of senior moms, because they have a different life experience than a lot of senior guys
in the room."

Against that backdrop, the private gatherings among the sisterhood are a source of
both power and perspective. They occur every few weeks or months, depending on the
need. Venues include the senators' homes—and occasionally the unlikely confines of the
Capitol's Strom Thurmond Room, a space named for one of the chamber's most notorious

Picture 10.2 Women Senators Go Bowling

Courtesy of Senator Claire McCaskill's office (http://hoh.rollcall.com/senate-women-strike-up-friendships-with-bipartisan-bowling/?dcz=emailalert).

womanizers. "We started the dinners 20 years ago on the idea that there has to be a zone of civility," says Mikulski. Not only do they have dinner together but also, in 2015, they even went bowling as a group. Once a year, the group also dines with the female Supreme Court justices. Dianne Feinstein, who chairs the Select Committee on Intelligence, holds regular dinners for women in the national security world. Even the female chiefs of staff and communications directors have started regular get-togethers of their own. In April, the Senate women breached their no-outsider rule by agreeing to dine at the White House with President Obama. Going around the table, California Senator Barbara Boxer remarked that one hundred years ago they'd have been meeting outside the White House gates to demand the right to vote. ("A hundred years ago, I'd have been serving you," Obama replied.) (Grand Forks Herald 2013).

This chapter considers various aspects of women's public leadership. It explores their leadership styles, movement into leadership positions, and effect on public policy. It then surveys public policy more generally aimed at women in the polity. It begins with an overview of Political Party's "Why Women?" question.

Normative Perspectives on Women's Representation

Political Parity lists fourteen ways in which women in public office have made a difference in democratic politics and policy making (see Text Box 10.1). Their first three ways, grouped under the rubric "100% of the talent pool," represent what are called normative concerns. Normative perspectives center on claims about how things should or ought to have stimulated much of the research on women's political participation. Part of

Text Box 10.1   Political Parity Answers the Why Women Question

100% of the Talent Pool

- A more representative government leads to policies that *represent more Americans.*
- Simply watching women run for office has been shown to *galvanize female citizens, making them more interested and actively involved in the political arena.*
- Having women as political leaders increases participation in our democracy and *inspires women of all sectors to take leadership roles.*

A New Style of Leadership

- Women, as a group, are more *partial to nonhierarchical collaboration, consensus building, and inclusion* than men, as a group, and they bring that style to politics.
- Female legislators *gather policy information from different sources* than men and rely on different types of information in making key decisions.
- Unlike their male colleagues, women in legislative and executive posts are *motivated most often by policy goals,* not power or prestige, in running for office and serving.
- Female lawmakers *open the legislative agenda* to new perspectives and issues.

Improved Policy Outcomes

- On average, women *sponsor and cosponsor more bills* than do men and are able to enlist more cosponsors.
- Across parties, women are, on average, 31 percent *more effective at advancing legislation* and see continued *success farther into the legislative process.*
- Congresswomen deliver 9 percent—or roughly $49 million—*more per year in federal programs* to their home districts than do congressmen.
- Women across the political spectrum are more likely than their male counterparts—of either party—to prioritize issues affecting *women, families, and children* on their legislative agendas.
- Regardless of party affiliation, women have voted more *consistently in favor of environmental protections* and policies than men have over the past twenty-five years in both the House and the Senate.

Greater Public Trust

- The American public rates women above or equal to men in seven of eight traits considered crucial for leadership—women are perceived as *outgoing, hardworking, honest, intelligent, creative, compassionate, and ambitious.*
- Women are ranked higher in public polling than men in four of seven key policy-making areas, including working out *compromises,* keeping government *honest, standing up* for what they believe in, and representing *constituents'* interests.

normative inquiries are questions of descriptive representation. Descriptive representation centers on the extent to which certain groups with particular characteristics in the populace are present among the public policy decision makers and how that matters. Substantive representation, a second aspect of normative concerns, focuses on how the decisions are made and whether the opinions distributed among the public are reflected in that decision-making process, regardless of how descriptively representative of the populace the decision makers are. From a women's rights perspective, descriptive representation concerns the extent to which women are present in political leadership positions and diversity among women in these positions. The substantive representation of women assesses the extent to which representatives act for women or on women's behalf. Activists argue that increased descriptive representation of women is expected to increase the substantive representation of women (Schwindt-Bayer and Taylor-Robinson 2011). The idea that women will "act for" or on behalf of other women links women's descriptive representation to their substantive representation (Cowell-Meyers and Langbein 2009). Electing more women to public office will "make a difference" for women in public policy. Sharing group membership means sharing experiences and policy goals, understanding perspectives, and prioritizing issues. Thus, having more women in legislative office will mean more advocates for women-friendly policies in the legislature and that more policy reflecting that agenda will be initiated and enacted.

The normative stimulus for studying women's quests for political leadership emerges from ideas about justice and fairness, women's symbolic importance as political leaders, and women's substantive impact on policy making. Justice and fairness arguments center on the concern of the unequal distribution of men and women in leadership positions. Justice requires that one half of the population not be excluded from political leadership, and fairness demands that men and women be present in roughly equal numbers among political elites. The gender, ethnicity, and race of elected representatives serve as evaluations of democratic political institutions. Implicit in these evaluations is the assumption that democratic political institutions, which lack any representatives from historically disadvantaged groups, are unjust and perceived as illegitimate. It is "grotesquely unfair for men to monopolize representation," Anne Phillips has argued in laying out the justice argument for gender parity in representation. She asks, "By what 'natural' superiority of talent or experience could men claim a right to dominate assemblies?" (Phillips 1998, 232). Phillips maintains that descriptive representatives are needed to compensate for past and continued injustices toward certain groups. According to this argument, the past and present betrayals of privileged groups create a belief that trust can be given only to descriptive representatives. The presence of descriptive representatives partially compensates for those betrayals.

Jennifer Lawless (2004) has also summarized this normative perspective, stating that "many scholars conclude that there appears to be something wrong with a political system that produces governing bodies dominated by men, when in fact, women comprise the majority of the population" (81). Discrimination has kept women from pursuing political leadership positions on an equal basis with men. Many historical examples exist of the prejudices women have faced when they left their traditional roles in the home and sought a place in the public sector. Indeed, it took over seventy years of campaigning for women just to get the right to vote, as Chapter 2 highlighted.

It might not matter whether public policies incorporated women's perspectives and interests if they were the same as men's. But we know that they have not been the same in the past; otherwise, why would women have organized, marched, and lobbied for an Equal Rights Amendment? Why would they have sued in court for equal rights and have needed special laws regarding violence, job security, and so on? The distinctive experiences of women's lives have also not been incorporated into the policy-making agenda and heard in legislative debates without the presence of women to express them (see, for example, Hawkesworth 2003 and Dodson 2006). The substantive importance of having a critical mass of women present as public policies are being made is an important representational issue. Female lawmakers have been shown to bring distinct policy preferences and ideas to the legislative agenda, policy debates, and problem solving.

A further argument advanced in support of the idea of descriptive representation is that female politicians serve as role models, inspiring other women to political activism and greater political competence. They perform a symbolic representational function. Women running and serving in high public office have an impact on their female constituents, stimulating greater interest and involvement in the electoral process, according to this perspective. Female leaders may impact people's attitudes toward government and their ability to influence it, seeing it as more accessible and open as it becomes more diverse. Their presence may especially affect women helping to close their deficit vis-à-vis men on political factors such as efficacy, interest, knowledge, and general political participation. These possible effects on women's engagement in the political process bring together descriptive and symbolic representation concerns in advocating for more women in political leadership positions. Several empirical studies have researched the symbolic connection between female political leaders and candidates and female constituents and voters (e.g., Atkeson 2003; Atkeson and Carrillo 2007; Lawless 2004; Wolbrecht and Campbell 2006).

Leadership Styles

The award story described in this chapter's introduction is about leadership style—that is, how lawmakers present themselves, engage in the policy-making process, work with their colleagues, and communicate with their constituents. Political Parity describes several ways in which women have brought "A New Style of Leadership," as listed in Text Box 10.1.

Political scientist Cindy Simon Rosenthal (1997, 2002) surveyed male and female state legislative committee chairs and conducted interviews with them, observed committee hearings, and organized focus groups in 1994 to explore the relationship between gender and leadership style. She concluded that female committee chairs in state legislatures were likely to use their leadership roles differently from their male colleagues. A desire to involve people in legislative deliberations motivated female committee chairs to use committee management practices that were inclusive of others. They reported a preference for more collaborative and accommodative conflict resolution styles and to be less comfortable with competitive or dominating leadership styles. Female committee chairs tended to demonstrate greater patience and better listening skills needed to work out differences of opinion.

Lyn Kathlene's (1994) study of discourse in the Colorado legislature—that is, verbal exchanges—revealed gendered patterns of speaking

> ### Sidebar 10.1 Representative Barbara Lee: "You Can't Rest"
>
> "You have to be the resistance," Representative Barbara Lee of California told her hometown paper, the *Oakland Tribune*. "You have to keep trying to work with the Republicans to do something that works for the country. You can't have a defeatist attitude. I think being a black woman in America, a double minority, I'm used to having to battle. It's another battlefront. You can't rest."
>
> (King 2016).

behavior. Men talked first, talked longer, took more speaking turns, and interrupted others four times more often than female committee members. Women, in contrast, used their fewer turns to be more facilitating. In a social network analysis of sponsorship and cosponsorship of legislation in the U.S. House of Representatives, female lawmakers were found to be more collaborative than their male counterparts (Von Hagel 2011).

A study of male and female U.S. senators' press releases has also shown that the sexes communicate differently with their constituents. Female senators were more likely to talk about communal issues such as education, health care, and the environment, whereas male senators spent significantly more time focusing on competitive issues like the economy and foreign policy, even when the authors controlled for party and seniority in the press releases. Male senators were also significantly more likely to mention the federal projects they have brought to their districts compared with female senators. Female senators emphasized their leadership positions in Congress more than male senators. Female senators took clearer positions when talking about matters of public policy than their male counterparts (Fridkin and Kenney 2014).

Scholars have also studied the influence of gender on several aspects of effectiveness in the legislative process. Some evidence suggests that women have been more effective lawmakers in Congress than men. Volden and colleagues (2013) developed a Legislative Effectiveness Score for each lawmaker in the U.S. House from 1973 through 2008 based on how many bills the legislator introduced as well as how many of those bills received action in committee, passed out of committee, received action on the floor of the House, passed the House, and then became law. Being a female legislator translated into a 10 percent increase in legislative effectiveness using this measure. Intriguingly, women in the minority party drove this overall finding of effectiveness. Women in both the majority and the minority party introduced more bills overall than their male colleagues. But as one moved through the legislative process, minority party women become more and more effective, whereas majority women's effectiveness relative to their male colleagues decreased. Volden et al. attribute the success of minority female legislators to their use of the consensus-building skills necessary to achieve success as members of the minority party.

From a different lens on effectiveness, one study has shown female U.S. representatives as being better at "bringing home the bacon"—that is, directing funds to their district and being more active sponsors of legislation. Anzia and Berry (2011) compared the relative success of male and female U.S. representatives in delivering federal spending to their districts. At the same time, female representatives sponsored and cosponsored more bills per Congress than their male counterparts. Anzia and Berry attribute female legislators' greater effectiveness as politicians in Congress to a sex-based selection process that requires female political aspirants to have more talent and be harder working to win the support of voters, campaign contributors, and party gatekeepers.

Moving from overall bill sponsorship to a focus on women's issues bills, Volden et al. (2016) found that, since the 1970s, congresswomen have also sponsored such bills at a significantly greater rate than men. Across nineteen different issue areas, these scholars have found that women substantially sponsored more bills on six issues, all of which correspond to issues scholars have labeled as women's issues. However, at the same time, they have found, these women's issues bills introduced by female legislators are significantly more gridlocked than other issues in Congress. On average, only 4 percent of bills introduced in Congress become law. In comparison, only 2 percent of women's issues bills become law, and only 1 percent of women's issues bills that women introduce have been enacted. Volden et al. (2016) conclude that "we are left with strong evidence that women sponsor bills on different issues than men and achieve less success on those women's issues" (21).

Formal Leadership

By far, the most significant event in women's legislative political leadership history in the United States was the "breaking of the ultimate marble ceiling" that occurred when Nancy Pelosi was elected Speaker of the U.S. House of Representatives at the beginning of the 110th Congress in 2007 after having served as a U.S. representative since 1987. Representative Pelosi had moved up the party organizational hierarchy, first being elected party whip in 2001 and then chair of the Democratic Caucus (or minority leader) in 2003. Her Democratic colleagues unanimously reelected her as Speaker of the House in the 111th Congress. By extension, she became the most politically powerful woman in American government, second in line for the presidency.

After the Democrats lost control of the House as a result of the 2010 election, her party caucus continued to elect Representative Pelosi as its leader—although not unanimously and not without dissension. Members had concerns about her being a lightning rod for conservative criticism and the party's loss of control of the House in the 2010 election. The Campaign Media Analysis Group reported that more than $65 million was spent on 161,203 ads targeting Representative Pelosi during the 2010 election year (Steinhauser and Livingston 2010). Karen Tumulty (2012) reported in the *Washington Post* that Pelosi "was portrayed as, among other things, a cackling witch." The Democratic Caucus elected her minority leader by a vote of 150 to 43 for Heath Shuler, a conservative Democrat in his third term from North Carolina. Although the Democrats were again soundly defeated across the country in the 2014 midterm elections, Representative Pelosi faced no opposition to being reelected as minority leader for the 114th Congress. After significant losses

Picture 10.3 Nancy Pelosi (D-CA) Celebrates Having Taken the Oath of Office as Speaker of the U.S. House of Representatives, January 2007

Photo 956688839

in the 2016 election, she faced a strong challenge to retain her position as minority leader but once again was reelected.

The Speakership of the U.S. House is the only formal position in the legislative branch of government described in the U.S. Constitution. But the political parties in both houses of Congress have created additional leadership positions. The U.S. Senate has the formal positions of majority and minority leaders. The senator holding either of these positions has been elected by his or her fellow party senators. No woman has ever been elected by her party caucus to either of these positions. No female senator has ever run for one of these positions.

In addition, the parties have developed leadership teams beyond the titular head of the party in each chamber. In the 114th Congress, Cathy McMorris Rodgers served as conference chair for the Republicans, ranking fourth in terms of formal party leadership. No woman serves in a formal position among the U.S. Senate Republicans, whereas Patty Murray of the state of Washington served as Democratic conference secretary in the 114th Congress. It is more common for women to be formal leaders in state legislatures. In 2015, four women were serving as Speakers of the House in state legislatures, and eighteen women were serving as presidents or presidents pro tempore in the state senates.

Other leadership positions include being a chair of a legislative committee or subcommittee. Speaker Pelosi immediately appointed close ally Representative Louise Slaughter of New York to chair the House Rules Committee in the 110th and 111th Congresses. The Rules Committee, once a powerful bastion of independence within the House, has now become an arm of the House leadership. The Rules Committee is a key actor in the structuring of floor activity, as it sets the terms of floor consideration of a proposed bill.

"Women Are Wielding Notable Influence in Congress," Ed O'Keefe wrote in an early 2014 *Washington Post* piece. He noted that "after decades of trying to amass power, several women have vaulted to the top of influential congressional committees, putting them in charge of some of the most consequential legislation being considered on Capitol Hill." The Democrats were still the majority party in the U.S. Senate at that time in the 113th Congress. Democratic female senators chaired the Appropriations Committee, the Budget Committee, the Agriculture Committee, and the Intelligence Committee. When the Republicans won control of the Senate as a result of the 2014 midterm elections, they did not select any women as committee chairs due in large part to their lack of seniority. One woman served as a committee chair in the U.S. House of Representatives in the 114th Congress, Republican Candice Miller, who chaired the Committee on House Administration.

Rights and Equity in Public Policies

In 1977, the federal government sponsored a national conference to celebrate International Women's Year and to identify goals for women for the next decade. Planning for the conference began with a series of "open town meetings" in each state and territory. These state meetings were generally more representative by age, race, economic status, ethnicity, and religion than the official legislatures making decisions in those same states. They selected two thousand delegates to the national conference, which was held in Houston, Texas (Steinem 1979). Funds were provided for transportation, lodging, and childcare to women who otherwise would not have been able to attend (Kalsem and Williams 2010).

The national conference met to construct a National Plan of Action for women to present to the Carter administration and to Congress. This meeting was the first and only national women's conference the federal government has sponsored. In addition to the delegates, fifteen thousand observers participated in events surrounding the conference. A good deal of ceremony and symbolism accompanied the conference. On September 29, a torch was lit at Seneca Falls, New York, the site of the 1948 first women's rights convention. It was carried by a relay of runners 2,600 miles to Houston, arriving the day before the conference began. Poet Maya Angelou wrote a new Declaration of Sentiments to parallel the one passed by the 1848 convention, which accompanied the torch on its journey. Formulating and adopting the National Plan of Action was the conference's main task. Conference leaders were committed in the plan not merely to acknowledge those "at the bottom" but also to give voice to their needs and concerns in the plan's planks. The conference itself came under attack from antifeminist opponents such as Phyllis Schafly. Hundreds of protesters who came to Houston proclaimed the conference "antifamily" and formed a counter conservative coalition called the pro-family movement.

The Plan of Action that was adopted spoke to the intersections of women's lives and addressed race, age, class, and sexuality issues. Conference participants recognized and highlighted the need for coalition building across lines of race, class, ethnicity, sexuality, age, and other categories of identity and experience. Leading feminist Gloria Steinem wrote the introduction to the official report, *What Women Want*, describing the conference as one of the few accounts of history being made from the bottom up.

The final plan consisted of twenty-six planks, ranging from better enforcement of existing laws to broad demands for a national health security system, full employment, peace, and disarmament. These planks could be considered an agenda of women's rights' policies. Of the twenty-six planks, only one on equal credit, which called for an end to discrimination in consumer credits practices, was approved unanimously. Large majorities passed another seventeen planks. But debate on topics such as abortion rights and sexual preference was intensely heated. The event was also one of the first times that the issue of sexual orientation within the women's movement was discussed on such a large scale.[1]

Black female delegates also challenged the conference, arguing that the initial National Plan of Action did not represent Black women adequately.

> Before these women emerged, the Plan of Action only included several brief paragraphs pertaining to minority women, the gist of which was simply: discrimination is unacceptable. Finding this to be insufficient, this group of black women traveled to Houston for the Conference and demanded that a separate "Black Women's Agenda" be included in the Plan of Action. The agenda was renamed the "Women of Color Agenda" and eventually "Minority Women" as a result of other women of color's desire to also be afforded separate space in the document to address their unique concerns. The minority caucus's substituted plank listed specific concerns of "American Indian and Alaskan Native women," "Asian/Pacific American women," "Black women," and "Hispanic women."[2]

The 1977 Plan of Action provides a comprehensive list of equality issues of distinct importance to women. A decade later, in 1978, the Institute for Women's Policy Research (IWPR), a nongovernmental organization, was founded with the mission of "informing policy, inspiring change, and improving lives." It has become the preeminent organization conducting and disseminating research "to address the needs of women, promote public dialogue and strengthen families, communities, and societies." Based largely on the Beijing Platform of Action described in Chapter 7, as well as on state advisory committees, IWPR has constructed a Status of Women in the States database comprising a checklist of women's resources and rights as a contemporary set of indicators of "women-friendly" public policies in the United States. Policy areas in this database include violence against women, child support, welfare policies, employment and unemployment benefits, sexual orientation and gender identity, and reproductive rights.

Women's rights activists have pursued a variety of legislative and judicial strategies in their quest for equal rights and gender equity in the United States. The women's rights movement has successfully lobbied the U.S. Congress to enact several major pieces of legislation mandating equality in the areas of economic and educational policies and violence against women. Table 10.1a lists those laws. Individual women and women's rights groups have also extensively challenged public policies in federal and state courts. Moreover, opposing groups have used the courts to challenge public policies enhancing women's rights and gender equity. Regarding judicial strategies, Table 10.1b lists the major Supreme Court decisions affecting women's rights and equality, some of which upheld women's rights and some of which limited their rights.

The 1960s through the 1990s were an especially activist era of policy making regarding women's status and equal rights. Public policies addressing pay discrimination among workers based on sex, work and family issues, educational opportunity, equal credit, and sexual intimidation were enacted. Women's rights' activists continue in contemporary congresses to introduce legislation that builds on these governmental policies regarding equity issues and economic disparities. They face opposition from conservatives seeking to limit government involvement in people's lives. Victories have been few in the most recent decades.

Women's rights policy issues have predominantly been defined in terms of role equity and role change issues based on the work of Joyce Gelb and Marian Lief Palley (1982). Role equity policies are policies that extend the same rights and benefits to women as men, such as access to credit, and that appear to be relatively delineated or narrow in their implications. They permit policy makers to seek advantage with feminist groups and voters with little or no controversy. Role change issues, in contrast, appear to produce change in the dependent role of wife, mother, and homemaker, holding out the potential of greater sexual

Table 10.1a–b Major Women's Rights Legislation and Supreme Court Decisions

Major Women's Rights Legislation

1963	Equal Pay Act
1964	Title VII of the Civil Rights Act
1972	Title IX of the 1972 Education Amendment Act (regulatory)
1974	Equal Credit Opportunity Act
1974	Women's Educational Equity Act (substantive)
1978	Pregnancy Discrimination Act
1993	Family and Medical Leave Act
1994	Violence Against Women Act (reauthorized in 2005 and 2013)
2009	Lilly Ledbetter Fair Pay Act

Major Supreme Court Decisions

1971	*Reed v. Reed* (equal protection)
1973	*Roe v. Wade* (abortion)
1975	*General Electric v. Gilbert* (employment)
1976	*Craig v. Boren* (equal protection)
1980	*Harris v. McRae* (abortion)
1983	*Akron v. Akron Center for Reproductive Health* (abortion)
1989	*Webster v. Reproductive Health Services* (abortion)
1992	*Planned Parenthood of Southeastern Pennsylvania v. Casey* (abortion)
1996	*United States v. Virginia* (military)
2007	*Ledbetter v. Goodyear Tire and Rubber Company* (employment)
2007	*Gonzales v. Carhart* (abortion)
2015	*Young v. UPS* (employment)

freedom and independence in a variety of contexts such as abortion rights and participation in the military. In general, policy making in the United States is incremental in nature, with the status quo being advantaged. This environment provides a major challenge to women's rights activists seeking large policy change.

Congressional Caucus for Women's Issues

The presence of a formal caucus is a way to achieve visibility and power in a legislature. "When a caucus bands together, the result is political clout" (Thomas 1991, 973). Twenty-two states have a formal women's caucus in their state legislatures to promote issues of special concern to women. In 1977, a bipartisan group of fifteen of the eighteen female members of the 95th Congress founded the Congressional Caucus for Women's Issues (CCWI), originally called the Congresswomen's Caucus, to discuss the status of women and to advance a women's rights policy agenda in the national legislature. Some representatives had sought to form a group to publicize women's concerns that grew out of the emerging women's rights movement in earlier congresses. But the formation of a caucus required the retirement of senior female members who were not ideologically attuned to feminism or to the forming of a group calling attention to gender. Outspoken and controversial Representative Bella Abzug's retirement and the election of new female representatives attuned to the women's rights movement facilitated the formation of the caucus in 1977. Outside feminist organizations were also instrumental in the caucus's formation. They had lobbied female members to form a group "to which they could communicate their objectives and through which they could make their goals part of the national agenda" (Gertzog 1995, 184).

The caucus, structured to work as a bipartisan organization and at times serving as a challenge to Congressional leadership, has had difficulties throughout its long tenure in remaining a viable organization affecting the congressional agenda and the enactment of public policies. But it has brought to public attention problems women face that otherwise would not have been on the Congressional agenda. In its early years, its major victory was the mobilization of fellow lawmakers to extend the life of the Equal Rights Amendment (ERA). When the ERA was adopted in the U.S. House and Senate in 1972, states were given seven years to ratify it. When time was running out and ratification was still three states short of the required three fourths necessary, Representative Elizabeth Holtzman introduced a joint resolution adding seven years, during which time states could endorse the measure. No precedent existed for extension of a proposed constitutional amendment. Caucus activists initiated an intensive campaign to achieve extension. Against major odds, they were successful in obtaining a three-year extension. For most caucus members, adoption of the ERA extension was a legislative highpoint of the 97th Congress (Gertzog 1995, 92).

Since then, the caucus has pressed for enactment of a variety of legislation providing greater opportunities for women in American society and promoting equality between the sexes. It was most active in terms of legislative proposals in the 1980s and 1990s. The Economic Equity Act, a signature omnibus bill consisting of twenty-two pieces of legislation, was the caucus's primary effort to achieve economic equality for women through the lawmaking process. This proposed legislation targeted women whose traditional roles and responsibilities had left them economically disadvantaged. They were deprived of pensions and annuities, employment and wages, capital for investment, and social security and insurance benefits (Gertzog 1995). According to Representative Margaret Heckler, its purpose was to counter "policies in the public and private sector that are completely at odds with work patterns determined by the realities of women's dual wage-earning and parenting roles" (Gertzog 1984, 155).

CCWI was also instrumental in putting women's health issues on the legislative agenda. A 1990 General Accounting Office report that the caucus had requested showed that women had been systematically excluded or underrepresented in numerous clinical studies whose subjects ranged from heart disease to the overuse of prescription drugs. As a result of the report and the national attention the caucus brought to it, the National Institutes of Health created an Office of Research on Women's Health that has now been in operation for over twenty-five years. In the 101st Congress, CCWI also introduced the omnibus Women's Health Equity Act consisting of eighteen items addressing inequities in the treatment of women's health issues.

In recent years, the caucus has become less central to the legislative work of the Congress's female members regarding the advancement of women's rights and equity bills. Female membership has grown in numbers, and female legislators have gained seniority and have moved into committee leadership positions from which they can sponsor and guide legislation, making the caucus less necessary to affect the legislative agenda. Female members have also become more polarized across the parties, making consensus within the caucus very difficult. In the most recent congresses, the caucus has been mainly engaged in task forces and briefings rather than in sponsorship of legislative bills as a group. The caucus continues to be headed in each Congress by two representatives, one from each party. The caucus in the 113th Congress organized seven task forces: women's health, women and the economy/business, international women's issues, women in the military/veterans, Afghan women, trafficking, and education/STEM. Republican Representative Kristie Noem and Democrat Doris Matsui were selected as chairs for the caucus in the 114th Congress.

Litigating Women's Rights

In addition to lobbying for and sponsoring legislation, women's rights activists have also looked to the judicial system for help, filing lawsuits to eliminate perceived discriminatory practices in the private and publics sectors. They have mounted legal challenges regarding various traditional aspects of U.S. society that they believed treated women differently from men, restricted their rights as citizens, and fought legal challenges to women's rights and equity.

In its rulings, the Supreme Court has developed a set of standards, termed *scrutiny*, used in making decisions in discrimination cases involving state actions. It uses a different and lower standard of review for sex discrimination claims under the 14th Amendment's equal protection clause than it does for claims of racial or religious discrimination. Whereas racial and religious discrimination are subject to "strict scrutiny," sex discrimination is subject to the lower standard of "intermediate scrutiny." This difference means that for cases involving racial or religious discrimination, the courts will look to see whether the law under challenge is *necessary* to achieve a *compelling* governmental interest, whereas for cases involving sex discrimination, the courts will look to determine whether the law under challenge bears a *substantial relationship* to important governmental interest. The governmental interest need not be "compelling," and the law that furthers this interest need not be "necessary" (Neuwirth 2015, 9).

The court once used what has been called rational basis scrutiny in upholding state policies involving a challenge of sex discrimination. Here discrimination must only bear a rational relationship to legitimate state objectives. The burden of proof is on the challenger to show that a particular policy has no relationship to a state objective; otherwise, the policy stands. Women's rights advocates have strived to get the court to apply a strict scrutiny standard as in race or religion discrimination cases to sex discrimination cases, but they have not yet achieved that goal. The court has moved from the rational scrutiny standard that advantages the retention of state policies to an intermediate standard in which sex classification must bear a *substantial relationship* to an important state objective. Here both the state and the challenger have the burden of proof.

Public Policies on Women and Work

Campaigns for equal pay laws and their enforcement have been a central focus of women's rights public policy advocacy throughout the history of the contemporary women's rights movement, beginning with the 1963 Equal Pay Act, which required equal pay for jobs that are equal in skill, effort, and responsibility. This law, however, said nothing about sex discrimination in hiring. Title VII of the Civil Rights Act of 1964 then banned discrimination in hiring on the basis of sex. The application of these laws has greatly diminished the disparity in men's and women's earnings, but women continue to earn considerably less than men, as discussed in Chapter 3. IWPR estimates that female full-time workers in 2014 made only seventy-nine cents for every dollar men earned, a gender wage gap of 21 percent. Women earn less than men in almost any occupation. Chapter 3 explored how sex segregation in the workforce continues to contribute to wage disparity.

But it is also the case that female workers have found that regardless of laws on the books, they continue to face discrimination in the workplace when it comes to being paid equally with their male colleagues. Many women have had to sue their employers in the courts to receive compensation for unequal pay. Pursuit of legal challenges in the courts is not an easy or inexpensive task. Nor has it always been successful. Chapter 3 described Lilly Ledbetter's suit against Goodyear Tire and Rubber Company for paying her significantly less than her male counterparts. Her challenge became a cause célèbre among women's rights' groups when, in 2007, the Supreme Court overturned a lower court ruling saying she had missed a statute of limitations. The court ruled in a 5–4 decision that the statute of limitations for presenting an equal-pay lawsuit begins at the date the pay was agreed upon, not at the date of the most recent paycheck, as a lower court had ruled. Women's advocates decried the decision as a setback for women, whereas business groups applauded the decision, calling it fair. Congressional Democrats immediately introduced the Lilly Ledbetter Fair Pay Act, which would effectively overturn the court's ruling. But it was not until 2009, with expanded Democratic majorities in both houses of Congress and a Democrat newly inaugurated as president looking for a significant bill to sign as his first presidential act, that the bill became law. The Lilly Ledbetter Fair Pay Act amended the Civil Rights Act of 1964, which had banned sex discrimination in employment. The bill mandated that the 180-day statute of limitations for filing an equal-pay lawsuit regarding pay discrimination resets with each new discriminatory paycheck.

The U.S. House voted 250–177 to pass the Lilly Ledbetter Fair Pay Act in a party line vote. All the Republican female members voting cast "no" votes, whereas all the female Democrats voted "yea." In the Senate, however, all the Democratic and Republican female members voted "yea." This legislative remedy to a Supreme Court decision came nearly fifty years after the Equal Pay Act of 1963 and the Civil Rights Act of 1964 banning sex discrimination in employment had been enacted.

The Lilly Ledbetter Fair Pay Act extended the statute of limitations but failed to deal with the underlying problem of lack of information about comparable salaries for female workers who believed they were being discriminated against. A coalition of feminist activists and labor organizations therefore has lobbied Congress to pass the Paycheck Fairness Act, first introduced in 2009, to close some of the remaining loopholes in the Equal Pay Act. It would discourage pay discrimination by empowering workers to share more wage information and provide women with more tools to challenge gender-based wage discrepancies. Sections of this proposed legislation aim to make wages more transparent, require that employers prove that wage discrepancies are tied to legitimate business qualifications and not gender, and prohibit companies from taking retaliatory action against employees who raise concerns about gender-based wage discrimination. Bill supporters have not been able to achieve enough votes in the U.S. House and Senate to pass it into law. Democrats have championed the bill, whereas Republicans have actively opposed it. Opponents of the bill argue that revealing salary information violates privacy, that more frivolous lawsuits would result, costing businesses undue expenses, and that the wage gap is a result of women's choices, not structural discrimination.

On October 5, 2015, Governor Jerry Brown signed into law the California Fair Pay Act at the Rosie the Riveter National Historical Park, legislation similar to the national proposed law banning paying women less than men for "substantially similar work." It shifts to employers the burden of showing that any differences in pay between the sexes are due to seniority, education, a merit system, or other acceptable factors. It is considered to be the strongest such legislation in the country. Republican and Democratic legislators voted for the act's passage, and the California Chamber of Commerce supported it.

Work and Family Policies

U.S. public policies are among the least family-friendly in terms of work and family in the developed world. It is the only high-income country and one of only eight countries in the world that does not mandate paid leave for mothers of newborns (Heymann and McNeil 2013). No federal law and only a few states provide a mechanism for mothers and fathers to take paid personal leave. Nearly every member of the European Union (EU) provides at least fourteen weeks of job-guaranteed paid maternity leave, during which time workers receive at least two thirds of their regular earnings (International Labour Organization 2010). Eighty-one countries extend paid leave to new fathers through paternity leave (specific to fathers), through parental leave that can be taken by either parent, or through some combination of the two (Heymann and McNeill 2013).

U.S. Representative Patricia Schroeder first introduced a version of a family and medical leave law into Congress in 1985. She stood alone in her advocacy. Eight years later, in 1993, Congress passed the landmark Family and Medical Leave Act (FMLA), and President Bill Clinton signed it into law. The FMLA applies only to public agencies and private employers with fifty or more employees. It requires that employees who have worked for the employer for at least one year and have averaged at least twenty-four hours of work a week be provided with twelve weeks of unpaid leave to care for a new child or a sick family member or to recover from their own illness. Thus, it only covers about one half of the workforce, and the leave also does not have to be paid. Thus, many workers, especially lower wage workers, find limited value in the FMLA. Efforts to expand its reach and mandate paid leave have been a central part of continued public policy debates regarding families and work. Both Democrat Hillary Clinton and Republican Donald Trump supported the enactment of some type of paid leave in the 2016 presidential campaign.

In 2002, California became the first state to create a Paid Family Leave (PFL) program, a family leave insurance program that provides income replacement to eligible workers for family caregiving or bonding with a new child. Massachusetts, New Jersey, Rhode Island, Connecticut, and several cities have since joined California in enacting paid family and medical leave or earned sick days laws. California expanded its Paid Family Leave program in 2014 to enable workers in that state to receive up to six weeks of wage replacement benefits to care for seriously ill siblings, grandparents, grandchildren, or parents-in-law.

Recent studies show that California's paid leave program has resulted in more parents taking leave during the period surrounding new births. The program appears to have increased leave-taking by all new mothers, including the economically less advantaged. In addition, the availability of paid leave appears to modestly increase the likelihood that working mothers in California will be on the job nine or more months after the births of their children. Some indications suggest that working new mothers are earning higher wages (Ruhm 2016).

On the federal level, Senator Kirsten Gillibrand (D-NY) and Representative Rosa DeLauro (D-CT) introduced the Family and Medical Insurance Leave (FAMILY) Act in 2013. The act would create a national insurance program funded by equal employer and employee contributions of approximately $1.50 a week for a median wage worker (National Partnership for Women and Families 2015). All workers who are insured for disability insurance benefits under the Social Security Act and who had earned income from employment during the twelve months prior to the month in which an application for family and medical leave insurance benefits was filed would be eligible to receive family leave benefits, and the program would not be limited to employees of a specific establishment size like the FMLA. The FAMILY Act would provide up to twelve weeks (or sixty workdays) of partially paid leave for workers while they care for themselves during a serious illness, for seriously ill family members, for a newborn or newly adopted child, and for injuries or other conditions and circumstances experienced by family members who are in the military (National Partnership for Women and Families 2015). The Family Act has not yet been voted on in Congress. Conservative groups such as the Independent Women's Forum oppose such legislation as expansions of federal government intrusion in the market and workplace.

Complicating the idea of women as workers similar to men has been the question of the implications of pregnancy on women workers and their equality in the workforce. How should pregnant workers be treated in the workforce? The concept of disability has framed public policies regarding pregnant workers. President Kennedy's Commission on the Status of Women (1961–1963) and its successor, the Citizen's Advisory Council on the Status of Women, developed the concept of pregnancy as a temporary physical disability, holding that "childbirth and complications of pregnancy are, for all job-related purposes, temporary disabilities and should be treated as such under any health insurance, temporary disability insurance or sick leave plan of an employer, union or fraternal society."

The Supreme Court ruled in the 1975 case of *General Electric v. Gilbert* that a policy that distinguishes between pregnant and nonpregnant persons does not constitute sex discrimination against women. The Gilbert case involved the exclusion of pregnancy as a disability under private employer benefit plans. General Electric's benefit plan provided all employees nonoccupational sickness and accident benefits, but disabilities arising from pregnancy were excluded. In response, Congress passed the Pregnancy Discrimination Act into law in 1978 as an amendment to Title VII of the Civil Rights Act of 1964. The Pregnancy Discrimination Act effectively overturned the Supreme Court decision in *General Electric v. Gilbert.* Before Congress passed the Pregnancy Discrimination Act of 1978 (PDA), it was common for employers to categorically exclude pregnant women from the workforce. This law prohibits discrimination against pregnant women in all areas of employment, including hiring, firing, seniority rights, job security, and fringe benefits. The PDA guarantees the right not to be treated adversely because of pregnancy, childbirth, or related medical conditions and the right to be treated at least as well as other employees "not so affected but similar in their ability or inability to work."

Yet pregnancy discrimination still persists more than a generation after the PDA's passage. The courts had opened loopholes in the PDA that too often left women who needed temporary work accommodations because of pregnancy without protection. Many women work through their pregnancies without any need for accommodation, but some pregnant workers, particularly those who work in more physically demanding or less flexible jobs, need some adjustments in work rules or duties. When their requests for reasonable accommodations—such as being allowed to carry a water bottle, refrain from climbing ladders, or avoid heavy lifting—are refused, pregnant workers often have to choose between their paychecks and healthy pregnancies, even when their employers provide similar accommodations to employees who need them because of disability or injury. Changes on both the legal front and in the legislative process suggest that pregnant workers will be treated more equitably and will be less likely to have to choose between a paycheck and a healthy pregnancy in the near future.

In the 2015 case of *Young v. UPS*, the Supreme Court addressed the question of whether the Pregnancy Discrimination Act requires an employer to provide the same work accommodations to an employee with pregnancy-related work limitations as to employees with similar but non-pregnancy-related work limitations. In 2006, UPS put a then-pregnant driver, Peggy Young, on unpaid administrative leave and eliminated her health insurance. Young's doctor had advised her not to lift more than twenty pounds during her pregnancy, something her job rarely required. She asked the company for a temporary light-duty assignment—an option extended to UPS workers injured on the job and even to those who have lost their commercial driver's license due to a DUI charge—or a plan to deal with the rare package on her route weighing more than twenty pounds. The company refused, saying Young was too much of a risk. UPS argued that its legal obligations regarding temporary light-duty assignments were limited to the injured and the disabled. The Supreme Court ruled in favor of Young, holding that when an employer accommodates workers who are similar to pregnant workers in their ability to work, it cannot refuse to accommodate pregnant workers who need it simply because it "is more expensive or less convenient" to accommodate pregnant women. The court also held that the employer who fails to accommodate pregnant workers violates the PDA when its accommodation policies impose a "significant burden" on pregnant workers that outweighs any justification the employer offers for those policies. As Justice Breyer asked in writing the court's majority opinion, "Why, when the employer accommodated so many, could it not accommodate pregnant women as well?" The Young case was a rare occurrence in which antiabortion organizations and groups that support abortion rights were on the same side of a legal debate, with both movements advocating for accommodations for pregnant workers.

Even with this court decision, many pregnant workers denied accommodations must go through a multistep evidentiary process to prove discrimination. Thus, in 2012, members of Congress introduced the Pregnant Workers Fairness Act (PWFA). The proposed PWFA would require an employer to make a reasonable accommodation for pregnancy, childbirth, and related medical conditions unless this creates an undue hardship on the employer. This legislation would require employers to make the same sorts of accommodations for pregnancy, childbirth, and related medical conditions that they do for other disabilities such as bathroom breaks, time for doctor's appointments, restrictions on lifting, and/or a nearby water bottle to remain hydrated.

The PWFA incorporates the accommodation language from the Americans with Disabilities Act to protect pregnant women with physical limitations from being pushed onto unpaid leave, transferred, or fired because they are pregnant. Where the Supreme Court's decision in *Young* might allow some employers to claim they are confused about their obligations, the PWFA makes obligations absolutely clear. The burden of proof in terms of discrimination would move from the pregnant worker to the employer. The PWFA was first introduced in Congress in 2012 and 2013 but failed each year to reach a floor vote.

Only Democrats supported the bill at that time. However, in the 114th Congress, several Republicans joined as sponsors, heightening the possibility that it could become law. However, it did not reach a vote in that Congress. As of the middle of 2015, thirty states had passed the PWFA. The conservative Independent Women's Forum supports the Supreme Court's decision in *Young*. Although not arguing against the PWFA, it does caution that

> it's important to consider carefully how such new laws will play out in the real world. Will they really help women by preventing discrimination and compensating those who are treated badly? Or will they do more damage to women's economic prospects by making employers more reticent to hire women of childbearing age in the first place?

The Pregnancy Discrimination Act mandates against such discrimination.

Reproductive Rights

The landmark 1973 Supreme Court decision in *Roe v. Wade* declared that the 14th Amendment's guarantee of liberty implied a right of privacy "broad enough to encompass a woman's decision whether or not to terminate her pregnancy." Restrictions on abortion, the court ruled, required a justification based on a compelling state interest. The *Roe v. Wade* decision divided pregnancy into three roughly equal time periods affecting states' constitutional powers to make policy regarding abortions, balancing women's privacy interests with the state's increasingly legitimate interest in protecting a fetus as it approached viability outside the womb. The trimester approach works in the following way:

1. In the first trimester, the state may not regulate or otherwise interfere with the decisions of the doctor and the patient to terminate her pregnancy.
2. In the second trimester, the state may regulate the medical conditions under which abortions are performed but may not restrict the practice.
3. In the third trimester, the state may prohibit abortion except to save the life or health of the mother.

Only a compelling state interest would justify restrictions on abortion. What might constitute a compelling state interest? Protecting maternal health would be one such interest. It becomes such a compelling interest only after the first trimester, when mortality rates from abortion become higher than mortality rates from childbirth. The state's interest in protecting fetal life becomes compelling at viability in the third trimester, when the fetus has the capability of meaningful life outside the womb. In the first trimester, a woman's right to make private choices is protected from state interference. But during the second and third trimesters, the state gains reasons to regulate abortion. In 1992, however, the Supreme Court introduced the "undue burden" test in deciding whether to uphold state regulations of abortion procedures. In writing the decision in the case of *Planned Parenthood of Southeastern Pennsylvania v. Casey*, Justice Sandra O'Connor wrote, "Only where state regulation imposes an undue burden on a woman's ability to make this decision does the power of the State reach into the heart of the liberty protected by the Due Process Clause." But no fixed, self-evident definition of what constitutes an "undue burden" exists. The courts decide on a case-by-case basis.

Medical advances since *Roe* have called into question the trimester framework. The *Roe* decision initiated some of the most sustained and strident controversies that the court has ever experienced, and myriad follow-up legal challenges have aimed at restricting access to abortion, including banning the use of federal funds for all nontherapeutic abortions. The legislative and election landscape continues to be embroiled in debates over women's reproductive rights. As Chapter 4 has shown, women (and men) have been and continue to be divided over abortion rights.

According to Guttmacher Institute statistics, a least half of American women will experience an unintended pregnancy by age forty-five, and at 2008 abortion rates, one in ten women will have an abortion by age twenty, one in four by age thirty, and three in ten by age forty-five. In 2011, 1.06 million abortions were performed, down 13 percent from 1.21 million in 2008. From 1973 through 2011, nearly fifty-three million legal abortions occurred (Guttmacher Institute 2014).

> **Sidebar 10.2 Abortion Statistics**
>
> Three in ten American women will have an abortion by age forty-five.
> Guttmacher Institute (www.guttmacher.org/united-states/abortion).

Activism on both sides of the issue has been multifaceted and intense, even deadly, with the shooting of abortion providers. Antiabortion activists have picketed doctors' offices, broken into clinics, and destroyed equipment. They have advocated for a constitutional amendment to prohibit abortion, mounted vigorous campaigns to elect pro-life legislators at the state and national levels, and campaigned for pro-life justices. Activists for women's rights have fought back. As was described in Chapter 8, groups such as EMILY's List, for example, support only pro-choice female candidates.

Antiabortion activists have succeeded in passing a broad spectrum of restrictive statutes designed to make abortion more costly and less accessible, especially at the state level. Conservative election successes in the 2010 and 2016 elections enhanced a positive climate in many states for the adoption of restrictive abortion procedures. Between 2010 and 2015, the Guttmacher Institute reports that the states passed 288 restrictions on abortion procedures; in 2015, fifty-seven new restrictions were enacted. They test the boundaries of how far states can limit access to abortion while *Roe v. Wade* still stands. Proposed restrictions have mainly centered on mandatory waiting periods, banning abortions after the first trimester, and medication abortions (the most commonly used first-trimester method). More than half of the states have enacted Targeted Regulation of Abortion Providers provisions, referred to as TRAP laws. Typically, TRAP provisions take two approaches: establishing stiff building codes and staffing standards and requiring abortion providers to have a formal relationship with a hospital. TRAP laws require women's health centers to follow regulations that other, similar outpatient medical facilities do not. These laws limit women's access to abortions by either forcing some centers to close because they cannot meet the new requirements or by driving up the cost of abortion procedures so much that some women can no longer afford them. Some proposed restrictions have been defeated in a few states.

Abortion rights activists have initiated legal challenges to many of these state laws restricting abortion access, arguing that they impose an "undue burden" on women seeking an abortion. The Supreme Court has ruled on several of these challenges, as indicated in Table 9.1. On June 26, 2016, in the case of *Whole Women's Health v. Cole* (later changed to *Whole Women's Health v. Helllerstedt*), in a 5–3 decision, the Supreme Court, overturned a Texas law requiring clinics that provide abortions to have surgical facilities and doctors to have admitting privileges at a nearby hospital. The law was predicted to close many clinics and to further reduce availability of abortion in Texas; the court has ruled the law violated the Constitution. The court ruled that both provisions constituted an undue burden and therefore were unconstitutional. Justice Stephen Breyer, in writing the majority opinion, noted that the restrictions "vastly increase the obstacles confronting women seeking abortions in Texas without providing any benefit to women's health capable of withstanding any meaningful scrutiny." Among the many friend-of-the-court documents submitted regarding this case was the Brief of Historians as Amici Curiae in Support of Petitioners. The *Washington Post* described this brief as "Laws written by men to protect women deserve scrutiny" (Barnes 2016). It was a compendium of historical laws substantively written to protect women but in reality worked to maintain male power and privilege.

Several female members of the U.S. House of Representatives also introduced the EACH Woman Act in the 114th Congress.[3] This act would mandate that every woman who receives health-care coverage through the federal government would have coverage for abortion care. It would dismantle the long-standing Hyde Amendment, which stipulates that Medicaid cannot pay for abortions. The bill would also prohibit interference with decisions by private health insurance companies to offer coverage of abortion care. In the current political climate, the act is not likely to advance through the legislative process.

Education Policy

As Chapter 3 shows, women have made major strides in formal education, now surpassing men in receiving postsecondary degrees. Nondiscriminatory federal financial aid programs such as Pell grants have played a major role in dramatically increasing women's access to a college education in the past half-century. In 1972, Title IX was added to the Higher Education Amendments Act, affecting a variety of aspects of sex discrimination in education. Title IX stated that "no person in the United States shall, on the basis of sex, be excluded from participation in, be denied the benefit of, or be subjected to discrimination under an educational program or activity receiving federal financial assistance" (20 U.S.C., Sec.1981, 15). Any educational institution receiving federal financial assistance must comply. Coverage extended beyond higher education to preschools, primary, secondary, and vocational schools. The sex discrimination sections of this piece of legislation received little attention as the bill made its way through Congress. The implementation of its sex discrimination regulations for schools and colleges, however, was filled with contentious debates. The conflicts had to do with how far toward integration of the sexes a school system has to go to achieve the stated goals of nondiscrimination (McBride and Parry 2011). No federal funds could go to educational institutions that practiced sex discrimination in any of their programs, including admissions, athletics, financial aid, counseling facilities, and employment. Under Title IX, schools are prohibited from discriminating against pregnant and parenting students. Schools dropped admissions quotas that limited the number of women enrolled in various programs. Admissions policies have been required to evaluate men and women under the same set of admission standards.

For many, Title IX is synonymous with expanded opportunities in athletics (National Coalition of Women and Girls in Education 2012). The debate over what constitutes nondiscrimination in schools' athletic programs has been particularly intense and has lasted for decades. Feminists wanted women to share equally in college and high school athletic resources. At stake was a potential redistribution of financial resources from males to females. The proposal to require equivalent expenditures for men's and women's sports creates considerable concern, particularly among schools with high-status intercollegiate football programs. In addition to equalizing expenditures, institutions had to establish and implement policies for accommodating increased interest in and abilities relevant to women's athletic programs. Opponents of Title IX argue that rather than mandating equality, it actually favors girls over boys. Champions of this legislation contend that it has made greater educational opportunities for students of both sexes. Forty years after Title IX was enacted into law, girls participating in high school athletics have increased tenfold, while six times as many women compete in college sports.

Title IX regulations provide three ways in which an institution can show it is providing equitable opportunities for women athletes (NCWGE 2012), as follows:

- A school can show that the percentage of its female athletes is substantially proportionate to the percent of women in its student body.
- The school has a history and continuing practice of programs that are demonstrably responsive to the developing interests and abilities of the members of the underrepresented sex.
- The institution's existing programs fully and effectively accommodate the interests and abilities of the underrepresented sex.

The Women's Educational Equity Act of 1974 created a series of programs to promote educational equity. It authorized funds to promote bias-free textbooks and curriculum, support research on gender equity, and revamp teacher-training programs. It established a National Equity Resource Center that for twenty-five years served as a clearinghouse for teacher training, developing equity curriculum materials and conducting research related to gender equity in education. Little effort was made to fund the act in the executive branch during the George W. Bush administration, and funding for the Equity Resource Center ended in 2003.

Picture 10.4 President Obama Honors the University of Connecticut Women's Basketball Team NCAA Champions, 2015

President Barack Obama joins the 2015 NCAA Women's Basketball Champion University of Connecticut Huskies in the East Room of the White House for a group photo during an event to honor the team for winning their championship title, September 15, 2015. Head Coach Geno Auriemma and UConn Chairman of the Board of Trustees Lawrence McHugh attend. (Official White House Photo by Chuck Kennedy.)

Violence against Women

The 1977 National Plan of Action declared wife beating a nationwide social problem and resolved that the president and Congress should declare the elimination of violence in the home to be a national goal. Nearly twenty years later, Congress acted on this plank with the passage of the Violence Against Women Act. The act, popularly known as VAWA, became law in 1994. Violence against women had historically been considered a private problem, namely as domestic abuse in the home. Moving the definition of the problem of domestic violence from the private sphere to the public sphere was a huge undertaking for the feminist community.

Addressing domestic violence at the federal level was especially problematic. VAWA was on the congressional agenda for four years before becoming law as part of the 1994 Crime Bill. The National Task Force to End Sexual Assault and Domestic Violence Against Women, a project of the National Organization for Women and its Legal Defense and Education Fund, took leadership in constructing the proposed legislation and lobbying it through Congress. Advocates for federal action presented masses of statistical evidence showing violence against women to be so pervasive that women were prevented from operating equally with men in society (McBride and Parry 2011, 301).

VAWA has five titles. Title I, Safe Streets for Women, increased sentences for repeat offenders who commit crimes against women. Title II, Safe Homes for Women, focuses on crimes of domestic violence. Title III, Civil Rights for Women, created the first civil rights remedy for violent gender-based discrimination. Title IV, Safe Campuses, grants funds to be spent on problems women faced on the nation's campuses. Title V, Equal Justice for Women in the Courts, provided training for state and federal judges to combat widespread gender bias in the courts.

The act charged the U.S. Department of Justice with collecting data on domestic abuse and provided money to state and local governments to fund efforts to offer services to victims and abusers. It identified domestic abuse as a gender-based crime that allowed victims to sue their batterers in federal court. It authorized grants to train judges and courts in domestic violence cases and to subsidize shelters. The act established a permanent women's policy agency, the Violence Against Women's Office (OVW), in the executive branch. OVW administers financial and technical assistance to communities around the country to facilitate the creation of programs, policies, and practices aimed at ending domestic violence, sexual assault, and stalking. In 2014, OVW reported that it had provided over $6 billion in grants and cooperative agreements.

An innovative aspect of VAWA was the extension of federal civil rights guarantees to victims of violent gender-motivated crimes such as rape. Under VAWA, victims could sue perpetrators for damages in federal court. The law applied to only violent crimes classified as felonies, and the victim would have to demonstrate that gender bias motivated the crime. Such action would be a civil suit, not a criminal one, and the victim could only obtain monetary damages. By definition, rape would be viewed as a crime against women, as feminists had long argued (McBride and Parry 2011, 288). Unfortunately for feminists, in 2000, the Supreme Court ruled in the case of *United States v. Morrison* that Congress had overstepped its authority in providing for this civil action. Congress had justified this action based on its powers to regulate interstate commerce and to enforce the 14th Amendment. The court ruled that any remedy due to the plaintiff had to be found in state legislatures and state courts, not in federal courts.

Twice, in 2000 and 2005, VAWA was reauthorized with bipartisan support and little opposition. Because of extensions added to it in the third renewal process, its reauthorization in 2012 was highly contentious. On February 2, 2012, the Senate Judiciary Committee approved its reauthorization on a 10–8 vote. All ten Democratic members voted for this reauthorization; all eight Republican members—all men—voted against it. It lost its bipartisan support because Democrats had added provisions to expand its coverage and to explicitly prevent grant recipients from discriminating against victims who were gay, lesbian, bisexual, or transgendered. It expanded the authority of Indian tribes to prosecute domestic violence. The new proposals also modified the U visa program to make it easier for law enforcement to gain the cooperation of victims in prosecuting dangerous perpetrators by allowing them to stay in the United States to assist law enforcement investigations. Democrats also argued that the reauthorization "consolidates programs and reduces authorization levels to address fiscal concerns while focusing on the programs that have been the most successful."

The tribal provision was controversial because it would allow tribes to prosecute offenders who are not American Indian or Alaska Native when their victims are and the violence happens on a reservation. This provision raised concern among some opponents about giving tribal courts increased power over defendants who are not tribal members. In 1978, the Supreme Court ruled that tribes do not have authority over people who are not American Indian, even when the crime happens on a reservation and involves a member of a tribe. According to the National Congress of American Indians, American Indian and Alaska Native women are 2.5 times more likely than other U.S. women to be battered or raped. Many are domestic violence victims whose abusers and assailants are not Native American. Tribal leaders argued that restrictions on prosecuting these abusers had prevented tribal officials from prosecuting abusers to help prevent repeat violence. They argued that "often the crimes are not serious enough for the federal government to step in. Violence often must escalate before a perpetrator is prosecuted" (Gamboa 2012). Representative Joe Baca articulated the Democratic perspective on the problem in his remarks during the House floor debate, stating that "many of the victims of domestic violence that live on the reservations are unable to hire legal counsel and can't travel hundreds of miles to Federal courts to petition for protection orders" (Congressional Record H2725).

The Associated Press described the 2012 VAWA debate on March 15:

> Senate Democrats fired the latest political shot in what they're calling the Republican "war against women" Thursday, pushing to renew and expand a law that fights violence against women and pays to help victims. They dared GOP senators to vote against it. Six female Democratic senators were joined by Sen. Lisa Murkowski of Alaska (R) on the Senate floor Thursday to offer their support for the Violence Against Women Reauthorization Act, which expired in September.[4]

The bill with the Democratic provisions eventually passed the Senate 68–31 but only after a group of mostly female Democratic senators engaged in a series of floor speeches, making

> a high-profile and at times emotional appeal to Republicans to support an expanded Violence Against Women Act. In doing so, they suggested Republicans were blocking the bill because it would extend its protections to illegal immigrants as well as gays and lesbians.
>
> (Barrett 2012)

Republicans angrily responded, accusing Democrats of playing election-year politics by trying to cast them as antiwomen. In the words of Republican Senator John Kyl, "I really resent the implication by some of my Democratic friends that if you're trying to improve the bill that somehow you are for violence against women. That's reprehensible" (Barrett 2012). The Democratic Senatorial Campaign Committee then used the issue in a fund-raising appeal, stating, "Today we're seeing another stunning GOP attack on women's rights," and asked for donations of five dollars or more for the committee's Protect Our Women's Rights Fund.

Republicans in the U.S. House of Representatives then moved a VAWA reauthorization bill forward without the Senate-passed Democratic provisions. In their floor speeches, Democrats continually described the Senate version as a bipartisan bill that all the female members of the Senate, Democrat and Republican, supported, even though the process in the Senate to reach that end was anything but bipartisan.

Republicans tapped first-term Florida Representative Sandy Adams to be the lead sponsor on the reauthorization bill in the House. She had been a victim of domestic abuse, thus making her leadership on this issue most poignant. As she described it,

> At an early age, I quit high school at 17 and joined the Air Force. Married by 18. During the marriage, I had a little girl, and I realized really soon that my husband had a penchant for drinking, and when he drank, he turned very mean, very violent.
>
> (States News Service 2012)

She took her daughter and left. She later worked as a law enforcement officer before winning a seat in the Florida State House and eventually running for the U.S. House.

At the same time, in a March 28 speech on the House floor, Democratic Representative Gwen Moore of Wisconsin recounted that she had been sexually assaulted as a child and raped as an adult. She led the Democratic advocacy of their version of the reauthorization bill during floor debate on adoption of the Republican version of VAWA reauthorization on May 16.

The GOP-dominated House Rules Committee adopted a closed rule for debate that did not allow any Democratic amendments. During the floor debate, forty-eight Democrats and twenty-two Republicans took to the microphone to speak with Republicans advocating for and Democrats arguing against the proposed bill.[5] All speakers supported reauthorization of VAWA. Republicans and Democrats competed for the mantle of being defenders of women against violence.[6] Debate centered on how best to achieve this goal. Democrats argued for the Senate-passed additions explicitly referencing violence against LBGT individuals and against Republican-imposed changes to the processing of cases involving immigrant women facing domestic violence and elimination of Democratic-inserted changes in the Senate bill allowing Indian tribes to prosecute non-Indians who had abused women on tribal lands. Each Democratic speaker explicitly argued for the importance of these changes and accused Republicans of weakening protections. The words of minority leader Nancy Pelosi illustrate the Democratic position:

> This legislation on the floor fails vulnerable people—members of the LGBT community, Native American women, and immigrant victims. All people deserve to be protected from domestic violence. There should be no exceptions to this law. We can't say women of America, we're passing a bill to protect you—not so fast in your applause if you happen to be a member of the LGBT community, an immigrant or otherwise, or a Native American woman.

Democrats emphasized the support of several hundred organizations and governmental groups in their remarks.

Republicans focused on the importance of not singling out specific groups. For example, Ann Marie Buerkle (R-NY) argued,

> When . . . we began discussing VAWA, we sat down with the understanding that Americans deserve equal protection under the law. We are not going to single out. We are not going to distinguish one victim from another. Any person who is a victim of domestic violence is a victim of domestic violence. Beyond that, it should be of no concern.

A second Republican theme in keeping with their more general philosophy regarding the scope of government was on program accountability and efficiency. For example, Representative Virginia Foxx (R-NC) stated, "With this bill, we have also worked to add accountability requirements to conduct the necessary oversight of VAWA grant recipients and programs. Our goal is to ensure that more money is spent on direct services and less on administrative bureaucracy." Representative Lynn Jenkins (R-KS) argued that "our legislation also goes beyond the Senate bill by ensuring that taxpayer resources help victims, not Washington bureaucrats, by limiting administrative expenses, requiring annual audits and combating fraud."[7]

No member, at least on the floor of the House or in the media, proposed that VAWA not be reauthorized or completely overhauled. No one seemed to vote against reauthorization because he or she opposed VAWA in principle. However, conservative women's groups *have* opposed VAWA and lobbied Congress not to enact this legislation. The Independent Women's Forum (IWF) has long argued against this act due to federal government involvement in what it believes should be states' functions and that it is too strongly antimale (Schreiber 2012). Concerned Women for America (CWA) also urged opposition. CWA senior fellow Janice Shaw Crouse's comment that "her group had been pressing senators hard to oppose reauthorization of legislation she called 'a boondoggle' that vastly expands government and 'creates an ideology that all men are guilty and all women are victims'" illustrated CWA's continued opposition (Weisman 2012). But these groups' views were not reflected in the reauthorization process.

The Republican version passed in the House 222–205, largely along party lines: twenty-three Republicans voted against the bill, and six Democrats voted for it. Two female Republicans, Judy Biggert and Ilena Ros-Lehtinen, voted against the Republican bill. Democrats used VAWA reauthorization to reinforce the idea of the Republican Party being antiwomen by adding measures aimed at specific groups of women that Republicans would be uncomfortable supporting. Legislators as a whole wanted to appear to be representing women when it came to violence against them. Both parties put female legislators in the forefront of the legislative process over reauthorization, linking descriptive with substantive representation and indirectly highlighting surrogate representation.

Because the House and Senate did not reconcile their differences by the end of the 112th Congress, the bill needed to be reintroduced in 113th Congress. The Democratic version, with some modifications, passed the Senate in February 2013, and that version then passed the House. President Obama signed the reauthorization into law on March 7.

A Continuing Activist Agenda

An activist agenda centering on federal government public policies continued into the second decade of the millennium. Liberal feminists continue to press for policies providing greater economic equity for women and sexual security. U.S. House Democrats launched a campaign in 2013 designed to "bolster economic opportunities for women." Under the leadership of House Minority Leader Nancy Pelosi (D-CA), the lawmakers pushed a series of bills to promote pay equity in the workplace, make childcare more affordable, and encourage a balance between jobs and family for the nation's working women. Legislation to affect gender equity and women's lives that has been introduced into Congress in the second decade of the millennium includes the Maternal Health Accountability Act, the Campus Sexual Violence Elimination Act, the Social Security Care Giver Credit Act, and the Zero Tolerance for Domestic Abusers Act.

Health care for women continues as an area of focus for women's rights activists. In the 114th Congress, Democratic Senators Patty Murray, Barbara Boxer, and Barbara Mikulski introduced the 21st Century Women's Health Act. In introducing this legislation, these senators stated that it

> invests in women's health clinics and the primary care workforce, and promotes critical preventive services like contraception coverage. The bill also works to provide compassionate assistance for survivors of rape by ensuring all hospitals provide emergency contraception, spreading awareness, and working with community-based groups to help prevent sexual violence.

The act would expand comprehensive preventive health services, including full access to contraceptive coverage for all women served by Medicaid, establish a women's health nurse practitioner training program to expand access to primary care, improve maternal safety and quality of care, create a new ombudsperson role to support women's access to health services, provide compassionate assistance and awareness for survivors of rape, help women report instances of inappropriate charges for birth control and other critical health-care needs, examine reproductive health access across the country, and launch a public awareness campaign for women's preventive services.

Women Matter

The presence and policy proposals of the Congressional Caucus for Women's Issues are evidence of women making a difference regarding public policy in the U.S. Congress. Research has shown that women "have mattered" in the U.S. Congress in a variety of additional ways. An important political science research volume published in 2002 asked the question "Are women transforming the U.S. Congress?" (Rosenthal 2002). The volume's chapters demonstrated the many ways in which female representatives and senators influenced the congressional policy-making process, especially in terms of affecting the agenda and debate around issues deemed to be of particular concern to women, so-called women's issues. Male and female legislators differed in their policy priorities, the interests represented, and their conceptualization of issues. Female legislators affected the agenda and sponsorship of legislation; they have influenced the committee decision-making process and floor debate. The chapters of *Women Transforming Congress* prominently described and analyzed these varied aspects of female legislators making a difference in the legislative process on issues especially affecting women. Michele Swers (2002, 280) concludes,

> The close examination of the importance of institutional position . . . that when women gained access to strategic positions of power, they became even more active advocates of policy initiatives on education, children and families, women's health, and general health than similarly situated men. Thus, Democratic and Republican women were more likely to take the lead in cosponsoring legislation on gender gap issues when they

were in the majority party. Therefore, in addition to electing more women to office, expanding the representation of women in strategic positions of power, including as members of the majority party and important committees, will enhance the quality of representation by increasing the diversity of viewpoints with a real influence on the congressional agenda.

Notes

1. The National Plan of Action can be found at http://1997-2001.state.gov/www/picw/archives/ npa.html. *Sisters of '77* is a documentary film released in 2005 and directed by Cynthia Salzman Mondell and Allen Mondell that chronicles the conference.
2. The Black Women's Agenda, Inc. (www.bwa-inc.org) is an organization in Washington, DC, whose purpose is to implement the recommendations in the Black Women's Action Plan. It is still active.
3. EACH stands for Equal Access to Abortion Coverage in Health Insurance.
4. The video of their remarks can be found at www.c-spanvideo.org/program/304925-5.
5. See the VAWA floor debate at www.c-spanvideo.org/program/HouseSession5333. The transcript of the House floor proceedings on the renewal of VAWA on May 16, 2012, can be found at http:// thomas.loc.gov/cgi-bin/query/D?r112:4:./temp/~r112cGZcFY.
6. Representative Virginia Foxx (R-NC) stated on the floor that "all Republicans are concerned about violence against anyone. Violence, we are very concerned about that. I personally won't even watch any kind of movie that has any kind of violence in it because I can't stand to see violence perpetrated on another human being. So Republican men and women both abhor violence against women."
7. See a video of their statements at www.youtube.com/watch?v=Sa8hOwweRDI.

Further Readings

Bingham, Clara and Laura Leedy Gansler. 2002. *Class Action: The Story of Lois Jensen and the Landmark Case That Changed Sexual Harassment Law*. New York, NY: Doubleday.

Lawless, Jennifer and Sean Theriault. 2016. "Sex, Bipartisanship, and Collaboration in the U.S. Congress." Political Parity. www.politicalparity.org/wp-content/uploads/2016/03/Sex_Bipartisanship_ Collaboration.pdf.

Ledbetter, Lilly with Lanier Scott Isom. 2012. *Grace and Grit: My Fight for Equal Pay and Fairness at Goodyear and Beyond*. New York, NY: Crown.

Milkulski, Barbara and Susan Collins. 2001. *Nine and Counting: The Women of the Senate*. New York, NY: Harper Perennial.

Verveer, Melanne and Kim K. Azzarelli. 2015. *Fast Forward: How Women Can Achieve Power and Purpose*. Boston, MA: Houghton Mifflin Harcourt.

Web Sources

"A History of Women in the U.S. Military," www.infoplease.com/us/military/women-history.html.

"Barriers and Bias: The Status of Women in Leadership." 2016. American Association of University Women. www.aauw.org/aauw_check/pdf_download/show_pdf.php?file=barriers-and-bias.

Political Parity. "Sex, Bipartisanship, and Collaboration in Congress." *Webinar*. www.youtube.com/ watch?v=pq7zcwg_gTM.

"President Obama's Record on Empowering Women and Girls." https://obamawhitehouse.archives. gov/node/355186.

Ross Godar, Julie. 2016. "Watch the SheKnows Media Town Hall Event with GOP Congresswomen." *SheKnows*, March 1. www.sheknows.com/living/articles/1114431/join-sheknows-media-for-a-live-town-hall-with-gop-congresswomen-on-march-2.

"What If Women Ruled the World?" 2014. *iKnow Politics*, April 1. http://iknowpolitics.org/en/ knowledge-library/video/what-if-women-ruled-world.

References

Anzia, Sarah and Christopher Berry. 2011. "The Jackie (and Jill) Robinson Effect: Why Do Congresswomen Outperform Congressmen?" *American Journal of Political Science*, 55, 3: 478–493.

Atkeson, Lonna Rae. 2003. "Not All Cues Are Created Equal: The Conditional Impact of Female Candidates on Political Engagement." *Journal of Politics*, 65: 1040–1061.

Atkeson, Lonna Rae and Nancy Carrillo. 2007. "More Is Better: The Influence of Collective Female Descriptive Representation on External Efficacy." *Politics & Gender*, 3, 1 (March): 79–103.

Barnes, Robert. 2016. "Laws Written by Men to Protect Women Need Scrutiny, Court Told." *The Washington Post*, February 8.

Barrett, Ted. 2012. "Accusations Fly in Senate Over Violence against Women Act." *CNN Wire*, March 15.

Cowell-Meyers, Kimberley and Laura Langbein. 2009. "Linking Women's Descriptive and Substantive Representation in the United States." *Politics & Gender*, 5, 4 (December): 491–518.

Dodson, Debra. 2006. *The Impact of Women in Congress*. New York, NY: Oxford University Press.

Fridkin, Kim L. and Patrick J. Kenney. 2014. "Different Portraits, Different Leaders? Gender Differences in U.S. Senators' Presentation of Self." In *Women and Elective Office: Past, Present, and Future*, eds. Sue Thomas and Clyde Wilcox. New York, NY: Oxford University Press, 126–144.

Gamboa, Suzanne. 2012. "Tribes Make Push for Violence against Women Act." *Salt Lake Tribune*, March 9.

Gelb, Joyce and Marian Leif Palley. 1982. *Women and Public Policies*. Princeton, NJ: Princeton University Press.

Gertzog, Irwin. 1984. *Congressional Women: Their Recruitment, Integration, and Behavior*. Westport, CT: Preager.

Gertzog, Irwin. 1995. *Congressional Women: Their Recruitment, Integration, and Behavior*. 2nd edition, revised and updated. Westport, CT: Preager.

Grand Forks Herald. 2013. "Bipartisanship lives, says Klobuchar, Heitkamp." October 22.

Guttmacher Institute. 2014. "Induced Abortions in the United States." www.guttmacher.org/factsheet/induced-abortion-united-states.

Hawkesworth, Mary. 2003. "Congressional Enactments of Race-Gender: Toward a Theory of Raced-Gendered Institutions." *American Political Science Review*, 97 (November): 529–550.

Heymann, Jody and Kristen McNeill. 2013. *Children's Chances: How Countries Can Move from Surviving to Thriving*. Cambridge, MA: Harvard University Press.International Labour Organization. 2010. "Maternity at Work: A Review of National Legislation: Findings from the ILO Database of Conditions of Work and Employment Laws." Geneva, Switzerland: International Labor Organization. www.ilo.org/wcmsp5/groups/public/@dgreports/@dcomm/@publ/documents/publication/wcms_124442.pdf.

Jackson, David. 2013. "Obama Jokes about 'Serving' Dinner Guests." *USA TODAY*, October 17.

Kalsem, Kristin and Verna L. Williams. 2010. "Social Justice Feminism." *UCLA Women's Law Journal*, 18, 1: 131–193.

Kathlene, Lyn. 1994. "Power and Influence of State Legislative Policymaking: The Interaction of Gender and Position in Committee Hearing Debates." *American Political Science Review*, 88: 560–576.

King, Jamilah. 2016. "How Black Women Like Me Reckon with America's Political Process." http://mic.com/articles/136045/how-black-women-like-me-reckon-with-america-s-political-process#.BFb0EGxZn.

Lawless, Jennifer. 2004. "Politics of Presence? Congresswomen and Symbolic Representation." *Political Research Quarterly*, 57: 81–99.

McBride, Dorothy E. and Janine A. Parry. 2011. *Women's Rights in the USA: Policy Debates and Gender Roles*, 4th edition. New York, NY: Routledge.

National Coalition of Women and Girls in Education. 2012. *Title IX and Athletics: Proven Benefits, Unfounded Objections*. http://ncwge.org/TitleIX40/Athletics.pdf.

National Partnership for Women and Families. 2015. "The Family and Medical Insurance Leave Act." www.nationalpartnership.org/research-library/work-family/paid-leave/family-act-factsheet.pdf.

Neuwirth, Jessica. 2015. *Equal Means Equal.* New York, NY: Free Press.

Newton-Small, Jay. 2013. "Women Are the Only Adults Left in Washington." *Time*, October 28. http://swampland.time.com/2013/10/16/women-are-the-only-adults-left-in-washington/.

O'Keefe, Ed. 2014. "Women Are Wielding Notable Influence in Congress." *The Washington Post*, January 16.

Phillips, Anne. 1998. "Democracy and Representation: Or, Why Should It Matter Who Our Representatives Are?" In *Feminism and Politics*, ed. Anne Phillips. Oxford, UK: Oxford University Press, 224–240.

Rosenthal, Cindy Simon. 1997. "A View of Their Own: Women's Committee Leadership Styles and State Legislatures." *Policy Studies Journal*, 5: 585–600.

Rosenthal, Cindy Simon. 2002. *Women Transforming Congress.* Norman, OK: University of Oklahoma Press.

Ruhm, Christopher. 2016. "What Americans Can Learn from California about the Advantages of Paid Parental Leave." www.scholarsstrategynetwork.org/brief/what-americans-can-learn-california-about-advantages-paid-parental-leave.

Schreiber, Ronnee. 2012. *Righting Feminism: Conservative Women & American Politics.* New York, NY: Oxford University Press.

Schwindt-Bayer, Leslie A. and Michelle M. Talyor-Robinson. 2011. "The Meaning and Measurement of Women's Interests: Introduction." *Politics & Gender*, 7, 3 (September): 417–418.

States News Service. 2012. "Adams Discusses VAWA and 'War on Women' on CNN's the 'Situation Room'." May 15.

Steinem, Gloria. 1979. "An Introductory Statement." *What Women Want.* New York: Simon and Schuster, 10–17.

Steinhauser, Paul and Amy Livingston. 2010. "Anti-Pelosi Ads Break Record." *CNN Politics*, November 8. http://politicalticker.blogs.cnn.com/2010/11/08/anti-pelosi-ads-break-records/.

Swers, Michele. 2002. "Transforming the Agenda: Analyzing Gender Differences in Women's Issue Sponsorship." In *Women Transforming Congress*, ed. Cindy Simon Rosenthal. Norman, OK: University of Oklahoma Press, 260–283.

Thomas, Sue. 1991. "The Impact of Women on State Legislative Policies." *Journal of Politics*, 53, 4 (November): 958–976.

Tumulty, Karen. 2012. "Twenty Years On, 'Year of the Woman' Fades." *The Washington Post*, March 24.

Volden, Craig, Alan E. Wiseman, and Dana E. Wittmer. 2013. "When Are Women More Effective Lawmakers Than Men?" *American Journal of Political Science*, 57, 2: 326–341.

Volden, Craig, Alan E. Wiseman, and Dana E. Wittmer. 2016. *Women's Issues and Their Fate in the United States Congress. Political Science Research and Methods.* https://my.vanderbilt.edu/alanwiseman/files/2016/03/VWW_Issues_201603.pdf.

Von Hagel, Alisa. 2011. "Gender Difference and Group Dynamics: The Impact of Women's Social Networks in the United States Congress." PhD Dissertation, Northern Illinois University, DeKalb.

Weisman, Jonathan. 2012. "Women Figure Anew in Senate's Latest Battle." *The New York Times*, March 15.

Wolbrecht, Christina and David Campbell. 2006. "See Jane Run: Women Politicians as Role Models for Adolescents." *Journal of Politics*, 68, 2 (May): 233–247.

11 Women's Political Participation in a Comparative Perspective

The chapters of this book have explored the myriad ways in which women have engaged in the practice of politics and sought equality with men in the political life of the United States and how economic inequality has impacted the quest for political equality. This final chapter begins with an exploration of the ways in which U.S. women's political engagement compares and contrasts with that of women in other nations. It then concludes by looking forward as the centennial of the women's suffragist amendment approaches.

Convention on the Elimination of All Forms of Discrimination against Women

In 1946, the United Nations established a Commission on the Status of Women (CSW) whose mission was ensuring women's equality and promoting women's rights. Its mandate was to "prepare recommendations and reports to the Economic and Social Council on promoting women's rights in political, economic, civil, social and educational fields" and to make recommendations "on urgent problems requiring immediate attention in the field of women's rights." In 1963, the General Assembly asked the commission to draft a Declaration on the Elimination of Discrimination against Women. The result was the United Nations' adoption of the Convention on the Elimination of All Forms of Discrimination against Women (CEDAW) in 1979 following the UN Decade for Women. CEDAW is an international bill of rights for women that obliges governments to take actions to promote and protect women's rights. The convention defines what constitutes discrimination against women and establishes an agenda for national action to end such discrimination. CEDAW defines discrimination as "any distinction, exclusion or restriction which has the effect or purpose of impairing or nullifying the recognition, enjoyment or exercise of . . . [the] human right of fundamental freedoms in the political, economic, social, cultural, civil or any other field." CEDAW works to ensure the right to vote and the right to work, to end forced marriages, to provide access to maternal health care and education, and to reduce sex trafficking and domestic violence.

Following CEDAW provisions, states that have ratified the convention submit reports to the United Nations every four years, providing detailed information about the measures they have taken to promote women's legal equality, eliminate discrimination rooted in customary and traditional practices, promote women's development and empowerment, and protect women's human rights (Hawkesworth 2012). The CEDAW committee charged with monitoring compliance has little actual power to compel states to comply with the obligations it assumed upon ratification of the treaty. It has no enforcement authority. It can only make recommendations highlighting areas where more progress is needed in a particular country. Each country decides how best to achieve implementation.

More than thirty years after the creation of CEDAW, the United States remains one of only seven nations that have not ratified this treaty. The other nonsignatory countries are Sudan, South Sudan, Somalia, Iran, and two small Pacific Island nations (Palau and Tonga). A total of 187 countries are signatories to the treaty.

In the United States, the U.S. Senate must ratify international treaties with two thirds of Senators present and voting in favor it. Before an international treaty reaches the Senate floor, the Senate Foreign Relations Committee typically reviews it and votes whether to send it forward for full Senate consideration. If it goes forward for a full Senate vote and the Senate consents, then the president deposits the instruments of ratification, signaling U.S. agreement to be bound by the treaty.

The Senate Foreign Relations Committee has twice voted favorably on the CEDAW treaty with bipartisan support, in 1994 with a vote of 13–5 and in 2002 with a vote of 12–7. But it has never been brought to the Senate floor for debate and a vote. U.S. women's rights advocates continue to call for America to ratify the convention. In 2014, as chair of the Subcommittee on International Operations and Organizations in the 113th Congress, U.S. Senator Barbara Boxer held a hearing on CEDAW, along with seven other female U.S. Senators. She called the U.S. lack of ratification "ridiculous, it's embarrassing, it is inexplicable that the United States has not joined 187 other countries in ratifying CEDAW."[1]

Lobbying efforts have been organized in the country to promote ratification. The Leadership Conference on Civil and Human Rights has established a CEDAW Task Force to lead a coalition effort engaging in outreach and education about U.S. ratification of CEDAW. It highlights what it considers to be instances in which countries advanced women's rights in a particular domain while working in partnership with CEDAW. For example, it credits the CEDAW Committee's recommendation to eliminate discriminatory provisions in its electoral law, with Kuwait's parliament voting to extend voting rights and the right to run for elective office to women in 2005. The electoral change followed a decades-long campaign by women's rights activists for full suffrage. How significant a role CEDAW actually played relative to other factors in gaining voting rights for women in Kuwait remains to be analyzed.[2]

Why has the United States not ratified the convention? Conservatives have been successful in keeping CEDAW from receiving a two-thirds majority in the U.S. Senate needed to ratify a treaty. They oppose the treaty for several reasons such as a concern about infringement on national sovereignty and that it would encourage abortion or interfere with the family and legalize prostitution, even though nothing in the treaty language indicates support for any of these concerns (Henderson and Jeydel 2007). Conservative groups such as Concerned Women for America (CWA) argue that, if adopted, then CEDAW would deny women basic freedoms and rights in the United States. It would violate constitutional rights of freedom and religion and subject American women to the supervision of a UN committee. CWA argues that the United States already provides legal protection to women (Wright 2010).

Against such concerns, it is important to note that CEDAW has no power to enforce changes in its laws or its constitution. How a nation responds to a CEDAW critique of its equal rights record is up to that nation. On the positive side, if the treaty were ratified, then executing the process of writing the four-year reports that CEDAW requires provides a country with the opportunity of surveying and assessing its policies for possible discrimination. By submitting them to the CEDAW Committee for review, the committee's response further provides a government an opportunity to reflect on its policies, defend them, and stimulate a public discussion about any seeming problems. In 1998, the city of San Francisco adopted the provisions of CEDAW into its local law, even though the United States had not yet ratified CEDAW. San Francisco acted in part to send a message to Washington, urging the federal government to ratify the treaty (Bellitto 2015).

Creating a Critical Mass of Female Leaders

Achieving a "critical mass" of female lawmakers has been high on the agenda of global women's rights advocates as part of the drive to eliminate discrimination against women. The equal participation of women and men in public life is one of the cornerstones of CEDAW. The 1995 UN Fourth World Conference on Women held in Beijing generated renewed pressure for the implementation of CEDAW provisions that, among other things, called for the equal participation of women and men in governmental decision making. The Beijing Platform for Action identified "inequality between men and women in the sharing of power and decision-making at all levels" and "insufficient mechanisms at all levels to promote the advancement of women" as two areas of significant concern where action was critical for women to achieve political equity. It mandated that governments work toward gender parity in public administrative institutions and legislative bodies. It encouraged governments to establish targets and to implement measures to integrate women into elected and nonelected public positions at levels comparable to those of men. Similarly, governments were to encourage nongovernmental organizations (NGOs), trade unions, political parties, and the private sector to promote the equal participation of men and women in decision-making positions (Tripp and Kang 2008).

The active participation of women and the inclusion of women's perspectives at all levels of decision making were necessary to achieve the goals of equality, development, and peace, the platform declared. Thus, the platform stated that the underrepresentation of women in elective and policy-making positions was a problem. The Beijing Platform described "discriminatory attitudes and practices" and "unequal power relations" that led to the underrepresentation of women in arenas of political decision making. Attention was directed toward institutional and cultural mechanisms of exclusion that prevented women from obtaining an equal share of positions in most political institutions in the world. It spoke of securing a critical mass of women in political leadership and of achieving the target the United Nations Economic and Social Council had endorsed in 1990 of having 30 percent women in positions at decision-making levels.[3] The idea of a critical mass of women in political leadership and as a goal to be achieved provides a context in which to assess the U.S. political system from a comparative perspective. Several countries have surpassed that critical mass goal and are much closer to gender equity in terms of formal elected leadership than the United States.

As noted in Chapter 7, training women in underdeveloped countries to run and win elective office has been a prominent activity of U.S. women's rights NGOs. Female elected officials have also worked with would-be female parliamentarians in these countries. For example, U.S. Representative Kay Granger (R-TX) has led congressional delegations to Jordan to help train Iraqi women leaders. These elected officials are viewed as experts when it comes to running for and being elected to public office. The U.S. government has also engaged in programs to help women increase their voices in the governments of other countries. For example, one such project has been the 2009 creation of the Women's Knowledge Network in partnership with Jordan's government. The U.S. Millennium Challenge Corporation (MCC) and the U.S. Agency for International Development (USAID) initiated this project with the goal of giving women opportunities to learn how to campaign for elected office and to develop effective public policies.

Ironically, however, the United States has been far less successful itself in reaching a critical mass of female elected officials. Its poor standing has received much critical commentary. The Inter-Parliamentary Union (IPU), located in Geneva, Switzerland, tracks and maintains a database on the number and percentage of women in national parliaments. It is the international organization of Parliaments. The IPU tracks women's membership in the parliaments across the globe. Its 2015 *Women in National Parliaments* accounting includes 192 countries. The United States ranked ninety-sixth in the world in the percentage of women in a nation's lower house of parliament. The average percent of women in lower or single house of parliaments globally is 22.9 percent, according to IPU calculations. In the United States, as noted in Chapter 8, women make up 19.4 percent of the U.S. House of Representatives. Of course, not all these countries are parliamentary democracies. Of the 125 countries Freedom House[4] characterizes as electoral democracies, the United States ranked seventy-third.

But these national legislatures also vary in the degree to which they are independent policy-making centers in their national governments. The U.S. Congress is one of the most powerful legislatures in the world. It is distinctive among national legislatures in the extent of its independent powers regarding making national policy and the degree to which its members can affect the policy-making agenda and introduce and pursue legislation (and have laws informally named after its members). It occupies the center stage in national policy making (Kernell and Jacobson 2003). Based on their comparative research, Smith, Roberts, and Vander Wielen (2007) concluded, "No other national legislature has greater power than the Congress of the United States" (1). In most parliamentary systems, the policy-making centers are solidly in the executive branch, which has a supportive majority in the parliament with limited powers and limited resources to pursue independent policy initiatives.

It is crucial, too, that beyond their numbers among elected officials, institutions are structured so that female members have opportunities for meaningful participation and effective leadership. In the U.S. Congress, although women constitute a smaller proportion of membership than do women in many other democratic legislatures, they have the opportunity to meaningfully affect public policy, more so than female members in many parliaments, as noted in Chapter 10. Not only numbers but also capacity for influence is important in measuring the progress women have made as national public officials in a comparative context and should serve as a frame of reference in assessing the meaningfulness of campaigns for and election of women to membership in the U.S. national legislature.

Joyce Gelb's (2002) research comparing the representation and influence of women in the British Parliament with the women in the U.S. Congress in the late 1990s illustrates this point. The number of women in the British Parliament doubled as a result of the 1997 election. Gelb found that changes in Labour Party rules, among other things creating all-women shortlists and targeting of winnable seats, created conditions that produced a dramatic increase in the number of women in the House of Commons in 1997 when the Labour Party won that year's election in a landslide. At the same time, the political opportunity structure of strong centralized parties in Britain's parliamentary system constrained the junior members and backbenchers' ability to achieve policy outcomes. Several female parliamentarians decided against running for reelection in 2001, citing negative masculine tendencies in the parliamentary culture. During the same period, although a smaller percentage of its membership, independent-minded female members of Congress, Gelb concludes, were producing a record of policy impact. Party strictures were less constraining on U.S. congresswomen than on their British sisters. "Even when numbers of women representatives are relatively small (e.g., do not constitute a 'critical mass') institutional realities of congressional seniority and relatively lax party control may yet yield opportunities for lasting impact on policy" Gelb (2002, 441) asserted. Changes in the political opportunity structure must affect both electoral and institutional structures for enhanced policy impact and real influence.

Electoral Systems and Women Parliamentary Representation

Chapter 8 described the significance of the single-member district electoral system and accompanying incumbent advantage that dominates in the United States in keeping women from coming anywhere near membership parity in the U.S. Congress. This system limits opportunities for both male and female newcomers. How electoral systems are constructed has a significant impact on women's representation in legislatures, according to the International Institute for Democracy and Electoral Assistance (IDEA), especially the distinction between single-winner and multi-winner districts. A 2005 IDEA report showed that countries using multi-winner districts elected up to 35 percent more women to their national legislatures between 1950 and 2004 than did countries using single-winner districts (Ballington and Karam 2015).

Electoral structures are key factors affecting the numerical representation of women in national parliaments. Electoral structures consist of such factors as the rules by which candidates get their names on the ballot, the role of party organizations in the electoral process, the votes it takes to win, and how many candidates for whom voters can cast ballots in particular districts. The U.S. single-member district electoral structure, often referred to as First Past the Post (FPTP), is the least conducive system to the election of women from a comparative electoral structure standpoint. List proportional representation systems, in contrast, do better when it comes to women's numerical representation. Proportional representation (PR) requires the use of electoral districts with more than one member. Under a List PR system, each party or grouping presents a list of candidates for a multimember electoral district, the voters vote for a party, and the parties receive seats in proportion to their overall share of the votes (Larserud and Taphorn 2007). The candidates actually elected to the legislature depend on their placement on the list. The greater the number of seats a party can win, the better the opportunity for female candidates in such systems (Matland 1993; Schwindt-Bayer 2009). The idea that electoral systems matter—in particular, that more women are usually elected to Parliament under party list proportional representation than under majoritarian electoral systems—has been confirmed by a long series of studies since the mid-1980s.

In the United States, not only do voters cast only one vote for a candidate but also the parties nominate only one candidate. That means it is impossible for them to present a balanced slate because they have only one candidate. In addition, one of the crucial factors that makes the U.S. system distinctive from other FPTP systems is the limited power the party has to select and to veto candidates that run under its label. The U.S. system is much more candidate centered than in other majoritarian countries, which makes it harder for the parties to increase representation, even if they are interested in achieving that goal. But as the description of Representation 2020's proposals for generating a more woman-friendly party system in Chapter 8 shows, the political parties could act positively toward a more gender-equitable nomination system.

Further, the candidate-centered single-member district system in the United States has contributed, among other factors, to incumbents being overwhelmingly advantaged. Also, because much of the history of the public realm has been a "men-only" domain, their domination as incumbents has created a major drag on women making much numerical progress in Congress.

In addition to Representation 2020's proposals for political party actions to enhance the nomination and election of women in the United States, it also advocates for structural changes to the U.S. electoral system to achieve greater gender equity in office holding (Terrell 2015). Building on the IDEA report, the primary structural change Representation 2020 advocates is the creation of multimember districts for legislative elections rather than the single-member district electoral system that now solely structures congressional elections and dominates among state legislatures. Whereas most elections for state legislative offices are single-member district affairs, eleven states use multimember districts to elect at least one house in their state legislatures. These eleven states, Representation 2020 reports, tend to rank among the highest for their percentage of legislators who are women. As of January 2015, three of the five states that are closest to gender parity in their state legislatures had multimember districts in at least one of their state legislative chambers (Vermont, Arizona, and Washington).

Multimember districts help women in several ways. When multiple candidates can win, a more diverse set of candidates are attractive for parties to place on the ballot. Making their parties more inclusive and representative of the voting population is easier when more candidates can win. Multimember districts also help lessen the power of incumbency, a particular problem for potential female candidates in the United States, as noted earlier. Multimember districts, Representation 2020 asserts, mean more winners in each district, which in turn means more candidates, more competition, and more diversity in each district. But instituting such a change in state legislatures, let alone in the U.S. Congress, would require a substantial learning curve among the public and expenditure of considerable resources to challenge entrenched interests in the status quo. The eleven states—Arizona, Idaho, Maryland, New Hampshire, New Jersey, North Dakota, Ohio, South Dakota, Vermont, Washington, and West Virginia—with some features of multimember districts in their state legislatures, provide real-life examples in any campaign to stimulate other states to adopt women-friendlier election systems.

Whereas structural changes are not on the radar of organizations promoting greater sex equity in elective office in this country, it is instructive to become knowledgeable about cross-country comparisons of electoral systems and their relation to women's membership in elected office, reflect on strategies to enhance women's presence that other countries have adopted, and look internally at the alternative ways of constructing electoral systems already present within the United States.

Representation 2020 has also constructed a Gender Parity Index to rank each of the fifty states. Gender parity is the point at which women and men are just as likely to hold elected office. The index includes the three most recent gubernatorial elections, their other current statewide elective executives, winners of the four most recent U.S. senator elections, the proportion of their U.S. House delegation that is female, the proportion of state legislative seats held by women, the sex of a state's Speaker of the House and state senate president, and the number of women elected in mayoral or county executive positions in the five largest local jurisdictions of the state. Each state is scored on a scale from 0 to 100. If a state has a score lower than fifty, then women are underrepresented in elected office in that state. If it has a score greater than fifty, then men are underrepresented. In 2015, New Hampshire ranked first with a score of fifty-seven. Mississippi ranked last with a score of seven.[5]

Quotas and the Election of Women

For decades, the Nordic countries had the highest political representation of women in the world. In 2005, women constituted over 45 percent of the members of Parliament in Sweden, 38 percent in Finland, 37 percent in Denmark, 36 percent in Norway, and 30 percent in Iceland following elections held between 2001 and 2005 (Dalerup 2005, 2014). Contrary to common perceptions, no constitutional clause or law demands a high representation—that is, legal quotas—of women in Scandinavia. For the most part, the high percentage can be attributed to sustained pressure by women's groups within parties as well as the women's movement in general. Women mobilized and organized to ensure that the political parties increased their number of female candidates and female candidates who had a fair chance of winning (see, for example, Sainsbury 1993). The real takeoff to the increase in women's representation in the Nordic countries happened in the 1970s before any party-installed candidate quotas.

The pressure to increase women's representation was applied to all political parties in Scandinavia. Some parties applied voluntary quotas, especially center-left parties in response to these demands. In three Scandinavian countries, quotas were introduced based on decisions made by the political parties themselves, first in parties to the left and in the social democratic parties during the 1970s, 1980s, and 1990s. Most center and right-wing parties, however, have considered quotas "un-liberal." It was not until 1993 that the Swedish Social Democratic Party introduced the principle of "every second on the list a woman." In a 50 percent quota system like this, the women are no more "quota women" than the men are "quota men."

Whereas the Scandinavian countries continue to be leaders in female membership in their national parliaments, the Rwandan parliamentary elections in 2003 resulted in that African country assuming the number one position when women won 48.8 percent of the seats in its lower house of Parliament. By 2015, the percentage of women in the lower house of the Rwandan Parliament had reached a remarkable 63.8 percent.

The 1994 genocide in Rwanda, perpetrated by Hutu extremists against the Tutsi minority and Hutu moderates, killed an estimated eight hundred thousand people (one tenth of the population). During the nine-year period of postgenocide transitional government, from 1994 to 2003, women's representation in Parliament (by appointment) reached 25 percent, and a new gender-sensitive constitution was adopted. The 2003 constitution increased exponentially the number of seats to be held by women in all structures of government. The lower house of the Rwandan Parliament consists of eighty members serving five-year terms, fifty-three of whom are directly elected through a PR system. The additional seats are contested as follows: twenty-four deputies (30 percent) are elected by women from each province and the capital city, Kigali; the National Youth Council elects two; and the Federation of the Associations of the Disabled elects one deputy. The twenty-four seats that are reserved for women are contested in women-only elections—that is, only women can stand for election, and only women can vote. The national system of women's councils coordinated the election for the women's seats, which took place in the same week as the general election in September 2003. Notably, in addition to the twenty-four reserved seats in the Chamber of Deputies, the elections saw an additional fifteen women elected in openly competed seats. Women thus had a total of thirty-nine out of eighty seats, or 48.8 percent.

While Rwanda elects members to its Parliament, it is not considered an electoral democracy because of constraints on broader political activity in that country. It ranks low on most measures of democracy. Freedom House rates Rwanda as "not free" in its annual report *Freedom in the World*. The increased presence of women also seems to have brought little change in the legislative process. Most legislation originates in the executive branch, and the majority female Parliament has created little legislation improving the status or rights of women. The executive branch also maintains tight control over civil society organizations, the media, and elections (Burnet 2011).

Among electoral democracies, Bolivia has moved ahead of the Nordic countries to rank first in the percentage of its national legislators who are women, 53.1 percent in 2015. Bolivia adopted a historic Quota Law in 1997 that was pushed by women's organizations. The law mandated that "the parties shall establish a quota of at least 30 percent women on all the party's decision-making levels and as regards the candidates for representative office." Political parties were commanded to include at least 30 percent female candidates.

However, in the succeeding elections, women were not placed in winnable positions for the most part but were primarily put in alternate deputy positions. Bolivia adopted a new constitution in 2009 that states that in the elections of representatives to the Plurinational Legislative Assembly, "the equal participation of men and women will be ensured." This mandate has been further specified in the election laws in effect.

According to International Democracy and Electoral Assistance (2015),

> The approval of the Political Constitution of Bolivia (2009), concurrent laws along with an extensive and sustained mobilization of different women's movements, gave way to achieve the recognition and application of the principles of parity and alternation to strengthen a more equitable participation between women and men. The election of 82 women out of 166 assembly members is the highest in Bolivian history. After 32 years of democracy, in 1982 the country went from having 2% representatives in the legislature, to reach parity in the political sphere of the national legislature.

Around the world, quotas have become a part of the electoral landscape. In the decade prior to 1985, four countries had introduced quotas. Between 1985 and 1994, twenty-one countries adopted quotas, whereas the former eastern bloc countries dropped them (Tripp and Kang 2008). In the following decade between 1995 and 2005, more than fifty-five countries adopted quotas. Now, over one hundred countries worldwide have adopted gender quotas of some form. Quotas are "fast-track" mechanisms for increasing women's representation (Schwindt-Bayer 2009). Quotas are principally a form of affirmative action to help women overcome the obstacles that have prevented them from entering politics in the same way as their male colleagues (Larserud and Taphorn 2007).

Gender quotas take three main forms. First, reserved seats are set aside for women in parliaments. Second, legislative quotas require a certain percentage of political party nominees to be women. Third, voluntary party quotas involve individual parties' nominees to be women (Bush 2011). Usually a target or minimum threshold is set for women and may apply to the number of female candidates a party proposes for election, or they may take the form of reserved seats in the legislature (Larserud and Taphorn 2007). In voluntary party quota systems, the political parties set the quotas themselves to guarantee the nomination of a certain number or proportion of women. As the name suggests, voluntary party quotas are not legally binding, and no sanctions exist to enforce them. They tend to be the most common type of quota (Tripp and Kang 2008).

Results-based quotas ensure that either a certain percentage (e.g., 20 percent) or a certain number (e.g., twenty out of one hundred) of the seats in a legislature are reserved for women. One form of results-based quotas is a separate "women-only" list or electoral district, or a "women-only" electoral tier, electing women to a predetermined number of seats. This form requires, as the name suggests, that only women are fielded as candidates in the district or tier in question.

Reserved seats are implemented through constitutional provisions, and occasionally electoral laws, setting aside parliamentary seats for women for which men are not eligible to contest, such as in the example of Rwanda cited earlier. They are found in Africa, Asia, and the Middle East. They first emerged in the 1930s, but since 2000, this quota system has become especially popular in countries with otherwise very low proportions of women in politics. Early policies reserved between 1 percent and 10 percent of seats for women, but more recent measures have entailed much larger provisions of 30 percent. Reserved seats can be implemented through either appointment or competitive election. A common concern regarding these measures is that they may serve as an inadvertent ceiling for women's participation, leading elites and citizens to assume that seats not explicitly reserved for women are therefore implicitly reserved for men.

Legal quotas, in contrast, are enacted through reforms to electoral laws and sometimes constitutions, requiring that all parties nominate a certain percentage of women candidates. They are found in many developing countries, especially Latin America—for example in Bolivia—and postconflict societies, primarily in Africa and the Middle East.

Legal quotas generally call for women to form between 25 and 50 percent of all parliamentary candidates nominated by political parties. In most instances, the language of these measures is gender neutral, speaking of women and men together or making reference to the "under-represented sex." Yet legal quotas vary in terms of how strictly their goals are articulated; some speak vaguely about "facilitating access," as is the case in France, whereas other countries offer concrete guidelines regarding the selection and placement of female candidates, as in countries like Argentina, Belgium, and Costa Rica.

Party quotas, in contrast, entail commitments by individual political parties that aim to include a specific proportion of women among their own candidates nominated to political office. Party quotas are most often implemented through party constitutions, statutes, and rulebooks. Party quotas typically set a goal of between 25 and 50 percent female candidates. All the same, the phrasing of this requirement varies: some policies identify women as the group to be promoted by the quota, for example, in Argentina, South Africa, and Spain, whereas others set out a more gender-neutral formulation, as in Italy and several Nordic countries. Party quotas govern the composition of party lists in countries with PR electoral systems, which is the case in much of the world, and are directed at collections of single-member districts in countries with majoritarian electoral arrangements, such as the United Kingdom. IDEA has constructed a list of pros and cons that have been put forward regarding the implementation of quota systems. Text Box 11.1 lists these pros and cons for readers' assessment of the value of quotas for enhancing the democratic nature of electoral institutions.

Text Box 11.1 IDEA Quota Project Pros and Cons

Pros

- Quotas for women do not discriminate but compensate for actual barriers that prevent women from their fair share of the political seats.
- Quotas imply that there are several women together in a committee or assembly, thus women have the right as citizens to equal representation.
- Women's experiences are needed in public life.
- Election is about representation, not educational qualifications.
- Women are just as qualified as men, but women's qualifications are downgraded and minimized in a male-dominated political system.
- It is in fact the political parties that control the nominations, not primarily the voters, who decide who gets elected; therefore, quotas are not violations of voters' rights.
- Introductory quotas may cause conflicts but may be only temporary.
- Quotas can contribute to a process of democratization by making the nomination process more transparent and formalized.

Cons

- Quotas are against the principle of equal opportunity for all, since women are given preference over men.
- Quotas are undemocratic because voters should be able to decide who is elected.
- Quotas imply that politicians are elected because of their gender, not because of their qualifications, and that more qualified candidates are pushed aside.
- Many women do not want to get elected just because they are women.
- Introducing quotas creates significant conflicts within the party organization.
- Quotas violate the principles of liberal democracy.

Although the implementation of quota laws has achieved substantial success in increasing the number of women in parliaments, neither the American political culture nor the structure of its electoral system is conducive to the introduction of legal quotas as a method of boosting the representation of women in the U.S. Congress or in lower level offices. The educational and economic advances American women have made in the latter part of the 20th century suggest that the idea that they need this extra help rather than achieving electoral office on their own merit would most likely not receive widespread support among the American citizenry, perhaps even among liberal feminists.

The Feminist Capital of the World

Iceland has been proclaimed the feminist capital of the world. On October 24, 1975,

> The women of Iceland went on strike—they refused to work, cook and look after children for a day. It was a moment that changed the way women were seen in the country and helped put Iceland at the forefront of the fight for equality.
>
> (Brewer 2015)

Ninety percent of the women in the country participated in the event, known in Iceland as the "Women's Day Off." Rather than going to the office or doing housework or childcare, they took to the streets to rally for equal rights with men.

Women obtained the right to vote in 1915 in Iceland, five years before the United States. In 1980, Vigdis Finnbogadottir was elected president. She was Europe's first female president, and the first woman in the world to be democratically elected as a head of state. She was reelected three times before retiring. In 1983, a new party, the Women's Alliance, won its first parliamentary seats. In 2009, Iceland elected Johanna Sigurdardottir, the world's first openly gay head of state and its first female prime minister. In 2000, it passed a law giving equal parental leave: three months for each parent, respectively. It banned strip clubs in 2010. The government pays 95 percent of kindergarten tuition. Boards of publicly owned companies as well as joint-stock companies with more than fifty employees are required to have 40 percent women. For six years in a row, Iceland has ranked highest in gender equality, according to the World Economic Forum's Global Gender Gap report, which is based on fourteen indicators divided into four subindexes— economic, educational, health based, and political—across 145 countries. The United States ranked twenty-eighth.[6]

Voting and Elections

Elections are a significant and indispensable element of democracy. Voting in elections is an exercise of a basic democratic right, and the extent to which legally enfranchised citizens exercise it is a key assessment of the health of a democratic nation. The role that women play as voters in elections one hundred years after obtaining the suffrage in the United States is the major "success" story in the history of women's participation in the political life of the nation. Chapter 4 showed trends in voting participation and described the ways in which "women matter" in contemporary elections. Women's turnout has gone from about one third of eligible voters at the dawn of suffrage to having a majority voting and turning out at higher levels than men.

At the same time, turnout rates in the United States are lower than in many other democracies. Men and women exercise this right to a lesser extent than citizens in most of the developed democracies. Based on the voting age population, the United States ranks thirty-first among the thirty-four countries in the Organization for Economic Cooperation and Development, most of whose members are highly developed democratic states in turnout in its most recent national election (53.6 percent in 2012) (DeSilver 2015). Voting is compulsory in some of these nations. Whereas compulsory voting laws are not always strictly enforced, their presence or absence can substantially impact turnout. In some countries, the government automatically enrolls individuals as voters. In the United States, registration to vote is mainly an individual responsibility. These structural differences contribute to lower rates of turnout in the United States compared with other democracies.

Is the contemporary gender gap in turnout favoring women a distinctive American phenomenon or part of a global trend? Unfortunately, no contemporary database provides data on turnout rates by sex across democratic elections since IDEA's 2000 report of turnout in seven nations. We can, however, compare generally U.S. rates with that of Great Britain and Canada. In Great Britain, the gender turnout trend tends to be in the opposite direction of that of the United States, with women turning out at lower rates than men (Cohen 2015; Independent 2015), whereas in Canada, women turn out at higher rates than men, similar to the United States (Block et al. 2012).

Gender Inequality and Income Inequality

How does gender inequality factor into income inequality? In addition to the World Economic Forum's Global Gender Gap Index, in 1995, the United Nations Development Program created the Gender-related Development Index and the Gender Empowerment Measure in an attempt to develop a comprehensive measure of gender inequality. In 2010, working from these initial measures, it created the Gender Inequality Index (GII). The GII is a composite measure of gender inequality in three areas: reproductive health (maternal mortality ratios and adolescent fertility rates), empowerment (share of parliamentary seats and education attainment at the secondary level for both males and females), and economic opportunity (labor force participation rates by sex). Using the UN's GII as a measure of gender inequality, the International Monetary Fund (IMF) has found that, globally, gender inequality is strongly associated with income inequality. Its research shows that gender wage gaps directly contribute to income inequality. Higher gaps in labor force participation rates between men and women are likely to result in inequality in earnings between the sexes, thus creating and exacerbating income inequality. Further, women are more likely to work in the informal sector in which earnings are lower, which widens the gender earnings gap and exacerbates income inequality.

The correlation between gender gaps in labor force participation and income inequality is strongest in high-income countries such as the United States compared with other country groupings. Because differences in levels of education and working conditions between men and women in these countries are less of a factor, they contribute less to income inequality. Also, less legal and other discrimination is found between men and women in employment. In these circumstances, gender gaps in labor force participation would translate directly into differences in earnings for men and women and thus increase income inequality.

Looking Ahead

The one-hundredth anniversary of women obtaining the right to vote will be celebrated in 2020. It is possible that once again a woman (or women) will be seeking the presidency in that year's election. Given Hillary Clinton's loss in 2016, it will still be a time of figuring out what it will take for a woman to crack this ultimate glass ceiling and why this challenge is so difficult to overcome in the United States.

Given the turn to the right in the 2016 election, it is highly unlikely that the U.S. Senate will ratify CEDAW as a symbolic part of the 19th Amendment one-hundred-year anniversary commemoration. Enactment of an Equal Rights Amendment to the Constitution has been revived as a political goal in recent years and may also be a central theme of this anniversary. Equal rights advocates propose two strategies for ratification. The first is the traditional process, as outlined in Article V of the Constitution, requiring a passage by two-thirds vote in both houses of Congress, followed by ratification by legislatures in three quarters of the fifty states. The second strategy calls for ratification by three more of the fifteen states that did not ratify the Equal Rights Amendment (ERA) during the 1972–1982 ratification campaign based on legal analysis that when three more states vote yes, this nontraditional amendment could withstand legal challenge and put the ERA into the Constitution.

Twenty states have adopted constitutions or constitutional ERAs mandating that equal rights under the law shall not be denied on account of sex. Wyoming and Utah gave women the right to vote and other legal rights when they first joined the union as states. Most states adopted constitutional amendments between 1971 and 1978. In 1998, two more states, Florida and Iowa, passed ERAs (Gladstone 2004).[7]

Some argue that given the many laws that have been enacted expanding women's rights, an ERA is not necessary. But setting women's equal rights in the Constitution would serve both as a symbol and as an extraordinarily forceful instrument when questions and acts of unequal treatment are put on the public agenda. As described in Chapter 10, several federal laws have been passed during the half-century of the second women's rights movement aimed at removing barriers to women achieving equity with men in the national economy. These laws are extremely important in the quest for gender equity. But as Jessica Neuwirth (2015, 10) writes in *Equal Means Equal,*

> While they have significantly helped women, these federal laws are not comprehensive, many are not fully inclusive, and one has been partially struck down by the Supreme Court for lack of a constitutional foundation. Most critically, none of these laws has the force of a constitutional amendment. That means they do not cover everyone and they can be rolled back at any time by a simple congressional vote.

Text Box 11.2 Why We Need the Equal Rights Amendment

- Without the ERA, the Constitution does not explicitly guarantee that the rights it protects are held equally by all citizens without regard to sex. The first—and still the only—right specifically affirmed as equal for women and men is the right to vote.
- The equal protection clause of the Constitution's 14th Amendment was first applied to sex discrimination only in 1971, and it has never been interpreted to grant equal rights on the basis of sex in the uniform and inclusive way that the ERA would.
- The ERA would provide a clearer judicial standard for deciding cases of sex discrimination, since federal and state courts (some working with state ERAs, some without) still reflect confusion and inconsistency in dealing with such claims. It would also clarify sex discrimination jurisprudence and forty years of precedent for Supreme Court Justice Antonin Scalia [sic], who claimed in an interview reported in the January 2011 *California Lawyer* that the Constitution, specifically the 14th Amendment, does not protect against sex discrimination.
- The ERA would provide a strong legal defense against a rollback of the significant advances in women's rights made in the past fifty years. Without it, Congress can weaken or replace existing laws on women's rights, and judicial precedents on issues of gender equality can be eroded or ignored by reactionary courts responding to a conservative political agenda.
- Without the ERA, women regularly and men occasionally have to fight long, expensive, and difficult legal battles in an effort to prove that their rights are equal to those of the other sex.
- The ERA would improve the U.S.'s human rights standing in the world community. The governing documents of many other countries affirm legal gender equality, however imperfect the global implementation of that ideal may be.

The Equal Rights Amendment (www.equalrightsamendment.org).

The Supreme Court has ruled in several cases that the equal protection clause of the 14th Amendment applies only to state actions and cannot be used in the case of individual actions, particularly in cases involving violence against women. An ERA would change that. It is also useful to consider the immense importance of the 2nd Amendment in structuring gun rights and its effect on debates about gun issues as a parallel to the significance of having equal rights for women mandated in the Constitution. Text Box 11.2 makes the case for ratification of the ERA.

The anniversary will also be a time of great retrospection on women's engagement and advancement in American politics in academic circles, within the activist community, and in the news and on social media. We can expect much commentary on the meaning of the one-hundredth anniversary regarding women's political participation and gender political equality. Some commentators will highlight and celebrate the gains women have made, whereas others will be more cautious in their reflections, noting the barriers that continue to impede political equity. Others still will focus on the relationship between equity in political leadership and women's lives more broadly viewed from the inequalities in the economic and social systems. Some will focus on the areas in which women now surpass men such as in higher education and college graduation rates. Others will highlight a continuing gender gap in pay and continued job segregation and the higher poverty levels of women.

Surveys will certainly abound about women's perspectives on equality and the quality of their lives. Pollsters will query women about their opinions regarding feminism and its meaning for their lives. Is feminism dead? If feminism is dead, then what does that mean? We would hardly expect that women want to return to a second-class status and reverse the gains that at least some women have made in the public and economic realms. Has the women's movement been successful? Has it stalled? What do women want? Will the political parties still be engaged in a rhetorical war on women? Each party will provide a rhetorical assessment of itself as a champion of women's rights. Will gains be viewed differently from an intersectional perspective with women at different places in the economic hierarchy and of diverse races and immigrant status having distinctive ideas about the gains women have made? The questions for discussion and debate are many and provocative.

> ### Sidebar 11.1 Ruth Bader Ginsburg on the Equal Rights Amendment
>
> "If I could choose an amendment to add to the Constitution, it would be the Equal Rights Amendment. I think we have achieved that through legislation, but legislation can be repealed, it can be altered.
>
> So I would like my granddaughters, when they pick up the Constitution to see that notion—that women and men are persons of equal stature—I'd like them to see that it is a basic principle of our society."
>
> September 13, 2014

The contemporary women's rights agenda can be assessed from several activist and governmental lenses. Many major current parliamentary initiatives at both the state and national levels were described in Chapter 10. Added to issues being addressed at the legislative level are contemporary executive branch initiatives. The Obama administration's National Council on Women and Girls (noted in Chapter 4) provides the most current such initiative. The council consisted of the heads of all the cabinet agencies to provide a wide focus on areas of concern about gender equity and the improvement of women's and girls' lives rather than a separate office on women's issues within the executive branch. Each of the cabinet departments and the major administrative agencies was required to submit reports on the status of women in its organization and to list the programs and initiatives it was undertaking to advance equity and improve the status of women and girls. These reports provide a comprehensive accounting of the wide range of issues still a part of the gender equity agenda. The council's 2014 report, *White House Council on Women and Girls Recent Agency Accomplishments*, is a particularly informative listing of priorities and actions of the executive branch regarding contemporary equity issues.

In 2012, the Commerce Department and the Office of Management and Budget submitted a report to the council on *Women in America: Indicators of Social and Economic Well-Being*. This report provided a statistical picture of women in America in five critical areas: demographic and family changes, education, employment, health, and crime and violence. The report's authors note that

> facts alone can never substitute for actions that directly address the challenges faced by women of all ages and backgrounds. But facts are deeply important in helping to paint a picture of how the lives of American women are changing over time and in pointing toward the actions and policies that might be most-needed.[8]

The data the administration assembled for the department reports and the council's initiatives provide a wealth of information for readers to review, reflect on, and evaluate regarding the status of women as the centennial anniversary of the 19th Amendment is observed.

In 2014, the Obama administration announced a new initiative, My Brother's Keeper, that would match $200 million over five years in private money with federal funds to provide mentorship and other support for at-risk young men of color. In response, Black women undertook a concerted public relations and lobbying effort, including an open letter to the President signed by one thousand women, advocating for inclusion of women and girls in the program.

> While we applaud the efforts on the part of the White House, private philanthropy, social justice organizations and others to move beyond colorblind approaches to race-specific problems, we are profoundly troubled about the exclusion of women and girls of color from this critical undertaking. The need to acknowledge the crisis facing boys should not come at the expense of addressing the stunted opportunities for girls who live in the same households, suffer in the same schools, and struggle to overcome a common history of limited opportunities caused by various forms of discrimination.
>
> We simply cannot agree that the effects of these conditions on women and girls should pale to the point of invisibility, and are of such little significance that they warrant zero attention in the messaging, research and resourcing of this unprecedented Initiative.[9]

Thus, the National Council issued a report highlighting the challenges facing women and girls of color. The 2015 report, *Advancing Equity for Women and Girls of Color: Addressing Challenges and Expanding Opportunities*, examined barriers and disparities women and girls of color face and highlighted initial steps the administration had taken to address these issues. The council then held a forum announcing that Prosperity Together, a group of women's foundations, would dedicate $100 million over the next five years to improve the economic status of low-income girls and women of color. The report outlined five main goals on which the White House initiative would focus: exclusionary school discipline practices such as suspension, offering emotional support to victims of abuse and trauma, incentivizing STEM education, sustained reduced rates of teen pregnancy, and tackling economic obstacles.

The feminist community advocates on behalf of these proposals as well as having an even more comprehensive agenda. The National Organization for Women (NOW), founded in 1968 and the first and most prominent continuing national women's rights organization, continues to advocate for the advancement of women's status in the United

Sidebar 11.2 Women in the Military

In December 2015, the U.S. Secretary of Defense announced that, starting in 2016, the Department of Defense would lift all gender-based restrictions on military service. This historic change clears the way for women to serve alongside men in combat arms units.

States. Its current issue agenda comprises six areas: reproductive rights and justice, economic justice, ending violence against women, racial justice, LGBTQ rights, and constitutional equality (i.e., passage of the ERA). Each domain covers a wide range of issues. The economic domain, for instance, calls for initiatives for welfare reform, livable wages, job discrimination, pay equity, housing, social security, and pension reform. Thus, many issues regarding women's domestic work and employment, privacy, rights, and equality continue to be at the center of public discussion, debate, and action. Women have made enormous gains in the public and private sectors, in both the individual and the group levels over the life of the second women's rights movement. But at the same time, the era of increasing income inequality has had differential effects *among* groups of women. Not all women have advanced equally. Class, race, ethnicity, and immigrant status have differentially impacted women's quest for political equality since the emergence of the second women's rights movement and continue to affect that quest a half-century later.

The Women's March on Washington

On November 9, 2016, the day after Donald Trump won the presidency, at least one woman was so distraught that she logged on to the Facebook group Pantsuit Nation and wrote, "I think we should march." A few hours later, ten thousand women had responded to her idea. Teresa Shook, a sixty-year-old retiree living in Hawaii, had ignited a process that by inauguration day would morph into a major political event: the Women's March on Washington.

The Women's March on Washington took place on Saturday, January 21, 2017, the day after the inauguration of Donald Trump as the forty-fifth president. About five hundred thousand women, men, and children converged on the Capital to march, sing, and listen and respond to inspirational speeches. (Some put the number of participants much higher.) Harry Belafonte and Gloria Steinem were honorary cochairs of the march. Additional marches and rallies took place in all fifty states, in thirty-three countries, and on all seven continents, including Antarctica. In total, over a million people participated in the various marches and rallies around the world. March organizers listed more than 670 "sister events" nationwide and overseas in cities including Tel Aviv, Barcelona, Mexico City, Berlin, and Yellowknife in Canada's Northwest Territories, where the temperature was six degrees below zero. Marchers in Cape Town, South Africa, for example, carried banners with slogans such as "Climate change is a women's issue" and "so over mediocre men running things" (Smith-Spark 2017).

The planned march's goal was to show

> strength, power and courage and demonstrate our disapproval of the new president and his values in a peaceful march. ALL women, femme, trans, gender non-conforming and feminist others are invited to march on Washington DC the day following the inauguration of the President-elect. This march is a show of solidarity to demand our safety and health in a time when our country is marginalizing us and making sexual assault an electable and forgivable norm.

The organizers stressed that the march was not so much anti-Trump but rather an affirmative message to the new administration that "women's rights are human rights." The event was promoted as a "march" or "rally" but emphatically not a "protest " (Crockett 2017). According to its statement of principles, the march was to be "a women-led movement bringing together people of all genders, ages, races, cultures, political affiliations and backgrounds."

The heart of the event was a demand for women's rights, but its guiding vision and principles encompassed a multifaceted list of values and principles. The platform was built on the basic premise that women's rights are human rights, and human rights are women's rights. It called for equal rights for women but also racial and economic equality; antidiscrimination protections for lesbian, gay, bisexual, and transgender Americans; access to affordable reproductive health care, including contraception and abortion; criminal justice reform; an increase in the federal minimum wage; immigration reform; and protections for the environment.[10]

The march emerged and developed as a social media phenomenon. It started with Facebook, as noted earlier, spread primarily through that medium, and gained structure through it. At the same time, mainstream media gave it scant coverage.[11]

> Taken collectively, the Women's March on Washington and its many affiliated "sister" marches were perhaps the largest single demonstration of the power of social media to create a mobilization. . . . [It] demonstrated that "organizers don't need media coverage anymore to reach large audiences and turn out large crowds for protests when people are passionate about issues and connect via social media."
>
> (Fahri 2017)

The march initially was called the Million Women's March. But that name was changed because a predominantly African American Million Women's March had already taken place in Philadelphia in 1997. Further, the original organizers were all White women. But some participants expressed concern about whether the march would have diverse leadership and take the concerns of women of color into account. Consequently, three prominent, experienced activists and organizers who were women of color joined as cochairs.

What will happen as a consequence of the march (see, for example, Przybyla 2017)? One commentator mused (Ramaswamy 2017), "Will the march translate into anything, or will it just be remembered as a feel-good event for the yoga pants and crunchy granola set?" Will the Women's March's momentum be sustained long after the march itself? Will it become an enduring opposition movement? Will its varied platform produce a cohesive

Picture 11.1 Rachel Hundley, Mayor of Sonoma, California, at a Women's March, January 21, 2017
Courtesy of Rachel Hundley.

plan to challenge President Trump's plans and actions?[12] Chapter 9 noted that one consequence of the election failing to produce the first female president was a surge in women's
interest in seeking elected office immediately following the election. EMILY's List reported
five hundred women attending its candidate training workshop the day after the march.
Planned Parenthood held a training session for two thousand organizers on how to build
support and to fight efforts to end its federal funding. Readers of this text should follow
up with a search for organizations, actions, and office seeking in their local and regional
communities to develop perspectives on these questions as the centennial anniversary of
women's right to vote nears.

Notes

1. The comment was made at a U.S. Senate Foreign Relations Subcommittee hearing on June 24, 2015. See www.womenspolicy.org/source/senate-committee-holds-hearing-on-cedaw/.
2. Other CEDAW actions the committee highlights include the following. Educational opportunities in Bangladesh used CEDAW to help attain gender parity in primary school enrollment and had as a goal for 2015 to eliminate all gender disparities in secondary education. Violence against women and girls, for example, cites Mexico's response to a destabilizing epidemic of violence against women by using CEDAW terms in a General Law on Women's Access to a Life Free from Violence. By 2009, all thirty-two Mexican states had adopted the measure. In the areas of marriage and family relations, it notes that Kenya has used CEDAW to address differences in inheritance rights, eliminating discrimination against widows and daughters of the deceased.
3. The Beijing Platform can be found at www.un.org/womenwatch/daw/beijing/platform/decision. htm.
4. Freedom House (www.freedomhouse.org) is an independent watchdog organization that conducts research and advocacy on democracy, politics, and human rights. It was founded in 1941 and is headquartered in Washington, DC.
5. Information on the construction of the index can be found at www.representation2020.com/gender-parity-index.html.
6. These rankings show the level of the gap between men and women. It does not rank countries on the overall levels of an indicator.
7. See Leslie Gladstone (2004) for the wording of the various state ERAs.
8. This report can be found at www.census.gov/library/publications/2011/demo/womeninamerica. html.
9. The letter can be found at www.aapf.org/2014/06/woc-letter-mbk/.
10. www.womensmarch.com/principles/.
11. Politifact monitored the three major networks—CNN, Fox, and MSNBC—from 7:00 a.m. to 2:00 p.m., tracking each time the words "women," "march," or "Women's March" were used. Left-leaning MSNBC provided the most dominant coverage, using the terms 114, 128, and 32 times, respectively. CNN followed closely behind, with mentions of "women" and "march" nearing 100 and "Women's March" said 23 times. But Fox's coverage clearly lagged, using the term "Women's March" 12 times on the air, with "women" and "march" said 28 and 32 times each.
12. See the following four "Monkey Cage" (*The Washington Post*) articles for academic perspectives on the likely consequences of the Women's March: (1) Emily Kalah Gade, "Why the Women's March May Be the Start of a Serious Social Movement," *The Washington Post*, January 30, 2017, www. washingtonpost.com/news/monkey-cage/wp/2017/01/30/why-the-womens-march-may-be-the-start-of-a-serious-social-movement/?utm_term=.436b03f48d3d&wpisrc=nl_cage&wpmm=1; (2) Corrine McConnaughy, "4 Lessons for Today's Women's Marchers from the Suffrage Movement," *The Washington Post*, January 26, 2017, www.washingtonpost.com/news/monkey-cage/wp/2017/01/26/4-lessons-for-todays-womens-marchers-from-the-suffrage-movement/?tid=a_inl&utm_term=.24f8b4ec7698; (3) Shom Mazunder, "Yes, Marches Can Make a Difference on These Three Factors," *The Washington Post*, January 27, 2017, www.washingtonpost.com/news/monkey-cage/wp/2017/01/27/yes-marches-can-really-matter-these-three-factors-make-the-difference/?tid=a_inl&utm_term=.557685cadc95; and (4) Dursum Peksen and Amanda Murdie, "The U.S. Was Ripe for a Women's Protest. And More Are Likely," *The Washington Post*, January 28, 2017, www.washingtonpost.com/news/monkey-cage/wp/2017/01/28/the-us-was-ripe-for-a-womens-protest-and-more-are-likely/?tid=a_inl&utm_term=.b89743ac0d17.

Further Readings and Other Resources

Dahlerup, Drude. 2013. *Women, Quotas, and Politics*. New York, NY: Routledge.

Franceschet, Susan, Mona Lena Krook, and Jennifer Piscopo, eds. 2012. *The Impact of Gender Quotas*. Oxford, UK: Oxford University Press.

Krook, Mona Lena. 2009. *Quotas for Women in Politics: Gender and Candidate Selection Reform Worldwide*. New York, NY: Oxford University Press.

Nwanevu, Osita. 2017. "I Ran for Office and Won." *Slate*, January 16. www.slate.com/articles/news_and_politics/politics/2017/01/i_ran_for_office_and_won_here_s_how.html?wpsrc=sp_all_article_storypromo.

Peksen, Dursun and Amanda Murdie. 2017. "The U.S. Was Ripe for a Women's Protest. And More Are Likely." *The Washington Post*, January 28. www.washingtonpost.com/news/monkey-cage/wp/2017/01/28/the-us-was-ripe-for-a-womens-protest-and-more-are-likely/?utm_term=.f26798050e12&wpisrc=nl_cage&wpmm=1.

Web Resources

International Institute for Democracy and Electoral Assistance (IDEA), www.idea.int.

Inter-Parliamentary Union (IPU), www.ipu.org.

"Women in America: Indicators of Social and Economic Well-Being." 2011. www.census.gov/library/publications/2011/demo/womeninamerica.html.

"Women's Leadership and Political Participation." *UN Women*. www.unwomen.org/en/what-we-do/leadership-and-political-participation.

References

Ballington, Julie and Azza Karam. 2005. *Women in Parliament: Beyond Numbers, a Revised Edition*. Stockholm, Sweden: International Institute for Democracy and Electoral Assistance.

Bellitto, Melissa. 2015. "Gender Mainstreaming in the United States: A New Vision of Equality." *UCLA Women's Law Journal*, 22, 2: 125–150.

Block, Clayton, Daniel Larrivee, and Stephen Warner. 2012. "Estimation of Voter Turnout by Age Group and Gender at the 2011 Federal General Election." *Elections Canada Working Paper Series*. www.elections.ca/res/rec/part/estim/estimation41_e.pdf.

Brewer, Kirstie. 2015. "The Day Iceland's Women Went on Strike." *BBC Magazine*, October 23. www.bbc.com/news/magazine-34602822.

Burnet, Jennnie. 2011. "Women Have Found Respect: Gender Quotas, Symbolic Representation, and Female Empowerment in Rwanda." *Politics & Gender*, 7: 303–334.

Bush, Sarah Sunn. 2011. "International Politics and the Spread of Quotas in Legislatures." *International Organization*, 65, 1: 103–137.

Cohen, Claire. 2015. "Almost 100 Years on from Winning the Vote, Women Shun the Polling Booths." *The Telegraph*, January 9. www.telegraph.co.uk/women/womens-politics/11333915/British-women-general-election-voters-shun-the-polling-booths.html.

Crockett, Emily. 2017. "'The Women's March on Washington' Explained." *Vox*, January 21.

Dalerup, Drude. 2005. "'Fast Track' to Equal Political Representation for Women: Why Scandinavia Is No Longer the Model." *International Feminist Journal of Politics*, 7, 1: 26–48.

Dalerup, Drude. 2014. "Increasing Women's Political Representation: New Trends in Gender Quotas." In *Women in Parliament: Beyond Numbers, a Revised Edition*, eds. Julie Ballington and Azza Karam. Stockholm, Sweden: International Institute for Democracy and Electoral Assistance.

DeSilver, Drew. 2015. "U.S. Trails Most Developed Countries in Voter Turnout." *Pew Research Center*, May 6. www.pewresearch.org/fact-tank/2017/05/15/u-s-voter-turnout-trails-most-developed-countries/.

Fahri, Paul. 2017. "How the Mainstream Media Missed the March That Social Media Turned into a Phenomenon." *The Washington Post*, January 22. www.washingtonpost.com/lifestyle/style/how-mass-media-missed-the-march-that-social-media-turned-into-a-phenomenon/2017/01/21/2db4742c-e005-11e6-918c-99ede3c8cafa_story.html?utm_term=.6921f1dfba11.

Gelb, Joyce. 2002. "Representing Women in Britain and the United States: The Quest for Numbers and Power." In *Women Transforming Congress*, ed. Cindy Simon Rosenthal. Norman, OK: University of Oklahoma Press, 422–444.

Gladstone, Leslie. 2004. "Equal Rights Amendments: State Provisions." *CRS Report for Congress.* http://digital.library.unt.edu/ark:/67531/metacrs7397/m1/1/high_res_d/RS20217_2004Aug23.pdf.

Hawkesworth, Mary. 2012. *Political Worlds of Women: Activism, Advocacy, and Governance in the Twenty-First Century.* Boulder, CO: Westview Press.

Henderson, Sarah and Alana S. Jeydel. 2007. *Participation and Protest: Women and Politics in a Global World.* New York, NY: Oxford University Press.

IDEA. 2015. "Bolivia: 51 Per Cent of Women Elected to Parliament." www.idea.int/news-media/news/bolivia-51-cent-women-elected-parliament%C2%A0.

Independent. 2015. "General Election 2015 Explained: Turnout." May 4. www.independent.co.uk/news/uk/politics/generalelection/general-election-2015-explained-turnout-10224278.html.

Kernell, Samuel and Gary C. Jacobson. 2003. *The Logic of American Politics.* Washington, DC: CQ Press.

Larserud, Stina and Rita Taphorn. 2007. *Designing for Equality: Best-Fit, Medium-Fit and Non-Favourable Combinations of Electoral Systems and Gender Quotas.* Stockholm, Sweden: International IDEA.

Matland, Richard. 1993. "Institutional Variables Affecting Female Representation in National Legislatures: The Case of Norway." *Journal of Politics*, 55, 3: 737–755.

Neuwirth, Jessica. 2015. *Equal Means Equal.* New York, NY: The Free Press.

Przybyla, Heidi. 2017. "Women's March Movement: What's Next and Can the Momentum Last?" *USA TODAY*, January 22. www.usatoday.com/story/news/politics/2017/01/22/womens-march-movement-able-transform-massive-crowds-into-lasting-legacy-trump/96920040/.

Ramaswamy, Venugopal. 2017. "Women's March Could Quickly Fade." *USA TODAY*, January 25. www.usatoday.com/story/opinion/nation-now/2017/01/25/womens-march-movement-or-fade-column/97011946/.

Sainsbury, Diane. 1993. "The Politics of Increased Women's Representation: The Swedish Case." In *Gender and Party Politics*, eds. Joni Lovenduski and Pippa Norris. London, UK: Sage, 263–289.

Schwindt-Bayer, Leslie. 2009. "Making Quotas Work: The Effect of Gender Quota Laws on the Election of Women." *Legislative Studies Quarterly*, 34, 1: 5–28.

Smith, Steven S., Jason M. Roberts, and Ryan J. Vander Wielen. 2007. *The American Congress.* 4th edition. New York, NY: Cambridge University Press.

Smith-Spark, Laura. 2017. "Protesters Rally Worldwide in Solidarity with Washington March." *CNN*, January 21. www.cnn.com/2017/01/21/politics/trump-women-march-on-washington/index.html.

Terrell, Cynthia. 2015. "The State of Women's Representation: A Blueprint for Reaching Gender Parity." www.c-span.org/video/?c4555732/women-elected-office.

Tripp, Aili and Alice Kang. 2008. "The Global Impact of Quotas: On the Fast Track to Increased Female Representation." *Comparative Political Studies*, 41, 3: 338–361.

Wright, Wendy. 2010. "Why the U.S. Has Not—And Should Not—Ratify CEDAW." www.cwfa.org/why-the-u-s-has-not-and-should-not-ratify-cedaw/.

Index